Grandmaster Secrets:

Winning Quickly at Chess

John Nunn

First published in the UK by Gambit Publications Ltd 2007
Original edition published as *101 Brilliant Chess Miniatures* in 1999

ISBN-13: 978-1-904600-89-3
ISBN-10: 1-904600-89-1
(First edition: ISBN-10: 1-901983-16-1; ISBN-13: 978-1-901983-16-6)

DISTRIBUTION:
Worldwide (except USA): Central Books Ltd, 99 Wallis Rd, London E9 5LN, England.
Tel +44 (0)20 8986 4854 Fax +44 (0)20 8533 5821. E-mail: orders@Centralbooks.com

Gambit Publications Ltd, 99 Wallis Rd, London E9 5LN, England.
E-mail: info@gambitbooks.com
Website (regularly updated): www.gambitbooks.com

Edited by Graham Burgess
Typeset by John Nunn
Cover image by Wolff Morrow
Printed in Great Britain by The Cromwell Press, Trowbridge, Wilts.

10 9 8 7 6 5 4 3 2 1

Gambit Publications Ltd
Managing Director: Murray Chandler GM
Chess Director: Dr John Nunn GM
Editorial Director: Graham Burgess FM
German Editor: Petra Nunn WFM
Webmaster: Dr Helen Milligan WFM

Contents

Symbols

+	check
++	double check
#	checkmate
x	capture
!!	brilliant move
!	good move
!?	interesting move
?!	dubious move
?	bad move
??	blunder
Ch	championship
corr.	correspondence game
1-0	the game ends in a win for White
½-½	the game ends in a draw
0-1	the game ends in a win for Black
(n)	*n*th match game
(D)	see next diagram

Preface

This book is an updated version of *101 Brilliant Chess Miniatures*, which was first published in 1999. Although the original '101' was moderately successful, I realized that the book could be improved. The rigid format did not lend itself particularly well to the contents of the book, with the result that the layout appeared dense and intimidating. When the idea of a new edition arose, I immediately decided to use a new layout for the book, which would make it much easier to follow the games and notes. I have also taken the opportunity to update some of the opening notes and to make a considerable number of analytical corrections to the notes of the first 101 games. There are also 24 new games, played between 1999 and 2007; taking advantage of the new layout, these games have been annotated in somewhat greater depth than the original collection. There is also a new introduction, which includes several additional lightly annotated miniature games. Altogether, the new edition is 120% larger than the 1999 version, as measured by total text area.

The intention of this book is to inform and educate in an entertaining way. Everybody has at times suffered the humiliation of a quick loss. Why does this happen and how can we avoid it happening in our own games? Conversely, how can we recognize and exploit errors by the opponent to score a quick win? This book aims to tackle these questions by presenting a collection of attractive games. Readers should note that there is no list of 'important points' at the end of each game. The reason is that the same points often occur in several games and it hardly makes sense to repeat again and again that it is usually a good idea not to get your king stuck in the centre. Instead I have written a lengthy introduction which collects all the important points together in one place. Readers are strongly advised to read this introduction before playing over the games themselves.

There is no generally-accepted definition of a miniature game and for this book I decided to make the limit 25 moves, which is perhaps the most commonly-used figure. The selection of the 125 games was made according to various criteria. In order to avoid repeating many over-familiar examples, the games are all relatively recent, having been played after 1970. The vast majority of games feature clashes between players with an Elo rating of at least 2500 (in the more recent games I raised this cut-off limit to reflect the increasing numbers of highly-rated players). The reason is that I wanted to present genuine contests, not crushes between players of widely different strengths. Most players find it easy to beat much weaker opponents – the problems only start to arise when you face opponents approaching your own strength. Since this is the scenario which is of most value to readers, I decided that the games should reflect a similar situation. I also tried to choose games containing a wide variety of motifs, so you won't find a long series of ♘d5 sacrifices in the Sicilian.

The analysis of these games revealed many interesting points. When one thinks of a miniature game, one tends to imagine a game in which one side greedily grabs material, neglects his development and it soundly crushed. Annotators of such games often assume that a quick loss must involve the winner playing good moves throughout, while the loser must have committed a series of errors. However, the reality is rather different and many of the following games don't fit this stereotyped pattern. Often, the struggle hangs in the balance until near the end because the loser's strategy was not fundamentally unsound, but required accurate follow-up play which was not forthcoming. Psychological factors are important in chess as a whole, and many quick defeats can be traced back not only to errors on the chessboard, but also to faulty chess thinking. I shall have more to say about this in the introduction.

John Nunn
Chertsey, 2007

Introduction

The basic principles of opening play are quite well-known – to develop your pieces, get castled and try to control the centre – so how is it that many players, even grandmasters, lose in under 25 moves?

There are many possible reasons for a quick defeat, of which the simplest is an outright blunder. Blunders are not restricted to the opening and can occur at any stage of the game, and for this reason we shall not address the subject of blundering in this book. In any case, the psychological aspects of blunders are covered in my book *Secrets of Practical Chess* (enlarged edition, Gambit, 2007).

Another reason is that a player falls into a known opening trap. Here again there isn't much to say; if you have prepared your openings well, then you should be aware of the potential pitfalls. Playing a sharp opening without reasonable preparation involves considerable risk and is best avoided. If you are interested in opening traps, then it may be worth studying *101 Chess Opening Traps* by Steve Giddins (Gambit, 1998).

In the current book, however, we shall be concerned with the most common and important case, namely that in which a player loses quickly without doing anything instantly fatal. You cannot lose quickly without making a mistake, but as we shall see the error is often not a single move, but a misconceived plan based on a major misjudgement. It is possible to learn to avoid this type of error, and that is partly what this book is about. We shall deal with the seven most common errors (summarized at the end of this introduction) but as they are often linked together, our examples will often feature more than one theme.

Material greed and poor development are often bound together. There is nothing wrong with gaining material if you do not thereby compromise your position, but it very often happens that a player will go to great lengths to win a pawn, only to ruin his position in the process. Pawn sacrifices in the opening are called gambits, and the compensation for the pawn often lies in a lead in development. This type of pawn sacrifice is restricted to the opening phase, because once both sides have developed all their pieces then you cannot sacrifice a pawn in return for a lead in development (although you may do so to misplace enemy pieces). Take a look at the following game. I shall withhold the names of the players for the moment; as you play it over, try to guess the year it was played.

1 e4 e5 2 f4 exf4 3 ♘f3 g5 4 h4 g4 5 ♘e5

The Kieseritzky Gambit, one of the most venerable lines in the King's Gambit.

5...h5?!

This line was played quite often in the 19th century, but it is hardly ever seen today. Black defends his attacked g4-pawn and, by controlling g4 and f3, hopes to force the e5-knight to retreat to an inconvenient square. The problem is that it is very slow, since it not only costs a tempo, it obliges Black to spend another tempo on his next move in order to defend f7. The main lines today are 5...♘f6 6 ♗c4 d5 7 exd5 and 5...d6 6 ♘xg4 ♘f6; in both cases Black returns his extra pawn in order to catch up with his development (for an example of the latter line, see Game 103).

6 ♗c4 ♘h6

Similar play arises after 6...♖h7 7 d4 d6 8 ♘d3 f3 9 gxf3 ♗e7 10 ♗e3.

7 d4 ♕f6?

Black follows up his strategy of hanging on to his extra pawn by defending the attacked f4-pawn, but this early development of the queen is against general principles and turns out badly. The main line is 7...d6 8 ♘d3 f3 9 gxf3 ♗e7 10

♗e3 ♗xh4+ 11 ♔d2, when White has a very dangerous lead in development but Black can still fight.

8 0-0

The simple 8 ♘c3 (intending ♘d5) is perhaps even stronger, since 8...♗b4 9 0-0 gives White an improved version of the game.

8...♕xh4 *(D)*

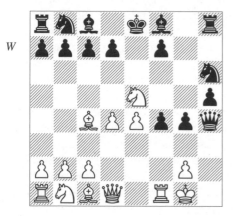

At first glance, Black might seem to be doing well in the diagram; he is still a pawn up, and White must watch out for traps such as 9 ♗xf4?? g3. But in fact Black is virtually lost. He has developed his queen but nothing else (the knight on h6 is only defending f7 and cannot count as 'developed'). In particular his entire queenside is still at home and cannot support his queen which, far from occupying a useful position, will soon be chased from pillar to post by White's minor pieces. On top of this, White dominates the centre with his pawns and Black has no safe place for his king.

9 ♖xf4 ♗d6

By pinning the e5-knight, Black indirectly defends f7, but his position is on the verge of collapse.

10 ♘f3 ♕g3?

The queen isn't doing anything here and is only in danger of being trapped. 10...♕d8 was a better chance, but after 11 e5 ♗e7 12 ♘c3! White has a massive attack (12...gxf3 13 ♕xf3 is disastrous for Black).

11 e5 ♗e7

Black starts going backwards. After 11...gxf3 12 ♖xf3 ♕g6 13 exd6 cxd6 14 ♘c3 Black's

position is a wreck, with a shattered pawn-structure, no development and an exposed king.

12 ♘h2

Now the threat is just ♘c3-e4, so Black decides to retract his earlier queen move.

12...♕h4

Leaving the queen where it is also offers no hope; for example, 12...d6 13 ♘f1 ♕h4 14 ♘bd2 ♕g5 15 ♘e4 ♕g6 16 ♘f6+ ♔f8 17 ♗d3 ♗f5 18 ♖xf5 ♘xf5 19 ♘g3 and White wins material.

13 ♘c3

Threatening 14 ♘f3 ♕g3 15 ♘e4, so Black creates a retreat-square for his queen.

13...♗d8 14 ♘e4 *(D)*

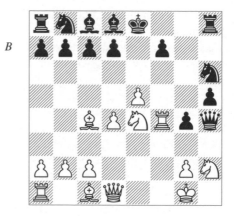

Compare this with the previous diagram. In five moves, Black has only managed to transfer his bishop from f8 to d8. White, on the other hand, is ready to play 15 ♘f3 ♕e7 16 ♘f6+, or simply 15 ♘f6+ at once.

14...♘c6 15 ♘f3 gxf3

Black prefers to surrender his queen immediately rather than submit to something like 15...♕e7 16 ♘f6+ ♔f8 17 ♘h4 d6 18 ♘g6+ fxg6 19 ♘g8+.

16 ♖xh4 ♗xh4 17 ♕xf3 ♘xd4 18 ♕xh5

Giving up his queen hasn't solved Black's problems and further material loss is inevitable.

18...♘df5 19 ♗xh6 d5 20 ♗xd5 ♖xh6 21 ♕xf7+ ♔d8 22 ♕f8+ 1-0

It is mate next move.

This one-sided game enables us to make some basic points. Black offended against several principles of opening play; he ignored the fight for the centre, clung to his extra pawn at the cost of development, exposed his queen to attack and had his king caught in the centre.

When did you think this game was played? 1850? 1860, perhaps? Actually, it was Mark Hebden – Jon Benjamin, 'Chess for Peace', London 1987. Although Black was doubtless well aware of the fundamental concepts of opening play, he nevertheless contravened them at almost every turn. This enables us to make an important point: it is not enough to be aware of the principles of opening play, you also have to put them into practice in your games. Under normal circumstances this is perhaps not too difficult, but if a player becomes flustered by something unexpected happening in the opening, it is surprising how often the basic principles are thrown out of the window and replaced by moves which, in a calmer moment, the player himself would doubtless recognize to be wrong. This game also emphasizes a point made earlier that it is very often not individual moves which are to blame so much as a faulty overall strategy. In this case, Black's desire to keep his extra pawn (5...h5?! and especially 7...♕f6?) drew him along a path that led only to disaster.

One of the basic aims of opening play is to find a safe spot for the king. In most cases, this means castling, although if the centre is blocked then the king may be safe in the middle for a time. The statistics for the 125 games in this book are revealing: the winner castled in 106 of the games (77 times on the kingside and 29 times on the queenside), but in these 106 games the loser only castled 39 times. Clearly, getting one's king stuck in the centre is a major factor in many quick losses. In some of these games the loser's failure to castle was involuntary; perhaps he was already under such a vicious attack that he had no time to castle, or he still had pieces on the back rank so that castling was physically impossible. In these cases the failure to castle was merely a symptom of the disease and not the primary cause; the real error occurred earlier. However, there are also some games in which the loser could perfectly well have castled, but chose not to (see Games 25, 45, 67, 87 and 97, for example). Here is an example in which a grandmaster fails to extract his king from the centre; it also allows us to introduce another important element into our discussion of quick losses: psychological factors.

John Nunn – Karl Robatsch
Clare Benedict Cup, Teesside 1979
Sicilian Defence, Sozin Attack

1 e4 c5 2 ♘f3 ♘c6 3 d4 cxd4 4 ♘xd4 ♘f6 5 ♘c3 d6 6 ♗c4 ♗d7 7 0-0 ♖c8

A slightly unusual line. 7...g6 8 ♘xc6 ♗xc6 9 ♗g5 ♗g7 10 ♘d5 ♗xd5 11 exd5 0-0 is more common, with just an edge for White.

8 ♗b3 g6 9 ♘xc6 ♗xc6 10 ♗g5 ♗g7 11 ♘d5 e6?!

Black allows his king to be trapped in the centre in order to achieve a strategic aim. This case is different from that of the previous game because Black's play has a valid goal and the question is whether White can exploit his temporary attacking chances before Black consolidates. It turns out that White can preserve some advantage, and so 11...♗xd5 12 exd5 0-0 is a

safer option, similar to the note to Black's 7th move.

12 ♘xf6+ ♗xf6 13 ♗xf6 ♕xf6 14 ♕xd6 ♕xb2

This is what Black was aiming for. He has broken up White's queenside pawns and if he could now play ...♕f6 followed by ...♕e7, he would have an undoubted strategic advantage. Note that 15 ♗xe6? loses to 15...♖d8.

15 ♖ad1 ♕f6 16 ♖fe1 *(D)*

This causes Black more problems than 16 ♗d5 ♕e7 17 ♗xc6+ bxc6, which led to a quick draw in Dochev-Stocek, Pardubice 2000: 18 e5 ♕xd6 19 ♖xd6 ♔e7 20 f4 ♖c7 21 ♖f3 ♖b8 22 ♖b3 ♖xb3 23 cxb3 ♖d7 24 ♖xc6 ♖d1+ ½-½.

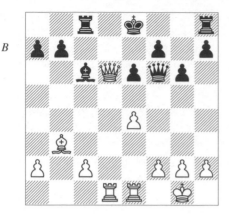

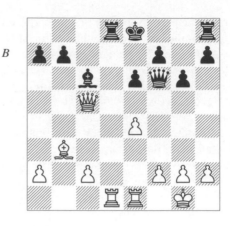

After the text-move, it turns out that Black's plan of playing ...♕e7 is not so easy to execute. 16...♕e7 at once is met by 17 ♕d4 0-0 18 ♕xa7 winning a pawn, although admittedly it wouldn't be easy to exploit the extra pawn in view of White's weak queenside structure. The alternative is to play 16...a6 or 16...b6 first, with the idea of playing ...♕e7 a move later. However, in these cases too White retains some advantage; for example, 16...a6 17 c4 ♖d8 18 ♕c5 ♖xd1 19 ♖xd1 ♕e7 20 ♕e5 0-0 21 c5 ♖d8 22 ♖d6 followed by ♕d4, or 16...b6 17 ♖d3 ♕e7 18 ♕f4 0-0 19 ♕h6 ♕f6 20 e5 ♕g7 21 ♕h4 with kingside pressure.

This is where psychology enters the equation. Black sees that he doesn't have a completely satisfactory continuation and realizes that the game hasn't gone as he intended. In this case it is easy to go round in circles looking at each move in turn, become frustrated, lose your sense of danger and play an inferior move. Instead of going for one of the above options, which would at least have enabled him to castle, Black only encourages White's initiative to grow.

16...♖d8?!

Exchanging rooks is a bad idea as it leaves Black's king with one less defender.

17 ♕c5 *(D)*

17...♖xd1 18 ♖xd1 a6?

Black has totally underestimated the danger posed by his exposed king. 18...♕e7 19 ♕xa7 0-0 was the last chance to save his king, although in this case 20 ♕e3 leaves Black worse off than if he had kept all the rooks on the board.

19 ♕d6

Switchbacks are often hard to see, and here the return of the queen to d6 seals Black's fate since ...♕e7 is no longer possible due to ♕b8+. The threat is 20 e5 ♕g5 21 g3 followed by f4 or h4.

19...♗xe4 *(D)*

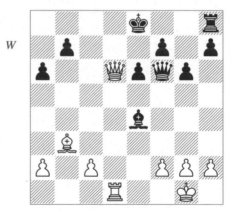

20 ♗xe6! 1-0

Black loses his queen after 20...fxe6 21 ♕b8+ ♔e7 22 ♕c7+ ♔e8 23 ♕c8+ ♔f7 24 ♖d7+.

One rather common situation is that a player is ready to castle immediately but the fact that his king is only one move away from safety creates a false sense of security. He then reasons that because he can castle at a moment's notice, it is safe to conduct some other operation first. This logic proves false when his opponent lashes out with some tactics which give him no time for the one tempo he needs. When your opponent's king lingers in the centre, it is worth looking to see if there is a sharp continuation which keeps him off-balance; sometimes even unlikely-looking ideas succeed, as in the following case.

John Nunn – Hans Karl
Lugano open 1984
Ruy Lopez, Open

1 e4 e5 2 ♘f3 ♘c6 3 ♗b5 a6 4 ♗a4 ♘f6 5 0-0 ♘xe4 6 d4 b5 7 ♗b3 d5 8 dxe5 ♗e6 9 ♗e3

At the time this game was played, 9 ♗e3 was an oddity, but since then it has become more popular, although it still has a long way to go to catch up with the main lines 9 c3 and 9 ♘bd2.

9...♗c5

A natural reaction, but the exchange of bishops tends to weaken the dark squares, especially c5, and so this is rarely played today. 9...♗e7 is the most common move.

10 ♕d3 ♗xe3?!

Already a mistake. The queen is drawn to the active square e3, where it helps to control c5, an important square in the Open Ruy Lopez. 10...0-0 is better, although after 11 ♖d1 White retains a slight advantage.

11 ♕xe3 *(D)*

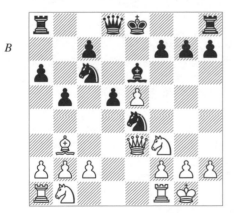

A key moment. Black can castle here, but after 11...0-0 12 ♘c3 ♘xc3 13 ♕xc3 ♕d7 14 ♕c5 White establishes a dark-squared blockade and has a clear advantage. Comforted by the thought that he can castle any time, Black

decides to play the otherwise desirable move 11...f5, so as to maintain his knight on e4. Perhaps 11...♘e7 is best, although 12 c3 0-0 13 ♘bd2 certainly favours White.

11...f5?

Losing by force.

12 exf6

In the later game Sadvakasov-Betaneli, Minneapolis 2005, White overlooked this forced win and preferred 12 ♖d1?, which leads to just a modest advantage for White.

12...♕xf6 *(D)*

There is no way out, since 12...gxf6 13 ♘c3 f5 14 ♖fd1 is disastrous for Black.

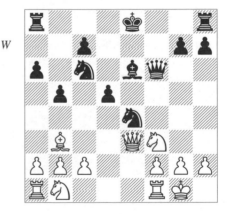

Black's position looks a little unstable with his king in the centre, a possible pin along the e-file and the c6-knight undefended. It was this last feature that alerted me to the possibility of the following move.

13 c4!

White strikes before Black has a chance to castle. 13...dxc4 14 ♕xe4 costs Black a piece so the reply is forced.

13...bxc4 14 ♗a4 ♗d7

14...♗f5 loses to 15 ♕d4 ♕d6 16 ♕e5+, but after the text-move the d5-pawn is undefended, which allows White to develop with gain of tempo.

15 ♘c3 ♕h6

Black tries to bail out by exchanging queens. The alternative 15...♕e6 is hopeless after 16 ♘xd5 ♕xd5 17 ♖ad1 ♕e6 18 ♖xd7 ♔xd7 19 ♗xc6+ followed by a knight fork.

16 ♕xh6 gxh6 17 ♘xd5 0-0-0?!

17...♔d8 is marginally better, but after 18 ♖ac1 ♘c5 19 ♗xc6 ♗xc6 20 ♖fd1 ♘d7 21 ♖xc4 ♗xd5 22 ♖xd5 White is a pawn up with a large positional advantage. After the text-move, White wins an exchange.

18 ♗xc6 ♗xc6 19 ♘e7+ ♔b7 20 ♘xc6 ♔xc6 21 ♘e5+ 1-0

After the king moves, White forks the rooks by 22 ♘f7, leaving Black a whole exchange down with a wrecked pawn-structure.

The various factors we have identified as prime causes of quick losses often go together; for example, spending a lot of time winning a pawn often leads to backward development and failure to castle. Although it may not be easy to isolate one particular element, many losses have pawn-grabbing as their primary cause, with the other factors being mere knock-on effects of the original mistake. This subject is particularly difficult because not all pawn-grabbing is wrong – one only has to think of the games of Fischer and Kasparov in the Poisoned Pawn. However, those considering snatching a pawn should be aware of the likely consequence that they will have to defend accurately for several moves in order to get away with it. One of the recurrent themes in this book is the practical difficulty of defending accurately for long periods – even grandmasters struggle to find a long series of 'only moves'. Therefore even pawn-grabs which in theory are probably satisfactory may be a poor bet in practice, because it is generally easier to attack than to defend.

It is quite revealing to look at the history of the Poisoned Pawn as an example of this theme. In the early days of the Poisoned Pawn, Black was often smashed rather quickly, but he also scored his fair share of wins. Fischer's games proved that grabbing the b2-pawn was a viable option even at the highest level. The theory of the line became more and more developed, with the main ideas for both sides worked out to great depth. The Poisoned Pawn remains a hot topic today; for example, it was played twice by Anand in the 2007 Corus tournament, once with White and once with Black. However, even today the chance of a painful loss remains for Black. Why, then, is it popular with Black? To answer this, take a look at the following game.

Rudolf Marić – Svetozar Gligorić
Belgrade 1962
Sicilian Defence, Najdorf Poisoned Pawn

1 e4 c5 2 ♘f3 d6 3 d4 cxd4 4 ♘xd4 ♘f6 5 ♘c3 a6 6 ♗g5 e6 7 f4 ♕b6 8 ♕d2 ♕xb2 9 ♖b1 ♕a3 10 ♗xf6

At the time this was one of White's main lines against the Poisoned Pawn. Later 10 f5 took over as the most popular continuation, but recently there has been a revival of interest in 10 e5, based on the line 10...h6 11 ♗h4 dxe5 12 fxe5 ♘fd7 13 ♘e4!? (both the Anand games mentioned above involved this continuation).

10...gxf6 11 ♗e2 ♘c6 12 ♘xc6 bxc6 13 0-0 ♕a5 14 ♔h1 ♗e7 15 f5

10 ♗xf6 has been out of favour for quite a long time and so there are many unexplored possibilities following it; for example, 15 ♕e3 h5 16 ♖b3 is an interesting idea with good practical results, which aims to develop White's initiative more slowly.

15...exf5

These days 15...h5 16 ♗f3 ♔f8 is considered the main line, but even here Black is not entirely safe, since 17 fxe6 ♗xe6 (17...fxe6 18 e5! dxe5 19 ♗xc6 ♖a7 20 ♕g5 f5 21 ♕g6 is very dangerous for Black) 18 ♖b7 is unclear.

16 exf5 ♗xf5 17 ♗f3?

White attacks the c6-pawn, but Black can simply give up this pawn in order to castle and take over the initiative. The critical line is 17 ♗xa6 ♕xa6 18 ♖xf5 d5 19 ♖e1, with considerable pressure in return for the pawn.

17...0-0 18 ♗xc6 ♖ac8

Black's king is now in safety and White must take care.

19 ♗b7?

White attempts to solve his problems by force, but the tactics rebound on him. He should have tried 19 ♗d5 ♕xc3 20 ♕xc3 ♖xc3 21 ♖xf5 ♖xc2 when, despite the two minus pawns, White has good drawing chances.

19...♖xc3 20 ♖xf5 (D)

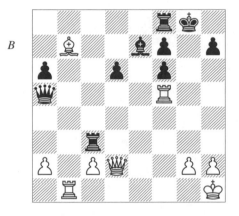

White intends 20...♕xf5 21 ♕xc3, when he is in no danger, but instead...

20...♖b3! 0-1

A beautiful finish, exploiting White's weak back rank to make decisive material gains.

You won't win like that if you play the Petroff Defence (1 e4 e5 2 ♘f3 ♘f6) or the Berlin Defence to the Ruy Lopez (1 e4 e5 2 ♘f3 ♘c6 3 ♗b5 ♘f6), two notoriously solid openings for Black. Economists will tell you that, in general, the only way you can get above-average returns from an investment is to take on above-average risk. A similar principle holds for chess openings. Black's score in the Poisoned Pawn is better than in most other openings, but in order to take advantage of this, Black must be prepared to accept the possibility of a nasty loss.

Whether the Poisoned Pawn appeals to you is a matter of taste; like investors, some players are more willing to accept risk than others. A further point is that playing very sharp openings involves a large amount of study, and not all players have the time or the inclination for this.

Snatching material in the opening may or may not be sound. There is a complete spectrum from relatively safe captures to suicidal greed. Popular opening lines such as the Poisoned Pawn naturally lie somewhere in the middle, because lines which clearly favour one colour are no longer played. In this book you will find plenty of examples of Black's queen taking the b2-pawn, not only in the Poisoned Pawn but also in various other openings; take a look at Games 11, 15, 29, 34, 35, 81 and 121. These range in soundness from the unclear lines of Games 29 and 34 to the extravagantly risky grab of Game 121. A final point is that you should not commit yourself to taking the b-pawn and then have second thoughts about it when the moment arrives. For example, if you have played ...♕b6 with the sole idea of preventing your opponent from developing his c1-bishop, and then he moves it anyway, it is a bit late suddenly to start thinking about whether ...♕xb2 is a good idea.

It is much easier to lose quickly with Black than with White; the large preponderance of wins by White in this book reflects this simple fact. White starts with a slight advantage, so an error with White may result in equality or at worst a slight disadvantage, but an error with Black will probably have more serious consequences. Moreover, many popular openings such as the Sicilian are based on the principle of counterattack. While such openings offer Black the chance to gain an advantage against inaccurate play, they also involve a higher than average risk.

Despite this, it is still possible to lose quickly with White; indeed, there is a particular danger which relates specifically to White: playing as if you have the advantage when you have not. Players at higher levels are particularly prone to this error, because possession of the white pieces is regarded as a very valuable asset. It is considered a failure if one emerges from the opening with 'only' an equal position. Examples of this phenomenon may be found, to a greater or lesser extent, in Games 12, 26, 38, 41, 67 and 86. As one plays over these games, a familiar pattern emerges. White makes an inaccuracy in the opening, which allows Black to equalize. However, White either does not appreciate the new situation or ignores it, and continues to play aggressively, often grabbing material. The result is a loss of the initiative and a savage attack by Black. It is quite easy to overestimate the advantage conferred by playing White; it is, after all, only one tempo and in unbalanced, dynamic positions other factors may be more important than a tempo (such as piece activity, king safety, etc.). Wishful thinking obviously also plays a part; the white player is unwilling to accept that he has done something wrong and lost his initial advantage, so his sense of danger is dimmed.

We have referred to psychological factors before, and now it is time to mention a common cause of quick losses: reacting badly to a surprise in the opening. Such a surprise can take various forms, such as an innovation or an unexpected choice of opening by the opponent. When your opponent plays an unfamiliar move in the opening, the tendency is to think there must be something wrong with it and look for a 'refutation'. This applies particularly if the move looks odd or counter-intuitive in some way. Here is an example.

John Nunn – Peter Large
British Ch, Chester 1979
Sicilian Defence, Velimirović Attack

1 e4 c5 2 ᐃf3 ᐃc6 3 d4 cxd4 4 ᐃxd4 ᐃf6 5 ᐃc3 d6 6 ᐃc4 e6 7 ᐃe3 ᐃe7 8 ᐃe2 0-0 9 0-0-0 a6 10 ᐃb3 ᐃe8

At the time, this was quite a popular method of meeting the Velimirović Attack.

11 f4

These days, 11 ᐃhg1 is practically the only move played, although White's modest 42% score with this move is not an especially favourable sign.

11...b5 12 f5 *(D)*

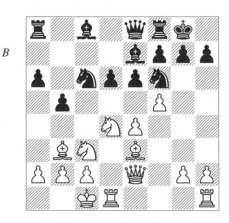

An over-the-board inspiration, which is in fact not particularly good. However, it immediately puts Black in a dilemma. Should he win a pawn with ...ᐃxd4 followed by ...exf5, or should he adopt a more cautious approach?

12...ᐃxd4

Objectively speaking, there's nothing much wrong with taking the pawn since it leads to a roughly level position. However, by accepting the sacrifice Black places himself under the burden of following up accurately. A simpler solution was 12...ᐃa5 13 fxe6 ᐃxb3+, followed by either ...fxe6 or ...ᐃxe6. In this case it isn't clear what White has achieved by pushing his f-pawn since he no longer has the b3-bishop that would have enabled him to exploit the slight loosening of Black's pawn-structure. It is quite possible that Black believed he should 'refute' White's rather dubious-looking plan, and it is often said that the only way to refute a sacrifice is to accept it. However, such general chess principles often have so many exceptions that they should be taken with a large pinch of salt.

13 ᐃxd4

The game G.Mainka-L.Kiss, Zurich 1988 continued 13 ♗xd4 exf5?! 14 exf5 ♗xf5 15 ♖de1 b4 16 ♕xe7 ♕xe7 17 ♖xe7 bxc3 18 ♗xc3 with a favourable ending for White. Here, too, Black made the mistake of believing that he should accept the pawn, when the simple 13...b4 14 ♘a4 e5 would have given him a satisfactory position.

13...exf5

13...e5 is riskier when White's knight can still go to d5; for example, 14 ♖dd1 ♗b7 15 ♘d5! ♘xe4 16 ♕f3! ♘c5 17 ♗h6! gives White a dangerous attack. One line is 17...♘xb3+ 18 ♕xb3 ♔h8 19 ♗xg7+ ♔xg7 20 f6+ ♗xf6 21 ♕g3+ ♔h8 22 ♘xf6 ♕e6 23 ♕h4 ♕f5 24 ♖hf1 ♕g6 25 ♖xd6 and White is better.

14 ♖f1 ♘xe4

This is more or less forced, since 14...♗e6 15 exf5 ♗xb3 16 axb3 definitely favours White.

15 ♘xe4 fxe4 16 ♖xe4 (D)

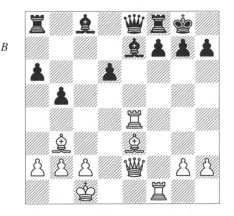

16...♗b7?!

Black aims to keep his extra pawn but by now he is playing with fire. The correct continuation was 16...♗e6! 17 ♗d4 (17 ♗xe6 fxe6 18 ♖xe6 ♖xf1+ 19 ♕xf1 ♕f7 is more or less equal) 17...♗g5+ 18 ♔b1 ♕c6 19 h4 ♖ae8! (19...♗h6? 20 ♖xe6! fxe6 21 ♖xf8+ ♖xf8 22 ♕xe6+ ♔h8 23 a3! rather surprisingly gives White a winning attack) and it's time for White to acquiesce to equality by 20 ♗xe6 fxe6 21 ♖e1 ♗f6 22 ♖xe6 ♗e5! 23 ♖xe8 ♖xe8 since the more ambitious 20 ♖xe6 fxe6 21 hxg5 ♕e4 22 ♖xf8+ ♖xf8 23 ♗e3 d5 can only lead to trouble for White.

17 ♖g4 d5

Blocking off the dangerous bishop is best, even though Black restricts his own bishop. 17...a5 18 ♕f2! ♗c8 loses spectacularly to 19 ♖xg7+! ♔xg7 20 ♕g3+ ♔h8 21 ♗xf7! ♖xf7 22 ♗d4+ ♗f6 23 ♖xf6.

18 ♗d4 (D)

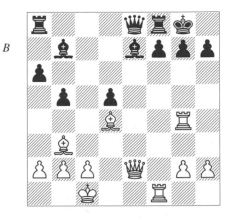

18...f6?

Black had to choose between ...f6 and ...g6 and he goes for the wrong one. At first sight 18...f6 looks the less weakening of the two because it erects a barrier to the d4-bishop, but it allows White to mount an attack against h7, a square which is almost impossible to defend. 18...g6 was correct; after 19 ♕e5 f6 20 ♕c7 ♗c6 21 ♖g3 White has strong pressure for the pawn, but Black is still fighting.

19 c3!

Black's lack of counterplay means that White can take his time. The bishop drops back to c2 to take aim against h7.

19...♕d7

After 19...♕f7 20 ♗c2, White's attack develops in much the same way; for example, 20...b4 21 ♕e3! and Black is faced with the deadly threats of 22 ♕h6 and 22 ♕h3.

20 ♗c2

The immediate threat is 21 ♖xg7+! ♔xg7 22 ♕h5.

20...g6?

Suicide, but Black's position was probably beyond saving in any case.

21 ♗xg6! hxg6 22 ♖xg6+ ♔f7 23 ♖gxf6+ ♗xf6 24 ♖xf6+ ♔g8 25 ♖g6+ 1-0

In this game we saw two important points; when faced with an unexpected move in the opening, it is often better to react safely and modestly rather than lash out with a risky attempt at a 'refutation'. The second point is that one should be flexible. Black played to win a pawn, which was not bad in itself; his mistake was grimly hanging on to it at all costs, when he could have equalized by returning it at the right moment. In some circumstances consistency is important, but stubbornness can be fatal.

The following example is based on a similar theme of an inappropriate response to an unexpected opening, coupled with material greed and neglect of development – a mixture of several motifs common to quick losses.

Alonso Zapata – John Nunn
Dubai Olympiad 1986
Ruy Lopez, Anti-Marshall

1 e4 e5 2 ᐅf3 ᐅc6 3 ♗b5 a6 4 ♗a4 ᐅf6 5 0-0 ♗e7 6 ♖e1 b5 7 ♗b3 0-0 8 a4 ♗b7 9 d3 ♖e8 *(D)*

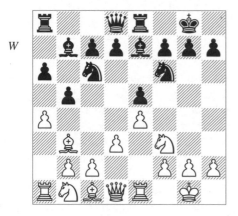

In 1986, this method of meeting the Anti-Marshall wasn't well known. The idea of the move, as opposed to the usual 9...d6, is that in some lines Black may be able to play ...d5 directly. This move was apparently new to White; how should he react? It is clear that there can't be anything wrong with simple development by 10 ᐅc3, 10 c3 or 10 ᐅbd2, and any of these would have been a reasonable choice. However, White was tempted by the poorly defended f7-pawn and decided to lash out with 10 ᐅg5. If, in fact, Black had been obliged to reply 10...♖f8 (as in the Flohr-Zaitsev), then there certainly wouldn't be any reason to criticize 10 ᐅg5, because at any rate White could repeat the position. However, Black is not forced to reply 10...♖f8 and then the idea of moving the knight to g5 starts to look dubious because White is moving the same piece twice while his queenside is still undeveloped.

10 ᐅg5?

These days 9...♖e8 isn't often played, because the simple 10 ᐅc3 and the rather more subtle 10 ᐅa3 are both believed to give White some advantage.

10...d5! 11 exd5 ᐅd4 *(D)*

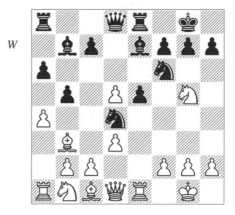

This pawn sacrifice is one of the points behind 9...♖e8. Exploiting the time White has wasted with ᐅg5, Black immediately seizes the initiative. It is doubtful if White can even equalize from this position, and even a slight slip will prove fatal.

12 ♗a2

12 d6? loses to 12...ᐅxb3 13 dxe7 ♕d5, while 12 ♖xe5 ᐅxb3 13 cxb3 ᐅxd5 14 ᐅc3

♕d7 is very good for Black. 12 c4 is one of White's better lines, but even here Black has some advantage after 12...♘xb3 13 ♕xb3 ♘xd5 14 ♘xf7 ♔xf7 15 cxd5 ♗xd5 16 ♕c2 b4.

12...♘xd5 *(D)*

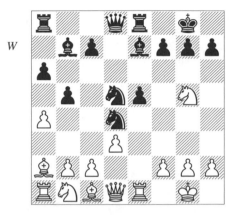

13 ♖xe5?!

White plays to win a pawn, but runs into still deeper trouble. The alternatives are:

1) 13 ♕h5? ♗xg5 14 ♗xg5 f6 wins for Black.

2) 13 ♘xf7?! (this is a critical try because it at least attempts to make use of the position of the knight on g5) 13...♔xf7 14 c3 ♘e6 15 ♕h5+ ♔g8 16 ♖xe5 (the pressure along the a2-g8 diagonal looks awkward, but Black can wriggle out) 16...♗g5! 17 ♗d2 (17 ♗xg5 ♘xg5 exploits White's weak back rank) 17...♗xd2 18 ♗xd5 ♗xd5 19 ♖xd5 ♕e7 20 ♘xd2 ♘f4 21 ♕f3 ♕e1+ 22 ♖xe1 ♖xe1+ 23 ♘f1 ♘e2+ 24 ♕xe2 ♖xe2 with a large advantage for Black.

3) 13 ♘f3 ♘b4 14 ♘xd4 ♘xa2 15 ♘f5 ♘xc1 16 ♘xe7+ ♖xe7 17 ♕xc1 ♖e6 and a draw was agreed at this point in Tal-Planinc, Moscow 1975, even though Black is clearly better.

4) 13 ♘c3 ♗xg5 14 ♗xg5 ♕xg5 15 ♗xd5 c6 16 ♘e4 ♕g6 17 ♗a2 c5 is at least slightly better for Black.

White should have conceded that he is now worse and played 13 ♘f3 or 13 ♘c3 but, as mentioned above, it is common for White to play 'by momentum' as if he were still better, even when he is not.

13...♗xg5 14 ♗xg5 ♕d7 *(D)*

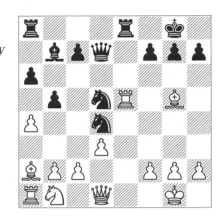

A look at the position shows that things have not gone well for White. All Black's pieces occupy active positions, while White has made little progress developing his queenside. The extra pawn provides little comfort.

15 ♖xe8+

White exchanges one of his few active pieces, but the alternative 15 ♗xd5 ♗xd5 16 ♖xe8+ (16 ♗f4 ♗xg2 17 ♔xg2 ♖xe5 18 ♗xe5 ♕d5+) 16...♖xe8 was also not very pleasant:

1) 17 ♗e3 ♕c6! (17...♗xg2 18 ♔xg2 ♕c6+ 19 ♔g1 ♘xc2 20 ♘c3 ♘xa1 21 ♕xa1 favours Black but is less clear – White even went on to win in Bacrot-Adams, European Internet blitz Ch 2003) 18 ♗xd4 ♗xg2 and White is defenceless.

2) 17 ♘d2 ♘e2+ 18 ♔h1 ♗xg2+ 19 ♔xg2 ♕g4+ 20 ♔h1 ♕xg5 21 axb5 ♕xb5 gives Black a clear advantage.

3) 17 ♘c3 ♗f3! 18 ♕f1 (18 gxf3 ♕h3 19 ♔h1 ♘xf3 20 ♗f4 ♘h4 21 ♕f1 ♕f3+ 22 ♔g1 ♕xf4 is also very good for Black) 18...♕g4 19 ♗e3 (19 ♗d2 b4 20 ♘c4 ♗xe4 21 dxe4 ♘f3+ wins for Black) 19...♘xc2 20 ♖c1 ♘xe3 21 fxe3 ♖xe3 22 axb5 axb5 23 ♘xb5 ♖xd3 24 ♘xc7 ♗e4 and Black has strong pressure.

15...♖xe8 16 ♘d2

More or less forced, since 16 ♘a3 b4 17 ♘c4 ♘e2+ 18 ♔h1 ♕g4 and 16 ♗e3 ♖xe3 17 fxe3 ♘xe3 win for Black.

16...♘b4 17 ♗b1? *(D)*

Instantly fatal, as is 17 ♘e4? ♘dxc2 18 ♖b1 ♗xe4. White should have tried 17 ♗b3, although even then 17...♘xb3 18 cxb3 (18 ♘xb3 ♕d5 19 ♕g4 ♘xc2 and Black wins) 18...♘xd3

19 ②f3 bxa4 20 bxa4 ♕f5 leaves him completely tied up.

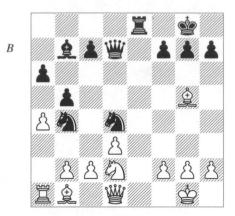

The diagram position represents a nightmare for White. His materialism and neglect of development have cost him dearly.

17...②e2+ 18 ♔f1 ♗xg2+

This combination exploits the undefended state of White's queen.

19 ♔xg2 ♕g4+ 20 ♔h1 ②g3+ 0-1

A further common error is that of removing an important defensive piece from the vicinity of one's king, or at any rate from a position where it can help in the defence of the king. Examples may be found in Games 21 (19 ②c4?), 45 (14 ②a4?), 93 (21...②ec6?) and 99 (17...②c4?). It is interesting to note that all these are knight moves. Repositioning a knight tends to be a more committal decision than repositioning a line-moving piece. If, for example, you move a queen from f6 to a6, it still controls some

squares on the kingside, such as g6 and h6, but if a knight moves from e5 to c4, then it no longer has any influence at all on the kingside and can only regain it by retracing its steps. In some of the above cases, the loser was motivated by the desire to generate some counterplay (Game 99, for example), but this has to be carefully judged. There is little point in arranging your pieces for active play on the queenside if you are mated on the kingside before this counterplay gets off the ground. In such cases one has to be pragmatic; if the active option doesn't work, then one should just settle for quiet, passive defence in the hope that things will take a turn for the better later on.

As a final topic, it is worth mentioning that the trend towards uncompromising play in the opening has increased the chances of losing quickly. Many modern openings involve a delicate balancing act; a concession is made in one area in order to gain a compensating advantage elsewhere. An example of this is the Sveshnikov Sicilian (1 e4 c5 2 ②f3 ②c6 3 d4 cxd4 4 ②xd4 ②f6 5 ②c3 e5 6 ②db5 d6 7 ♗g5 a6 8 ②a3 b5 9 ♗xf6 gxf6) in which Black accepts doubled f-pawns and a weak d5-square in return for some time (because the a3-knight must be re-activated) and eventual dynamic chances based on the two bishops and extra central pawn. Such openings, while they offer dynamic play and winning chances, place a considerable burden on the player adopting them. If the 'compensating advantages' are not exploited effectively, then the concessions which have been made may prove rapidly fatal. The following game provides a good example.

Veselin Topalov – Miguel Illescas
Linares 1995
Sicilian Defence, Sveshnikov Variation

1 e4 c5 2 ②f3 ②c6 3 d4 cxd4 4 ②xd4 ②f6 5 ②c3 e5 6 ②db5 d6 7 ♗g5 a6 8 ②a3 b5 9 ♗xf6 gxf6 10 ②d5 ♗g7 11 c3 f5 12 exf5 ♗xf5 13 ②c2 0-0 14 ②ce3 ♗e6 15 ♗d3 f5 *(D)*

A typical Sveshnikov position. White has manoeuvred his knights to gain secure control

of d5, while in the meantime Black has eliminated his doubled pawns and gained a 2-0 central pawn-majority. Control of d5 is a critical factor, because if White loses his control then Black's central pawns will be a massive force. For Black's part, it is unlikely that he will be

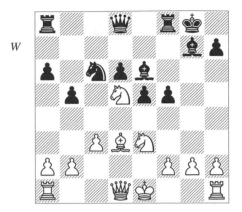

W

able to wrest control of d5 directly; instead, he must try to develop play somewhere so as to try to draw White's pieces away from d5.

16 ♗c2

16 0-0 and 16 ♕h5 are the other main continuations.

16...♗h6

At the time a new idea; Black intends an aggressive plan based on a direct kingside attack. 16...♖a7, 16...f4 and 16...♔h8 are playable alternatives, but Black should avoid 16...♘e7? due to 17 ♘xe7+ ♕xe7 18 ♗xf5! and the possible fork on d5 nets White a pawn. After Black's crushing defeat in the current game, the whole plan with 16...♗h6 more or less vanished, but it might in fact be playable, provided Black follows it up correctly.

17 0-0 (D)

17 ♕h5 is another idea, with perhaps an edge for White after 17...♗xe3 18 ♘xe3 ♕e8 19 ♕xe8 ♖axe8 20 0-0-0.

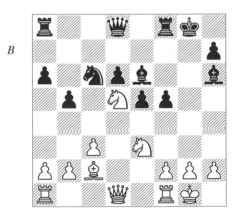

B

17...♖a7?!

This was Black's idea; he wants to swing his rook over to g7 to launch a direct attack on the white king. However, it was at this point that Black could have justified his previous play by 17...f4!, and now:

1) 18 ♕h5 ♕g5 (18...fxe3? 19 ♕xh6 exf2+ 20 ♖xf2 gives White a winning attack) 19 ♕xg5+ ♗xg5 20 ♘c7 ♗f7 21 ♘xa8 fxe3 22 ♘b6 exf2+ with good play for Black.

2) 18 ♘g4 ♗g7 19 ♕f3 leads to an unclear position. Note that 19...h5? is bad due to 20 ♕e4.

18 f4 ♕h4 19 g3 ♖g7? (D)

Black plays consistently for the attack, but with all his pieces stuck on the kingside, his central position is highly vulnerable. 19...♕h3 is better, with a slight advantage for White after 20 a4.

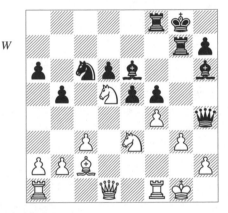

W

20 ♘c7!

Topalov pinpoints the flaw in Black's plan. With d6 and e6 under attack, Black's position is collapsing and he can only hope for salvation in tactics.

20...exf4

White consolidates his extra material after 20...♖xg3+ 21 hxg3 ♕xg3+ 22 ♘g2 ♗c4 23 ♕f3 or 20...♗c4 21 ♘xf5 ♖xf5 22 ♗xf5 ♖xg3+ 23 hxg3 ♕xg3+ 24 ♔h1 ♕h4+ 25 ♔g2 ♗xf1+ 26 ♕xf1 ♗xf4 27 ♕f3.

21 ♘g2 ♕h3

21...♕e7 22 ♘xe6 ♕xe6 23 ♗b3 costs Black his queen.

22 ♖xf4! (D)

An absolutely correct decision. By offering the exchange, White brings Black's attack to a dead halt, leaving him facing disaster in the centre. Not 22 ♘xe6?? fxg3 23 hxg3 ♗e3+! and Black wins, nor 22 ♘xf4? ♗xf4 23 ♖xf4 ♖xg3+ 24 hxg3 ♕xg3+ 25 ♔h1 ♕h3+ with a draw.

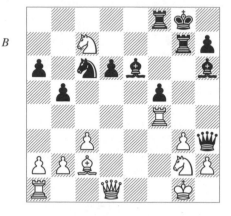

B

22...♗xf4

Or 22...♖xc7 23 ♖h4 and Black's queen is trapped.

23 ♘xf4 ♖xg3+ 24 ♔h1! (D)

The last finesse. 24 hxg3? ♕xg3+ 25 ♘g2 ♘e5! 26 ♘xe6 ♘f3+ 27 ♕xf3 ♕xf3 28 ♘xf8 ♕e2 is a likely draw.

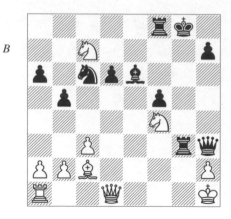

B

Now Black has several pieces hanging and heavy material loss is inevitable.

24...♕h6 25 ♕xd6 1-0

If you decide to adopt such double-edged opening systems, then it is necessary not only to prepare specific lines but also to have a good understanding of the general principles behind the opening. When 'double-edged opening systems' are mentioned, one tends naturally to think of openings such as the Sicilian and the Grünfeld, where an imbalance is part of the very nature of the opening. However, other openings include lines in which disaster is only one mistake away.

John Nunn – Migchiel de Jong
Leeuwarden 1995
French Defence, Winawer Variation

1 e4 e6 2 d4 d5 3 ♘c3 ♗b4 4 e5 ♘e7 5 a3 ♗xc3+ 6 bxc3 b6

The 3...♗b4 line of the French Defence is a perfectly respectable and solid opening, but even here Black has to take care not to allow his potential dark-square weaknesses to become serious. Thanks to the blocked centre, Black can often leave his king in the middle for some time, but this is another possible danger area since if the position should suddenly open up, then the king may be exposed to attack.

7 ♕g4 ♘g6 8 h4 h5 9 ♕d1 ♗a6 10 ♗xa6 ♘xa6 11 ♗g5 f6

This line has been played a number of times, but I don't like it for Black. Allowing the centre to be opened while his king is unable to castle quickly strikes me as asking for too much from the position. I prefer the alternative 11...♕d7 12 ♘e2 ♘e7 13 ♘f4 g6 which, while involving a further dark-square weakening, at least keeps the centre closed.

12 ♕d3

Forking the two undefended knights, but White does not win material because his own bishop is hanging.

12...♔f7 13 ♖h3 (D)

White utilizes the tactical point 13...fxg5? 14 ♖f3+ ♘f4 15 hxg5 ♕xg5 16 ♘h3 to keep his bishop on g5 for the moment. 13 ♘h3 is based on a similar idea and is also promising for White.

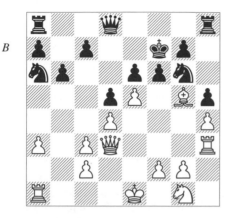

13...♕c8?

We are still in the opening and Black already makes a fatal error. It is essential for Black to keep his pawn on f6 so as to retain some dark-square control. Therefore he must play 13...♘b8 14 ♖f3 ♘d7 to support the f6-square. I believe that White is still better after 15 exf6 (not 15 ♘h3? ♘dxe5 16 dxe5 ♘xe5 17 ♕e2 ♘xf3+ 18 ♕xf3 ♕d6 with advantage to Black) 15...gxf6 16 ♘h3 ♕e7 17 ♔f1, followed by ♖e1, but anything is better than the catastrophe which now unfolds.

14 exf6 gxf6 *(D)*

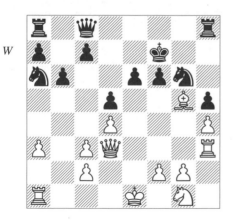

15 ♖f3

Now Black has no choice but to push the f-pawn, but this leaves the dark squares around his king seriously weakened.

15...f5 16 ♖g3 *(D)*

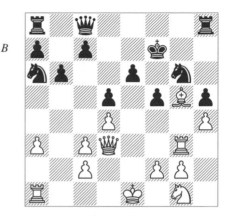

Clearing the way for ♘f3, taking aim at the weak e5- and g5-squares.

16...c6

In addition to Black's problems on the king-side, he still has to bring the out-of-play knight on a6 back into the game.

17 ♘f3 ♘c7 *(D)*

The bid for counterplay by 17...e5 18 ♘xe5+ ♘xe5 19 dxe5 ♘c5 20 ♕d4 ♘e4 is insufficient after 21 ♖e3 ♖g8 22 f3; for example, 22...♘xg5 23 hxg5 ♖xg5 24 e6+ ♔g8 25 ♕f6.

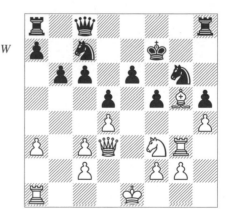

After the text-move White only has to occupy the weakened e5-square and Black's position will collapse. He achieves this with a surprising temporary piece sacrifice.

18 ♗f4! ♘xf4

Declining the sacrifice is little better; for example, 18...♖g8 19 ♘e5+ ♘xe5 20 ♗xe5 ♖g4 21 ♖xg4 hxg4 22 ♕e3 and the queen penetrates to h6.

19 ♘e5+ ♔e8 20 ♕f3

White regains the piece, whereupon his dominant e5-knight and control of the g-file quickly finish the game.

20...♘b5 21 ♕xf4 ♕c7 22 ♖g6 ♕d6 23 ♕g5 ♖f8 24 ♖g7 1-0

To summarize, the most common reasons for quick losses are:

1) Unwise pawn-grabbing.

2) Neglect of development.

3) Leaving the king in the centre for too long.

4) Moving an important defensive piece away from the king.

5) Reacting badly to a surprise in the opening.

6) Inappropriate play resulting from a failure to evaluate the position objectively.

7) Playing a double-edged opening without knowing what you are doing.

In many cases, more than one of these sins is committed simultaneously. If you avoid all of them, then your chances of reaching a reasonable middlegame position will be much improved. Conversely, if you feel that your opponent is guilty of one or more sins, then it is worth looking to see if you can exploit the situation. Many players fail to exploit mistakes in the opening because they do not react with sufficient energy. Ask yourself if you can open the centre or make a sacrifice to attack the enemy king. Then you will not only avoid some quick losses, but also score some quick wins.

Game 1
Eigil Pedersen – Peter Gallmeyer
Denmark 1971
Sicilian Defence, Najdorf Variation

1 e4 c5 2 ♘f3 d6 3 d4 cxd4 4 ♘xd4 ♘f6 5 ♘c3 a6 6 ♗g5 e6 7 f4 b5 8 e5 dxe5 9 fxe5 ♕c7 10 exf6 ♕e5+ 11 ♗e2 ♕xg5 12 0-0 ♕e5 13 ♗f3?!

13 ♔h1 and especially 13 ♘f3! are currently believed to be more dangerous for Black.

13...♖a7 14 ♘c6!? ♕c5+?!

According to present-day theory, 14...♘xc6 15 ♗xc6+ ♗d7 16 ♗xd7+ ♖xd7 17 ♕f3 ♗d6 is fine for Black.

15 ♔h1 ♖d7 (D)

Not 15...♘xc6? 16 ♘e4 ♕b6 (after 16...♕d4 17 ♘d6+! ♕xd6 18 fxg7 ♖g8 19 gxf8♕+ ♕xf8 20 ♗xc6+ ♗d7 21 ♕f3 Black will suffer due to his exposed king) 17 fxg7 ♗xg7 18 ♘d6+ ♔e7 19 ♗xc6 f5 20 ♘xf5+! exf5 21 ♖e1+ ♔f6 (21...♔f7 22 ♕d5+ ♔g6 23 ♕d6+ transposes, as 23...♗f6 loses to 24 ♗e8+) 22 ♕d6+ ♔g5 23 h4+! with a decisive attack.

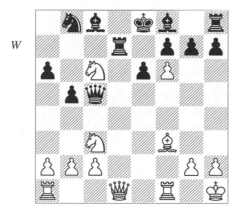

16 ♘xb8!

This queen sacrifice, first played in the current game, is the only way for White to continue his attack. Contrary to R.Marić's analysis in *Informator 12*, it should lead to a draw against best defence.

16...♖xd1 17 ♖axd1

The threat of 18 ♗c6+ forces Black's reply.

17...gxf6 18 ♘e4 (D)

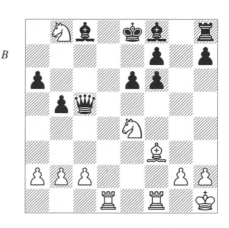

18...♕c7?

The fatal error. 18...♕f5! is the best defence. After 19 ♖d3 (19 ♘xf6+ ♕xf6 20 ♗c6+ ♔e7 21 ♖xf6 ♔xf6 is equal) 19...♕f4! White is forced into the drawish liquidation with 20 ♘xf6+, etc.

19 ♘xf6+ ♔e7 20 ♗h5!

Threatening a beautiful mate in four by 21 ♘c6+ ♕xc6 22 ♘g8+ ♖xg8 (22...♔e8 23 ♗xf7#) 23 ♖xf7+ ♔e8 24 ♖g7#.

20...♗g7 (D)

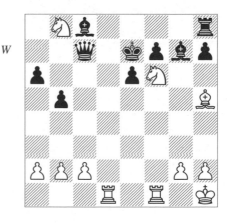

21 ♘c6+! ♕xc6

Or 21...&f8 22 ♘d7+ ♗xd7 23 ♖xf7+ ♔g8 24 ♘e7#.

22 ♘g8+! ♔e8

22...♖xg8 23 ♖xf7+ ♔e8 24 ♖c7+ ♔f8 25 ♖d8+ and mate next move.

23 ♗xf7+ ♔f8 24 ♖d8+ 1-0

Game 2
Mikhail Tal – Wolfgang Uhlmann
Moscow 1971
French Defence, Tarrasch Variation

1 e4 e6 2 d4 d5 3 ♘d2 c5 4 ♘gf3 ♘c6 5 ♗b5

It is hard to surprise Wolfgang Uhlmann in the French Defence, which he has played throughout his long career, but Tal apparently succeeded with this move since the East German grandmaster now thought for 20 minutes. In fact the move had been played before, but only very infrequently.

5...dxe4

These days 5...a6 is considered to be a simpler method of equalizing.

6 ♘xe4 ♗d7 7 ♗g5! *(D)*

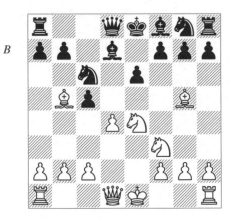

B

As usual, Tal plays for rapid piece development.

7...♕a5+ 8 ♘c3 cxd4

A few years later, in the game Ničevski-Uhlmann, Skopje 1976, Uhlmann improved by 8...a6 9 ♗xc6 ♗xc6 10 d5 (10 dxc5 ♗xc5 11 ♕e2 ♘f6 is equal) 10...♗xd5 11 0-0 ♗c6 12 ♘e5 ♕c7 13 ♖e1 ♘f6 14 ♗xf6 gxf6 15 ♘xc6 ♕xc6 16 ♕h5 ♗e7, and this time Uhlmann went on to win.

9 ♘xd4

Tal relates that at first he was attracted by the piece sacrifice 9 ♗xc6 ♗xc6 10 ♕xd4 ♗xf3 11 gxf3, but 11...♕xg5 12 ♕a4+ b5! 13 ♘xb5 ♕e5+ 14 ♔f1 ♔e7 seemed insufficient for White. In addition, Black could play safe with 11...♕b4, quenching White's attacking ambitions.

9...♗b4?! *(D)*

Black plays for the win of a pawn, but the resulting dark-squared weaknesses give White ample compensation. 9...♗e7 is sounder; after 10 ♕d2 (10 ♗e3 ♕c7 11 ♕e2 ♘f6 12 0-0 0-0-0 is level) 10...♘f6 (but not 10...♗xg5 11 ♕xg5 ♘xd4?? 12 ♗xd7+) 11 0-0-0 a double-edged position arises.

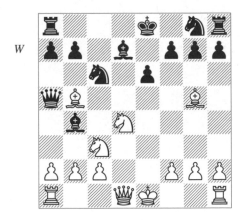

W

10 0-0! ♗xc3 11 bxc3 ♕xc3? *(D)*

Consistent, but far too risky (especially when facing Tal). The continuation 11...a6 12 ♗xc6 ♗xc6 was better, and now:

1) 13 ♘xc6 ♕xg5 14 ♕d6! ♕d5! (14...♘h6 15 ♖fd1! bxc6 16 ♖ab1 and 14...♘e7 15 ♖fd1! ♘xc6 16 ♕d7+ ♔f8 17 ♕xb7 are both excellent for White) 15 ♕xd5 exd5 16 ♖fe1+ ♔f8 17

♘b4 ♘f6 and White can win the d5-pawn, but in view of his broken queenside pawns it is very unlikely that this will be sufficient to win.

2) 13 ♕g4 ♗d5 14 c4! ♗xc4 15 ♖fe1 gives White an ominous initiative in return for a pawn.

Or 14...♘f6 15 ♖ad1 (the threat is 16 ♗xf6 gxf6 17 ♖xe6+! fxe6 18 ♕xe6+ ♔f8 19 ♖d7 mating) 15...a6 16 ♖xe6+ fxe6 17 ♕xe6+ ♔f8 18 ♗c4 ♘e5 19 ♕d6+ ♔e8 20 ♗xf6 1-0 Mulder van Leens Dijkstra-Balkowski, corr. 1985. It is amazing that this losing line should reappear in a postal game played 14 years later!

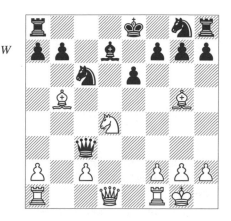

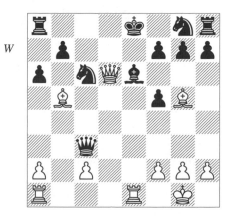

12 ♘f5!!

White must continue energetically; this beautiful sacrifice both gains time and opens the e-file.

12...exf5

Forced, as 12...♕c5 13 ♘d6+ ♔f8 14 ♘xf7 ♔xf7 (14...♕xb5 loses to 15 ♕xd7) 15 ♕xd7+ ♘ge7 16 ♗xc6 bxc6 17 ♗xe7 ♕xe7 18 ♕xc6 gives White a clear extra pawn.

13 ♖e1+ ♗e6 14 ♕d6 (D)

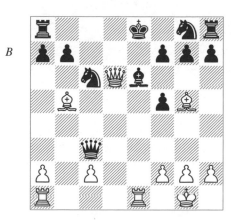

With two threats: one the simple 15 ♖ad1 and the other to transfer the g5-bishop to b4 via d2.

14...a6 (D)

15 ♗d2!

Threat No. 2 is executed. Such attacks may look easy, but there are many false paths; here, for example, 15 ♗a4? b5 16 ♗d2 ♕c4 17 ♗b3 ♖d8! 18 ♕c7 ♖d7 is a draw by repetition.

15...♕xc2 16 ♗b4! (D)

Not 16 ♖ac1? ♕xc1! 17 ♖xc1 axb5 18 ♖xc6 ♖d8! and Black wins.

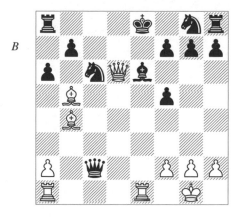

16...axb5

Black may as well take the piece as he cannot stop the check on f8.

17 ♕f8+ ♔d7 18 ♖ed1+!

18 ♖ad1+ ♔c7 19 ♕xa8 ♘f6 20 ♗d6+ ♔b6 21 ♕xh8 ♘e4 gives Black a little counterplay.

18...♔c7 19 ♕xa8 1-0

Slightly early, but after 19...♕a4 (19...♘f6 20 ♕xh8 ♘e4 21 ♗e1 now wins easily; 19...♕e4 20 ♗d6+ ♔b6 21 ♕f8 ♕h4 transposes) 20 ♗d6+ ♔b6 21 ♕f8 ♕h4 (21...♕g4 22 ♗c5+ ♔c7 23 ♕d6+ ♔c8 24 ♗b6 mates) 22 ♗c5+ ♔c7 23 ♖ab1 b4 24 ♗d6+ ♔b6 25 ♗xb4 the attack is decisive.

Game 3
Albin Planinc – Miguel Najdorf
Wijk aan Zee 1973
Sicilian Defence, Najdorf Variation

1 e4 c5 2 ♘f3 d6 3 d4 cxd4 4 ♘xd4 ♘f6 5 ♘c3 a6 6 ♗g5 ♘bd7 7 f4 e6 8 ♕f3 ♗e7 9 0-0-0 ♕c7 10 ♗d3 h6

The Browne System, currently considered Black's safest response to the 10 ♗d3 line. The main idea is that after 11 ♗h4 g5 12 fxg5 ♘e5 13 ♕e2 ♘fg4 Black will regain the pawn and establish a knight on the powerful central square e5. The only real problem with this plan is that Black's king is condemned to stay in the centre for some time. However, the current view is that White has no way of exploiting this factor.

11 ♕h3 *(D)*

B

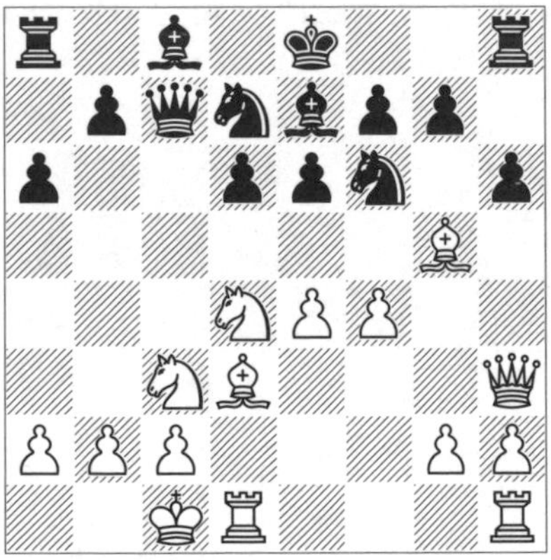

This move attempts to cross Black's plan of forcing through ...g5, or at least to extract a concession if he goes ahead with it.

11...♘c5?!

In 1973, it was early days for this line and it was not yet established that 11...♘b6 is the best move. The point of playing the knight to b6 is to increase Black's control of d5 so that a later ...e5 cannot be met by ♗xf6 followed by ♘d5.

12 ♖he1

12 f5 is another possibility, when Black's best may be the surprising 12...♘d5!?.

12...♖g8?! *(D)*

Black wants the g5-bishop to make up its mind; if it retreats to h4, then Black can continue with 13...g5. 12...♗d7 is a more solid alternative.

W

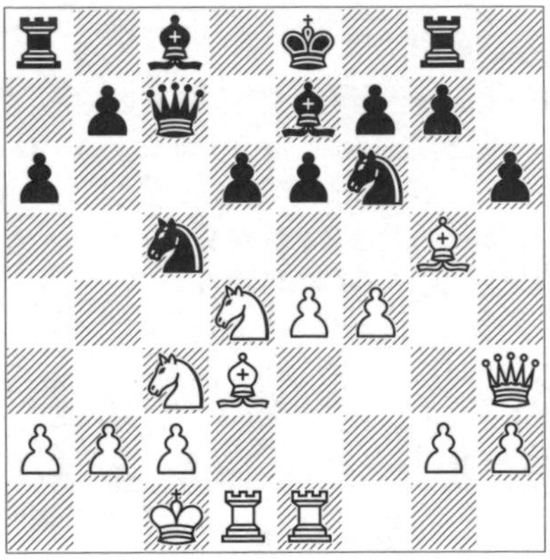

13 e5!?

White simply leaves his bishop on g5 and uses the tempo to crash through in the centre. The resulting open lines more than compensate for the pawn sacrificed.

13...dxe5

Or 13...hxg5 14 exf6 ♗xf6 (after 14...gxf6 15 ♕h7 ♖f8 16 ♘f5 White has a very strong attack) 15 ♘d5 ♕d8 16 ♘xf6+ ♕xf6 17 ♗h7 ♖h8 18 ♘f5 with dangerous threats for White.

14 fxe5 *(D)*

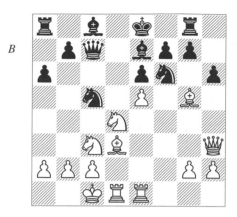

14...hxg5

Certainly not 14...♘d5? 15 ♗xe7 ♘xe7 (or 15...♘xc3 16 ♗xc5 ♘xd1 17 ♗d6 and White wins) 16 ♕g3 ♘xd3+ 17 ♖xd3 followed by ♘e4-d6.

15 exf6 ♗xf6

This game is often portrayed as a complete whitewash, probably due to the notes in *Informator 15*, where 13 e5 was already given as 'winning'. However, this is a bit of an exaggeration although there is no doubt that White's attack is extremely dangerous. The alternative 15...gxf6 is met by 16 ♕h7 ♘xd3+ 17 ♖xd3 ♖f8 18 ♕h5! with a tremendous initiative for White.

16 ♘d5 ♕d8 *(D)*

16...♕a5 is well met by 17 ♗c4! ♗xd4 18 b4 ♕d8 19 ♖xd4 ♔f8 20 bxc5 exd5 21 ♕a3 with a strong initiative.

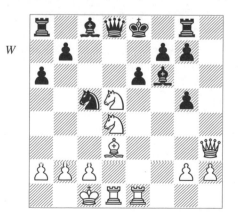

17 ♗h7?

An imaginative idea, which in the game succeeds dramatically. However, it would have been stronger to continue 17 ♕h7! ♘xd3+ (17...♔f8 18 ♘xf6 ♕xf6 19 ♖f1 ♘xd3+ 20 ♕xd3 ♕e7 21 ♘f3 also favours White) 18 ♖xd3 ♔f8 19 ♘xf6 ♕xf6 20 ♘f3 b5 21 ♘e5 with a clear advantage.

17...♖h8?

After this Black is indeed in trouble. There often comes a point when the defender has to sacrifice material himself to prevent the attacker's initiative from getting out of hand. Here Black should have played 17...♕xd5 18 ♗xg8 (or 18 ♘xe6 ♕xd1+! 19 ♔xd1 ♗xe6 20 ♖xe6+ ♘xe6 21 ♗xg8 0-0-0+ and the unusual fork wins for Black) 18...♕xa2 19 ♗xf7+ (otherwise White would be worse) 19...♔xf7 20 ♕h5+ ♔g8 with a draw.

18 ♘f5 *(D)*

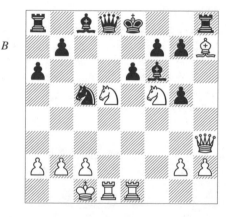

18...g4

There is no longer any defence, although this move does make life fairly easy for White. 18...♘a4 is the best try, but even then 19 ♘d6+! ♔f8 20 ♘xf6 ♕xf6 21 ♘c4 ♕f4+ (21...♕e7 22 ♖f1 e5 23 ♖xf7+! ♕xf7 24 ♕a3+ ♕e7 25 ♖d8+ ♔f7 26 ♘d6+ wins for White) 22 ♖d2! ♕xc4 23 ♕a3+ ♘c5 (23...♔e8 24 ♕d6 ♗d7 25 ♕xd7+ ♔f8 26 ♖f2 is decisive) 24 ♖d8+ ♔e7 25 ♖xh8 is very good for White.

19 ♕g3

Now Black faces the threat of 20 ♘c7+.

19...♔f8 20 ♘xf6 1-0

Owing to 20...♕xf6 21 ♕d6+ ♔e8 22 ♘xg7+ mating.

Game 4
Yuri Balashov – Ulf Andersson
Wijk aan Zee 1973
Sicilian Defence, Scheveningen Variation

1 e4 c5 2 ♘f3 e6 3 ♘c3 ♘c6 4 d4 cxd4 5 ♘xd4 a6 6 ♗e2 ♕c7 7 0-0 ♘f6 8 ♗e3 d6 9 f4 ♗e7 10 ♕e1 0-0 11 ♕g3 ♘xd4 12 ♗xd4 b5 13 a3 ♗b7 14 ♗d3

These days 14 ♔h1 is overwhelmingly the most popular move, with 14 ♖ae1 in second place.

14...g6

14...e5! 15 fxe5 ♘h5 followed by 16...dxe5 is the correct antidote to White's plan, since after this Black has equalized completely. For this reason 14 ♗d3 is almost never played today.

15 f5 ♖ae8?!

Not a very good move as it exposes Black to the possibility of ♗e3-h6, trapping the rook. 15...♘h5 16 ♕h3 e5 17 ♗e3 ♘f4 18 ♗xf4 exf4 19 ♖xf4 ♗f6 is better, with good dark-squared play for the pawn.

16 ♕h3 *(D)*

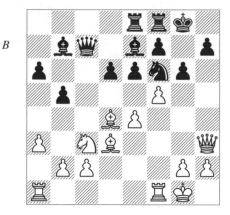

Attacking e6.

16...gxf5?

This certainly meets the threat of 17 fxe6, but at what a cost! 16...e5 17 ♗e3 ♖c8 18 ♗h6 ♖fe8 is better, although 19 ♗g5 gives White some advantage.

17 ♕h6

Not 17 exf5 e5, when the diagonals leading to Black's king are blocked.

17...e5

17...♕d8 loses to 18 ♖f3.

18 ♖xf5 ♘g4

This must have been the defence Andersson was counting on. It seems that the result will be the exchange of the d4-bishop for the g4-knight, when Black's grip on the dark squares gives him good chances of holding on.

19 ♕h3 exd4 *(D)*

19...♘f6 20 ♘d5 ♗xd5 21 exd5 exd4 22 ♖xf6 wins for White.

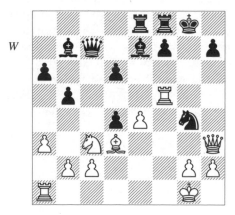

20 ♘d5!

White does not take the g4-knight but simply presses home his attack.

20...♕d7

After 20...♗xd5 21 exd5 Black is powerless to defend h7.

21 e5!

Again White refuses the knight and sets up the usual attack against h7.

21...♔h8

21...♘xe5 22 ♖g5+ wins the queen.

22 ♖h5 f5 23 e6 1-0

As 23...♕xe6 24 ♖xh7+ ♔g8 25 ♖h8+ ♔f7 26 ♕h7# is mate.

Game 5
William Lombardy – Miguel Quinteros
Manila 1973
Sicilian Defence, Najdorf Variation

1 e4 c5 2 ♘f3 d6 3 d4 cxd4 4 ♘xd4 ♘f6 5 ♘c3 a6 6 ♗g5 e6 7 f4 ♗e7 8 ♕f3 h6 9 ♗h4 ♕c7 10 0-0-0 ♘bd7

These days Black usually waits for ♗d3 before playing ...h6.

11 ♗e2!

And this is why. Against ...h6, the f1-bishop is better placed on e2.

11...♖b8

Spending an extra tempo preparing ...b5 is unappealing, but after the immediate 11...b5 White can utilize the weakness of g6; e.g., 12 ♗xf6 ♘xf6 13 e5 ♗b7 14 ♕g3 dxe5 15 fxe5 ♘d7 16 ♘xe6 fxe6 17 ♕g6+ ♔d8 18 ♕xe6 ♖e8 19 ♕f5 with a massive attack.

12 ♕g3 ♖g8

All these rook moves are not a good sign.

13 ♖hf1 b5 *(D)*

13...g5 is the alternative, but then 14 fxg5 ♘e5 15 ♘f3 favours White.

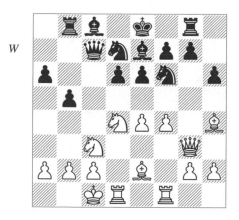

14 ♘xe6!

Again exploiting the weakness created by ...h6.

14...fxe6 15 ♕g6+ ♔d8

15...♔f8 loses to 16 e5 dxe5 17 f5 ♕d8 18 ♗xf6 gxf6 19 ♕xh6+ ♖g7 20 fxe6.

16 e5 dxe5 *(D)*

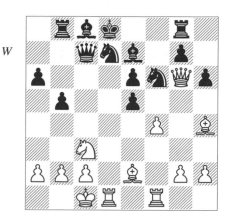

17 f5? *(D)*

Not the most incisive continuation of the attack. The alternatives are:

1) 17 ♗xf6 ♗xf6 18 ♕f7 ♖e8! (18...♖h8 19 ♘e4 gives White a very strong attack) 19 ♗h5 ♖h8 20 ♘e4 ♗e7 21 ♕xg7 ♖f8 is unclear.

2) 17 fxe5! ♕xe5 18 ♗g3 ♕e3+ 19 ♔b1 b4 20 ♗f4 ♕a7 21 ♘e4 ♘xe4 22 ♕xe4 is very dangerous for Black as there are many open lines in front of his king.

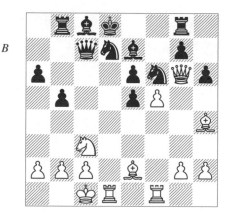

17...exf5

17...♕c6 18 ♕f7 ♖f8 19 ♕xg7 b4 20 ♗f3 ♕b6 is also unclear.

18 ♗xf6?

A further error. This exchange relieves much of the pressure on Black's position, which White could have maintained by 18 ♕f7! ♖e8 (or 18...♖f8 19 ♕xg7) 19 ♖xf5. This line would have left White with sufficient compensation for the piece, whereas now things swing (temporarily!) Black's way.

18...♗xf6 19 ♘d5 ♕c6 20 ♖xf5 ♖f8?

20...♕e6! is much better, as after 21 ♗g4 Black can run White's queen out of squares by 21...♕e8 22 ♕h7 ♖h8. In this case White would be struggling for equality.

21 ♗g4 ♖b6? *(D)*

Black collapses. 21...♕e6 (21...♖b7 is also better than the text-move) 22 ♖f3 (22 ♖h5 ♕c6 leaves White with nothing better than repetition) 22...♕e8 was the correct defence, with a roughly equal position.

22 ♖xf6!

Crushing.

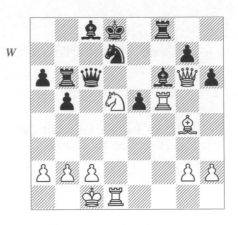

W

22...gxf6

Or 22...♖xf6 23 ♕xg7 ♖e6 24 ♕f7 and wins.

23 ♕g7 ♖b7

Black cooperates in making the game a miniature. 23...♖e8 loses to 24 ♘xb6 ♕xb6 25 ♖xd7+ ♗xd7 26 ♕xd7#.

24 ♕e7# (1-0)

Game 6

Boris Spassky – Nukhim Rashkovsky

USSR Ch, Moscow 1973

Sicilian Defence, Najdorf Variation

1 e4 c5 2 ♘f3 d6 3 d4 cxd4 4 ♘xd4 ♘f6 5 ♘c3 a6 6 ♗g5 e6 7 f4 ♕c7 8 ♗d3 *(D)*

B

An interesting line against 7...♕c7; for the moment White does not commit his queen.

8...♘bd7

This may already be inaccurate, since it allows White to develop his queen to e2 and prepare for e5 more quickly than usual. After 8...♗e7 White would be more or less forced to transpose into normal lines by 9 ♕f3 because 9 ♕e2?! h6 10 ♗h4? loses a pawn to 10...♘xe4.

9 ♕e2 b5 10 0-0-0 ♗b7 11 ♖he1

In contrast to the line with the queen on f3, the e4-pawn is not pinned and therefore White is already threatening 12 e5.

11...♗e7 12 e5 dxe5 13 fxe5 ♘d5 *(D)*

14 ♗xe7

Perhaps slightly inaccurate, although it requires exceptionally deep analysis to show this. The alternative 14 ♘xe6! seems to give White the advantage in every line. Then 14...fxe6? is very bad due to 15 ♕h5+ ♔d8 (or 15...g6 16 ♗xg6+ hxg6 17 ♕xh8+ ♘f8 18 ♗xe7 ♕xe7 19 ♘e4 leading to a clear advantage for White) 16 ♘xd5 ♗xd5 17 ♗xe7+ ♔xe7 18 ♕h4+! (the

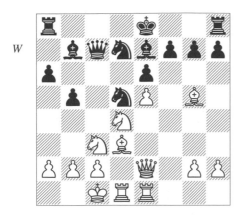

key move; if Black's king moves to e8, the h-pawn is pinned and thus ♗g6+ is possible) 18...♔e8 (18...g5 19 ♕xg5+ ♔e8 20 ♕g7 ♖f8 21 ♗xh7 ♕a5 22 ♗e4! ♕xa2 23 ♗xd5 exd5 24 e6 ♘c5 25 e7 wins for White) 19 ♗g6+ hxg6 20 ♕xh8+ ♘f8 21 ♖f1 ♘c5 22 ♕g8 ♔e7 23 ♖f2 followed by 24 ♖df1 and wins. Thus Black has to try 14...♗xg5+ 15 ♘xg5 ♘xc3 16 bxc3! (16 ♕f2 0-0-0! 17 bxc3 ♕xc3 18 ♘xf7 ♖hf8 leads to unclear complications) 16...♕xc3 17 ♕g4! with a very dangerous attack; for example, 17...♘c5 18 ♖e3! ♕a3+ 19 ♔d2 ♕a4 20 ♕f5! and Black will not be able to defend.

14...♘xc3 (D)

14...♔e7 loses to 15 ♕g4 ♘xc3 16 ♘xe6 ♕c6 17 ♕g5+, while 14...♘xe7 15 ♗xb5 axb5 16 ♘cxb5 ♕b6 17 ♘d6+ ♔f8 18 ♖f1 ♘f5 19 ♘4xf5 ♖xa2 20 ♘c4 ♕b4 (20...♖a1+ 21 ♔d2 ♕b4+ 22 c3 ♖xd1+ 23 ♖xd1 is also very good for White) 21 ♔b1 gives White a large advantage, since 21...♕a4 is calmly met by 22 b3!.

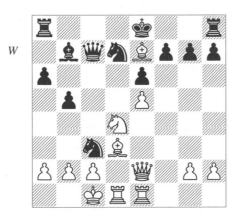

15 ♕g4 (D)

15 bxc3 ♔xe7 16 ♕g4 ♗d5 17 ♗e4 ♗xe4 18 ♘xe6 ♕xc3 is unclear.

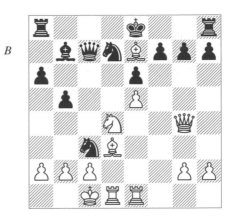

15...♘xd1

The best chance, because 15...♘xe5 16 ♕xg7 ♘xd1 17 ♖xe5 ♕xe7 18 ♕xh8+ ♔d7 19 ♕g7 ♘f2 20 ♗xh7 certainly favours White.

16 ♘xe6! (D)

Not 16 ♗d6? ♘xe5! 17 ♗xe5 ♘f2 18 ♘xe6 (if 18 ♕xg7, then 18...♘xd3+ 19 ♔b1 ♘xe5 20 ♕xh8+ ♔e7 21 ♕xe5 ♕xe5 22 ♖xe5 ♗xg2 wins for Black) 18...♘xd3+ (18...fxe6 19 ♕xe6+ ♕e7 20 ♕xe7+ ♔xe7 is also slightly better for Black) 19 ♔b1 ♕xe5 20 ♖xe5 ♘xe5 21 ♕xg7 ♘g6 22 ♘c7+ ♔e7 23 ♘xa8 ♖xa8 and Black has an edge.

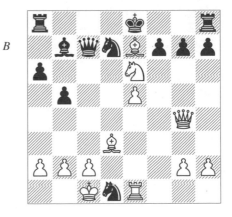

16...♕c6?

Black collapses under the sustained tactical barrage. He had to accept the knight by 16...fxe6

17 ♗d6 ♛b6 (17...♛c6 loses to 18 ♛g5 ♘f6 19 ♗e4 ♛d7 20 ♗xb7 ♛xb7 21 exf6) and now White has a choice of lines, but no clear route to an advantage:

1) 18 ♛g5 ♘f6 19 exf6 ♛xd6 (19...0-0-0 20 fxg7 ♖hg8 21 ♗e5! is very good for White) 20 fxg7 ♖g8 21 ♖xd1 most likely leads to a draw; e.g., 21...♛c7 22 ♛h5+ ♚e7 23 ♛g5+ with perpetual check.

2) 18 ♛xe6+ ♚d8 19 ♗f5 ♗c6 (19...♛c6? 20 ♛e7+ ♚c8 21 e6 wins for White) 20 ♛e7+ ♚c8 21 e6 ♘f6 is tremendously unclear.

17 ♘xg7+ ♚xe7 18 ♛g5+ *(D)*

White now wins by force.

18...f6

18...♚f8 19 ♘f5 wins after 19...♛g6 20 ♛e7+ ♚g8 21 e6 fxe6 22 ♖xe6, 19...♛xg2 20

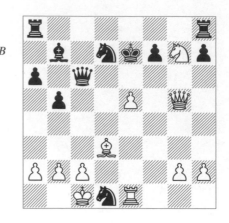

B

♛e7+ ♚g8 21 e6 or 19...♘f2 20 e6 ♘xd3+ 21 ♚b1.

19 exf6++ ♚d8 20 f7+ ♚c7 21 ♛f4+ 1-0

Game 7

Dragoljub Velimirović – Evgeny Vasiukov
USSR – Yugoslavia match, Tbilisi 1973
Sicilian Defence, Taimanov Variation

1 e4 c5 2 ♘f3 ♘c6 3 d4 cxd4 4 ♘xd4 e6 5 ♘c3 a6 6 ♗e2 ♛c7 7 0-0 b5

The most common line today is 7...♘f6.

8 ♘xc6 ♛xc6?!

Nowadays, if Black does play 7...b5, then here he recaptures with the d-pawn. The problem with the text-move is that the queen is tactically vulnerable on c6, both to ideas on the long diagonal and to possible ♘d5 tricks.

9 ♗f3 ♗b7 10 ♗f4 d6

After 10...♖c8 both 11 ♖e1 and 11 e5 ♛c7 12 ♘e4 are good for White.

11 ♖e1

White is already threatening 12 a4 b4 13 ♘d5.

11...e5 *(D)*

12 a4!

This innovation put the whole line out of business for Black. Hitherto, the less incisive 12 ♗d2 had given White little after 12...♘f6.

12...b4

12...exf4 13 e5 d5 14 ♘xd5 0-0-0 15 axb5 ♛xb5 16 c4 ♛e8 17 ♛b3 gives White a crushing attack.

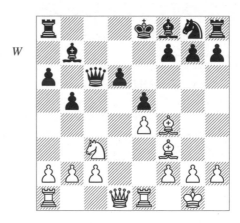

W

13 ♘d5 exf4 *(D)*

14 c3!

An amazingly calm move. 14 e5 appears more natural, but after 14...0-0-0 15 ♘e7+ ♘xe7 16 ♗xc6 ♘xc6 the position is far from clear, as Black's minor pieces could become very active.

14...b3?

A hopeless attempt to keep the queenside files closed. 14...bxc3 is the best chance, but even then 15 ♖c1 ♛d7 (15...♖b8 16 ♖xc3 ♛d7

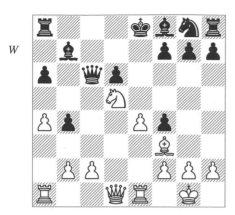

W

17 ♘c7+ ♚d8 18 ♕b3 and White wins) 16 e5 dxe5 17 ♖xc3 ♗xd5 18 ♗xd5 ♖d8 19 ♖xe5+ ♗e7 20 ♗c6 ♕xc6 21 ♖xd8+ ♚xd8 22 ♖xc6 ♘f6 23 ♖xa6 gives White the advantage thanks to his active rooks and two connected passed pawns.

15 e5! 0-0-0

Or 15...♚d8 16 ♕xb3 ♖b8 17 ♘e7! and Black's position collapses.

16 ♕xb3 *(D)*

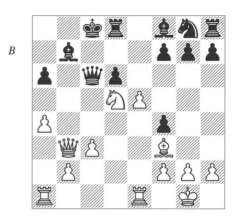

B

16...♚b8 17 ♘b4 ♕d7 18 ♗xb7 ♚xb7 19 ♘d5+ ♚a8 20 ♘b6+ ♚a7 21 ♘xd7 ♖xd7 22 ♖ad1 1-0

Game 8
Evgeny Vasiukov – Dragoljub Velimirović
USSR – Yugoslavia match, Tbilisi 1973
Sicilian Defence, Rossolimo Variation

It only seems fair to give Vasiukov's revenge!

1 e4 c5 2 ♘f3 ♘c6 3 ♗b5 e6 4 ♗xc6

One of the two main moves in this position, the other being 4 0-0.

4...bxc6

Certainly the right recapture. Taking with the d-pawn does not fit together with ...e6, which blocks in the c8-bishop.

5 0-0

These days 5 d3 is more popular.

5...♕c7 *(D)*

Any move which fights for control of e5 cannot be bad, but it is more flexible for Black to bring his kingside pieces out by 5...♘e7 6 b3 ♘g6 7 ♗b2 f6, followed by ...♗e7 and ...0-0, with every chance of equality.

6 d3 d6 7 ♘c3 ♘f6 8 ♕e2

Threatening to play 9 e5; the resulting exchange of pawns would leave Black's c-pawns looking particularly weak.

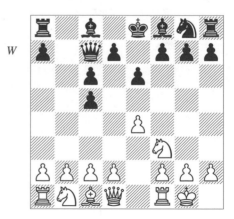

W

8...e5

More or less forced to block White's threatened e5, but this extra pawn move leaves Black somewhat behind in development. The closed nature of the position means that this is not necessarily disastrous, but he has to take care.

9 ♘h4 *(D)*

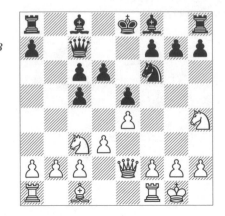

White seeks to exploit his lead in development by opening the position up with f4.

9...g6

9...♗e7 10 f4 exf4 11 ♗xf4 0-0 12 ♔h1 gives White an edge as he has the simple plan of ♗g3 followed by ♘f5, with pressure along the f-file and a more active bishop.

10 f4 exf4 *(D)*

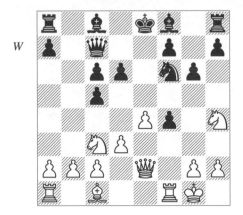

11 e5?!

A very dynamic continuation, although perhaps not objectively best. The simple 11 ♗xf4 ♘h5 12 ♗g5 ♗g7 13 ♘f5 (13 g4? h6) 13...♗e5 14 ♘h6 f6 15 ♗e3 is better, with a rather unclear position in which both knights on the h-file are oddly placed.

11...dxe5?!

Black misses the chance to exchange off his light-squared bishop, which is otherwise in serious danger of being blocked in by ...♘d7. 11...♗g4! would have exploited White's optimism; after 12 ♘f3 (12 ♕e1 dxe5 13 ♗xf4 ♘d7 is fine for Black) 12...♗xf3 13 ♖xf3 (13 ♕xf3 dxe5 14 g3 g5 is unconvincing) 13...dxe5 14 ♗xf4 ♘d7 15 ♘e4 f5 I cannot see any good way for White to stop Black completing his development by ...♗g7 (or ...♗e7) followed by ...0-0.

12 ♗xf4 ♘d7 13 ♖ae1

White has sufficient play for the pawn but no more.

13...♗g7 14 ♘f3 f6 15 ♘e4 0-0 16 ♗e3 *(D)*

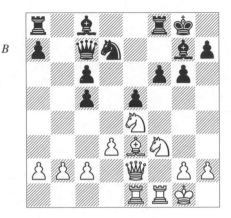

16...♖e8 17 g4

Recapturing the c5-pawn is at best equal for White, so he decides to continue on the kingside. There is little risk in this approach, as the c5-pawn is doomed anyway.

17...f5

An ambitious and risky move, but not yet an error. 17...♘f8 is a safer option, heading for e6. Then 18 ♘fd2 f5 19 gxf5 gxf5 would be unclear.

18 gxf5 gxf5 19 ♘fg5! *(D)*
19...♘f6?

Only this move gives White the chance to press home his kingside attack. 19...h6 is also bad after 20 ♕h5 ♖e7 21 ♖xf5! hxg5 (21...♘f8 22 ♖xf8+ ♔xf8 23 ♖f1+ ♔g8 24 ♕g6 hxg5 25 ♘f6+ ♔f8 26 ♘h7++ ♔g8 27 ♖f8#) 22 ♕g6 ♕d8 (22...♔h8 23 ♘xg5 ♘f8 24 ♖xf8+ ♗xf8 25 ♖f1 and White wins) 23 ♘xg5 ♘f8 24 ♖xf8+ ♔xf8 25 ♖f1+ mating. Black's correct defence is 19...♘f8! 20 ♕h5 ♖e7 21 ♗xc5! h6!

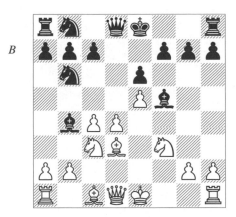

(21...fxe4 loses to 22 ♗xe7 ♕xe7 23 ♖f7 ♕c5+ 24 ♔h1) 22 ♘g3 hxg5 (22...f4 23 ♗xe7 ♕xe7 24 ♘f3 fxg3 25 hxg3 is also unclear) 23 ♗xe7 ♕xe7 24 ♘xf5 ♗xf5 25 ♖xf5 ♘e6 with an unclear position.

20 ♘xf6+ ♗xf6 21 ♕h5 ♖e7 *(D)*
22 ♘xh7! ♖g7+

22...♖xh7 23 ♕e8+ ♔g7 24 ♖e2! ♖h4 (White also wins after 24...♕f7 25 ♖g2+ ♗g5 26 ♖xg5+ ♔f6 27 ♕xc6+) 25 ♖g2+ ♖g4 26 ♖xg4+ fxg4 27 ♗h6+! ♔xh6 28 ♖xf6+ mates.

23 ♔h1 ♕f7 24 ♘xf6+ ♖xf6 25 ♖g1 1-0
Since 25...♗e6 26 ♖xg7+ ♕xg7 27 c4! gives White a decisive attack.

Game 9

Borislav Ivkov – Jan Timman
Amsterdam (IBM) 1974
Alekhine Defence, Four Pawns Attack

1 e4 ♘f6 2 e5 ♘d5 3 d4 d6 4 c4 ♘b6 5 f4 ♗f5 6 ♘c3 e6 7 ♘f3 dxe5 8 fxe5 ♗b4?

In the early 1970s, ...♗b4 was played in various positions of the Alekhine Four Pawns Attack. This idea is viable when White's bishop is on e3, but here White can use the extra tempo to launch a vicious attack by sacrificing his d-pawn.

9 ♗d3! *(D)*

This plan had been played before, as we shall see, but the current game gave it such a high profile that ...♗b4 disappeared virtually overnight against non-♗e3 lines.

9...♗xd3

9...c5 10 ♗xf5 exf5 11 d5 ♘xc4 12 0-0 also gives White a very strong initiative.

10 ♕xd3 c5 11 0-0 cxd4 12 ♘e4

White already has two very strong threats: 13 ♘fg5 and 13 c5 followed by 14 ♘d6+.

12...♘6d7

Or 12...♘8d7 (12...0-0 loses to 13 ♘fg5 ♘8d7 14 ♘d6 g6 15 ♕h3 h5 16 ♘gxf7) 13 a3 ♘c5 14 ♘xc5 ♗xc5 15 ♘g5 ♖f8 16 ♘xh7 with a horrible position for Black, Vetemaa-Ma.Tseitlin, Pärnu 1973.

13 ♘fg5!

White consistently sacrifices a second pawn to further his attack.

13...♘xe5 14 ♕g3 ♘bd7 (D)

Forced, as 14...♘bc6 loses to 15 ♘xe6 fxe6 16 ♕xg7.

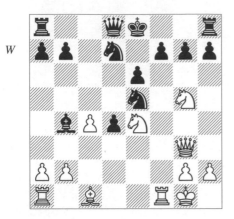

15 ♗f4

Once the e5-knight gives way, White will crash through on f7.

15...♕b6

Black tries to defend tactically. 15...♕a5 16 a3 ♗e7 17 b4 is also very bad, while 15...0-0 16 ♗xe5 ♘xe5 fails to 17 ♘f6+! ♔h8 18 ♘fxh7.

16 ♗xe5 f6 17 ♗d6

17 c5 is also decisive.

17...fxg5 18 ♗xb4 ♕xb4 19 ♘d6+ ♔e7

After 19...♔d8 20 ♘f7+ White wins a whole rook.

20 ♖f7+ ♔d8 21 ♕xg5+ ♔c7 22 ♘b5+ ♔c8 23 ♖af1

Now White threatens both 24 ♖xd7 and 24 a3.

23...b6 (D)

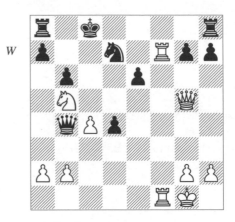

24 ♖xd7 ♔xd7 25 ♕xg7+ 1-0

It is mate or loss of the queen after 25...♕e7 26 ♖f7.

Game 10

Miguel Quinteros – Zoltan Ribli

Montilla 1974

Nimzo-Indian Defence, Classical Variation

1 d4 ♘f6 2 c4 e6 3 ♘c3 ♗b4 4 ♕c2

The Classical Variation, by which White prepares 5 a3 ♗xc3+ 6 ♕xc3, thereby avoiding doubled c-pawns. The cost is a loss of time; White has to move his queen twice, and on c3 it is exposed to further attack by ...♘e4. The theme of positional advantage versus lead in development is central to this game.

4...c5 5 dxc5 0-0 6 ♗f4 (D)

An unusual move which has now largely disappeared from practice. 6 a3 ♗xc5 7 ♘f3 b6 is currently preferred, with a slight advantage for White.

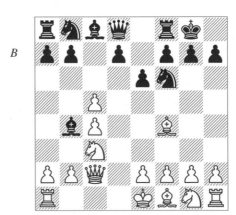

6...♘a6

Better than 6...♗xc5 7 ♘f3 ♘c6, which is similar to the last note except that White has managed to avoid playing a3.

7 a3

7 ♗d6 is tempting, but White cannot maintain his extra pawn after 7...♖e8 8 a3 ♕a5 9 ♖c1 ♗xc3+ 10 ♕xc3 ♕xc3+ 11 ♖xc3 ♘e4. The continuation 12 ♖c2 ♘axc5 13 ♗xc5 ♘xc5 leads to an equal endgame.

7...♗xc3+ 8 ♕xc3 ♘e4 *(D)*

Black can also play the safer line 8...♘xc5 9 b4 ♘ce4, followed by ...d5, with comfortable equality.

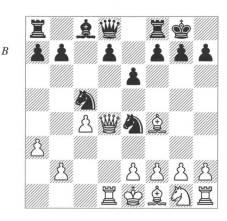

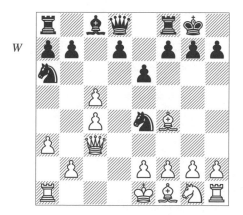

The text-move is more double-edged, but probably about equally strong.

9 ♕d4 ♘axc5 10 ♖d1 *(D)*

This is rather slow and allows Black to take the initiative in the centre. 10 b4 is the critical move, when the main line runs 10...♘b3 11 ♕xe4 ♘xa1 12 ♗e5 (White must round up the knight quickly, or else Black may rescue it by ...a5-a4; if 12 ♕b1, then 12...♕f6 and it is not clear how White will catch the knight) 12...a5 13 ♗xa1 (13 ♕b1 axb4 14 axb4 ♕b6 15 ♗xa1 ♖xa1 16 ♕xa1 ♕xb4+ 17 ♔d1 ♕b3+ 18 ♔d2 d5 gives Black enough for the piece) 13...axb4 14 ♕d4. In this key position either 14...f6 or 14...♕g5 leads to an unclear situation.

10...d5

The rest of the game centres around the black knights. If White can drive them back and complete his development, then the two bishops will give him a clear advantage. Black's aim is to strike before White's remaining pieces enter the game. This is another example of the quite common situation in which it is the owner of the two knights who has to open up the position.

11 b4

White ambitiously attempts to drive the knights away before completing his development, but the result is that they move forward to occupy even more advanced posts. 11 cxd5 (not 11 f3? ♘b3 followed by 12...♕a5+ and Black wins) 11...exd5 12 e3 (12 ♕xd5? ♕b6! gives Black excellent play for the pawn) is much safer. Without being too ambitious, White just prepares to develop his kingside. This would lead to approximate equality.

11...♘a4 12 f3? *(D)*

It is a mistake to force the other black knight forwards. This was the last chance for White to play safe by 12 cxd5 or 12 ♖c1.

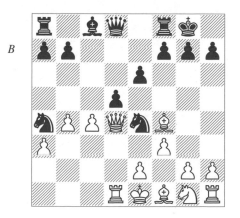

12...♘ec3

Not 12...♘f6? 13 e4, which would be excellent for White.

13 ♖d3

13 ♖c1 dxc4 14 ♕xc4 ♗d7 followed by ...♖c8 only increases Black's lead in development.

13...f6 *(D)*

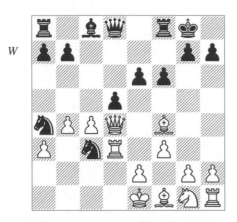

Black once again foils White's attempts to get rid of the intrusive knights; if now 14 ♖xc3, then 14...e5 wins the exchange.

14 ♗d2 e5 15 ♕h4 d4

Threatening 16...♗f5.

16 e3

At last the e-pawn moves, but too late.

16...♗f5 17 ♗xc3

17 exd4 loses material to 17...♗xd3 18 ♗xd3 e4.

17...♘xc3

Not 17...♗xd3? 18 ♗xd3 and White has at least a draw.

18 ♖d2 dxe3!

18...♘b1 is also very good, but is not as forcing as the text-move.

19 ♖xd8 ♖axd8

Black's queen sacrifice is decisive.

20 ♗e2 ♖d2 *(D)*

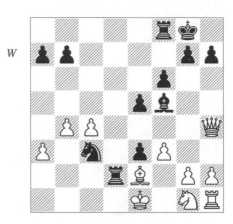

With the deadly threats of 21...♖fd8, followed by 22...♖d1+, and 21...♗d3.

21 g4 ♗d3

Now the e2-bishop falls.

22 ♔f1 ♘xe2 23 ♘xe2 ♖xe2 24 ♔g1 ♖d8 0-1

There is no answer to the threat of moving the bishop, followed by ...♖d1#.

Game 11

Rafael Vaganian – Viktor Kupreichik

USSR Ch, Leningrad 1974

Trompowsky Attack

1 d4 ♘f6 2 ♗g5 c5 3 d5

A sharp alternative to the quieter 3 ♗xf6.

3...♕b6

This must be the critical test of 3 d5 as White is forced to sacrifice his b-pawn.

4 ♘c3 ♕xb2 5 ♗d2 ♕b6 6 e4 d6

An alternative idea is to block the centre by 6...e5; e.g., 7 f4 d6 8 fxe5 dxe5 9 ♘f3 ♘bd7 with unclear play.

7 f4 g6? *(D)*

It is a mistake to allow White to break through in the centre. Black should have put up a fight for the e5-square by 7...♘bd7 8 ♘f3 ♕c7.

8 e5

An early central advance can sometimes rebound on the attacker, but not here as White has a lead in development to back up his aggression.

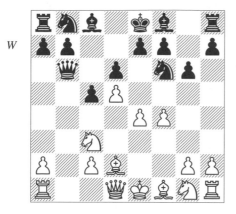

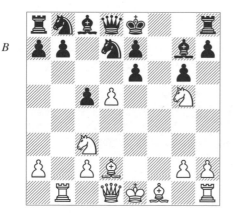

8...dxe5

8...♘fd7 9 ♘f3 ♗g7 10 ♖b1 ♕d8 11 e6 fxe6 12 ♘g5 also gave White a vicious attack in the slightly earlier game Vaganian-Jansa, Kraguje-vac 1974. Note the recurrent theme of using the e-pawn to prise open Black's position.

9 fxe5 ♘fd7 10 ♘f3 ♗g7 11 ♖b1 ♕d8 12 e6!

White strikes quickly before Black can castle.

12...fxe6 13 ♘g5! *(D)*

The advancing pawns have torn holes in Black's defences; now the heavier pieces move up to exploit the weaknesses.

13...♘f6 14 ♗b5+ ♔f8

Interposing on d7 allows 15 ♘xe6.

15 dxe6 a6?!

15...♕d4 would have been a better chance, but even so the position after 16 ♘e2 ♕d5 17 0-0 is very unpleasant for Black.

16 ♗e3! ♕a5

Or 16...♕c7 17 ♗c4 b5 18 ♗d5 ♘c6 19 0-0 ♗b7 20 ♘ce4 with an enormous initiative.

17 0-0 *(D)*

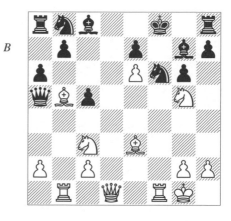

White's attack is so strong that he can afford to offer the bishop.

17...h6

17...axb5 loses to 18 ♖xb5 ♕c7 19 ♘d5 ♕e5 20 ♗xc5.

18 ♕d3

Exploiting Black's new weakness at g6.

18...♔g8 19 ♕xg6 ♗xe6 20 ♘xe6 ♖h7 21 ♖xf6 ♘d7 22 ♗xd7 1-0

It's quite nice to take three enemy pieces on consecutive moves without any reprisal.

Game 12
Rafael Vaganian – Albin Planinc
Hastings 1974/5
English Opening

1 d4 ♘f6 2 c4 c5 3 ♘f3 cxd4 4 ♘xd4 e6 5 ♘c3 ♗b4 6 ♘b5

An ambitious attempt to gain the two bishops without conceding doubled pawns, the defect being the time it costs. 6 g3 is considered better today.

6...0-0 7 a3 ♗xc3+ 8 ♘xc3 d5 9 ♗g5 *(D)*

The only try for the advantage. After 9 e3 ♘c6 White's dark-squared bishop is blocked in and Black has no problems.

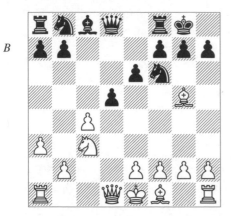

9...h6 10 ♗xf6 ♕xf6 11 cxd5

11 e3 is possible, with a likely transposition to the next note.

11...exd5 12 ♕xd5?

Too greedy, as Black's lead in development provides excellent compensation for the pawn. 12 e3 is better. If 12...♖d8 then 13 ♕d4 blocks the d-pawn, while after 12...♘c6 13 ♕xd5 ♖d8 14 ♕f3 White's chances are much better than in the game, as Black's queen can no longer swing over to b6.

12...♖d8 13 ♕f3 ♕b6 *(D)*

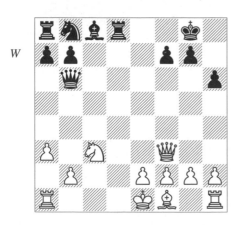

Gaining time by attacking the b2-pawn.

14 ♖d1

14 b4 is certainly no better. After 14...♘c6 15 e3 ♗e6 16 ♗e2 a5 17 b5 ♘e5 Black has more than enough for the pawn (indeed, he will soon win one of White's queenside pawns).

14...♖xd1+ 15 ♘xd1 ♘c6 16 ♕e3

Trying to defend by tactical means, which is always dangerous when one is behind in development. However, even after the marginally better 16 e3 ♗e6 17 ♗e2 ♖d8 18 0-0 ♖d2 Black will soon regain the pawn with good play.

16...♘d4! *(D)*

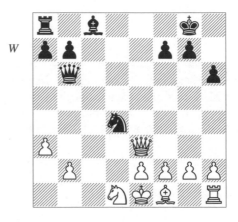

17 ♕e8+

White frees his e-pawn with gain of tempo, but his queen proves tactically vulnerable on e8.

17...♔h7 18 e3

If 18 ♕xf7, then 18...♗f5 19 e3 ♘c2+ 20 ♔d2 ♗g6 21 ♕c4 ♖d8+ 22 ♔c1 ♘a1 wins.

18...♘c2+ 19 ♔d2 ♗f5! *(D)*

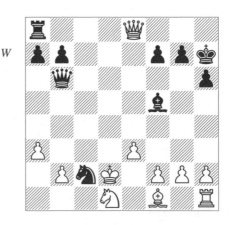

This rook sacrifice gives Black the advantage in every variation.

20 ♕xa8

20 ♕xf7 ♗g6 transposes into the previous note.

20...♕d6+ *(D)*

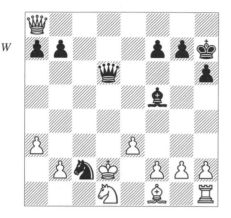

21 ♔c1

First of all, 21 ♔e2 allows an attractive forced mating line: 21...♕d3+ 22 ♔f3 ♕xd1+ 23 ♗e2 ♘d4+! 24 exd4 ♕b3+ 25 ♔f4 g5+ 26 ♔xf5 ♕e6#.

21 ♔c3 also loses, although the winning method is not at all simple. Here is a summary of the analysis: 21...♕e5+! and now:

1) 22 ♔b3 ♘a1+ 23 ♔b4 (23 ♔a2 ♕d5+ transposes to the analysis of 22 ♔d2 below) 23...b6 24 ♕c6 ♗d7! 25 ♗d3+ g6 26 ♗xg6+ ♔g7 wins for Black.

2) 22 ♔c4 ♕c7+ 23 ♔b3 ♗e6+ 24 ♔a4 ♕b6 is also decisive.

3) Therefore, White has to try 22 ♔d2, but even here 22...♕d5+ 23 ♔c3 (23 ♔c2 ♕d3+ wins as after 21 ♔e2 above) 23...♕a5+ 24 b4 (Black also wins after 24 ♔b3 ♘a1+ 25 ♔a2 ♕d5+ 26 ♗c4 ♕xc4+ 27 ♔xa1 ♕c1+ 28 ♔a2 ♗e6+ 29 b3 ♕c2+ 30 ♔a1 ♕xb3 31 ♘c3 ♕xc3+ 32 ♔b1 ♗f5+ 33 ♔a2 ♕c2+ 34 ♔a1 ♗e6) 24...♕xa3+ 25 ♔d2 ♕xb4+ 26 ♔c1 (26 ♘c3 ♘a3 gives Black a winning attack; e.g., 27 ♔e2 ♕xc3 28 ♕d8 ♘c4 29 ♕d4 ♕c2+ 30 ♔e1 ♘b2) 26...♘a1 27 f3 ♘b3+ 28 ♔b2 ♘d2+ 29 ♔c1 ♘xf1 is hopeless for White.

21...♘a1 *(D)*

22 ♕xb7?

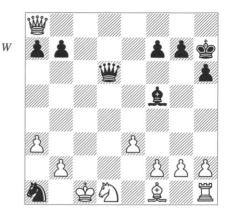

Up to here White has defended quite well, but now he loses in one (admittedly attractive) move. 22 ♗c4 ♕c5 23 ♘c3 ♕xc4 24 ♕d8 is a much better defence, which is conveniently ignored in most annotations of this game. Black should continue 24...♘b3+ 25 ♔d1 ♕g4+ 26 ♘e2 (26 ♔e1 ♕xg2 27 ♖f1 ♗h3 28 ♕d3+ f5 should be winning for Black as White is paralysed and can hardly meet the threat of ...♘a1-c2+ forcing a decisive liquidation) 26...♕e4! (taking the g-pawn only increases White's defensive chances) 27 ♔e1 ♕b1+ 28 ♕d1 ♕xb2 29 ♘d4 (29 ♘g3 ♕c3+ 30 ♔e2 ♕c4+ 31 ♔e1 ♗c2 wins for Black) 29...♘xd4 30 exd4 ♕xa3 with a clear advantage as White will find it very hard to stop the connected passed pawns while his king is so exposed.

22...♕c7+! *(D)*

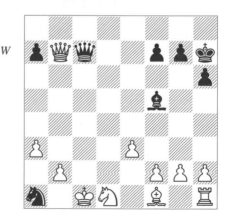

Winning the queen or mating.

0-1

Game 13
Mikhail Tal – Fridrik Olafsson
Las Palmas 1975
Modern Defence

1 e4 d6 2 d4 g6 3 ♗c4 ♘f6

The move-order is unusual, and White should now transpose back to normal lines with 4 ♘c3. Instead, he attempts to pursue an independent path but only makes Black's task easier.

4 ♕e2?! *(D)*

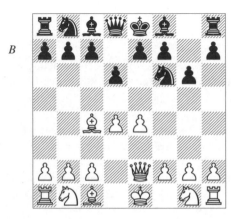

This move seems inaccurate as it gives Black the opportunity to launch an early attack on d4 by missing out ...♗g7.

4...♘c6! 5 ♘f3 ♗g4

Now White must spend time defending d4.

6 c3

6 ♗b5 is no better; 6...♘d7 7 c3 e5 8 d5 ♘cb8 9 h3 ♗xf3 10 ♕xf3 ♗e7 11 g3 ♗g5 was equal in Tal-Matulović, Skopje Olympiad 1972.

6...e5

Black consistently pursues his attack on d4.

7 ♗b5

7 d5 ♘e7 8 ♗g5 ♗g7 9 ♘bd2 h6 10 ♗e3 c6 is equal.

7...exd4 8 cxd4 ♘d7

White has still not solved his problems with the d4-pawn.

9 ♗e3 ♗g7 *(D)*

Finally the pressure against d4 forces White to exchange on c6. The resulting position is very pleasant for Black. He has the two bishops, an

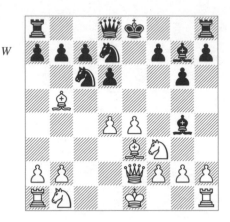

open b-file for his queen's rook and the chance to open the diagonal for his dark-squared bishop by playing a later ...c5. White is not yet worse, but he certainly has to take care.

10 ♗xc6 bxc6 11 ♘bd2 0-0 12 ♖c1

Better than 12 0-0, when 12...♖b8 would be awkward as 13 b3 would run into 13...c5. Also, by attacking c6, White forces Black's hand.

12...c5 13 dxc5 ♗xb2 14 ♖c2 ♗g7 15 0-0 ♖e8 *(D)*

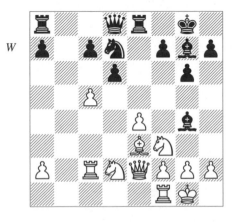

Black's position is very comfortable; he only has to play the most natural moves.

16 ♖d1

16 cxd6 cxd6 17 h3 ♗xf3 18 ♕xf3 is a safer route to equality; after 18...♘e5 19 ♕e2 d5 20 exd5 ♕xd5 21 ♘c4 a draw is not far away.

16...♘xc5

Now White has to part with his other bishop, but in compensation he gains some time.

17 ♗xc5 dxc5 18 ♖xc5?

It is the knight rather than the rook which belongs on c5 and so White should have played 18 ♘b3 ♕e7 19 ♘xc5. After 19...♖ad8 20 ♖xd8 ♖xd8 21 h3 ♗xf3 22 ♕xf3 ♕d6 23 g3 the position is equal.

18...♕d6 19 ♖dc1

Admittedly, White now has pressure against c7, but winning this pawn means little if Black's bishops are allowed to develop their full power.

19...♗h6 (D)

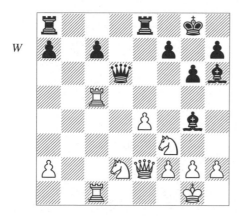

20 ♖xc7?!

After 20 ♖1c2 ♗xd2 21 ♕xd2 ♖xe4 22 ♖xc7 ♗xf3 23 gxf3 ♖d4 Black has a clear advantage, but anything is better than a forced loss.

20...♖ad8

Not 20...♗xf3? 21 ♕xf3 and the attack on f7 allows White to escape.

21 ♖1c2

The stage is set for a spectacular combination based on White's weak back rank. The alternative 21 ♖7c2 ♗xf3 22 gxf3 ♕d3! 23 ♔f1 ♗xd2 24 ♕xd3 ♖xd3 25 ♖d1 ♖xf3 26 ♖dxd2 ♖xe4 leaves Black with a clear extra pawn.

21...♗xd2 22 ♕xd2 (D)

22...♕f4!! 23 ♖e7

A tricky Tal defence. 23 ♕e1 ♖xe4 and 23 ♕c1 ♗xf3 24 gxf3 ♕xf3 are dead lost.

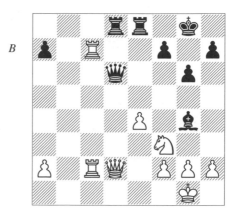

23...♖f8!

An equally tricky reply. Although Black can no longer play ...♖xe4, the loose rook on e7 represents a tactical weakness. Both 23...♖xd2 24 ♖xe8+ ♔g7 25 ♘xd2 and 23...♕xd2 24 ♖xd2 would even have given White the advantage.

24 ♕a5

There is no reasonable square for the white queen; for example, 24 ♕e2 ♗xf3 25 ♕xf3 (25 gxf3 ♕g5+ picks up the rook) 25...♕d6 threatens both 26...♕d1+ and 26...♕xe7, or 24 ♕c1 ♗xf3 25 gxf3 ♕xf3 26 ♖d2 ♕f4 27 ♖c2 ♕g4+ and Black wins.

24...♖d1+

The immediate 24...♕g5 is equally good.

25 ♘e1 ♕g5! (D)

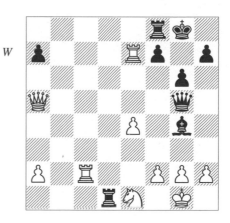

0-1

The final exploitation of White's back rank also takes advantage of the undefended pieces on a5 and e7.

Game 14
Mikhail Tal – Robert Byrne
Biel Interzonal 1976
Sicilian Defence, 4 ♕xd4

1 e4 c5 2 ♘f3 d6 3 d4 cxd4 4 ♕xd4 ♘c6 5 ♗b5

White is prepared to surrender the two bishops to keep up the momentum of his development. However, this line is not regarded as very threatening for Black.

5...♗d7 6 ♗xc6 ♗xc6 7 ♘c3 ♘f6 8 ♗g5 e6 9 0-0-0 ♗e7 10 ♖he1 0-0 11 ♕d2

Preparing ♘d4 followed by f3 or f4.

11...♕a5?!

Not the most accurate, as after ♔b1 the black queen will be exposed to ♘d5 tricks. 11...♕c7 12 ♘d4 ♖fd8 is better, with equality.

12 ♘d4 ♖ac8 13 ♔b1 *(D)*

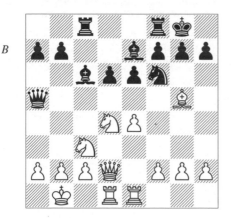

Now 14 ♘d5 is a real threat, and meeting it costs Black a tempo.

13...♔h8

If 13...♖fd8, then 14 ♘d5 ♕xd2 15 ♘xe7+ ♔f8 16 ♖xd2 ♔xe7 17 f4 with the awkward threat of 18 e5.

14 f4

Now White can choose whether to continue with e5 or f5, depending on Black's response.

14...h6?!

14...♖fd8 is best, securing the d6-pawn and preparing to answer 15 e5 by 15...dxe5 16 fxe5 ♘g8.

15 h4! *(D)*

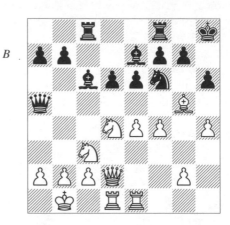

Naturally, Tal does not retreat the bishop but maintains it on g5.

15...hxg5?

This move is crushingly refuted. 15...♖fd8 was still best.

16 hxg5 ♘xe4 *(D)*

Black tries to exchange queens by returning the piece, but White is having none of it! 16...♘h7 fails to 17 g4 ♔g8 (17...♘xg5 18 ♖h1+ wins for White) 18 ♕h2 ♗xg5 19 ♖h1 ♗h6 20 g5 ♘xg5 21 fxg5 ♕xg5 22 ♖dg1 and wins.

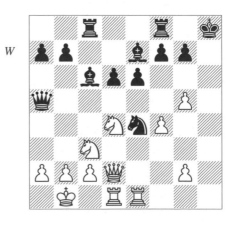

17 ♕d3!

Black is defenceless.

17...♗xg5

Or 17...♘xc3+ 18 bxc3 ♔g8 19 ♖h1 f5 20 g6, winning.

18 ♘xe4 ♗xe4

18...♗xf4 loses to 19 ♖h1+ ♗h6 20 ♘f6.

19 ♖xe4 ♗h6 20 g4 f5 21 ♖xe6 ♗xf4

Or 21...fxg4 22 ♖h1 ♖c7 23 ♕g6 ♖fc8 24 ♖e8+ ♖xe8 25 ♕xe8+ ♔h7 26 ♘e6 and White wins.

22 ♘xf5 1-0

There are just too many threats: 23 ♖h1+, 23 ♘e7 and 23 ♕h3+, for example.

Game 15
Walter Browne – Robert Byrne
USA Ch, Mentor 1977
Dutch Defence, 2 ♘c3

1 d4 f5 2 ♘c3 ♘f6 3 ♗g5 d5

3...e6 is a solid alternative, avoiding the doubled pawns. After 4 e4 fxe4 5 ♘xe4 ♗e7 theory considers the position to be roughly equal.

4 ♗xf6 exf6 5 e3 ♗e6 6 ♗d3 *(D)*

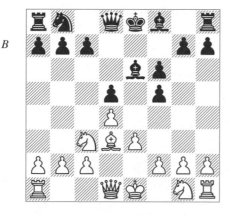

6...g6?!

Black adopts an entirely passive stance, simply supporting his d5- and f5-pawns by ...c6 and ...g6. It is much more dynamic to defend the pawns by ...♕d7, using the extra time for piece development. Perhaps 6...♘c6 7 ♕f3 ♕d7 is most accurate, with a roughly level position.

7 ♕f3 c6 8 ♘ge2 ♘d7 9 h3

This exposes the dark side of Black's plan. Although his pawn-structure appears solid, White can undermine it with h3 and g4; if Black then exchanges on g4, White's h1-rook will be very well placed to exploit the weakness of Black's h-pawn.

9...♕b6 *(D)*

After 9...h5, 10 g4 hxg4 11 hxg4 fxg4 12 ♗xg6+ ♔e7 13 ♕g2 ♗h6 14 ♘g3 (14 0-0-0?! is less accurate as 14...f5 prevents White from occupying f5) is very unpleasant as Black's king is a target and the f5-square is weak.

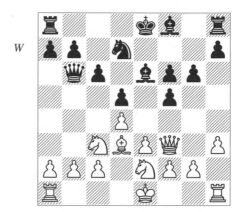

10 g4!

An excellent and courageous move, especially as White had a perfectly safe alternative in 10 0-0-0.

10...♕xb2?

Of course this is consistent with his previous move, but, just as in Game 11, taking the b2-pawn turns out badly for Black. He should have cut his losses with 10...fxg4 11 hxg4 ♗f7 (11...♕xb2 is bad here because of 12 ♖b1 ♕a3 13 ♗xg6+) 12 0-0-0 0-0-0 13 ♖h3, but even in this case White can develop kingside pressure by doubling on the h-file.

11 ♖b1 ♕a3 12 gxf5 ♗f7

12...gxf5 13 ♖b3 ♕a5 14 ♖xb7 ♗b4 15 ♔d2 0-0-0 16 ♖xb4 ♕xb4 17 ♗a6+ ♔c7 18 ♖b1 is similar to the game.

13 ♖xb7 ♗b4

Black has to go in for this, otherwise he remains a pawn down.

14 0-0 *(D)*

14 ♔d2 ♕b2 15 ♖c7! is also promising for White.

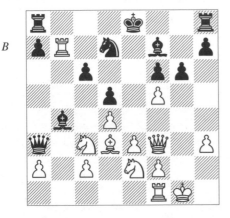

14...0-0-0

If 14...♗xc3, then 15 ♖b3 ♕xa2 16 ♘xc3 ♕a5 17 ♖fb1 is clearly better for White. After the text-move, the rook on b7 is trapped, and the knight on c3 is hanging. However, this is precisely the moment when White can launch a vicious attack by sacrificing the exchange.

15 ♖xb4!

In *Informator 24*, Byrne and Mednis give the line 15 ♗a6 ♗xc3 16 ♕g3 ♘e5 as clearly better for Black, even though White can win straight away by 17 ♖xa7+ ♔b8 18 ♖xf7 and Black will be lucky to escape with the loss of only a piece. Instead, Black should meet 15 ♗a6 by 15...♗d6!, after which the bishop and rook battery is surprisingly ineffective. Indeed, White would be forced to give up the exchange by 16 ♖xa7+ ♔b8 17 ♖xd7 ♖xd7 18 ♖b1+ and although this line still favours White, the text-move is far more clear-cut.

15...♕xb4 16 ♗a6+ ♔c7 17 ♖b1 ♕d6

Black must prevent the deadly threat of 18 ♕g3+.

18 ♖b7+ ♔c8 *(D)*

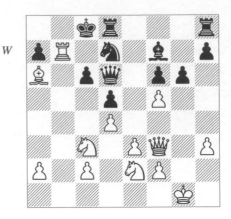

At first sight Black is hopelessly lost, but it proves surprisingly tricky to finish him off.

19 ♖b3+

19 ♖b6+ ♔c7 20 ♘b5+ cxb5 21 ♖xd6 ♔xd6 22 ♗xb5 certainly favours White, but he should be hoping for more from such a position. To begin with, White repeats moves.

19...♔c7 20 ♖b7+ ♔c8 21 e4

The strongest continuation. White threatens not only 22 exd5, but also 22 ♘b5! cxb5 23 ♕c3+ ♘c5 24 ♖b6+, etc.

21...♘b8 *(D)*

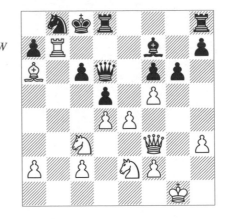

As good or bad as any other defence.

22 ♘b5!

An elegant conclusion.

22...cxb5 23 ♕c3+ ♘c6

Or 23...♕c6 24 ♖xa7+ mating.

24 e5

A killer move. Black's queen has no reasonable way to maintain its defence of c6.

24...♕c7

White also wins after 24...fxe5 25 dxe5 d4 26 ♘xd4.

25 e6 1-0

A cruel finish. White is attacking both bishop and queen and, now that d7 is covered, has the even more serious threat of 26 ♖b6+. There is no defence.

Game 16

Boris Spassky – Bent Larsen

Bugojno 1978

Caro-Kann Defence, 4...♗f5

1 e4 c6 2 d4 d5 3 ♘c3 dxe4 4 ♘xe4 ♗f5 5 ♘g3 ♗g6 6 ♘f3 ♘d7 7 ♗d3

An unusual plan. White almost always plays h4, either here or on the previous move, in order to gain space on the kingside.

7...♕a5+?!

7...e6 is safer; after 8 0-0 ♘gf6 9 c4 ♗d6 (or 9...♗e7) the position is equal.

8 ♗d2 ♕c7

Black's idea is that because White's queen is no longer guarding the d3-bishop, White is more or less forced to exchange bishops himself. Whilst this aim is desirable, it is not worth giving White the free tempo ♗d2.

9 ♗xg6 hxg6 10 ♕e2 e6

10...♘gf6 11 0-0-0 is also awkward for Black, as 11...0-0-0 loses to 12 ♘g5.

11 ♘e4 *(D)*

11...0-0-0

11...♘gf6 12 ♘eg5 ♗e7 runs into 13 ♘xf7! ♔xf7 14 ♘g5+ ♔e8 15 ♘xe6 ♕b6 16 0-0-0 with a very dangerous attack.

12 g3

Preparing ♗f4.

12...c5?!

12...♘df6! 13 ♘eg5 (13 ♗f4 can be met by 13...♕a5+) 13...♗d6 would have been much better; White retains slight pressure, but Black will be able to develop his remaining pieces by ...♘h6-f5, with reasonable play.

13 ♗f4 ♕c6

13...♕a5+ 14 c3 cxd4 15 ♕c4+ ♘c5 16 ♘xd4 ♖h5 17 0-0 is also good for White.

14 0-0-0 c4 *(D)*

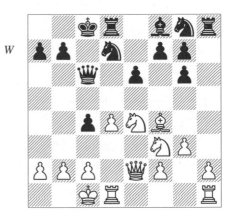

15 ♘c3!

Black is powerless to prevent White's breakthrough by d5.

15...♘h6

15...♘gf6 is still met by 16 ♘g5 attacking the weak f7-pawn.

16 d5! exd5 17 ♖xd5 *(D)*

Black's attempt to block the position has failed and White powers through in the centre.

17...♗c5

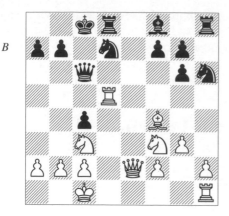

17...♘f5 18 ♘b5 ♗c5 19 ♕xc4! wins as 19...♗e3+ 20 fxe3 ♕xc4 21 ♘xa7# is mate.

18 ♖hd1 f6 *(D)*

18...♖he8 loses to 19 ♖xd7.

19 ♖d6!

A forceful conclusion.

19...♗xd6 20 ♖xd6 ♕c5 21 ♖d5 1-0

As 21...♕c6 22 ♘b5 is decisive.

Game 17

Boris Gulko – Vladimir Savon

Lvov Zonal 1978

Modern Benoni, Taimanov Attack

1 d4 ♘f6 2 c4 e6 3 ♘c3 c5 4 d5 exd5 5 cxd5 d6 6 e4 g6 7 f4 ♗g7 8 ♗b5+

This is currently thought to be the sternest test of the Modern Benoni, although it is an option only available in move-orders without an early ♘f3.

8...♘fd7 9 a4

The most flexible line; White waits for ...a6 before deciding where to put the bishop. Depending on Black's exact moves, the destination could be f1, e2 or d3, or White might even exchange on d7.

9...0-0

9...♕h4+ 10 g3 ♕e7 is another possibility.

10 ♘f3 ♘a6 11 0-0 ♘c7

11...♘b4 is tempting, but on b4 the knight often proves to be out on a limb.

12 ♗d3 a6 *(D)*

13 ♕e1

Even today it isn't clear which is the strongest move. 13 ♘d2 is well met by 13...♘f6!, but 13 ♔h1 is also very logical.

13...♖b8 14 e5!?

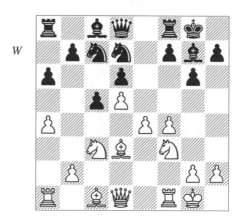

White goes straight for Black's throat. Those of a calmer disposition might prefer 14 a5, which gives White a slight advantage. However, White cannot expect to continue positionally for long, as a breakthrough by e5 or f5 is an essential component of this system.

14...♘b6 *(D)*

The only reasonable move; Black homes in on White's weak d5-pawn.

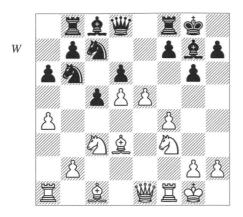

15 f5!

White's last move has effectively committed him to play for the attack, regardless of any sacrifices involved. He cannot hope for an advantage after the timid 15 ♗e4 (15 ♘e4 is answered by 15...♗f5) 15...f5 16 exf6 ♕xf6 17 a5 ♘c4 18 ♕e2 b5 19 axb6 ♘xb6.

15...dxe5 16 fxg6 fxg6! *(D)*

Not 16...hxg6? 17 ♘g5 ♘bxd5 (17...f6 18 ♘h7! ♔xh7? 19 ♕h4+ ♔g8 20 ♗xg6 ♖f7 21 ♕h7+ ♔f8 22 ♗h6 is decisive) 18 ♕h4 ♘f6 19 ♗e3! (19 ♖xf6? ♕d4+ 20 ♕xd4 cxd4 kills the attack) 19...♘ce8 (19...♕xd3 20 ♖xf6 ♕xe3+ 21 ♔h1 ♕xg5 22 ♕xg5 ♗xf6 23 ♕xf6 is very good for White) 20 ♖ad1 with a crushing attack.

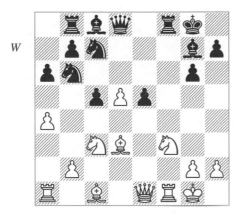

17 ♗g5 ♕d6

There is no ideal square for the black queen. Here it is exposed to attack by ♘e4, while after 17...♕d7 the c8-bishop is blocked in, a factor

White can exploit by 18 a5 ♘bxd5 19 ♗c4 ♕c6 20 ♗e7! ♖f5 21 ♘xd5 ♘xd5 22 ♗xd5+ ♕xd5 23 ♖d1 followed by a winning penetration to d8.

18 ♕h4 *(D)*

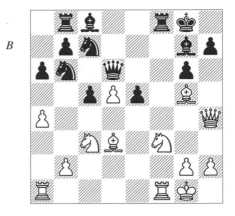

18...♘cxd5

This move was criticized by Gulko in *Informator 25*, but I believe that the real error comes later. After 18...♘bxd5, Gulko gave 19 ♖ad1 ♗e6 20 ♗c4 ♕c6 21 ♗h6 as unclear, but it seems to me that White is in very bad shape after 21...♘xc3 22 bxc3 ♗xh6 23 ♗xe6+ ♘xe6 24 ♕xh6 e4 25 ♘e5 ♕xa4. Instead, White should reply 19 ♘e4 ♕c6 20 ♖ac1 b6 21 ♗h6, with a strong attack in return for the two pawns.

19 ♖ad1 c4! *(D)*

19...♗e6 20 ♘e4 ♕c6 21 ♗h6 gives White enough for the pawns.

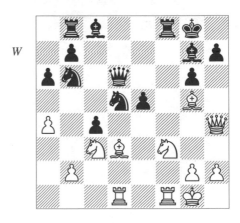

20 ♘xd5

20 ♗e4 ♕c5+ 21 ♔h1 has been recommended, but it seems worse than the text-move;
e.g., 21...♗e6! (21...♘f6 is also playable) 22
♘xd5 (22 ♗e3? ♘xe3 23 ♘g5 h6 24 ♘xe6
♘xd1 25 ♖xd1 ♕f2 and Black wins) 22...♘xd5
23 ♗xd5 ♗xd5 24 ♗e7 ♕c6 25 ♗xf8 ♖xf8
with an advantage for Black.

20...cxd3?

Only this move costs Black the game. The
correct line is 20...♘xd5! (not 20...♕xd5? 21
♗xg6! ♕c5+ 22 ♔h1 hxg6 23 ♗e7 followed by
♘g5 and White wins) 21 ♗xc4 ♗e6 22 ♔h1
(or 22 ♕e4 ♕c5+ 23 ♔h1 ♘f4 24 ♗xe6+ ♘xe6
with an edge for Black) 22...♕c6 23 ♖fe1 ♘f4
24 ♗xe6+ ♘xe6 and, if anything, Black is
slightly better.

21 ♘e7+ ♔h8 22 ♘xe5! (D)

This crushing blow lands on an apparently
well-defended square.

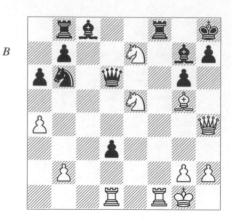

22...♗f5

After 22...♕xe5 23 ♘xg6+ Black loses his
queen, but even the move played costs Black a
piece.

23 ♖xf5 ♗xe5 24 ♖xe5 ♖f7 1-0

Game 18

Walter Browne – Ljubomir Ljubojević

Tilburg 1978

Nimzo-Indian Defence, Rubinstein Variation

**1 d4 ♘f6 2 c4 e6 3 ♘c3 ♗b4 4 e3 0-0 5
♗d3 c5 6 ♘f3 d5 7 0-0 cxd4 8 exd4 dxc4 9
♗xc4 b6 10 ♗g5 ♗b7 11 ♖e1 ♘bd7 12 ♖c1
♖c8** (D)

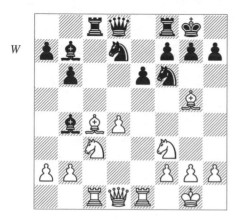

13 ♕b3!?

An innovation at the time of this game – for-
merly White had played 13 ♗d3. These days

neither move is thought to give White any advantage; for example, the continuation 13 ♗d3
♖e8 14 ♕e2 ♗xc3 15 bxc3 ♕c7 is approximately equal.

13...♕e7?!

Browne's novelty reaps an instant reward,
but it was not easy to find a good continuation
at the board. 13...♕c7? loses to 14 ♘b5!, while
13...♗a5 14 ♘e5 ♘xe5 15 dxe5 ♕d4, which
was recommended by Ljubojević in *Informator
26*, is bad in view of 16 ♗xe6! ♘g4 17 ♗e3
♘xe3 18 ♗xc8, when White wins material.
Black's most solid line is 13...♗xc3 14 ♖xc3
h6, with equality.

14 ♗d5! (D)

14 d5 is the more obvious method of trying
to exploit the e-file pin, but it fails to 14...♕c5
15 ♘a4 ♕a5 16 dxe6 ♗xe1 and White cannot
justify his sacrifice.

14...♗a6?!

Black cannot fully equalize, whatever he
plays. After 14...♗xd5 15 ♘xd5 Black has to

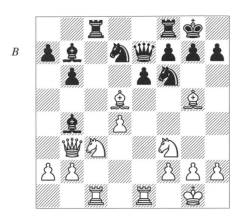

give up his queen, while if 14...罩b8, then 15 ♗xb7 ♗xc3 16 豐xc3 罩xb7 17 d5! ♘c5 18 b4 and Black cannot avoid having his pawn-structure damaged by dxe6. 14...♗xc3!? is probably the best defence, but after 15 ♗xb7 (not 15 ♗xf6? ♗xe1! 16 罩xc8 ♗xf2+ 17 ♔xf2 ♘xf6 and Black wins a pawn) 15...♗xe1 16 罩xc8! (White must avoid 16 ♗xc8? ♗xf2+!, when 17 ♔xf2 loses a pawn to 17...♘e4+ 18 ♔g1 ♘xg5, while 17 ♔f1 ♗xd4! 18 ♘xd4 ♘c5 19 ♘c6 豐c7 favours Black) 16...h6 17 ♗h4 罩xc8 18 ♗xc8 ♗a5 Black does not fully equalize as his bishop is badly placed on a5.

15 豐a4 (D)

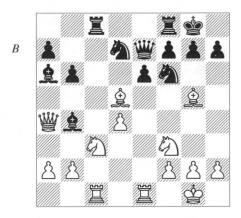

15...♗xc3

15...♘b8 16 ♗xf6 gxf6 17 ♗e4 豐d6 18 ♗b1 is good for White in view of Black's weakened kingside, while after 15...♗a5 16 a3 Black's bishops are very clumsily placed.

16 bxc3 ♘b8

After 16...♗d3, 17 ♗b3 followed by ♘e5 gives White the advantage, but not 17 豐xa7? 豐d6, when White's queen is in trouble.

17 ♗b3

Threatening 18 d5. Black's problem is that preventing d5 generally involves allowing White to break up his kingside by ♗xf6.

17...b5

Or 17...豐d7 18 豐a3 and Black can hardly avoid doubled f-pawns.

18 豐a5 (D)

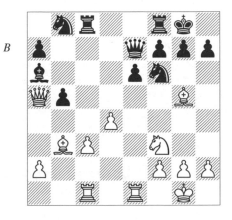

18...豐b7?!

This leads to a rapid disaster, but even after 18...豐c7 19 豐a3, followed by ♗xf6, Black is in a bad way.

19 ♗xf6 gxf6 20 d5! (D)

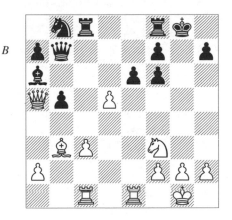

The thematic central breakthrough comes even though Black's queen is no longer on the e-file. White's idea is twofold: first of all he

intends to weaken the f5-square and secondly he opens the fourth rank for a lightning queen switch to the kingside.

20...exd5

20...e5 21 ♕b4 leaves Black in deep trouble.

21 ♕b4

Also here Black is helpless; his shattered kingside is totally devoid of defensive pieces, while White's queen, bishop and knight are all poised to attack.

21...♕d7

Or 21...♖fe8 22 ♕g4+ ♔h8 23 ♕h5 ♔g7 24 ♗c2 ♖xe1+ 25 ♖xe1 ♖h8 26 ♘d4 and White wins.

22 ♕h4 ♔g7

22...♖ce8 23 ♗c2 f5 24 ♕g5+ ♔h8 25 ♖xe8 ♖xe8 26 ♗xf5 ♕e7 27 ♕h5 f6 28 ♗xh7 is decisive.

23 ♘d4 *(D)*

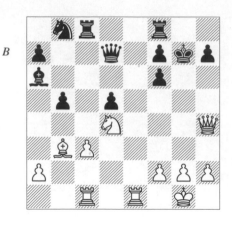

B

1-0

At first sight an early resignation, but Black cannot meet the twin threats of 24 ♗c2 and 24 ♖e7. For example, 23...♘c6 24 ♗c2 or 23...h6 24 ♖e7.

Game 19

Werner Hug – Viktor Korchnoi
Switzerland 1978
Catalan Opening

1 ♘f3 e6 2 g3 d5 3 ♗g2 c5 4 0-0 ♘c6 5 c4 dxc4

A rather unusual move.

6 ♕a4

Black's move-order could have been better exploited by 6 ♘a3 followed by ♘xc4.

6...♗d7 7 ♕xc4 ♖c8 8 ♘c3

8 d4 b5 9 ♕d3 (9 ♕xb5? ♘b4 wins material) 9...cxd4 10 ♘xd4 ♘b4 11 ♕d1 e5 12 a3 is unclear.

8...♘f6 9 d4

Transposing into the normal Catalan.

9...b5 10 ♕d3 cxd4

10...c4! 11 ♕c2 ♗e7 is a safer line, with equality.

11 ♘xd4 ♘e5

11...♘xd4 12 ♕xd4 ♗c5 13 ♕d3 is also slightly better for White.

12 ♕d1 ♕b6 *(D)*

13 ♗g5?!

Too slow. A few years later, in Ribli-Unzicker, Lucerne Olympiad 1982, White gained a slight

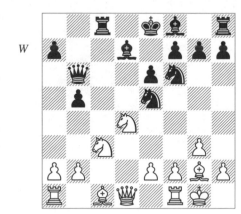

W

advantage by 13 a4! bxa4 14 ♘xa4 ♕b8 15 ♗f4 ♗d6 16 ♘c3.

13...♗e7 14 ♖c1 0-0

Black has completed his development and the position is now equal.

15 ♘f3 ♘xf3+ 16 ♗xf3 ♖fd8 17 ♕b3?!

17 ♘e4 ♗c6 18 ♕e1 is better, forcing exchanges.

17...b4 18 ♘e4? *(D)*

18 ♗xf6 ♗xf6 19 ♘e4 ♗e7 may be slightly better for Black, but it is certainly preferable to the text-move.

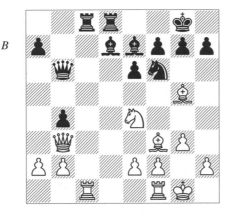

18...♘xe4!

The start of a combination which gives Black a winning position.

19 ♗xe7 ♖xc1 20 ♖xc1 ♕xf2+ 21 ♔h1

White is attacking rook and knight, but Black has a way out.

21...♖c8! 22 ♕d1

22 ♖d1 loses to the attractive knight manoeuvre 22...♘d2! 23 ♕d3 ♘f1 24 ♗g2 ♘e3,

while 22 ♖xc8+ ♗xc8 23 ♕d1 ♕xf3+! 24 exf3 ♘f2+ drops a piece.

22...♖xc1 23 ♕xc1 ♗c6!

Setting up a threat which White fails to notice.

24 ♗xb4? *(D)*

Oddly enough, 24 ♕a1 is the best defence, taking the queen well out of range of Black's knight, although even here 24...a5 should win comfortably.

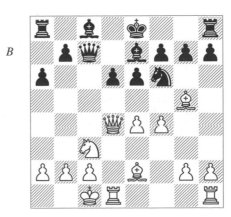

24...♕xe2! 0-1

As 25 ♗xe2 ♘xg3++ 26 ♔g1 ♘xe2+ wins a piece.

Game 20
Mikhail Tal – Bent Larsen
Montreal 1979
Sicilian Defence, Richter-Rauzer Attack

1 e4 c5 2 ♘f3 ♘c6 3 d4 cxd4 4 ♘xd4 ♘f6 5 ♘c3 d6 6 ♗g5 e6 7 ♕d2 ♗e7 8 0-0-0 a6 9 f4 ♕c7

A rather unusual system which has never gained any real popularity.

10 ♗e2 ♘xd4?!

When this system is used today, it is almost always with 10...♗d7, although 11 ♗f3 is then slightly better for White.

11 ♕xd4 *(D)*

Black's premature exchange has made it much easier for White to play e5.

11...b5

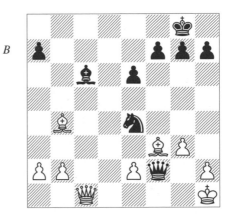

11...0-0 12 e5 dxe5 13 ♕xe5 ♕b6 14 ♘e4 gives White a slight advantage.

12 e5 dxe5 13 fxe5 ♘d5 14 ♗xe7 ♘xc3

At first sight White has no good follow-up, but his next move puts Black in trouble. After 14...♘xe7? White wins by 15 ♗xb5+ axb5 16 ♘xb5.

15 ♗f3! *(D)*

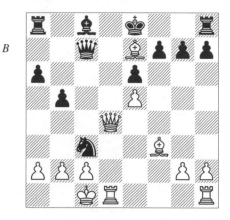

15...♘xd1?

This greedy response leads to catastrophe. 15...♗b7? loses a piece to 16 ♗d6 ♗xf3 17 bxc3!, and 15...♔xe7? 16 bxc3 ♖a7 17 ♗c6! f6 18 exf6+ gxf6 19 ♖hf1 gives White a decisive attack. 15...♘e2+! is the only way to continue; after this Tal gave 16 ♗xe2 ♕xe7 17 ♗f3 ♗b7 18 ♗xb7 ♕xb7 19 ♕d6 ♖c8 (not 19...♕xg2? 20 ♕d7+ ♔f8 21 ♖hg1 ♕e4 22 ♖gf1, winning) 20 ♖d2 ♕c6 21 ♖hd1 ♕xd6 22 ♖xd6 ♖a8 23

♖b6 as clearly better for White in his *Informator 27* notes. This whole line occurred some 18 years later in McDonald-S.Pedersen, London 1997, when Black did eventually draw, but only after defending carefully until move 67.

16 ♗d6 ♕c4 *(D)*

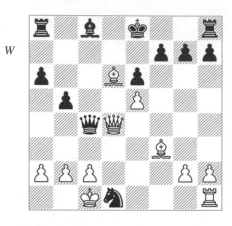

17 ♕b6!

Winning quickly as Black is facing too many threats: 18 ♗xa8, 18 ♖xd1 and 18 ♗c6+ ♗d7 19 ♗xd7+ ♔xd7 20 ♕b7+ are just samples.

17...♘f2

17...♘e3 18 ♕xe3 traps the rook. After the text-move, 18 ♕xf2 may be met by 18...♕f4+ 19 ♔b1 ♗d7, but one of White's other threats proves effective.

18 ♗c6+ ♗d7 19 ♗xd7+ ♔xd7 20 ♕b7+ ♔d8 21 ♕xa8+ ♕c8 22 ♕a7 1-0

As White is forking e7 and f2.

Game 21

Boris Spassky – Mikhail Tal

Montreal 1979

Queen's Indian Defence, Classical System

1 d4 ♘f6 2 c4 e6 3 ♘f3 b6 4 e3 ♗b7 5 ♗d3 d5 6 b3 ♗d6 7 0-0 0-0 8 ♗b2 ♘bd7 9 ♘bd2

A harmless system for White.

9...♕e7

This position has turned up now and again for over 140 years; the first example I can find is Paulsen-Kolisch, match (23), London 1861.

10 ♖c1 *(D)*

10 ♘e5 is another possibility, but 10...c5 equalizes.

10...♖ad8

Tal suggested 10...c5 and 10...♘e4 as possible alternatives, but the text-move was also played in the only other example of this position I could find: Colle-Yates, Karlsbad 1929.

11 ♕c2

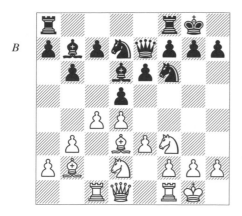

11 ♕e2 is well met by 11...♘e4; for example, 12 cxd5 exd5 13 ♗a6 ♗xa6 14 ♕xa6 ♘xd2 15 ♘xd2 c5 with equality. Therefore Spassky plays to prevent ...♘e4. Colle preferred 11 ♘e5 and went on to win after some weak play by Black.

11...c5 *(D)*

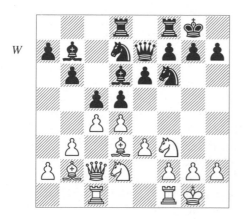

12 cxd5

White makes the double-edged decision to inflict 'hanging pawns' on Black. Whether these pawns are strong or weak depends largely on the relative piece activity of the two players. Here Black should have no cause for concern as none of White's minor pieces is actually attacking the pawns. 12 ♘e5 is a safer option, but White cannot really hope for an advantage.

12...exd5 13 dxc5 bxc5 14 ♕c3

Another double-edged move. White wants to rule out ...♘e4, but the queen is now exposed to the typical liberating thrust ...d4.

14...♖fe8 15 ♖fd1 *(D)*

15 ♖fe1 runs into tactical difficulties after 15...c4!; for example, 16 bxc4 ♗b4 17 ♕c2 dxc4 18 ♗xc4 ♗xf3 19 gxf3 ♗xd2 20 ♕xd2 ♘e5 and Black wins.

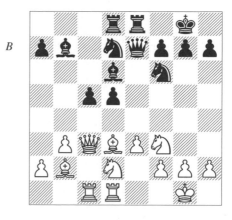

15...d4?!

Perhaps the dubious symbol is rather severe, as this sacrifice led to a quick win. However, in the harsh light of home analysis, it is revealed as not fully correct.

16 exd4 cxd4 *(D)*

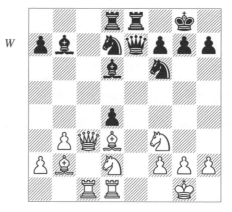

17 ♕a5?

Only this move gives Black the advantage. Having played so provocatively, White should have been consistent and taken the pawn, not by 17 ♕xd4? ♘c5 18 ♖e1 ♘xd3! 19 ♖xe7 ♗xe7 20 ♕c3 ♗b4 21 ♕c7 ♗xd2 22 ♘xd2 ♘xb2 23 ♕xb7 ♖xd2 with a large advantage for Black, but by 17 ♘xd4!. Then Black has various continuations, but nothing very convincing; for example, 17...♗xh2+ (17...♕e5 18 ♘4f3! ♕h5 19 ♗e4! defuses Black's attack) 18 ♔xh2 ♘g4+ 19 ♔g1 (19 ♔g3 ♕e5+ 20 f4 ♕e3+ 21 ♘2f3 ♗xf3 22 ♘xf3 ♘df6 23 ♗xh7+ also favours White) 19...♕h4 20 ♘2f3! (20 ♘4f3? ♕xf2+ 21 ♔h1 ♘de5! wins for Black) 20...♕xf2+ 21 ♔h1 ♖e5 (21...♘de5 22 ♖d2 ♕e3 23 ♗f5 doesn't help Black) 22 ♗f5 ♖c5 23 ♗xg4 ♖xc3 24 ♗xc3 and White wins.

17...♘e5

Now Black obtains a dangerous attack without any sacrifice.

18 ♘xe5

18 ♖e1 ♗xf3 19 ♘xf3 ♘xf3+ 20 gxf3 ♕b7 favours Black.

18...♗xe5 (D)

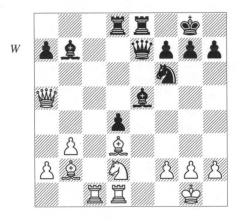

19 ♘c4?

Moving this knight further away from the kingside is asking for trouble, especially against

Tal! There are many other false paths: 19 ♗a3? ♕e6 20 ♘f1 ♗f4!, with ...♕g4 to come, is very good for Black; 19 ♖e1?! ♕d6 20 ♘f1 ♘g4 gives Black a dangerous attack; and 19 ♗b5 ♖d5 is similar to the game. 19 ♘f1! is relatively the best defence, although Black still has some advantage.

19...♖d5 20 ♕d2 (D)

There is no defence; e.g., 20 ♗a3 ♗xh2+ 21 ♔xh2 ♘g4+ 22 ♔g3 ♕f6 23 ♕d2 ♘xf2! or 20 ♕xa7 ♗xh2+ 21 ♔xh2 ♘g4+ 22 ♔g3 ♖h5, winning in both cases.

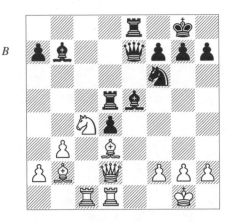

20...♗xh2+! 21 ♔xh2 ♖h5+!

Even more convincing than 21...♘g4+.

22 ♔g1

Or 22 ♔g3 ♘e4+ 23 ♗xe4 ♕h4+ 24 ♔f3 ♕xe4+ 25 ♔g3 ♕h4#.

22...♘g4 0-1

There is no defence to the twin threats of 23...♕h4 and 23...♖h1+.

Game 22

Gennadi Sosonko – Robert Hübner

Tilburg 1979

Catalan Opening

1 d4 ♘f6 2 c4 e6 3 g3 d5 4 ♗g2 dxc4 5 ♘f3 a6 6 0-0 b5

This attempt to hold on to the pawn is risky, and these days Black usually opts for the safer 6...♘c6.

7 ♘e5 ♘d5

This is the main line, but 7...c6!? 8 b3 cxb3 9 ♘xc6 ♕b6 10 ♘a5 ♖a7 is an interesting alternative.

8 ♘c3 (D)

8 a4 is the current preference.

8...c6?

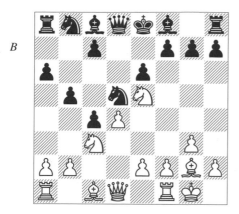

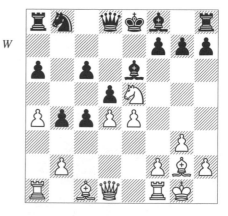

White) 11 ♗xe4 ♖a7 12 ♗c6+ ♘d7 13 d5 leads to a very strong attack.

10 e4 ♗e6 11 a4 b4 *(D)*

11...♗e7 12 axb5 cxb5 13 exd5 ♗xd5 14 ♘xf7! and 11...f6 12 exd5 cxd5 13 ♕h5+ g6 14 ♘xg6 are both lost for Black.

According to theory, Black should continue 8...♗b7 9 ♘xd5 exd5 (9...♗xd5? 10 e4 ♗b7 11 ♕h5 g6 12 ♘xg6 fxg6 13 ♕e5 wins for White) 10 e4 dxe4 11 ♕h5 g6 (11...♕e7? 12 ♗g5 ♕e6 13 ♖ae1 is very dangerous for Black) 12 ♘xg6 fxg6 13 ♕e5+ ♗e7 14 ♕xh8 ♘d7 15 h4 0-0-0 16 ♗h3 ♖e8 with good compensation for his small sacrifice – indeed, practical results from this position have favoured Black. White should probably prefer 16 ♗g5 ♕f7 17 ♗xd8 ♗g7 18 ♕xh7 ♘f8 19 ♕xg7 ♕xg7 20 ♗g5, although he cannot hope for an advantage even with this line.

9 ♘xd5 *(D)*

9 e4 has also been played with success.

12 exd5 ♗xd5

After 12...cxd5 White can choose between a clear positional plus after 13 ♘xc4 and the more ambitious 13 f4 ♖a7 14 f5 ♗c8 15 ♕f3.

13 ♕g4! h5 *(D)*

13...♗xg2 14 ♖e1! ♗e7 15 ♕xg7 ♖f8 16 ♔xg2, 13...♗e6 14 ♕h5 ♕c7 15 ♖e1 ♗e7 16 ♘xc6! ♘xc6 17 ♖xe6 and 13...♖a7 14 ♗xd5 cxd5 15 ♖e1 ♖e7 16 ♗g5 are also lost for Black.

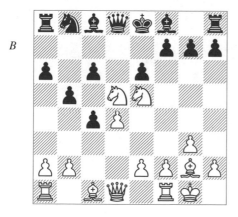

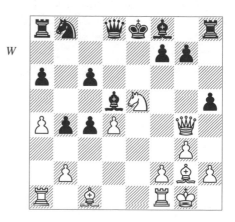

9...exd5

9...cxd5 is no better; for example, 10 e4 dxe4 (10...♖a7 11 exd5 exd5 12 ♖e1 ♗e7 13 ♘xf7! is very dangerous, while 10...♗b7 11 ♕h5 ♕c7 12 exd5 ♗xd5 13 ♗xd5 exd5 14 ♖e1 wins for

14 ♗xd5! cxd5

Or 14...hxg4 15 ♗xf7+ ♔e7 16 ♗g5+.

15 ♕f5 ♖a7 16 ♖e1 ♖e7 17 ♗g5 g6 18 ♗xe7 1-0

Game 23
Gyula Sax – Ljubomir Ljubojević
London (Phillips & Drew) 1980
Sicilian Defence, c3

1 e4 c5 2 ♘f3 e6 3 c3 d5 4 e5 d4

A more ambitious plan than 4...♘c6, which transposes into the Advance French after 5 d4.

5 ♗d3

5 cxd4 cxd4 6 ♗b5+ ♗d7 7 ♘xd4 ♗xb5 8 ♘xb5 ♘c6 is at least equal for Black.

5...♘c6 *(D)*

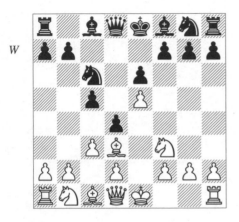

6 ♕e2?

The start of a bad plan. Natural development is best here; after 6 0-0 ♘ge7 7 ♖e1 ♘g6 8 g3 ♗e7 9 h4 White is slightly better.

6...♘ge7 7 0-0 ♘g6

Threatening 8...♘f4.

8 ♕e4

White intends to besiege the d4-pawn by ♘a3-c2, with the aim of forcing ...dxc3. Although this plan fails, the text-move does not deserve a question mark since White had already gone wrong at move six.

8...♗e7

8...dxc3 9 dxc3 ♘gxe5 10 ♘xe5 ♘xe5 11 ♗b5+ ♘d7 12 ♖d1 is dangerous for Black.

9 ♘a3 0-0 10 cxd4 cxd4 11 ♘c2 ♕c7 *(D)*

12 ♖e1

The problem becomes clear. After 12 ♘cxd4 ♘cxe5 White has an isolated pawn and his queenside development is very difficult.

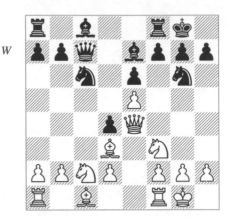

12...♖d8

Now the d4-pawn is secure as 13 ♘cxd4 loses a piece to 13...♘xd4 14 ♘xd4 ♕d7. Meanwhile, Black intends to attack the e5-pawn by 13...♖d5.

13 h4

Not 13 b3 ♖d5 14 ♗c4? ♘cxe5! 15 ♗xd5 exd5 16 ♕xd5 ♘xf3+ 17 gxf3 ♕xc2 18 ♖xe7 ♕d1+ and Black wins.

13...h5! *(D)*

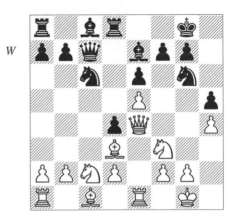

Renewing the threat of ...♖d5, rounding up the e5-pawn.

14 g4?

White panics. 14 b3 ♖d5 15 ♗b2 ♘cxe5 favours Black, but White should have tried it. Note that 16 ♘xe5 ♖xe5 17 ♕xd4 is impossible due to 17...♖xe1+ 18 ♖xe1 ♗f6.

14...hxg4 15 h5 *(D)*

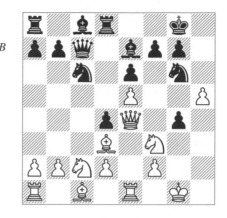

15...♘cxe5!

An attractive and devastating combination.

16 ♘xe5 f5 17 ♕e2 ♘f4 18 ♕f1

White's moves are forced.

18...b5 0-1

White is helpless against the threats on the long diagonal. A typical line is 19 ♘a3 a6 20 b3 ♗d6 21 ♘g6 ♘h3+ 22 ♔g2 ♗b7+.

Game 24
Viktor Korchnoi – Robert Hübner
Johannesburg 1981
Queen's Indian Defence

1 d4 ♘f6 2 c4 e6 3 ♘f3 b6 4 ♘c3 ♗b7 5 ♗f4

A distinctly unusual line.

5...♗e7 6 ♕c2 ♘h5?!

This loses time, and allows White to transpose into a relatively favourable variation of the Queen's Indian. 6...0-0 is better.

7 ♗d2 d5 8 cxd5 exd5 9 g3 0-0 10 ♗g2 ♘f6 11 0-0 *(D)*

By means of an unusual move-order, we have reached a position which more often arises after 4 g3 ♗b7 5 ♗g2 ♗b4+ 6 ♗d2 ♗e7 7 ♘c3

0-0 8 0-0 d5 9 cxd5 exd5 10 ♕c2 (of course the move-numbers differ by one). This position is thought to give White a slight advantage.

11...♖e8?!

A rather artificial move. Of the various lines tried here, perhaps 11...c5 12 ♖ad1 ♘bd7 offers the best chances of equality.

12 ♘e5 *(D)*

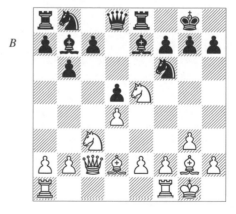

Coupled with ♕b3, this sets up a latent threat against f7 which exploits the rook's absence from f8.

12...a6

Black wants to play ...♘bd7 in a position where he can meet ♕a4 by ...b5, hence this preparatory move. White is also better after 12...♘bd7 13 ♕a4 ♘xe5 14 dxe5 ♘e4 15 ♘xe4 dxe4 16 ♖fd1, so 12...♗d6 was the best chance, intending to meet 13 ♘c4 by 13...♗e7.

13 ♕b3 ♘bd7

13...c5 14 dxc5 ♗xc5 15 ♘d3 favours White.

14 ♖ad1 b5 (*D*)

15 ♘xd5!?

A truly amazing combination. It is certainly hard for Black to find the correct reply from many plausible defences, and even then White keeps an edge. Korchnoi recommended 15 ♗g5 ♘b6 16 ♘d3, which is good enough for an edge, but 15 ♗f4! is probably objectively strongest. One variation runs 15...c6 (15...♘f8 16 e4 ♘e6 17 exd5 ♘xf4 18 d6! ♘xg2 19 ♘xf7 and White wins) 16 e4 ♘f8 17 ♘xc6! ♗xc6 18 exd5 ♗b7 19 d6 ♗xg2 20 dxe7 ♖xe7 21 ♔xg2 and White has won a pawn in return for minimal compensation.

15...♘xd5 16 ♗a5 (*D*)

The point of White's play. By opening the d-file, White threatens to take the d5-knight. 16 ♗xd5 ♗xd5 17 ♕xd5 ♘xe5 18 ♕xd8 ♗xd8 19 dxe5 ♖xe5 is only equal.

16...♘7f6?!

16...♗d6? 17 ♘xd7 ♕xd7 18 ♗xd5 loses a pawn, and 16...♘7b6 17 ♗xb6 cxb6 18 e4 ♗f6 19 exd5 ♕d6 20 ♘c6 is better for White, so the best defence is 16...♗f6!. After 17 f4 ♘7b6 18 ♗xb6 (18 e4 ♗xe5 19 dxe5 ♘c4 20 ♗b4! also gives White an edge, but not 20 ♗c3? ♘xc3!)

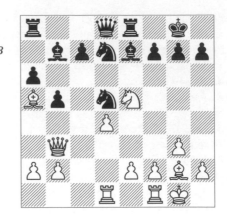

18...cxb6 19 e4 ♕d6 (19...♘c7 is unclear after 20 ♘xf7 ♕d7 or 20 ♕xf7+ ♔h8 21 ♕h5 ♔g8) 20 exd5 ♖ad8 21 ♘c6 ♗xc6 22 dxc6 ♗xd4+ 23 ♔h1 the advanced c-pawn gives White an edge.

17 e4

White's threat is not so much to take the d5-knight immediately, but rather to step up the pressure by ♖c1 first.

17...♖c8

Black anticipates White's attempts to exert pressure along the c-file.

18 ♖c1! (*D*)

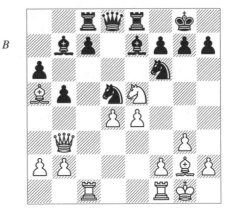

Now White threatens to take on d5, when Black will be weak at both c6 and c7. A further idea is simply to build up by ♖fd1 before regaining the piece.

18...♘xe4?

Black panics and returns the extra piece unfavourably. 18...♗d6! was best; after 19 exd5

♗xe5 20 dxe5 ♖xe5 21 ♗h3! ♖h5 22 ♗xc8 ♕xc8 23 f3 ♗xd5 24 ♕c2 c6 25 ♖ce1 Black obviously has some compensation, but it is not enough to offset his material disadvantage.

19 ♗xe4

Now Black is in real trouble as c6 and f7 are serious weaknesses.

19...g6 *(D)*

19...♕d6 is no better; e.g., 20 ♖c5 ♖cd8 (or 20...c6 21 ♗f5 ♖a8 22 ♗d7) 21 ♖xc7! ♘xc7 22 ♕xf7+ ♔h8 23 ♗xb7 and White wins.

20 ♖c6!

A deadly move. One might have expected White to occupy the c6-weakness with his knight, but the rook is even more effective as the knight can stay on e5 to maintain the pressure against f7.

20...♘f6

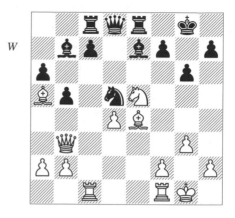

The knight must move, but now the f7-square collapses.

21 ♘xf7 ♕xd4 22 ♘g5+ ♔h8 23 ♗c3 1-0

Total destruction.

Game 25

Alexander Beliavsky – Bent Larsen

Tilburg 1981

Caro-Kann Defence, 4...♗f5

1 e4 c6 2 d4 d5 3 ♘c3 dxe4 4 ♘xe4 ♗f5 5 ♘g3 ♗g6 6 h4 h6 7 ♘f3 ♘d7 8 h5 ♗h7 9 ♗d3 ♗xd3 10 ♕xd3 ♘gf6 11 ♗f4 e6

The other main line is 11...♕a5+ 12 ♗d2 ♕c7, followed by queenside castling. With 11...e6 Black is aiming to castle kingside.

12 0-0-0 ♗e7 13 ♘e5 *(D)*

13...a5

13...0-0 is more accurate, waiting to see White's response before committing himself.

14 ♖he1 a4?

One liberty too many. 14...0-0 would still reach a playable position for Black.

15 ♘g6!

Now Black will definitely not be able to castle!

15...♘d5 *(D)*

15...fxg6 is bad in view of 16 ♕xg6+ ♔f8 17 ♖xe6 ♕e8 18 ♘f5! ♘xh5 (18...♕xg6 19 hxg6 ♗d8 20 ♗d6+ ♔g8 21 ♖de1 mates) 19 ♕xe8+ ♖xe8 20 ♖xe7 ♖xe7 21 ♗d6 ♔f7 22 ♘xe7 ♖e8 23 ♘f5 ♖e2 24 ♖f1 followed by 25 ♔d1 and White consolidates his extra pawn.

15...a3 is a tricky move. Then White should not be seduced by 16 ♘xh8? axb2+ 17 ♔b1 ♖a3 18 ♘xf7 ♕a8! 19 ♕g6 ♘f8 20 ♘d6++ ♔d7, when Black has dangerous counterplay. Instead 16 b3! is correct, with very similar play to the game.

16 ♘f5!

Another forceful blow.

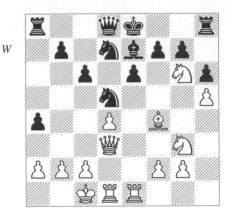

16...♗f8

A very bad sign, but 16...exf5 17 ♘xe7 ♘xe7 18 ♗d6 ♘e5 19 dxe5 0-0 20 e6 is hopeless for Black.

17 ♗d6

Now that the bishop is not hanging on f4, White genuinely threatens to capture the h8-rook.

17...♖g8

Forced, but it gives White another tempo for his attack.

18 c4

Dislodging Black's only well-placed piece.

18...♘b4 19 ♕h3 *(D)*

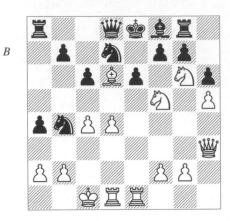

Taking aim at e6.

19...fxg6

There is nothing better.

20 ♖xe6+ ♔f7 21 hxg6+! ♔xe6 22 ♖e1+ ♘e5 23 ♗xe5 1-0

In view of 23...♘d3+ 24 ♔b1! ♘xe5 25 ♖xe5+ ♔d7 26 ♘xg7+ winning the queen.

Game 26

Lev Psakhis – Efim Geller

Erevan Zonal 1982

Queen's Gambit Declined, Tartakower Defence

1 d4 d5 2 c4 e6 3 ♘c3 ♗e7 4 ♘f3 ♘f6 5 ♗g5 h6 6 ♗h4 0-0 7 e3 b6 8 ♗xf6

The most common lines are 8 cxd5, 8 ♖c1, 8 ♗e2 and 8 ♗d3, but there are a number of side-lines for White, including the text-move.

8...♗xf6 9 cxd5 exd5 10 ♕d2

White intends to exert pressure on d5, so as to prevent the freeing thrust ...c5.

10...♗e6!

10...♗b7 can be met by either 11 b4 c5 12 bxc5 bxc5 13 dxc5 ♕a5 14 ♖c1 or simply 11 ♖d1, effectively restraining ...c5.

11 ♖d1 ♕e7 12 g3

This is the critical move because after 12 ♗e2 ♖d8 13 0-0 ♘d7 14 ♕c2 c5 Black frees himself and equalizes.

12...c5!

12...♘d7 13 ♗g2 ♖fd8 is also possible, although it is less dynamic than the text-move.

13 dxc5? *(D)*

Again the critical move, because if Black is allowed to play ...c5 without a fight, White's plan of ♕d2 and ♖d1 looks rather pointless. However, it turns out that the tactics are on Black's side, so White should have aimed for equality with 13 ♗g2 ♘c6 14 0-0 cxd4 15 ♘xd4 ♘xd4 16 exd4 ♕d7.

13...♖d8!

This is the point of Black's play. Black secures the d5-pawn, and now threatens 14...bxc5 with a good game because he has retained his dangerous dark-squared bishop.

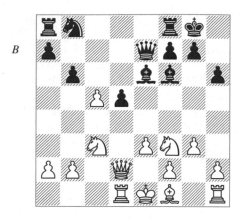

B

14 cxb6

Consistent, but White is really playing with fire.

14...d4! *(D)*

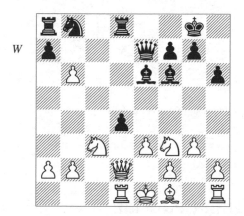

W

15 ♗g2

There is no really satisfactory continuation:

1) 15 ♘e4? ♗d5 16 ♘xf6+ ♕xf6 17 ♕xd4 ♕xf3 18 b7 ♖d7! 19 ♗b5 (19 bxa8♕ ♗xa8 and 19 ♕a4 ♗xb7 also win for Black) 19...♕xh1+ 20 ♔d2 ♕xd1+ 21 ♔xd1 ♗f3+ and Black wins.

2) 15 ♘xd4 ♗xd4 16 ♗g2 ♗xb6 17 ♕c2 ♘d7 18 ♗xa8 ♖xa8 19 0-0 ♗h3 20 ♖fe1 ♗g4 with advantage to Black in view of the weak light squares around White's king.

3) 15 ♘e2 ♗d5 16 ♗g2 axb6 17 a3 ♘c6 with a very strong initiative for Black.

4) 15 ♗e2 ♘c6 16 ♘xd4 ♘xd4 17 exd4 ♗xd4 and White will have to give up his queen for a rook and a piece.

15...♘c6 16 ♘xd4

16 ♘e4 dxe3 17 ♕xe3 ♖xd1+ 18 ♔xd1 axb6 is clearly very good for Black, while 16 exd4 ♗b3+ 17 ♘e5 (after 17 ♕e3 ♗xd1 18 ♕xe7 ♘xe7 19 ♔xd1 axb6 the endgame is clearly favourable for Black) 17...♘xe5 18 ♕e3 ♗xd1 19 dxe5 ♗xe5 20 0-0 ♗h5 gives White insufficient compensation for the piece.

16...♘xd4 17 exd4 *(D)*

17 ♗xa8 ♖xa8 18 exd4 ♗d5+ 19 ♕e2 ♗xh1 20 ♕xe7 ♗xe7 21 bxa7 ♖xa7 favours Black. The three pawns do not provide enough compensation for the piece when Black has two bishops against a knight.

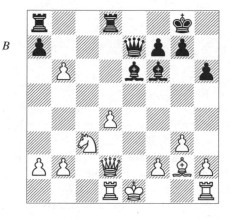

B

17...♗h3+ 18 ♔f1

18 ♗e4 ♗xd4 19 ♕e2 ♗xc3+ 20 bxc3 ♖e8 21 f3 axb6 is bad for White.

18...♖xd4 *(D)*

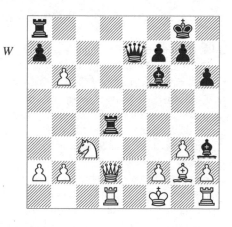

W

19 ♕e3

19 ♕xd4 ♗xd4 20 ♖xd4 ♕f6 21 ♖f4 (21 ♖d3 ♕f5 22 ♖e3 axb6 23 ♗xh3 ♕xh3+ is similar) 21...♕c6 22 ♖g1 ♗xg2+ 23 ♖xg2 axb6 gives Black excellent winning chances.

19...♕b7 (D)

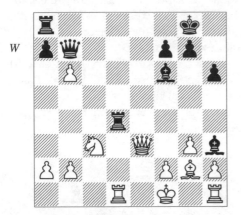

20 f3?

White has defended well after his dubious opening, but now makes a further error which loses quickly. 20 ♖g1! ♖xd1+ 21 ♘xd1 is correct, when Black cannot achieve more than a modest advantage; for example, 21...♗xg2+ 22 ♖xg2 ♕a6+ 23 ♕e2 ♕xa2 24 ♖g1 axb6 25 ♔g2 ♖d8 26 ♖e1 or 21...♖d8 22 ♕e2 (but not 22

♘c3? ♗xg2+ 23 ♖xg2 ♗xc3 24 bxc3 ♕a6+! 25 ♔e1 ♕xa2 and Black wins) 22...♗xg2+ 23 ♖xg2 ♕xb6 24 f3 (24 ♖g1 ♕a5 25 ♔g2 ♕xa2 26 ♖e1 is clearly better for Black) 24...♕c6 25 ♘c3 ♗xc3 26 bxc3 ♕xc3 27 ♖f2 with only a slight advantage for Black.

20...♖xd1+ 21 ♘xd1 ♕a6+ 22 ♔g1

22 ♔f2 ♖d8 23 b7 ♕xb7 is also winning for Black.

22...♖d8 (D)

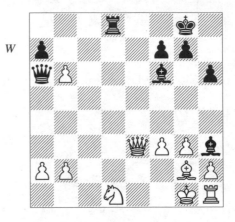

23 ♘f2 ♗d4 24 ♕e1 ♗xf2+! 0-1

25 ♔xf2 (25 ♕xf2 ♖d1+) 25...♕xb6+ 26 ♔f1 (26 ♕e3 ♖d2+) 26...♗c8! wins for Black.

Game 27

Garry Kasparov – Tigran Petrosian

Bugojno 1982

Bogo-Indian Defence

1 d4 ♘f6 2 c4 e6 3 ♘f3 ♗b4+ 4 ♗d2 ♕e7 5 g3 ♗xd2+ 6 ♕xd2 0-0 7 ♗g2 d5 (D)

These days this variation of the Bogo-Indian is played almost exclusively with the idea of ...d6 and ...e5. It is logical for Black to put his pawns on dark squares, given that he has exchanged off his dark-squared bishop.

8 0-0 dxc4

Black is aiming to liquidate all the central pawns, but the danger is that White's g2-bishop will exert nagging long-term pressure against Black's queenside. The alternative plan is to support the d5-point by, for example, 8...♖d8 9

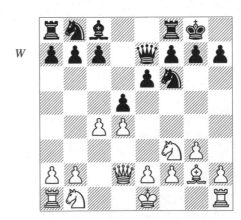

♖c1 c6. Although Black's position is solid, White has a small but long-term advantage due to his more active bishop.

9 ♘a3 *(D)*

9...c5?

But this is definitely wrong. As explained above, the whole plan of liquidating the centre has its dangers for Black; to make matters worse, Black executes this plan in a way which costs valuable time. 9...♖d8 is better; for example, 10 ♕c2 (or 10 ♘xc4 c5 11 ♖fd1 ♘a6 with just an edge for White) 10...c5 11 dxc5 ♕xc5 12 ♖fd1 offers White no more than a slight advantage.

10 dxc5!

10 ♘xc4 allows Black to transpose into the previous note by 10...♖d8.

10...♕xc5

After 10...♖d8 White can keep the advantage by either 11 ♕e3 ♘d5 12 ♕d4 or 11 ♕b4 ♘a6 12 ♕xc4 ♕xc5 13 ♕xc5 ♘xc5 14 ♘e5.

11 ♖ac1 ♘c6 12 ♘xc4

Sooner or later Black will have to move his queen again; this loss of time explains why his 9th move was a mistake.

12...♕e7 *(D)*

12...♖d8 13 ♘f4 ♕e7 (after 13...♘d5?! 14 ♕h4 ♕e7 15 ♕xe7 ♘dxe7 16 ♖fd1 White has strong pressure in the endgame) 14 ♘fe5 ♘xe5 15 ♘xe5 gives White the same type of pressure as in the game.

13 ♘fe5 ♘xe5 14 ♘xe5

It is not at all clear how Black can develop his queenside pieces.

14...♘d5 15 ♖fd1

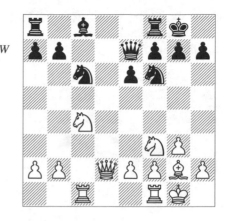

Stepping up the pressure. 15 ♗xd5 ♖d8 lets Black off the hook.

15...♘b6

Black hopes to play ...f6 and ...e5, so as to develop the c8-bishop, but this plan doesn't even get off the ground.

16 ♕a5! *(D)*

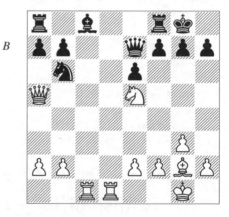

Despite White's pressure, accuracy is necessary to prevent Black from freeing himself. This move stops 16...f6 on account of 17 ♘c4 ♘xc4 18 ♖xc4 followed by penetration on c7.

16...g6

The immediate 16...♖d8 fails due to Black's weak back rank: 17 ♘c4! ♖xd1+ (17...♘d5 18 ♗xd5 exd5 19 ♘b6 wins for White) 18 ♖xd1 ♘d7 19 ♕c7 is decisive. The move played prepares ...♖d8.

17 ♖d3!

Again preventing 17...♖d8, this time owing to 18 ♕c5! (there is now no capture on d1 with check) 18...♕xc5 19 ♖xd8+ ♕f8 20 ♖xf8+ ♔xf8 21 ♖c7 and White wins.

17...♘d5 18 e4 (D)

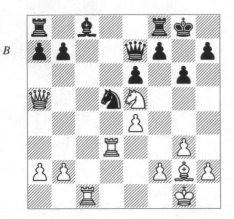

Blocking the fianchettoed bishop, but only for a moment. Of course, White has no interest in winning a pawn on d5, as Black would gain some freedom – White's position is so strong that he can play for more.

18...♘b6

18...♕b4? loses to 19 ♖xd5.

19 ♗f1! ♖e8

Black was intending 19...f6, but now this move fails to 20 ♘c4 ♘xc4 (20...♗d7 21 ♘xb6 axb6 22 ♕xb6 ♗c6 23 a3 gives White a pawn more with a good position) 21 ♖xc4 b6 22 ♕c3 ♗a6 23 ♖c7 since the d3-rook is defended.

White's prophylactic play reminds one of ... Petrosian!

20 ♖dd1!

Another useful move, activating the f1-bishop. Black is now totally paralysed.

20...♖f8

20...♗d7 loses after 21 ♘xd7 ♘xd7 22 ♖c7.

21 a3! ♔g7 22 b3

White slowly but surely prepares a4-a5.

22...♔g8 23 a4 ♖d8 (D)

Or 23...♔g7 24 ♕d2, followed by a5.

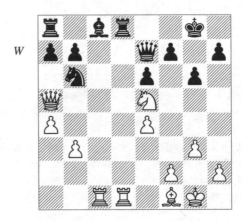

24 ♕c5! 1-0

After 24...♕xc5 (if 24...♕e8, then 25 ♘g4 wins) 25 ♖xd8+ ♕f8 26 ♖xf8+ ♔xf8 27 ♖c7 it is only a question of how many pawns Black is going to lose.

Game 28
Mikhail Tal – John van der Wiel
Moscow Interzonal 1982
English Opening

1 c4 ♘f6 2 ♘c3 e6 3 ♘f3 b6 4 e4 ♗b7 5 ♗d3

White intends to form a powerful centre by ♗c2 and d4, so Black must react quickly.

5...c5 6 0-0 ♘c6 7 e5 ♘g4 8 ♗e4 ♕c8?!

Current theory prefers 8...f5 9 exf6 ♘xf6 10 ♗xc6 ♗xc6 11 d4 ♗xf3 12 ♕xf3 cxd4 13 ♘b5 with just an edge for White.

9 d3 (D)

9...♘gxe5?!

It is risky to accept the pawn. 9...f5 10 exf6 ♘xf6 11 ♗f4 ♗e7 12 ♘b5 0-0 is safer, with at worst a slight disadvantage.

10 ♘xe5 ♘xe5 11 f4

Black's king is still far from safety.

11...♘c6?!

11...♗xe4 12 ♘xe4 ♘c6 13 f5 ♗e7 is better; White has a dangerous attack, but nothing clear-cut.

12 f5 g6

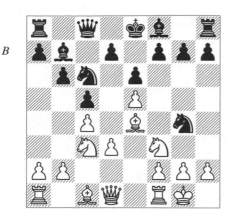

B

There is nothing better:

1) 12...♗e7?! 13 ♕g4 ♗f6 14 ♘b5 0-0 15 fxe6 fxe6 16 ♕h3 g6 (16...h6 17 ♗xh6) 17 ♗h6 ♗g7 18 ♗xg7 ♔xg7 19 ♘d6 ♕c7 20 ♘f7! ♖xf7 21 ♖xf7+ ♔xf7 22 ♕xh7+ and White wins.

2) 12...♘d4 13 ♕h5 ♗xe4 14 ♘xe4 exf5 15 ♗g5 h6 16 ♖ae1 ♘e6 17 ♗h4 g6 18 ♘f6+ ♔d8 19 ♘d5+ ♔e8 20 ♕f3 gives White a very strong attack.

13 ♗g5 gxf5 14 ♗xf5! ♗e7?

The only chance was 14...exf5, but after 15 ♕e2+ ♘e7 16 ♖ae1 ♖g8 17 ♗xe7 ♖xg2+ 18 ♕xg2 ♗xg2 19 ♗h4+ ♗e4 20 ♘xe4 fxe4 21 ♖xe4+ ♗e7 22 ♖xe7+ ♔d8 23 ♖fxf7 ♔c7 24 ♗g3+ ♔b7 (after 24...♔c6 25 ♖xh7 a5 26 h4 Black is tied up and can hardly oppose the advance of White's h-pawn) 25 ♖xd7+ ♔a6 26 a3! followed by b4 White has a large advantage.

15 ♕h5
Decisive.
15...♗xg5
15...exf5 16 ♖ae1 ♔d8 17 ♘d5 wins for White.
16 ♕xg5 ♘e7
16...exf5 17 ♖ae1+ ♔f8 18 ♕h6+ ♔g8 19 ♘d5 and 16...♕c7 17 ♖ae1! (threatening 18 ♘d5) 17...♘e7 18 ♗e4 ♗xe4 19 dxe4, intending e5 coupled with ♘e4 or ♘b5, are hopeless for Black.
17 ♗e4
Threatening 18 ♘b5.
17...♗xe4 18 ♘xe4 ♕c6 (D)

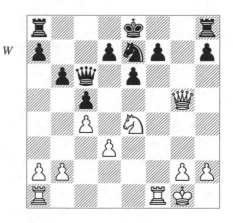

W

19 ♖xf7!
An attractive finish.
19...♔xf7 20 ♕f6+ ♔g8 21 ♕xe7 ♖f8 22 ♖f1! 1-0

Game 29
John van der Wiel – Lubomir Ftačnik
Århus 1983
Sicilian Defence, Najdorf Poisoned Pawn

1 e4 c5 2 ♘f3 d6 3 d4 cxd4 4 ♘xd4 ♘f6 5 ♘c3 a6 6 ♗g5 e6 7 f4 ♕b6 8 ♕d2 ♕xb2 9 ♖b1 ♕a3 10 ♗e2

This line against the Poisoned Pawn suddenly materialized in the early 1980s. After initial successes, antidotes were found and it is now rarely seen.

10...♗e7 11 0-0 ♘c6?

Black has a number of playable lines, including 11...h6, 11...♕c5, 11...♘bd7 and 11...♕a5, but this isn't one of them.

12 ♘xc6 bxc6 13 e5! dxe5 14 fxe5 ♕c5+ 15 ♔h1 ♕xe5 16 ♗f4 (D)
16...♘e4

There is nothing better; e.g., 16...♕a5 17 ♗f3 ♗d7 (17...0-0 18 ♘d5) 18 ♖b7 ♕d8 and

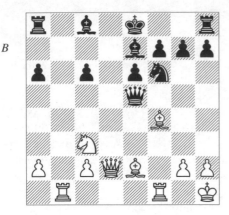

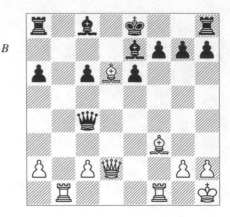

now White can choose between 19 ♘a4, 19 ♘e4 and 19 ♖d1, all of them very unpleasant.

17 ♘xe4 ♕xe4 18 ♗f3 ♕c4

After 18...♕a4 19 ♕c3 ♗d7 20 ♕xg7 ♖f8 21 ♗h5 the f7-square will collapse.

19 ♗d6! *(D)*

19...f5?!

Losing by force, as does 19...f6 20 ♗h5+ g6 (20...♔f8 21 ♖xf6+! mates) 21 ♗xe7 ♔xe7 22 ♕h6. 19...♖a7 is the best chance, although after 20 ♗xe7 ♖xe7 21 ♕d6 f6 (21...f5 22 ♗xc6+ ♔f7 23 ♖xf5+ exf5 24 ♗d5+ ♕xd5 25 ♕xd5+ ♗e6 may be Black's best chance, although this should be a win for White) 22 ♗h5+ g6 23

♖xf6! ♕d5 (23...gxh5 24 ♖b8 mates, while 23...♖f7 24 ♖xf7 ♔xf7 25 ♕c7+ ♔f6 26 ♖e1! gives White a winning attack) 24 ♕b8 ♕d7 (or 24...♕d8 25 ♗f3 ♖c7 26 ♕b2! ♖g8 27 ♕e5 with crushing pressure) 25 ♗f3 ♖f7 26 ♖xf7 ♔xf7 27 ♕f4+ ♔g8 28 ♖f1 White has a paralysing bind and should win.

20 ♖fd1 ♖a7

20...♗xd6 21 ♕xd6 ♔f7 22 ♕c7+ ♔f6 23 ♖b6! ♕c5 24 ♖xc6 ♕a7 25 ♕d6 followed by 26 ♖c7 wins for White.

21 ♖b4 ♕xa2 22 ♗xe7 ♔xe7 23 ♕d4 1-0

The fork of the a7-rook and the g7-pawn wins a rook.

Game 30

Ljubomir Ljubojević – Garry Kasparov

Nikšić 1983

King's Indian Attack

1 e4 c5 2 ♘f3 e6 3 d3 ♘c6 4 g3 d5 5 ♘bd2 g6 6 ♗g2 ♗g7 7 0-0 ♘ge7 8 ♖e1 b6!? *(D)*

An instructive move. If Black plays 8...0-0, then White replies 9 e5 with an automatic kingside attack by ♘f1, h4 and ♘h2-g4.

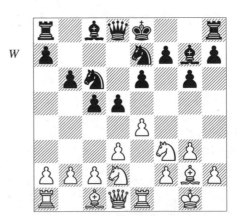

Black delays castling so as not to present White with such an obvious target. Only after Black has developed counterplay in the queenside or centre will he consider castling. Of course, one must always take care when leaving one's king in the centre, but here the risk is small. Black is ready to castle if things should start looking dangerous; for example, if White opens the e-file by exd5, thereby giving up the option of e5, Black will probably castle very quickly.

9 h4

9 c3 a5 10 a4 ♗a6 is similar to the game.

9...h6

Now h5 can be answered by ...g5.

10 c3

If White plays 10 e5, then Black changes plan and aims for queenside castling. After 10...♕c7 11 ♕e2 ♗b7 12 ♘f1 0-0-0, for example, White's set-up, which would be very effective against kingside castling, looks somewhat out of place.

10...a5

White's last move weakened d3, so Black both gains queenside space and prepares for ...♗a6. It would be a mistake to play 10...♗a6 as 11 exd5 exd5 12 ♕a4 would be very unpleasant.

11 a4

11 e5 ♕c7 is a little awkward for White as 12 d4 cxd4 13 cxd4 would be well met by 13...♘b4.

11...♖a7 *(D)*

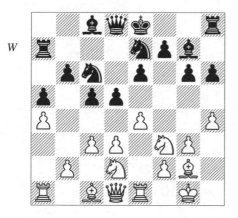

Black consistently aims to play as many useful moves as possible before castling; now he intends ...♖d7 and ...♗a6.

12 ♘b3

An inaccuracy. White should have tried either 12 exd5 exd5 13 ♘b3 0-0 14 ♗f4 or 12 e5 ♗a6 13 ♘f1, with a roughly equal position in either case.

12...d4!

Black immediately exploits White's omission of exd5. If the e-pawns had been exchanged,

White would be able to develop his bishop at f4, whereas now this would be pointless as Black can just reply ...e5.

13 cxd4

13 e5 dxc3 14 bxc3 ♖d7 15 d4 cxd4 16 cxd4 0-0 is fine for Black.

13...cxd4 14 ♗d2? *(D)*

A serious positional error. It was essential to play 14 e5 to gain some space, when 14...♗a6 15 ♖e4 ♖d7 16 ♗f4 is unclear.

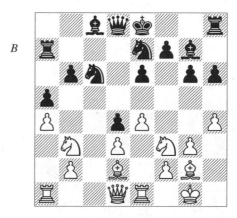

B

14...e5!

Now White is in trouble. Black has more space and can develop his remaining pieces easily. White, on the other hand, is completely tangled up: where can his minor pieces move to?

15 ♘c1 ♗e6 16 ♖e2

White tries to solve the puzzle of rearranging his pieces, but his contortions contrast sharply with Black's comfortable development.

16...0-0 *(D)*

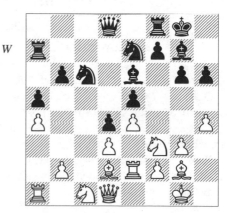

W

Black finally castles. Needless to say, White no longer has any attacking chances on the kingside; indeed, thanks to the weakening advance h4, it is White's kingside which is in danger.

17 ♗e1 f5 18 ♘d2

18 exf5 gxf5 doesn't help.

18...f4

Black's space advantage increases. Now he threatens 19...fxg3 followed by 20...♗g4.

19 f3

Or 19 gxf4 exf4 20 ♘f3 ♘e5 followed by ...♘7c6 and Black secures his knight on e5.

19...fxg3 20 ♗xg3 g5

The direct attack starts.

21 hxg5 (D)

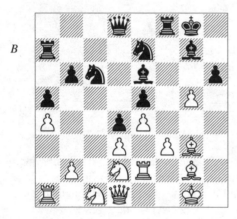

21...♘g6!

Black would much prefer to take on g5 with his queen.

22 gxh6 ♗xh6

The pawn is irrelevant as White's kingside is on the point of collapse. Eleven moves ago, when Kasparov played ...♖a7, he could hardly have imagined that this rook would now be swinging across to join in a kingside mating attack!

23 ♘f1 ♖g7 24 ♖f2 ♗e3 25 b3

25 ♘xe3 dxe3 26 ♖f1 (26 ♖e2 ♕g5 27 ♕e1 ♘d4 and Black wins) 26...♕g5 27 ♘e2 ♘f4 finishes White off.

25...♘f4 (D)

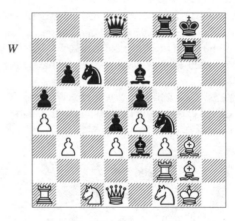

0-1

26 ♖a2 ♘xg2 27 ♔xg2 ♕h4 is catastrophic for White.

Game 31

Jan Timman – Lev Polugaevsky

Tilburg 1983

Nimzo-Indian Defence, Sämisch Variation

1 d4 ♘f6 2 c4 e6 3 ♘c3 ♗b4 4 e3 c5 5 ♗d3 0-0 6 a3 ♗xc3+ 7 bxc3 ♘c6 8 ♘e2 b6 9 e4

A typical Sämisch Nimzo-Indian position; Black aims to win the c4-pawn with ...♗a6 and ...♘a5, while White plays for a kingside attack. Here Black must prevent a deadly pin by 10 ♗g5, but 9...h6 must be avoided as it seriously weakens Black's kingside.

9...♘e8 (D)

The correct solution, side-stepping the pin without creating a weakness.

10 0-0 ♗a6 11 f4

At first sight White's attack, based on f5-f6, looks very dangerous, but with accurate play Black can defend.

11...♘a5?!

A rather risky plan which allows White to advance his f-pawn. 11...f5 is a safer alternative,

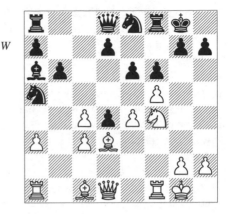

stopping White's f-pawn one move earlier than in the game. Theory regards the resulting position as unclear.

12 f5 f6 *(D)*

Black must prevent f6 by White; for example, 12...鱼xc4 13 f6 ②xf6 14 鱼g5 gives White an extremely dangerous attack.

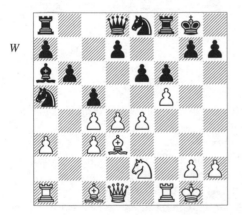

13 ②f4

13 罝f3 cxd4 14 罝h3 exf5 15 exf5 led to a win for White in Cvitan-H.Grünberg, Polanica Zdroj 1985, but at this stage the position is just unclear.

13...cxd4 *(D)*

13...exf5 14 exf5 鱼xc4 is inferior because of 15 鱼xc4+ ②xc4 16 dxc5 threatening 17 豐d5+.

14 豐h5

14 fxe6 dxc3 15 e5 looks dangerous, but after 15...fxe5 16 鱼xh7+ (16 豐h5 ②f6 17 豐xe5 dxe6 18 豐xc3 豐d6 also defends) 16...含xh7 17 豐h5+ 含g8 18 ②g6 Black has a neat defence in

18...罝xf1+ 19 含xf1 豐f6+ 20 含g1 豐xe6 21 鱼g5 ②f6 22 鱼xf6 豐xf6 23 罝f1 c2! 24 罝xf6 c1豐+ 25 罝f1 豐h6. This line shows that Black's pawn captures are not only motivated by the desire for material gain – sometimes they provide a mechanism for counterplay.

However, 14 cxd4 exf5 15 鱼d2! (15 exf5 鱼xc4 16 鱼xc4+ ②xc4 17 豐h5 ②ed6 18 ②g6 豐e8 gave Black a clear advantage in Ker-Hellers, Gausdal 1986) is an interesting and possibly dangerous idea. After 15...②xc4 16 鱼b4 罝f7 17 豐e2 罝c8 18 exf5 White has strong pressure in return for the pawn.

14...exf5 *(D)*

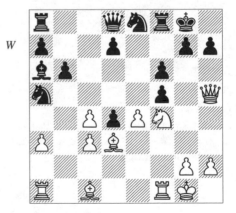

15 exf5?

White plays for mate, but this is too ambitious. He should have continued 15 豐xf5 ②d6 (15...dxc3 16 e5 g6 17 ②xg6 and White wins after 17...罝f7 18 exf6 罝xf6 19 豐d5+ 含g7 20 ②f4 or 17...②g7 18 ②e7+ 豐xe7 19 豐xh7+

&f7 20 exf6) 16 ♕d5+ ♘f7 17 cxd4 ♖c8 18 c5!
♗xd3 19 ♘xd3, when White's active queen
gives him a slight advantage.

15...♘d6!

Cool defence, clearing e8 for the black queen.
Occupying this square will not only force White
to spend a tempo avoiding the queen exchange,
but the action of Black's queen along the e-file
will provide counterplay.

16 ♖f3 ♕e8

The immediate 16...♗xc4 allows 17 ♖h3 h6
18 ♘g6 ♗xd3 19 ♖xd3, when a sacrifice on h6
is threatened; e.g., 19...♖e8? 20 ♗xh6 gxh6 21
♖g3! ♖e3 22 ♕xh6 ♘xf5 23 ♘e7++ ♔f7 24
♕h7+ ♔e6 25 ♘xf5 with a decisive attack for
White.

17 ♘g6 *(D)*

After 17 ♕h4 ♗xc4 18 ♖h3 h6 19 ♘g6
♗xd3 the situation is entirely different, as the
f5-pawn is *en prise*.

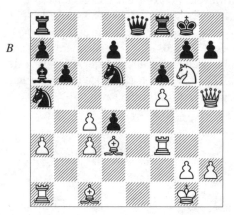

17...♗xc4

The cavalry arrives just in time; Black is
threatening 18...♗xd3 19 ♖xd3 ♕e1#, so White
has to interrupt his attack.

18 ♗f4

18 ♗xc4+ ♘axc4 19 cxd4 ♘xf5 20 ♕xf5
hxg6 leaves White with little to show for the
two pawns.

18...♗xd3

Not only removing an attacking piece, but
also bearing down on the important g6-square.
Now White's attack collapses.

19 ♖h3 *(D)*

White's last desperate chance, as 19 ♗xd6
hxg6 and 19 ♖xd3 ♘xf5 are easily winning for
Black.

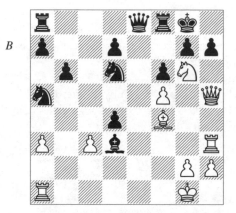

19...♗xf5!

Not 19...h6? 20 ♖xd3 and White is suddenly
better.

20 ♕xh7+

White finally breaks through to h7, but the
cost has been too high.

20...♔f7 21 ♖g3 ♘e4 22 ♘e5+

22 ♖e1 ♘xg3 23 ♖xe8 ♗xg6 gives Black far
too much for the queen.

22...♔e6 0-1

White will be at least a piece and two pawns
down.

Game 32

Boris Spassky – Yasser Seirawan

Zurich 1984

Pirc Defence

**1 e4 d6 2 d4 ♘f6 3 ♘c3 g6 4 ♘f3 ♗g7 5 h3
0-0 6 ♗e3**

This system became popular in the 1980s but
is less often seen these days. White delays the

development of his f1-bishop until he has a better idea where it will be well placed.

6...a6 7 a4 b6 8 &c4 &b7?!

It is risky to allow White to advance in the centre. 8...e6 is currently regarded as giving Black a comfortable position.

9 e5 ♘e4

9...dxe5 10 dxe5 ♕xd1+ 11 ♖xd1 is simply bad for Black as 11...&xf3 loses material after 12 exf6, while 9...♘e8 10 e6 f5 11 d5 c6 12 h4 gives White a very dangerous attack.

10 ♘xe4 &xe4 (D)

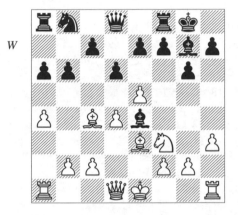

11 ♘g5!

At the cost of the g-pawn, White opens a file towards Black's king and gains a number of tempi for his attack.

11...&xg2?!

11...d5? 12 &b3 &xg2 13 ♖g1 &e4 14 ♘xe4 dxe4 15 ♕g4 regains the pawn with tremendous pressure on the light squares. 11...&b7 12 ♕g4 e6 offers better defensive chances, but this is still a pretty grim prospect for Black.

12 ♖g1 &c6 13 ♕g4 (D)

White threatens 14 e6 f5 15 ♕h4 h6 16 ♘f7 with a decisive attack, so Black is obliged to make another non-developing move to prevent the advance of White's e-pawn.

13...e6

13...dxe5 14 ♕h4 h6 runs into the combination 15 ♘xf7! ♖xf7 16 ♖xg6 &d5 17 dxe5 &xc4 18 ♕xc4 c6 (Black must try to free his f7-rook; this threatens 19...♕d5) 19 ♖d1 ♕c7 20 ♕e6 with total paralysis.

14 0-0-0

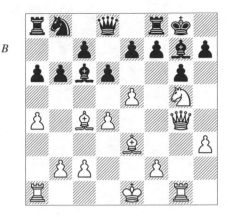

White completes his development. The threat is 15 h4 and if Black replies 15...h5, weakening g6, then White has only to retreat his queen to be threatening a deadly piece sacrifice on e6.

14...♘d7 (D)

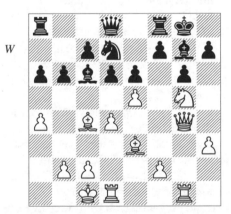

15 h4

15 ♘xf7 ♖xf7 16 ♕xe6 ♕f8 17 ♕xf7+ ♕xf7 18 &xf7+ ♔xf7 19 d5 &xd5 20 ♖xd5 ♘xe5 would be extremely difficult to win, so White goes for more.

15...dxe5

15...h5 16 ♕g3 ♕e7 (trying to support e6) 17 ♘xe6 fxe6 18 ♕xg6 wins for White.

16 dxe5

16 ♘xe6 looks promising, but is not so clear after 16...fxe6 17 ♕xe6+ ♔h8 18 ♕xc6 exd4 19 &xd4 (or 19 ♖xd4 ♕f6) 19...&xd4 20 ♖xd4 ♕f6!.

16...♕e7 (D)

17 ♖xd7!?

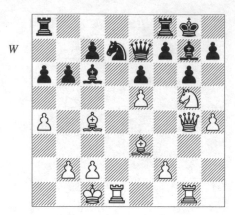

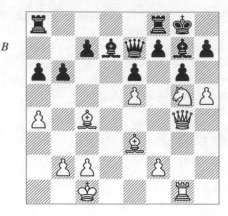

An imaginative sacrifice to gain a tempo for h5. This move can hardly be criticized, because it gives White the advantage. However, it is worth mentioning that the simpler 17 f4 would have given White a very strong attack without any additional material investment.

17...♗xd7

17...♕xd7 18 h5 is no better for Black:

1) 18...♖fe8 19 ♘xh7! ♔xh7 20 hxg6+ ♔g8 21 gxf7+ ♕xf7 22 ♗h6 ♖e7 23 ♗xg7 ♕xg7 24 ♗xe6+ ♔h8 25 ♕h4+ ♕h7 26 ♕f6+ ♖g7 27 ♗f5 and wins.

2) 18...♗d5 19 ♗d3 h6 allows White a truly spectacular win by 20 ♘h7!! (20 hxg6 hxg5 21 ♗xg5 fxg6 22 ♗xg6 lets Black escape after 22...♖f5! 23 ♗f6 ♖xf6 24 exf6 ♗xf6 25 c4 ♗xc4) 20...♔xh7 21 hxg6+ ♔h8 22 ♕h4 f5 23 ♗xh6 ♔g8 24 ♗g5 ♖fe8 25 ♗f6 and Black is powerless to prevent ♖g3-h3, followed by mate on h8.

18 h5 *(D)*
18...f5?!

Losing quickly, but Black's other defences offered little hope:

1) 18...♖fd8 19 ♘xh7 ♗xe5 loses to 20 hxg6 f5 21 ♕xf5 ♗xb2+ 22 ♔xb2 ♕b4+ 23 ♗b3 ♕xb3+ 24 cxb3 exf5 25 ♗h6! and White gains too much material.

2) 18...♗xe5 19 ♘xh7 ♕b4 (19...♖fd8 transposes to the previous line) 20 ♗d4! ♕xc4 21 ♗xe5 ♕xg4 22 ♘f6+ ♔g7 (22...♔h8 loses to 23 ♘xg4+) 23 h6+! ♔h8 (23...♔xh6 24 ♘xg4+ mates in a few moves) 24 ♖xg4 ♗c6 25 h7, followed by ♖h4, and White wins.

3) 18...h6 19 hxg6! hxg5 20 ♗xg5 ♕c5 (20...♕e8 21 gxf7+ ♖xf7 22 ♗f6 ♕f8 23 ♕g6 followed by 24 ♗d3 wins for White) 21 ♗f6 ♕xf2 22 ♗xg7 ♖xg7 23 gxf7+ ♔xf7 24 ♖f1 ♕xf1+ 25 ♗xf1 is very unpleasant for Black in view of his exposed king, but nevertheless this was the only chance to play on.

19 ♕h3 f4

19...h6 loses to 20 hxg6 ♗xe5 21 ♘f7.

20 hxg6 ♗xe5 21 ♘xe6

21 ♘f7 also wins.

21...♗xe6 22 ♗xe6+ ♔g7

22...♔h8 23 ♖h1 wins for White.

23 gxh7+ 1-0

Game 33

John Nunn – Gennadi Sosonko

Thessaloniki Olympiad 1984

Sicilian Defence, Velimirović Attack

1 e4 c5 2 ♘f3 ♘c6 3 d4 cxd4 4 ♘xd4 ♘f6 5 ♘c3 d6 6 ♗c4 e6 7 ♗e3 a6 8 ♕e2 ♕c7 9 0-0-0 ♘a5 10 ♗d3 b5 11 a3 *(D)*

11...♗b7

11...♖b8 is the main alternative, but Black is still not threatening ...b4 because this would

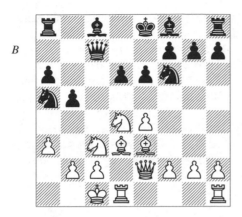

B

leave the a6-pawn hanging. Thus White has time to play g4.

12 g4 d5

This looks like the critical move, generating counterplay in the centre before White drives away the knight by g5. However, it allows White to make a dangerous sacrifice, so more recent games have focused on the alternatives 12...罩c8 and 12...公d7.

13 exd5 公xd5 (D)

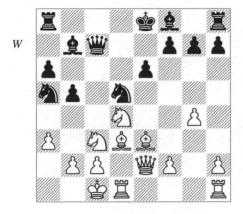

W

Everything looks fine for Black; he has managed to force through ...d5, and the open diagonal from b7 to h1 means that the h1-rook is exposed to attack.

14 公dxb5!

Were it not for this tactical point, White's whole plan would indeed be misconceived.

14...axb5

There is not much to choose between this and 14...豐b8. After the queen move, 15 公xd5

公xd5 16 公c3 盒xh1 17 罩xh1 gives White fair compensation for his small sacrifice. Objectively the position should probably be assessed as 'unclear', but in practice it is much easier to play the white side. 14...豐e5? is bad in view of 15 公xd5 盒xd5 16 盒b6! 豐f4+ (16...豐xe2 loses to 17 公c7+) 17 含b1 罩c8 18 盒xa5 盒xh1 19 罩xh1 axb5 20 盒xb5+ 含e7 21 盒b4+ 含f6 22 盒d2 with a decisive attack.

15 盒xb5+ 含d8

Forced, as 15...盒c6 16 公xd5 exd5 17 盒b6+ 豐e7 18 盒xa5 豐xe2 19 盒xc6+ 含e7 20 罩he1 and 15...公c6 16 公xd5 exd5 17 盒c5+ 盒e7 18 盒xc6+ 盒xc6 19 罩he1 win for White.

16 公xd5 (D)

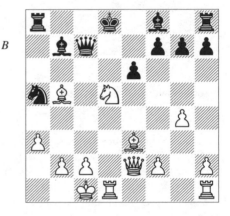

B

16...exd5

Best. After 16...盒xd5 17 罩xd5+! exd5 18 罩d1 White has a clear advantage:

1) 18...盒e7 19 罩xd5+ 含c8 20 豐f3 (threatening 21 罩d7) 20...罩b8 21 盒a6+ wins.

2) 18...公b7 19 盒g5+ 含c8 20 豐e8+ 公d8 21 罩xd5 also wins.

3) 18...公c6 19 豐c4! 公e7 20 罩xd5+ is decisive.

4) 18...含c8 19 罩xd5 盒d6 20 盒a6+ 公b7 21 盒xb7+ 含xb7 22 豐b5+ 含c8 23 盒b6 罩b8 (23...豐d7 24 豐c4+ 含b7 25 罩b5 罩a6 26 盒c7+ 含a7 27 盒xd6 wins because Black cannot recapture the bishop) 24 豐a6+ 豐b7 25 豐xb7+ 含xb7 26 罩xd6 and, with three connected passed pawns for the exchange, White has a winning position.

5) 18...盒d6 19 罩xd5 公b7 (relatively best; 19...含c8 transposes to line '4') 20 盒a6 罩xa6

(20...Rb8 21 Bxb7 Rxb7 22 Wd3 Kd7 23 Bc5 Rb6 24 Wf5+ Kd8 25 Bxb6 Wxb6 26 c4 and White wins) 21 Wxa6 Ke7 22 We2 gives White three pawns and a continuing attack for the piece.

17 Rd3! *(D)*

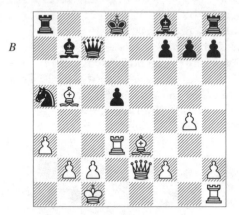

The rook switch to c3 cuts off the black king's escape route via c8 and b8.

17...Nc4!

Again Black finds the best defence. 17...Bd6 18 Rc3 Nc4 19 Rd1 Kc8 20 Bxc4 dxc4 21 Wxc4, 17...Wd6 18 Rc3 Be7 19 Re1 Nc6 20 Bb6+ Kd7 21 Wf3 and 17...Bc5 18 Rc3 Bxe3+ 19 Wxe3 Wd6 20 b4 are all lost for Black.

18 Rc3

The alternatives 18 Bxc4 Wxc4 19 Bb6+ Kd7 20 Wf3 Rc8 21 Wxf7+ Be7 and 18 Re1 Nxe3 19 Wxe3 Be7 are unclear.

18...Bb4? *(D)*

Only this mistake costs Black the game. 18...Bxa3! is the correct defence, whereupon 19 bxa3 (19 Bxc4? loses to 19...Bb4!) 19...Rxa3 20 Rxa3 (20 Rxc4 dxc4 21 Rd1+ Kc8 22 Rd7 Ra1+ 23 Kb2 Ra2+! 24 Kb1 Ra1+ is perpetual check) 20...Nxa3 21 Re1 (the threat is 22 Bg5+ followed by 23 We8+) 21...Kc8 (21...Nxb5 22 Wxb5 Wc6 is also only very slightly better for White) 22 Wd3 Nxb5 23 Wxb5 Wc4 24 Wxc4+ dxc4 25 Bd4 leads to an insignificant endgame edge for White.

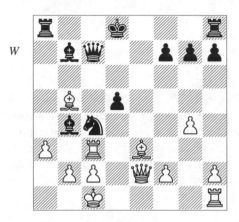

19 Rxc4!

This further sacrifice proves decisive.

19...dxc4 20 Rd1+ Kc8 21 Rd4

The most convincing win; Black must return a piece, but then material is equal while White's attack persists.

21...Bd5 22 Rxd5 Bd6 23 Rd4 1-0

Further material loss is inevitable.

Game 34
Jan Timman – Ljubomir Ljubojević
Linares 1985
Sicilian Defence, Najdorf Poisoned Pawn

1 e4 c5 2 Nf3 d6 3 d4 cxd4 4 Nxd4 Nf6 5 Nc3 a6 6 Bg5 e6 7 f4 Wb6 8 Wd2 Wxb2 9 Rb1 Wa3 10 Be2 Be7 11 0-0 Nbd7

We have the same line of the Poisoned Pawn as in Game 29. As was mentioned there, 11...h6, 11...Wc5 and 11...Wa5 are also possible. The move played appears most natural,

but allows a surprising breakthrough in the centre.

12 e5 dxe5 13 fxe5 Nxe5 14 Bxf6 Bxf6 *(D)*

Currently theory gives 14...gxf6 15 Ne4 f5 16 Rb3 Wa4 as best, with an unclear position. However, Ljubojević can hardly be criticized for the natural text-move.

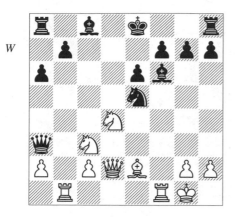

15 ♖xf6 gxf6 16 ♘e4 ♘d7?

But this is definitely wrong. 16...♕e7 17 ♕f4 ♔d8 18 ♘xf6 ♘d7 19 ♘xd7 ♗xd7 20 ♖xb7 is the best continuation, when White is slightly better.

17 ♖b3 ♕xa2

After 17...♕a4, 18 ♕c3 (threatening 19 ♖a3) 18...e5 19 ♘f5 gives White an enormous attack; e.g., 19...♕c6 20 ♕b4 ♘c5 21 ♘g7+ ♔f8 22 ♘xc5 ♔xg7 23 ♘e6+ fxe6 24 ♖g3+ ♔f7 25 ♗h5#.

It is now too late for 17...♕e7 in view of 18 ♘c6! bxc6 19 ♘d6+ ♔d8 (19...♔f8 allows mate in two) 20 ♕a5+ ♘b6 21 ♕xb6+ ♔d7 22 ♘e4! ♖d8 23 ♖d3+ ♔e8 24 ♕xc6+ ♗d7 25 ♖xd7 and White wins.

18 ♘d6+ ♔f8

After 18...♔e7 19 ♕b4 ♕a1+ 20 ♔f2 Black is totally defenceless.

19 ♕c3 *(D)*

19...♔g7?

This allows a forced mate. Black should have tried giving up a piece to safeguard his king by 19...♖g8 20 ♘xc8 ♔g7 (20...♘e5 21 ♖xb7 is very good for White). Then 21 ♘d6

♘e5 22 ♗c4 is very unpleasant for Black, but at least he could continue the game.

20 ♘4f5+ exf5

20...♔f8 loses to 21 ♕c7.

21 ♘xf5+ ♔g6

21...♔f8 22 ♕b4+ mates.

22 ♕h3! *(D)*

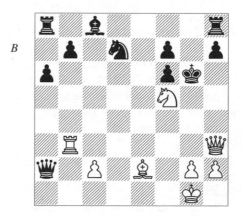

1-0

Black cannot meet the threats of 23 ♖g3#, 23 ♕g4# and 23 ♕h5#.

Game 35

Artur Yusupov – Jesus Nogueiras

Montpellier Candidates 1985

Queen's Gambit Declined, Exchange Variation

1 d4 d5 2 c4 e6 3 ♘c3 c6 4 ♘f3 ♘f6 5 ♗g5 ♘bd7 6 cxd5 exd5 7 e3 ♗d6

Black intends the ambitious plan of ...♘f8-g6, followed by ...h6, forcing the exchange of

White's dark-squared bishop. The defect is that his king has to stay in the centre for a long time.

8 ♗d3 ♘f8 *(D)*

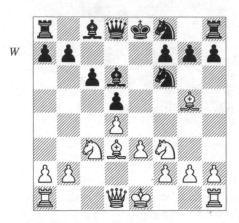

9 ♘e5

The sharpest reply; White intends f4, cementing his knight on e5.

9...♕b6

A rather greedy move aiming at the b2-pawn (we have already seen a number of fatal b2-pawn grabs in this book!). 9...♕e7 is a playable alternative, when 10 f4 h6 11 ♗h4 g5 12 fxg5 hxg5 13 ♗xg5 ♖g8 14 ♗h4 ♗xe5 15 dxe5 ♕xe5 16 ♕f3 is unclear, but an attacking player would favour White as Black's king is trapped in the centre for the time being.

10 0-0

White does not want to spend a tempo covering his b-pawn.

10...♗xe5

10...♕xb2 11 ♖c1 is very dangerous; for example, 11...♘g6 12 f4 0-0 13 ♖c2 ♕b6 14 ♗xf6 gxf6 15 ♘g4 ♗xg4 16 ♕xg4 with a very strong attack, Timman-Ljubojević, KRO match (5), Hilversum 1987. Black therefore decides to eliminate the dangerous knight, but this has the effect of weakening his dark squares. Black is not yet seriously worse, but the fact that his king is still in the centre means that even a slight misstep could prove fatal.

11 dxe5 *(D)*

11...♘g4?

This move is a mistake because of White's strong reply. 11...♘6d7 is correct, when 12 ♗f4 (12 ♕a4 is dubious due to 12...♘e6) 12...♘c5

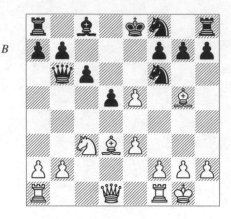

13 ♘a4 ♘xa4 14 ♕xa4 ♘e6 was unclear in Gulko-Smagin, Moscow 1984.

12 ♕a4! *(D)*

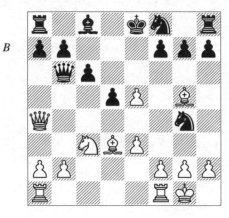

This exposes the weakness of Black's previous move: 12...♘xe5 loses to 13 ♘xd5, while 12...♘e6 is impossible because the g4-knight hangs.

12...♕xb2

After 12...♗d7 White can gain a large advantage by either 13 e6 ♗xe6 14 ♘xd5 ♗xd5 15 ♕xg4 or 13 ♕a3 f6 14 exf6 gxf6 15 ♗f4. Since the alternatives are out of the question, the text-move is practically Black's only constructive possibility. However, the dangers are obvious.

13 ♖ac1 *(D)*

Not, of course, 13 ♘xd5? ♕xe5 and the threat of mate at h2 turns the tables. 13 ♘b5 is also inferior because 13...cxb5 14 ♗xb5+ ♗d7 15 ♖ab1 ♗xb5 16 ♕xg4 ♗d7! is unclear.

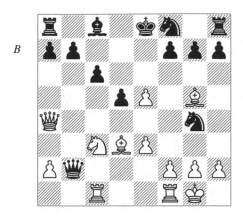

13...♗d7

13...♘xe5 loses to 14 ♖c2 ♕b6 15 ♘xd5, while 13...a5 14 ♘b5! ♘e6 15 ♘d6+ ♔f8 16 ♕xg4 ♕xe5 17 ♘xc8 h5 18 ♘b6 won for White in Hjartarson-Ljubojević, Tilburg 1989 – another zero for Ljubo in this line.

14 ♕d4! *(D)*

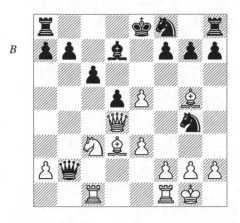

Sometimes it is the relatively quiet-looking moves which turn out to be the most deadly. By lining up the two queens on the same diagonal, White sets up the threat of 15 ♘xd5 (15 ♘e4 and 15 ♘b5 are also threatened). In addition, Black has to worry about the possibility of 15 e6 ♗xe6 16 ♕xg7, trapping the rook.

14...f6

There is no defence; for example, 14...♘g6 15 e6 ♗xe6 16 ♗xg6 hxg6 17 ♕xg7 ♔d7 18 ♖b1 and White wins, or 14...♗c8 15 h3 ♘h6 (15...♘xf2 fails to 16 ♕c5) 16 ♕c5 ♘g8 (the position of Black's knights is comical, at least for everybody except Nogueiras) 17 ♕d6 ♘e6 (17...♘d7 18 e6 fxe6 19 ♕xe6+ ♔f8 20 ♗f4 is decisive) 18 ♘xd5 cxd5 19 ♖b1, followed by 20 ♗b5+.

15 exf6 gxf6 16 ♗xf6 ♖g8 *(D)*

Or 16...♘xf6 17 ♕xf6 ♖g8 18 ♘xd5.

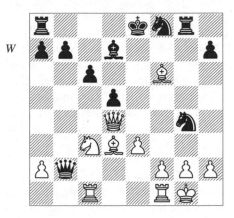

17 ♘b5!

The discovered attack motif arises in any case. Now Black loses his queen.

17...♕xb5

17...♕xd4 18 ♘d6# is an attractive mate.

18 ♗xb5 ♘e6 19 ♕b2 cxb5 20 ♗h4 1-0

Game 36

Mikhail Tal – Viktor Korchnoi

Montpellier Candidates 1985

Sicilian Defence, Richter-Rauzer Attack

1 e4 c5 2 ♘f3 d6 3 d4 cxd4 4 ♘xd4 ♘f6 5 ♘c3 ♘c6 6 ♗g5 e6 7 ♕d2 ♗e7 8 0-0-0 0-0 9 ♘b3 a5 10 a4 d5 11 ♗b5! *(D)*

This move, originally an idea of Vitolinš, came to prominence as a result of the current game. Today it is regarded as White's best move

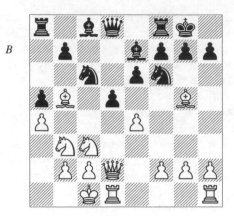

B

and is the reason why the variation with 9...a5 10 a4 d5 is now rarely seen.

11...dxe4

11...♘b4 may be Black's best chance, although White can retain an edge with either 12 e5 ♘d7 13 ♗xe7 ♕xe7 14 f4 or simply 12 ♖he1.

11...♘xe4 12 ♘xe4 dxe4 13 ♕xd8 ♗xd8 14 ♗xd8 ♘xd8 15 ♘c5 f5 16 ♖d6 gave White some advantage in the earlier game Tal-Sisniega, Taxco Interzonal 1985. Korchnoi attempts to improve on this, but his move also fails to solve Black's main problem – his inability to develop the c8-bishop.

12 ♕xd8 ♗xd8 (D)

After 12...♖xd8 Tal gave 13 ♘xe4 ♘xe4 14 ♗xe7 ♖xd1+ 15 ♖xd1, but this does not appear especially clear after 15...♘xf2. Therefore 13 ♖xd8+ ♗xd8 14 ♖d1 ♗e7 15 ♗xc6 bxc6 16 ♘xe4 is better, with an advantage for White.

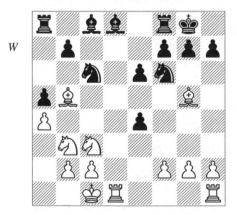

W

13 ♖he1

13 ♗xf6 ♗xf6 14 ♘xe4 also gives White an edge.

13...♘a7

The alternatives also fail to equalize. After 13...♗b6 14 ♗xf6 gxf6 15 ♘xe4 f5 16 ♘f6+ ♔g7 17 ♘d7 ♗xf2 18 ♘xf8 ♗xe1 19 ♘xe6+ White retains an advantage whichever way Black recaptures, 13...h6 14 ♗xf6 ♗xf6 15 ♘xe4 gives White a useful extra tempo over the previous note and, finally, 13...♘g4 14 ♗xd8 ♖xd8 15 ♘xe4 is clearly better for White.

14 ♗c4 h6

14...♘c6 15 ♘c5 also favours White.

15 ♗xf6 gxf6

Or 15...♗xf6 16 ♘xe4 ♗e7 17 ♘bc5 and Black's development is still difficult; for example, 17...b6 18 ♘d7 ♗xd7 19 ♖xd7 with advantage to White.

16 ♘xe4 (D)

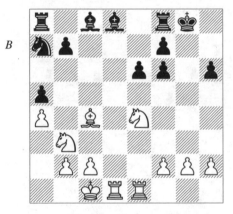

B

16...f5 17 ♘d6 ♗c7

Black intends 18...♖d8, forcing the knight either to retreat or to be exchanged off for the troublesome bishop.

18 g3

The immediate 18 ♘c5 b6 19 ♘xc8 ♗f4+! (not 19...♖axc8 20 ♘xe6) 20 ♔b1 ♖axc8 21 ♘xe6 ♖xc4 22 ♘xf8 ♔xf8 23 ♖d7 ♘c6 is unclear. White therefore cuts out the check on f4 which proved so useful to Black in this line.

18...b6? (D)

This runs into a surprising combination. 18...♖d8 is the best defence; however, even in this case 19 ♘b5! (19 ♘xf5 ♖xd1+ 20 ♔xd1 exf5 21 ♖e7 ♗b6 22 ♖xf7 ♔h8 is unclear)

19...♘xb5 20 ♗xb5 gives White the advantage; for example, 20...♖xd1+ 21 ♖xd1 e5 22 ♘c5 with continuing pressure.

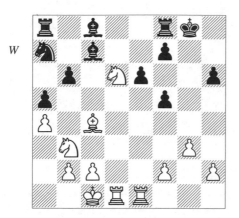

W

19 ♘xf5!

This unexpected move exchanges two minor pieces for a rook and a pawn. However, in the resulting position White's rooks will be extremely active.

19...exf5 20 ♗d5 ♗e6

The only move, as 20...♖b8 loses to 21 ♖e7.

21 ♗xa8 ♖xa8

21...♗xb3 is no better; for example, 22 ♖d7! ♗xa4 23 ♖xc7 ♖xa8 24 ♖ee7 ♘c6 25 ♖xf7 and Black will lose more pawns.

22 ♘d4 (D)

Black's poorly coordinated minor pieces are in no position to resist White's pressure along the central files. The knight on a7 is particularly ineffective.

22...♗d5?!

Loses more material, but there is no saving the game; for example, 22...♖e8 23 ♘xe6 fxe6 24 ♖d7 ♗b8 25 ♖b7 ♘c6 26 ♖xb6 ♘d4 27 c3 ♗a7 28 ♖a6 and again Black's pawns are falling.

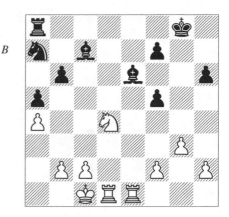

B

23 ♖e7 ♖c8

Both 23...♗d8 24 ♘xf5! ♗e6 25 ♖e8+ ♔h7 26 ♘e3 (so that ...♗g5 isn't check) 26...♘c6 27 ♖d6 and 23...♗d6 24 ♖d7 are easy wins for White.

24 ♘b5 (D)

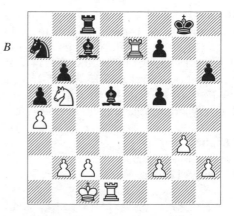

B

1-0

As 24...♘xb5 25 ♖xd5 ♘d6 (or 25...♘a7 26 ♖dd7) 26 ♖xc7 ♖xc7 27 ♖xd6 leads to an easily won rook ending.

Game 37

Rainer Knaak – Andras Adorjan

Szirak 1985

Nimzo-Indian Defence, Rubinstein Variation

1 d4 ♘f6 2 c4 e6 3 ♘c3 ♗b4 4 e3 b6 5 ♘e2 ♗a6 6 ♘g3 0-0 7 e4 ♘c6 8 ♗d3 ♘a5?

An error which is severely punished by White. Black heads off to win the c4-pawn, but leaves White a free hand in the centre. 8...e5 is better, preventing the further advance of White's e-pawn.

9 ♗g5

Setting up a very awkward pin.

9...h6 10 h4! *(D)*

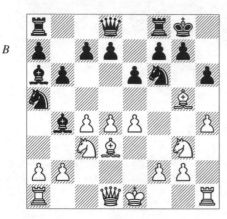

10...d6

Accepting is no better; e.g., 10...hxg5 11 hxg5 g6 (11...♘e8 12 ♕h5 f5 13 g6 mates) 12 gxf6 ♕xf6 13 e5 ♕g7 (after 13...♕f4, 14 ♘h5 wins outright) 14 ♘e4 ♗e7 15 ♕f3 f5 16 exf6 ♗xf6 17 ♘xf6+ ♕xf6 18 ♕h3 ♖f7 19 0-0-0 with a very strong attack for no material sacrifice.

11 ♘h5

Forcing Black's hand.

11...hxg5 12 hxg5 ♘xe4

Or:

1) 12...♘h7 13 e5 ♕xg5 14 ♗xh7+ ♔xh7 15 f4! ♕h6 16 ♘f6+ gxf6 17 ♕d3+ wins for White.

2) 12...♘e8 13 ♕g4 f5 (forced) 14 exf5 exf5 15 ♗xf5 ♖xf5 16 ♕xf5 gives White a large advantage; e.g., 16...♗xc4 17 ♘f4 ♕c8 18 ♖h8+! ♔xh8 19 ♕f8+ and 20 0-0-0, winning.

13 ♗xe4 *(D)*

Threatening 14 ♘f6+ followed by 15 ♕h5.

13...♕xg5

The rook on a8 is the least of Black's worries. If 13...♖e8, then 14 ♘xg7! ♔xg7 15 ♖h7+ ♔f8 16 ♕h5 mates.

14 f4 ♕h6

A desperate attempt to hang on.

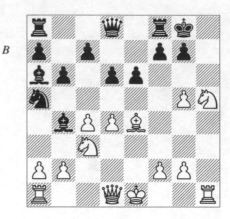

15 ♕f3

White could have won more quickly by 15 ♘f6+ ♕xf6 16 ♗h7+ ♔h8 17 ♗g6+ ♔g8 18 ♖h8+ ♔xh8 19 ♕h5+ ♔g8 20 ♕h7#.

15...d5 16 ♗h7+

16 ♘f6+ would still have been effective.

16...♔h8

Or 16...♕xh7 17 ♘f6+ gxf6 18 ♖xh7 ♔xh7 19 ♕h5+ ♔g7 20 ♕g4+ and 21 ♔f2, with a mating attack.

17 ♗c2 ♔g8 *(D)*

17...♗e7 18 0-0-0 ♔g8 19 ♘f6+ ♗xf6 20 ♖xh6 gxh6 21 cxd5 is also hopeless.

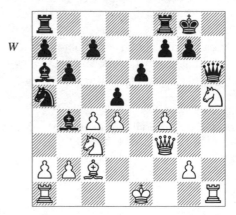

18 ♘f6+!

Finally White sees it!

18...♕xf6 19 ♗h7+ ♔h8 20 ♗g6+ ♔g8 21 ♖h8+! 1-0

Black was definitely not OK in this game, but in Game 66 Adorjan makes a better case for the advantages of the black pieces.

Game 38
Viktor Korchnoi – Alon Greenfeld
Biel 1986
English Opening

1 ♘f3 ♘f6 2 c4 c5 3 d4 cxd4 4 ♘xd4 e6 5 ♘b5?

A very unusual move. It is wrong to move the d4-knight again without any particular reason. While grandmasters know all sorts of exceptions to the standard principles of chess, this move is not one of them, and not even Korchnoi can offend against basic opening principles without being punished at least occasionally. 5 ♘c3 and 5 g3 are the most common moves.

5...d5

5...♗b4+ 6 ♗d2 ♗xd2+ 7 ♕xd2 d5 8 cxd5 a6 is a safe equalizing line.

6 cxd5

6 ♗f4 ♗b4+ 7 ♘1c3 0-0 8 ♘c7 ♘h5 is fine for Black as the knight will never emerge from a8.

6...a6 *(D)*

After 6...♘xd5 7 e4 White is slightly better, but 6...exd5 7 ♘1c3 a6 8 ♘d4 ♗c5 9 e3 0-0 10 ♗e2 ♘c6 11 ♘xc6 bxc6 12 0-0 ♗d6 led to equality in Smyslov-Furman, USSR Ch 1961.

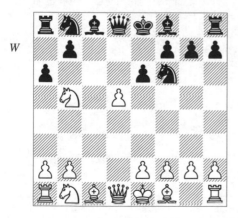

7 ♘5c3?!

7 ♘d4 would be an admission that the knight's foray to b5 was a mistake. Then, as in Smyslov-Furman above, Black would gain easy

equality. However, this might have been better than the game continuation.

7...exd5 8 ♗e3

After 8 ♗g5 d4 9 ♗xf6 ♕xf6 10 ♘d5 ♕e5 Black is clearly better.

8...♘c6 *(D)*

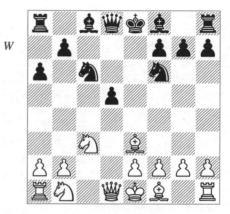

Now White suffers from his lack of control of d4 and is forced into artificial measures to prevent the advance of Black's d-pawn.

9 ♗d4 ♘xd4 10 ♕xd4 ♕c7

Black continues the fight for d4 by preparing ...♗c5.

11 e3 ♗c5 12 ♕a4+

12 ♘xd5 ♘xd5 13 ♕xd5 gives Black a very strong initiative for the pawn after 13...0-0 or 13...♗e6 14 ♕e4 ♕b6.

12...b5! *(D)*

Black must be prepared to sacrifice in order to keep the initiative. 12...♗d7?! can be met by 13 ♗b5, after which Black can only claim an edge.

13 ♗xb5+

White has little choice but to accept the sacrifice. The other way to win the exchange was 13 ♘xb5, but after 13...♕e5! 14 ♘c7++ (both 14 ♘5c3+ ♗d7 15 ♕a5 d4 and 14 ♘d6++ ♔e7 15 ♘xc8+ ♖hxc8 16 ♘d2 ♕xb2 17 ♖b1 ♕c3

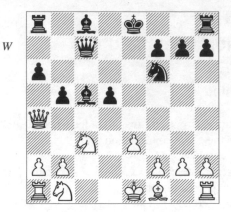

Black regains all his sacrificed material while retaining a very strong attack. Finally, 15 0-0 ♘g4 16 g3 ♗b7 17 ♘xb5 ♕c6 18 ♕a4 d4 19 f3 dxe3 gives Black a winning attack.

The text-move is an attempt to deflect Black's bishop from the a7-g1 diagonal before entering this last line.

15...♗xb4 16 0-0 ♘g4 *(D)*

White's bare kingside, poor development and misplaced queen give Black too strong an attack. Note that 16...♗xc3? 17 ♘xc3 ♕xc3 loses to 18 ♖ac1.

18 ♖b7+ ♔f8 clearly favour Black) 14...♔e7 (not 14...♔f8? 15 ♘xa8 ♕xb2 16 ♗d3 ♗d7 17 ♕b3 ♕xa1 18 ♘b6! and White is better) 15 ♘xa8 (15 ♕a5 ♕d6 and Black wins) 15...♕xb2 16 ♗d3 (or 16 ♘c7 ♗b4+ 17 ♔d1 a5 18 ♗d3 ♕xa1 19 ♕c2 ♗g4+ 20 f3 ♗d7 and Black has a large advantage) 16...♗b4+! (Black plays for the attack while keeping the capture of the a1-rook in reserve) 17 ♔f1 ♗g4 18 ♔g1 (18 f3 loses to 18...♖c8, which explains why the king had to go to e7 at move 14) 18...♖xa8 White is in serious trouble.

13...axb5 14 ♕xa8 0-0 *(D)*

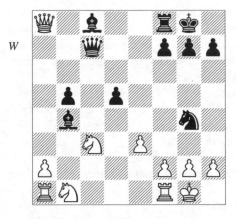

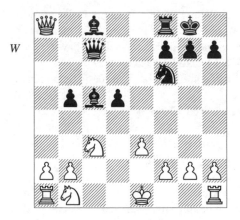

15 b4

Ingenious, but ultimately unsuccessful. 15 ♘d2 is bad after 15...♗b7 16 ♘xb5 ♕b6 17 ♕a4 ♗c6, winning the knight on b5 while at the same time trapping White's king in the centre. Another possibility is 15 ♘xd5 ♘xd5 16 ♕xd5, but after 16...♗b7 17 ♕b3 ♗xg2 18 ♖g1 ♕xh2

17 g3

Or 17 f4 ♗xc3 18 ♖c1 ♕a5 and Black wins.

17...♗b7 18 ♘xb5

18 ♕a7 ♗c5 19 ♘xb5 ♕c6 wins as in the analysis of 15 0-0 given above.

18...♕c6 19 ♕a4 d4 20 f3

White's moves are all forced.

20...♕h6! *(D)*

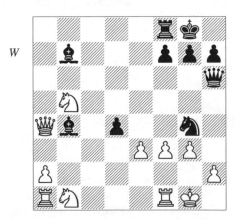

Even with the bishop on b4 rather than c5, Black has a winning attack.

21 ♕c2

There is no way out, since 21 fxg4 ♕xe3+ 22 ♖f2 ♕e4 forces mate.

21...d3 22 ♕g2

Or 22 ♕b2 d2.

22...♘xe3 0-1

It is not often that such a skilled defender as Korchnoi loses so quickly.

Game 39
Murray Chandler – Rafael Vaganian
Dubai Olympiad 1986
French Defence, Winawer Variation

1 e4 e6 2 d4 d5 3 ♘c3 ♗b4 4 e5 b6 5 a3 ♗f8

Black intends to keep his 'good' dark-squared bishop and exchange off his 'bad' light-squared bishop by ...♗a6.

6 ♘f3 ♕d7 7 ♗b5!? *(D)*

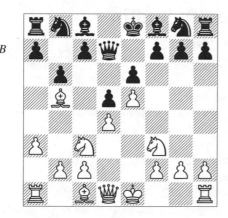

The manoeuvre ♗b5-a4 appeared in the early 1980s and immediately caused problems for Black. White's idea is simply to avoid the exchange of his light-squared bishop, thereby nullifying Black's whole opening strategy.

7...c6 8 ♗a4 ♗a6 9 ♘e2

Not only enabling castling, but also preparing to reactivate the a4-bishop by c3 followed by ♗c2.

9...h5?

Black wants to secure his knight on f5, but ...h5 permanently weakens the kingside dark squares. 9...♗b5 is probably the best try; if then 10 ♗b3, Black can start immediate counterplay by 10...c5.

10 0-0 ♘h6 11 ♖e1 ♗e7

11...♘f5 12 c3 ♗e7 13 ♗g5 favours White. Far from exchanging his 'bad' bishop, Black faces the exchange of his 'good' bishop.

12 c3 g6 13 ♘f4 ♘f5 14 ♘h3

Preparing ♗g5.

14...♗b5 15 ♗c2 c5 16 ♗g5 ♘c6 *(D)*

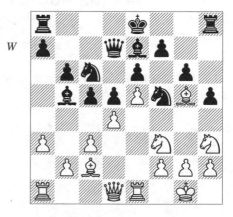

17 ♗f6!

Even better than exchanging bishops.

17...♗xf6

After 17...♖g8 18 ♘fg5 White is already threatening 19 ♗xf5.

18 exf6 ♕d8

18...cxd4 19 ♗xf5 gxf5 20 ♘xd4 leaves Black's position riddled with dark-squared weaknesses.

19 dxc5 bxc5 20 ♘f4

Attacking d5.

20...♕xf6 21 ♕xd5?!

21 ♘xe6! (21 ♘xd5? ♕d8 lets Black off lightly) 21...fxe6 22 ♕xd5 would have been more destructive since 22...♘fe7 23 ♖xe6 ♕f7

24 ♖ae1 0-0 25 ♕xc5 leads to catastrophic material loss for Black.

21...♖c8?

This loses forthwith. 21...♘fe7 was the only chance, but even then 22 ♕xc5 ♕xf4 23 ♕xb5 ♖b8 24 ♕a4 ♕xa4 25 ♗xa4 leaves White a pawn up with a favourable position (note that 25...♖xb2 loses the pinned knight to 26 ♘e5 ♖b6 27 ♖ab1).

22 ♕xc5 a6

22...♗a6 23 ♗a4 ♘fe7 24 ♘e5! wins more material.

23 a4 ♘ce7

Black attempts to rescue the trapped bishop tactically.

24 ♘d5! *(D)*

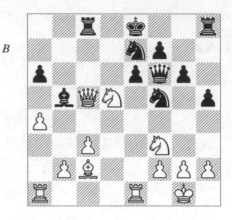

This attractive blow wins a piece.

1-0

Game 40

Andras Adorjan – Sergey Kudrin

New York Open 1987

Queen's Indian Defence

1 d4 ♘f6 2 ♘f3 e6 3 c4 b6 4 g3 ♗a6 5 ♘bd2 ♗b7 6 ♗g2 c5 7 e4 *(D)*

7...cxd4

The greedy 7...♘xe4? is not a good idea: 8 ♘e5 d5 (8...♘c3 9 ♕h5 g6 10 ♕h3, 8...♘d6 9 ♗xb7 ♘xb7 10 ♕f3 and 8...f5 9 ♘xe4 followed by 10 ♕h5+ are all winning for White) 9 cxd5 exd5 (9...♘xd2 loses to 10 ♘xf7!) 10 ♕a4+ ♘d7 11 ♘xe4 dxe4 12 ♗h3 ♗c8 13 ♕c6 ♖b8 14 ♘xf7 and White wins.

8 e5 ♘g4?!

8...♘e4 is the contemporary preference, with roughly equal chances.

9 0-0 ♕c7

Other moves have been tried, with equal lack of success.

10 ♖e1 ♗c5? *(D)*

Trying to keep the extra pawn is too greedy. Black's best chance is 10...h5 11 h3 ♘h6 12 ♘xd4 ♗xg2 13 ♔xg2 ♘c6, when White may be able to maintain an edge, but not more.

11 ♘e4!

Black's development does not look too bad, but he suffers from the poorly placed knight on g4, and the fact that the e5-pawn drives a wedge into his position. Note that 11 h3? is bad due to 11...♘e3!.

11...d3

Other moves are no better; e.g.:

1) 11...♘c6 12 ♗f4 0-0 13 h3 ♘h6 14 ♗xh6 gxh6 15 ♘f6+ ♔g7 16 ♕d3 ♖h8 17 ♘h5+ ♔f8 18 ♕d2 with a large advantage for White.

2) 11...♗xe4 12 ♖xe4 f5 13 exf6 ♘xf6 14 ♗f4 ♕c8 15 ♘xd4 ♘xe4 16 ♗xe4 ♘c6 (White also wins after 16...♘a6 17 ♕h5+ ♔f8 18 ♘xe6+ dxe6 19 ♕f3) 17 ♘xc6 dxc6 18 b4! ♗xb4 (18...♗e7 19 ♕h5+ ♔f8 20 ♕f3 ♗f6 21 ♖d1 is very good for White) 19 ♕a4 ♗c3 20 ♗xc6+ ♔f7 21 ♖d1 ♖d8 22 ♗xa8 ♖xd1+ 23 ♕xd1 ♕xa8 24 ♕d3 and White wins a pawn for nothing.

12 ♘fg5? *(D)*

A brave move, but it is not necessary to give up the important e-pawn. 12 ♕xd3 would have given White a clear advantage at no risk; for example, 12...♘xe5 13 ♘xe5 ♕xe5 14 ♗f4, 12...0-0 13 ♘xc5 ♕xc5 14 ♖e2 ♘c6 15 ♘g5 g6 16 ♘e4! ♕xe5 17 h3, or 12...♗xe4 13 ♕xe4 ♗xf2+ 14 ♔f1 ♗xe1 15 ♔xe1 – White is better in every case.

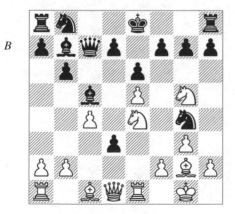

12...♘xe5 13 ♗f4

Threatening 14 ♘xc5.

13...d6

13...f6 loses to 14 ♕h5+ ♔e7 15 ♘xf6! gxf6 16 ♖xe5! fxe5 17 ♕f7+ ♔d6 18 ♗xe5+, while

13...♗e7 14 ♕h5 g6 15 ♕h6 ♗f8 16 ♘f6+ ♔e7 17 ♕h4 gives White an enormous attack.

14 ♕h5

The storm clouds are gathering. The immediate threat is to the e6-pawn.

14...♔f8?

A major concession. 14...d2? is also bad in view of 15 ♘xe6! dxe1♕+ 16 ♖xe1 ♕e7 17 ♘6xc5 ♗xe4 18 ♘xe4 ♘bc6 19 ♘xd6+ ♕xd6 20 ♗xe5 and White wins.

Black's best defence is 14...g6! and now:

1) 15 ♕h6 ♘bd7! (not 15...♗xe4? 16 ♘xe4 ♘bc6 17 ♘f6+ ♔e7 18 ♕h4 ♕c8 19 ♗xe5 dxe5 20 ♘g4+, when White wins after 20...♔f8 21 ♕f6 ♖g8 22 ♕f3 or 20...♔d6 21 ♗xc6 ♕xc6 22 ♘xe5 ♕b7 23 ♕f4) 16 ♕g7 0-0-0, and White is struggling to equalize.

2) 15 ♕h3! (aiming for a sacrifice on e6 or f7) 15...♘bd7 16 ♘xf7 ♔xf7 (16...♘xf7 17 ♕xe6+ ♔f8 18 ♘g5 is also about equal) 17 ♘g5+ ♔g8 18 ♕xe6+ ♔f8 19 ♗xe5 ♘xe5 20 ♕f6+ ♔g8 21 ♗h3 ♗c8 22 ♗g2 ♗b7 with a draw by repetition.

15 ♘xc5 bxc5 *(D)*

16 ♖xe5!

The start of a combination shattering Black's position.

16...dxe5

16...♗xg2 loses to 17 ♖xc5!.

17 ♗xe5 ♕d7 18 ♗xb7 ♕xb7 *(D)*

19 ♘xe6+!

Another forceful blow. Black cannot play 19...fxe6 due to 20 ♗d6+, so his king has to move again.

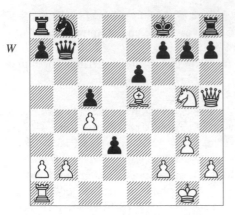

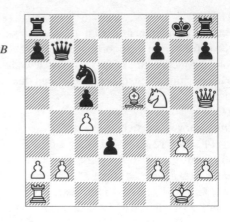

19...⬛g8 20 ♘xg7

20 ♗xg7 fxe6 21 ♗e5 also wins.

20...♘c6

Black's queenside development comes too late to help save his king. 20...♘d7 also loses to 21 ♘f5.

21 ♘f5! *(D)*

White's final sacrifice.

21...♘xe5

Or 21...f6 22 ♘h6+ ⬛f8 (22...⬛g7 23 ♕g5+) 23 ♗d6+ ⬛g7 24 ♕g4+ ⬛xh6 25 ♗f4#.

22 ♕g5+ ♘g6 23 ♕f6 1-0

Since 23...⬛f8 24 ♕g7+ ⬛e8 25 ♘d6+ picks up the black queen.

Game 41

Yasser Seirawan – Alexander Beliavsky

Brussels (World Cup) 1988

Slav Defence, Exchange Variation

1 d4 d5 2 c4 c6 3 ♘c3 ♘f6 4 cxd5 cxd5 5 ♗f4 ♘c6 6 e3 ♗f5 7 ♘f3 e6 8 ♗b5 ♘d7 9 0-0

9 ♕a4 is another major line.

9...♗e7 10 ♗xc6

White exchanges on c6 before Black can play ...♖c8, when he would be able to take back with a piece.

10...bxc6 11 ♖c1 ♖c8

11...g5?! 12 ♗g3 h5 13 h3 g4 14 hxg4 hxg4 is premature as 15 ♘d2 followed by e4 opens the centre before Black's h-file attack has really got going.

12 ♘a4?! *(D)*

Playing the knight to the far edge of the board allows Black to start a kingside attack. 12 ♘e5 ♘xe5 13 ♗xe5 f6 14 ♗g3 c5 is equal. If White had time to exploit the c5-square, then his strategy would be justified, but Black takes action before White can consolidate his grip.

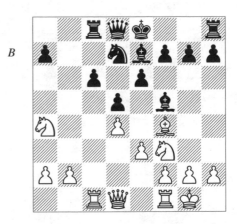

12...g5!

Unexpected and very strong. This attack is fully justified as Black's king is safe, his central pawn-structure is solid and White cannot quickly open the position by playing e4.

13 ♗g3 h5 14 h3?

The usual principle about not moving pawns in front of your king holds here. Pushing the h-pawn just makes it easier for Black to open a file on the kingside. 14 ♘c5 was much better, restricting Black to an edge after 14...♘xc5 (14...h4? 15 ♘b7) 15 dxc5 h4 16 ♗d6.

14...g4 15 hxg4 hxg4 16 ♘e5

White is in trouble as there is no decent square for this knight. 16 ♘h2 ♘f6! 17 ♘c5 ♗xc5 18 dxc5 ♘e4 favours Black as 19 ♘xg4? loses to 19...♕g5, while 16 ♘d2 ♗b4! opens the way for ...♕g5-h5.

16...♘xe5 17 ♗xe5 (D)

17 dxe5 c5 gives Black a positional advantage thanks to his active bishops and attacking chances along the h-file.

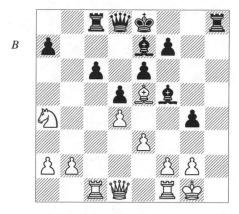

17...f6 18 ♗g3 ♔f7

Creating a path for the queen to reach the h-file.

19 ♖e1?

19 f3 gxf3 20 ♕xf3 is better, although Black is on top after 20...♕g8.

19...♖h5!

Black prepares to double on the h-file, while retaining the option of ...♕a5 (see the following note).

20 ♕d2

20 ♔f1 ♕a5! cuts off the king's escape route as 21 ♔e2? leads to mate after 21...♕b5+ 22 ♔d2 ♕d3#.

20...♗e4!

If Black can conquer the e2-square, White's king will be cornered.

21 ♔f1 (D)

21 ♘c3 ♕h8 22 ♔f1 ♗f3 leads to a quick mate.

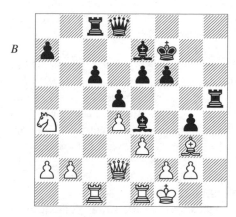

21...♗f3! 0-1

It is mate in a few moves.

Game 42

Jaan Ehlvest – Ulf Andersson
Belfort (World Cup) 1988
Sicilian Defence, Taimanov Variation

1 e4 c5 2 ♘f3 e6 3 d4 cxd4 4 ♘xd4 ♘c6 5 ♘c3 a6 6 ♗c2 ♕c7 7 f4 ♘xd4 8 ♕xd4 b5 9 ♗e3 ♗b7 10 0-0-0

A double-edged line in which White aims for rapid development at the cost of putting his king in the c-file firing-line.

10...♖c8 11 ♔d2

Necessary to meet the threat of ...b4, but this move appears slightly artificial.

11...♘f6 12 ♗f3 ♗e7 (D)

12...♕a5 13 ♕a7!? is complex, while after 12...♗c5 13 ♕xc5 ♕xc5 14 ♗xc5 ♖xc5 15 ♖e1 White has an edge.

13 ♖hd1?!

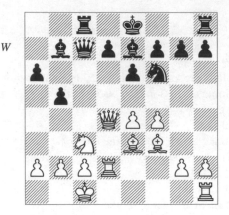

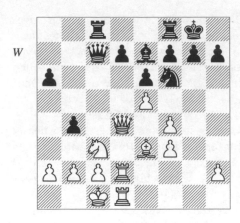

Despite its success in this game, the text-move is today regarded as inaccurate. The main line runs 13 g4 d5 (13...♗c5 14 ♕xc5 ♕xc5 15 ♗xc5 ♖xc5 16 ♖hd1 is unclear) 14 exd5 b4 15 ♘a4 ♗xd5, which led to a draw in Nijboer-J.Polgar, Wijk aan Zee 1998.

13...0-0 14 e5 ♗xf3?

This natural move is an error. Instead, Black should play the immediate 14...b4! 15 ♘a4 (15 ♗xb7 ♕xb7 is slightly better for Black, while 15 exf6 bxc3 16 ♕xc3 ♕xc3 17 fxe7 ♕xe3 18 exf8♕+ ♔xf8 0-1 was Hector-P.Cramling, Valby 1991) 15...♗xf3 16 gxf3 (16 exf6 ♗xf6 wins for Black) 16...♘d5 17 ♘b6 ♘xb6 18 ♕xb6 ♕c4 with an unclear position.

15 gxf3 b4? *(D)*

The exchange on f3 has serious consequences for Black owing to the open g-file. 15...♘h5 16 ♕xd7 favours White, so Black should have tried 15...♘e8 16 ♕xd7 ♗b4 17 ♕xc7 ♘xc7 18 ♖d3 ♗xc3 19 ♖xc3 ♘d5 with just an edge for White.

16 exf6 bxc3 17 ♖g2!

The point.

17...♕b7

17...cxb2+ 18 ♔b1 ♗c5 19 ♖xg7+ ♔h8 20 ♕d3 mates.

18 ♖xg7+ ♔h8 19 ♖g8+! *(D)*

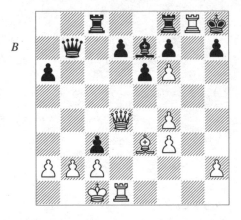

1-0

As 19...♖xg8 (19...♔xg8 20 ♖g1+ ♔h8 21 fxe7+ wins for White) 20 fxe7+ ♖g7 21 ♖g1 ♕xb2+ 22 ♔d1 ♕b1+ 23 ♗c1 forces mate.

Game 43

Sergey Kudrin – Daniel King

London (NatWest Young Masters) 1988

Caro-Kann Defence

1 e4 c6 2 d4 d5 3 ♘c3 dxe4 4 ♘xe4 ♘f6 5 ♘xf6+ exf6

At first sight, this line appears anti-positional, as White's queenside majority can create

a passed pawn, while Black's crippled kingside majority cannot. In the Exchange Variation of the Spanish, where a similar transformation of the pawn-structure occurs, Black has the two bishops as compensation, which is not the case here. However, it is not easy for White to exploit his better pawn-structure since the endgame is still a long way off, and Viktor Korchnoi has achieved some success on the black side.

6 c3 ♗d6 7 ♗d3 0-0 8 ♕c2 ♖e8+ 9 ♘e2 g6? *(D)*

An error, since this gives White a target for his kingside attack. Both 9...h6 and 9...♔h8 are more solid than the text-move.

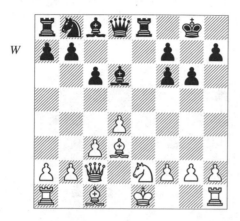

10 h4 ♗e6 11 h5

White already threatens to win by taking twice on g6.

11...f5 *(D)*

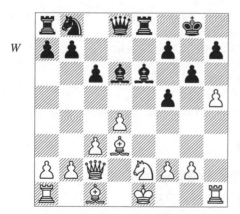

12 hxg6

The preliminary exchange is important. 12 ♗h6? is a serious mistake because after 12...g5 there is no good defence to Black's threat of 13...♕f6. In 1988, Julian Hodgson won two

games thanks to this mistake: Abramović-Hodgson, London 1988 continued 13 ♕d2 f4 14 g3 ♗g4 15 gxf4 ♗xf4 16 ♕xf4 gxf4 17 ♖g1 ♕h4 18 0-0-0 ♔h8, while Pereira-Hodgson, Almada 1988 went 13 ♗xf5 ♕f6 14 ♗xh7+ ♔h8 15 ♗g6 ♗c4 16 ♗d3 ♗xd3 17 ♕xd3 ♕xh6, with a winning position for Black in both cases.

12...fxg6 13 ♗h6 *(D)*

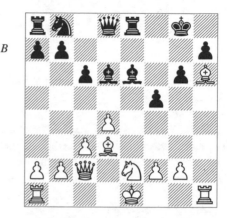

Developing the bishop to an active square and preparing to castle queenside.

13...♘d7?!

13...♕f6 is better, defending g6 so that g4 can be met by ...fxg4. Although White still has dangerous threats after 14 0-0-0, Black has more defensive chances than in the game.

14 g4!

White strikes before Black can reinforce his kingside with 14...♘f6.

14...♗d5

At first sight this disrupts White's attack, as the rook has no safe square on the h-file. However, White's attack is now so dangerous that he can afford to invest some material.

15 0-0-0! *(D)*

15...♗xh1

Black faces considerable problems and all his options appear unattractive. 15...♗f8 was an alternative, but after 16 ♗xf8 ♘xf8 17 gxf5! ♗xh1 18 ♖xh1 Black is still struggling; for example, 18...♕d5 19 ♘g3 ♕xa2 20 fxg6 hxg6 21 ♗xg6 ♖e7 22 ♕d3 and White has a vicious attack.

16 ♖xh1

The light-squared weaknesses give White's attack more to bite on.

16...♗f8 (D)

16...♕f6 17 gxf5 gxf5 18 ♗xf5 ♘f8 offers White several ways to maintain the advantage; e.g., 19 ♗xf8 ♔xf8 20 ♖h5 with a continuing attack. Of course, 16...fxg4 fails to 17 ♗xg6.

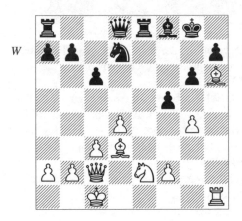

17 ♗d2

Now this is even better than exchanging on f8. The main threat is 18 gxf5, but White might also simply strengthen his attack by 18 ♘f4.

17...fxg4?

Loses straight away. 17...♘b6 is only slightly better, as 18 ♘f4 (18 gxf5 ♕d5! is less clear) 18...♘d5 (not 18...fxg4 19 ♗xg6 hxg6 20 ♕xg6+ ♗g7 21 ♘h5 ♕e7 22 ♗h6 ♕f7 23 ♕xg4 and White wins) 19 gxf5 ♘xf4 20 ♗xf4 ♕d5 21 f3 gives White a massive attack. Therefore 17...♘f6 was the best chance, but 18 ♕b3+ ♘d5 19 gxf5 remains extremely unpleasant for Black.

18 ♕b3+ ♔g7 (D)

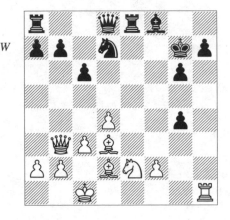

19 ♖xh7+!

White finishes the game off with an attractive rook sacrifice.

19...♔xh7 20 ♕f7+ ♔h8

White also wins after 20...♗g7 21 ♕xg6+ ♔g8 22 ♗c4+.

21 ♘f4 1-0

Black has no reasonable way to defend g6.

Game 44

Jaan Ehlvest – Garry Kasparov
Reykjavik (World Cup) 1988
English Opening

1 c4 ♘f6 2 ♘c3 e5 3 ♘f3 ♘c6 4 e3 ♗b4 5 ♕c2 0-0 6 d3

A rather timid continuation instead of the critical move 6 ♘d5.

6...♖e8 7 ♗d2 ♗xc3 8 ♗xc3 d5 9 cxd5 ♘xd5 10 ♗e2 (D)

A type of reversed Sicilian Scheveningen has been reached, although with one pair of

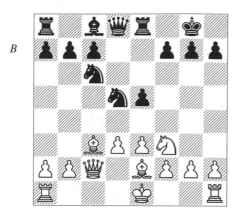

B

minor pieces removed. As so often happens with reversed openings, White has no problems gaining equality, but playing for an advantage proves more difficult.

10...♗f5

10...♕d6 is also adequate for equality.

11 ♖d1

White takes time out to counter the possibility of ...♘db4. After 11 e4 ♘f4!? (11...♘xc3 12 bxc3 ♗g4 13 0-0 ♘a5 is roughly level, Taimanov-Kuzmin, USSR Ch, Leningrad 1974) 12 exf5 ♘d4 13 ♗xd4 exd4 14 ♘g1 (14 0-0 ♖xe2 15 ♕b3 ♕d5 favours Black) 14...♕d5 15 0-0-0 ♕xa2 the position is unclear. 11 0-0 is playable and probably safest, because 11...♘db4 12 ♗xb4 ♘xb4 13 ♕c3 ♘xd3 14 ♖fd1 e4 15 ♘e1 is just dead equal.

11...a5 12 0-0 ♕e7 13 a3

13 e4 leads to nothing after 13...♘db4! 14 ♕b1 ♗g4.

13...a4 *(D)*

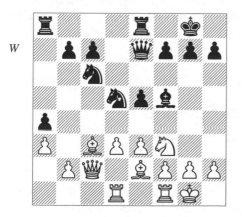

W

14 ♗e1?!

White would like to improve the position of his pieces by ♘d2-e4, but it is not so easy to achieve this; e.g., 14 ♘d2 ♘xc3 (14...♘d4 is less effective as 15 exd4 exd4 16 ♗f3 dxc3 17 ♗xd5 cxd2 18 ♗xb7 is fine for White) 15 ♕xc3 ♘d4 and Black is slightly better. However, nothing good can come from the textmove. Although White preserves his two bishops, he delays his development by several moves. 14 ♖fe1 is best; White improves the position of his rooks and waits to see Black's plan before committing himself.

14...♗g6

Black easily sidesteps the threat of 15 e4.

15 ♕c4

15 ♘d2 is still bad, this time because of 15...♘f4.

15...♖ed8 16 ♘d2? *(D)*

White thinks the time is ripe to reposition his knight, but he runs into a tactical storm. 16 d4 ♘b6 (or 16...e4 17 ♘d2 ♕g5 straight away) 17 ♕c3 e4 18 ♘d2 ♕g5 19 ♘c4 ♘d5 20 ♕c1 ♖e8 would have restricted Black to an edge.

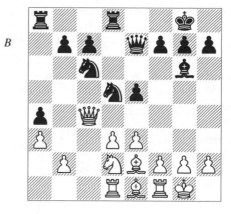

B

16...♘d4!

A typical Kasparov move.

17 exd4

White must accept as 17 ♗f3 ♘b6 18 ♕c3 ♘b5 followed by ...♗xd3 wins for Black.

17...♘f4 18 ♗f3 ♖xd4 *(D)*

19 ♕b5

After this White's queen is trapped, but after 19 ♕a2 (19 ♕c3 ♗xd3 20 g3 ♘e2+ 21 ♗xe2 ♗xe2 is also very good for Black) 19...♗xd3 20

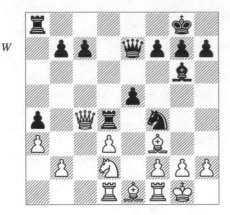

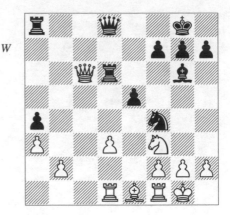

♞g6+ and White mates) 27 ♔h1 ♞xc3 28 ♕xf7+ ♔h8, winning for Black.

24...e4 (D)

Even stronger than 24...♗xd3.

♗xb7 ♜ad8 is very bad for White; e.g., 21 ♜a1 (in order to recapture on f1 with the knight; 21 ♗f3 ♗xf1 22 ♔xf1 e4 23 ♗e2 ♕g5 wins for Black) 21...♕d7 (threatening 22...c6) 22 ♞f3 ♕b5! 23 ♞xd4 exd4 24 ♗d2 ♗xf1 25 ♜xf1 ♞e2+ 26 ♔h1 ♞g3+ 27 hxg3 ♕xf1+ 28 ♔h2 ♕xf2 the black d-pawn will be decisive.

19...c6 20 ♗xc6

Or 20 ♕b6 ♜a6 and there is no escape.

20...bxc6 21 ♕xc6 ♕d8

The imminent loss of the d3-pawn is the least of White's worries. The congested mass of white pieces means that he will be hard-pressed to avoid the loss of the exchange after ...♗xd3.

22 ♞f3 ♜d6 (D)

White's difficulties with his queen are not over and now Black gains time by chasing it around.

23 ♕b5

23 ♕b7 loses to 23...♜b6.

23...♜d5

23...♗xd3 24 ♕xe5 is less clear.

24 ♕b4

Or 24 ♕b7 ♗xd3 25 ♗c3 ♗xf1 26 ♞xe5 ♞e2+ (but not 26...♜xd1?? 27 ♕xf7+ ♔h8 28

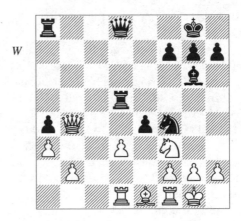

25 ♗c3

25 ♞d2 loses after 25...♕h4! 26 g3 (26 ♞xe4 ♞e2+ 27 ♔h1 ♕xh2+! 28 ♔xh2 ♜h5#) 26...♕h3 27 gxf4 ♜h5 forcing mate. If 25 ♜d2, then 25...♞xd3 finishes White off.

25...♞e2+ 0-1

Game 45

Rainer Knaak – Jon Speelman

Thessaloniki Olympiad 1988

Queen's Pawn

1 d4 d6 2 c4 e5 3 ♞f3 e4 4 ♞g5 f5 5 ♞c3 c6 6 ♞h3 ♞a6 7 e3 ♞f6 8 d5 (D)

Perhaps a slightly inaccurate move. White should prefer 8 ♞f4, and only play d5 when

Black is committed to ...♘c7 (ruling out ...♘c5) or ...♗e7 (excluding the possibility of ...g6 and ...♗g7). 8 ♗e2 is another popular move, again waiting for Black to declare his intentions.

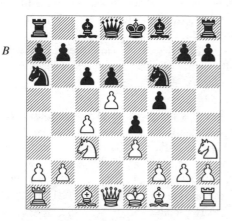

8...g6

Black immediately takes the opportunity to develop his bishop on the long diagonal, which White has opened by advancing his d-pawn.

9 b3 ♗g7 10 ♗b2 0-0 *(D)*

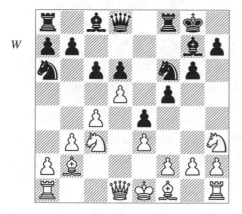

Now that White has played d5, Black is happy to leave his knight on a6 since it has a possible future at c5.

11 ♕d2

Another slight slip. Individually, these small errors are not especially noteworthy, but taken together their effect is significant. White should prefer 11 ♗e2, preventing Black's next move in the game. At first sight this seems bad because of 11...♕a5 (11...cxd5 12 ♘xd5 gives White an

edge) 12 ♕d2 cxd5, but this may be met by 13 ♘xe4!.

11...♘g4! *(D)*

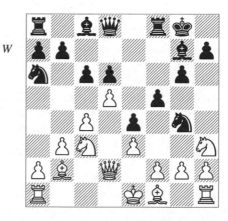

A good move. Black gives White cause to worry over the eventual destination of his king. If he plays 0-0, Black has an automatic attack by ...♕h4 and ...♗e5, while 0-0-0 is not very tempting as White's king can also become exposed on the queenside; e.g., 12 0-0-0 ♘c5 13 ♔b1 (or 13 dxc6 bxc6 14 ♕xd6 ♘d3+ 15 ♖xd3 exd3 16 ♕xd3 ♕e7 and Black is a little better) 13...♕b6 14 dxc6 bxc6 15 ♕xd6 ♖b8 lining up for a sacrifice on b3. Therefore White leaves his king in the centre.

12 ♗e2 ♘c5 *(D)*

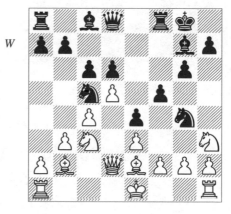

13 ♖d1?!

Stepping up the pressure against the d6-pawn, but it turns out that White has no time to take this pawn. 13 0-0-0?! is also dubious after

13...♘e5 aiming at d3, while 13 b4 ♘d3+ 14 ♗xd3 exd3 15 ♕xd3 f4!? 16 ♘xf4 g5 17 ♘h3 ♘e5 gives Black good compensation for the two pawns. In fact, this was the right moment for 13 0-0! since 13...♕h4 can be countered by 14 dxc6 bxc6 15 ♕xd6. Instead 13...♗e5!? leads to an unclear position. White's failure to castle here costs him dearly.

13...♕h4! 14 ♘a4?

Alarmed by the increasing pressure, White heads for liquidation, but this decentralizing move gives Black the chance to launch a decisive attack. 14 dxc6 bxc6 15 b4 (15 ♕xd6 ♘xe3! 16 ♕xc5 ♘xg2+ 17 ♔d2 ♕xh3 18 ♕xc6 ♖b8 is very good for Black) is also bad since Black can break through by 15...f4!, so White should have tried 14 0-0 ♗e5 15 ♗xg4 fxg4 16 ♘f4 g5 17 g3 ♕h6 18 ♘fe2 ♘d3 19 ♗a1. Then Black would have a slight advantage, but White would still be in the game.

14...f4! *(D)*

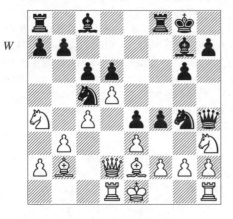

W

With a winning attack.

15 ♗xg7

Forced, since 15 exf4 e3, 15 0-0 f3 and 15 ♗xg4 ♘d3+ are all hopeless for White.

15...fxe3 16 ♕c3

There is no defence. It makes little difference whether the queen moves to b2, c3 or d4.

16...♖xf2

After this Black has many threats, the most deadly being 17...♖xg2+ 18 ♔f1 and now either 18...♕xh3 or 18...♘xh2+.

17 ♗h8 *(D)*

White has the pleasure of threatening mate in one himself, but it is too easy for Black to block the long diagonal. However, other moves are no better; e.g., 17 ♘xc5 ♖xg2+ 18 ♔f1 ♕xh3 19 ♗xg4 ♖xg4+ 20 ♔e2 ♕f3+ mating, or the neat line 17 g3 ♕xh3 18 ♗f1 (18 ♗h8 ♖xe2+) 18...♘xh2!.

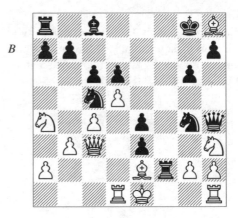

B

17...♖xg2+ 18 ♔f1 ♘e5! 0-1

This move, combining defence and attack, leaves White helpless; e.g., 19 ♗xe5 ♗xh3 20 ♕xe3 ♖f8+, etc.

Game 46

Ivan Sokolov – Vitaly Tseshkovsky

Wijk aan Zee 1989

English Opening

1 c4 e5 2 g3 d6 3 ♗g2 g6 4 e3 ♗g7 5 ♘e2 h5!?

With the knight committed to e2, it is not so easy to deal with the advancing h-pawn.

6 d4 h4 7 ♘bc3 ♘h6

Aiming to exert pressure on d4 by ...♘c6 and possibly ...♘f5.

8 e4?!

Ambitiously trying to sideline the knight on h6, but d4 is weakened.

8...♗g4

Already threatening to take on d4.

9 ♕d3

Unpinning the knight and preparing to drive Black back by f3. The immediate 9 f3? is met by 9...h3.

9...♘d7! *(D)*

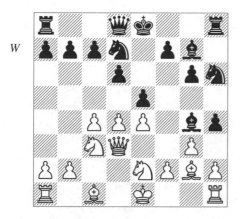

Again preventing 10 f3, this time due to 10...exd4 11 ♘xd4 h3 12 ♗f1 ♗xd4 13 ♕xd4 ♘e5.

10 d5

Now White need not worry about the pressure against d4, but Black gains more time.

10...♘c5 11 ♕e3 h3 12 ♗f1 f5 13 f3 fxe4! *(D)*

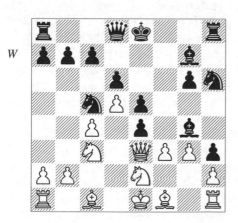

A correct sacrifice, which White should not have accepted.

14 fxg4?

Now Black's initiative proves too strong. 14 fxe4? is also bad; e.g., 14...0-0 15 ♘g1 ♕f6! 16 ♗e2 (16 ♗xh3 ♘d3+! 17 ♕xd3 ♕f2#) 16...♗xe2 17 ♕xe2 ♘d3+ 18 ♕xd3 ♕f2+ 19 ♔d1 ♕g2 and Black wins.

14 ♘xe4! is correct, when 14...0-0 15 ♘xc5 and 14...♗xf3 15 ♕xf3 ♖f8 16 ♘f4 exf4 17 ♘xc5 dxc5 18 ♕e4+ favour White. 14...♘f5 15 ♕a3 ♘xe4 16 fxg4 ♘e7 is the best reply, with an unclear position.

14...♘xg4 *(D)*

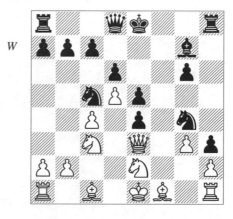

15 ♕g1

15 ♕g5 loses to 15...♘d3+ 16 ♔d1 ♘df2+ 17 ♔c2 ♕xg5 18 ♗xg5 ♘xh1.

15...♕f6

There is no defence.

16 ♘d1 *(D)*

16 ♘b5 ♘d3+ 17 ♔d2 ♕e7 18 ♔c3 ♘df2 seals White's kingside in completely.

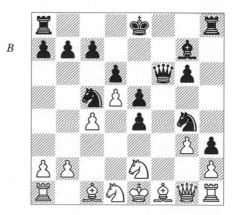

16...♘d3+ 17 ♔d2 ♕f3

Threatening 18...♗h6+ 19 ♔c2 ♘b4+ followed by mate.

18 a3

This does not meet the threat, but after 18 ♘ec3 ♘gf2 Black picks up a whole rook.

18...♗h6+ 19 ♔c2 ♘b4+ 0-1

As 20 axb4 ♕d3# is mate.

Game 47
Garry Kasparov – Jon Speelman
Barcelona (World Cup) 1989
Modern Defence

1 d4 d6 2 e4 g6 3 c4 e5 4 ♘f3 exd4 5 ♘xd4 ♗g7 6 ♘c3 ♘c6 7 ♗e3 ♘ge7 8 h4!? *(D)*

The most direct plan. White aims to exploit the absence of a black knight from f6.

8...h6

Intending to meet h5 by ...g5. 8...f5!? and 8...h5 are playable alternatives, although White has good chances to retain a slight advantage after any move.

9 ♗e2

An awkward reply for Black. The weakening of the kingside created by ...h6 rules out ...0-0, but it is not easy for Black to organize ...0-0-0 because his queen is in the way.

9...f5

The correct choice, because Black must develop his pieces.

10 exf5 ♘xf5 11 ♘xf5 ♗xf5 12 ♕d2 *(D)*

12...♕d7?

12...♕f6!? offered better chances, keeping an eye on the h4-pawn and exerting pressure on the long diagonal.

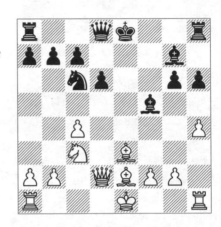

13 0-0 0-0-0

A critical moment. White must act quickly, or he will come to regret playing h4. In the game Black never gets a chance to exploit the slight weakening of White's kingside because he is too busy on the other side of the board.

14 b4! *(D)*

The most vigorous. The slower 14 ♖ac1 ♔b8 15 b4 ♘xb4 16 ♗f3 ♘a6 17 ♘b5 ♘c5 18 ♘xa7! ♕a4! (18...♔xa7? 19 ♗xc5+ dxc5 20 ♕a5+ ♔b8 21 ♗xb7 c6 22 ♗a6 ♔a8 23 ♖b1 ♗xb1 24 ♖xb1 wins for White) 19 ♘b5 g5 proved less effective in Epishin-Hedke, Groningen 1996.

14...♘xb4

14...♔b8 is no better; e.g., 15 b5 ♘e5 16 ♘d5 g5 (16...♘g4 17 ♗xg4 ♗xg4 18 ♖ab1, intending 19 ♖b3, also gives White a very dangerous attack) 17 a4 ♘g4 18 ♗xg4 ♗xg4 19 ♗xa7+ ♔xa7 20 b6+ cxb6 21 a5 b5 (21...♖xa1 22 axb6+ ♔b8 23 ♖xa1 threatens 24 ♖a8+ and if 23...♕f7, then 24 ♕a5 ♔c8 25 ♕b5! ♔b8 26 ♘c7 ♕xc7 27 ♖a8+ ♔xa8 28 bxc7 and mate

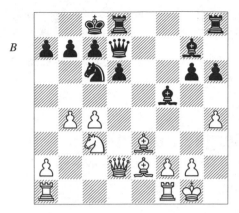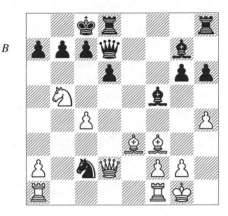

next move) 22 ♕e3+ ♚b8 23 a6 ♕c6 (23...bxa6 loses to 24 ♖xa6) 24 a7+ ♚a8 25 ♖a5! with a decisive attack for White, Schön-Danner, Budapest 1989.

15 ♘b5! (D)

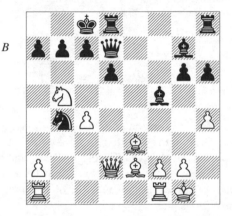

15...♘c2

Or 15...♗xa1 16 ♕xb4 ♗e5 17 ♗f3 c5 18 ♘xa7+ ♚b8 19 ♕a3 (threatening 20 ♘b5) 19...♕c7 20 g4 (in order to gain b1 for the rook) 20...♗d7 (not 20...♗c2 21 ♖c1 ♖hf8 22 ♘b5 ♕b6 23 ♗d5 trapping the bishop) 21 ♖b1 ♖df8 22 ♗d5!, intending ♕a6, and Black is in serious trouble.

16 ♗f3 (D)

16...d5

There is no promising move; for example:

1) 16...♗xa1 17 ♘xa7+ ♚b8 18 ♖b1! c5 19 ♘c6+ ♚c8 20 ♕a5 ♘b4 (or 20...♕xc6 21 ♗xc6 bxc6 22 ♕a7 and White wins) 21 ♖xb4 cxb4 22 ♕a8+ ♚c7 23 ♗b6+! ♚xb6 24 ♕a5#.

2) 16...♘xe3 17 ♕xe3 ♗xa1 18 ♕xa7 ♕g7 19 ♕xb7+ ♚d7 20 ♖e1! ♖c8 21 ♘xd6 wins for White.

3) 16...c5 17 ♖ad1 ♗e5 18 ♘xa7+ ♚b8 19 ♘b5 results in material equality and a continuing strong attack for White.

4) 16...♘xa1 17 ♘xa7+ ♚b8 18 ♕a5 and now, although there are many variations, White clearly has a very strong attack. One line runs 18...♖de8 19 ♘b5 ♕d8 and now the attractive blow 20 ♗b6! wins on the spot.

5) 16...♖de8 is the best defence, but even here 17 ♘xa7+ ♚d8 18 ♗xb7 ♖xe3 19 fxe3 ♗xa1 20 ♗d5 ♕g7 21 ♘c6+ ♚c8 22 ♖xf5 gxf5 23 ♕xc2 gives White a very strong attack for a minimal material investment.

17 ♗xd5 ♘xa1

Both 17...c6 18 ♘xa7+ ♚b8 19 ♗f4+ and 17...♗xa1 18 ♘xa7+ ♚b8 19 ♖b1 b6 20 ♕a5 are winning for White.

18 ♘xa7+ ♚b8 19 ♕b4! (D)

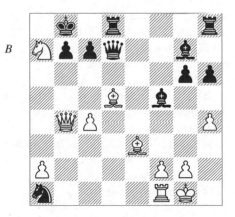

19...♕xd5

This only prolongs the game slightly. 19...c5 20 ♗f4+! ♔a8 21 ♕a5 also wins, while 19...c6 20 ♗f4+ ♔a8 21 ♘b5 forces mate.

20 cxd5 ♘c2 21 ♕a5 ♘xe3 22 fxe3

In addition to his material advantage, White retains a strong attack. The game did not last long.

22...♖he8 23 ♘b5 ♖xd5 24 ♕xc7+ ♔a8 25 ♕a5+ 1-0

Game 48

Lev Polugaevsky – Sergey Kudrin

New York Open 1989

Grünfeld Defence, Exchange Variation

1 d4 ♘f6 2 c4 g6 3 ♘c3 d5 4 cxd5 ♘xd5 5 e4 ♘xc3 6 bxc3 ♗g7 7 ♗c4 c5 8 ♘e2 ♘c6 9 ♗e3 0-0 10 ♖c1!? *(D)*

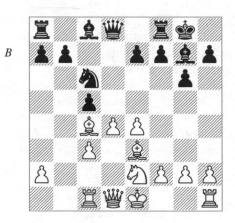

An interesting idea pioneered by Polugaevsky. For decades White had automatically castled here, but 'Polu' realized that there are some merits to moving the rook first.

10...cxd4

One important point is that if Black continues as if White had castled, by 10...♗g4?! 11 f3 ♘a5 12 ♗d3 cxd4 13 cxd4 ♗e6, then 14 d5! no longer involves an exchange sacrifice.

11 cxd4 ♕a5+

The most natural attempt to exploit the fact that White has not castled.

12 ♔f1! *(D)*

The key point of White's idea. It does not matter that White blocks in his h1-rook, as his plan is to start a kingside attack by h4-h5, and this will activate the rook *in situ*.

12...♗d7

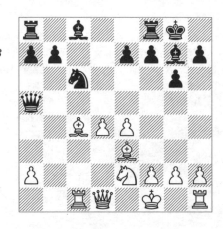

12...♕a3!? is currently considered a critical move. The point is that after 13 h4 ♗g4! White can no longer play f3. Therefore, White may have nothing better than 13 ♕b3, but the exchange of queens removes a lot of the sting from White's plan.

13 h4 ♖ac8?!

13...e5?! 14 d5 ♘d4 15 ♘xd4 exd4 16 ♗xd4 ♗xd4 17 ♕xd4 led to a win for White in Polugaevsky-Korchnoi, Haninge 1989. However, 13...♖fc8!? is probably better than the text; White's attack involves h5 and hxg6, followed by transferring the queen to the h-file. Giving the king a free square on f8 means that this will not threaten mate.

14 h5 e5

14...e6 15 hxg6 hxg6 16 e5 ♘e7 17 ♕d3 ♖fe8!? 18 ♗d2! ♕a4 19 ♗b3! ♖xc1+ 20 ♗xc1 ♕b4 21 ♕h3 proved extremely unpleasant for Black in H.Grünberg-Gauglitz, East German Ch (Zittau) 1989.

15 hxg6 hxg6 16 d5! *(D)*

16 ♗d2 had been played in an earlier game Guseinov-Khuzman, Baku 1988. Typically for 'Polu', he was ready with a deep improvement.

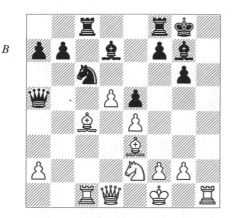

16...♘d4

16...♘e7 17 ♗g5 also favours White.

17 ♘xd4 *(D)*

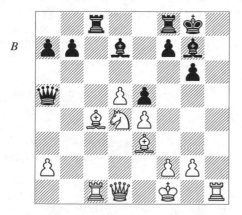

17...♖xc4?

The critical position arises after 17...exd4 18 ♗xd4 ♗b5 (or 18...♖xc4 19 ♖xc4 and now 19...♕a6? 20 ♕d3 transposes to the game, while 19...♗b5 20 ♗xg7 transposes to the main line of this note) 19 ♗xg7 ♖xc4 20 ♖xc4 ♗xc4+ 21 ♔g1 ♔xg7 *(D)*.

Here White must play accurately to secure any advantage:

1) 22 ♕c1 f6 23 ♖h3 ♕c5! 24 ♕h6+ ♔f7 25 ♕h7+ ♔e8 26 ♕xb7 ♗xd5! and Black is saved by the perpetual check on c1 and f4 (White cannot meet ...♕f4+ by ♖g3 due to ...♖h8+).

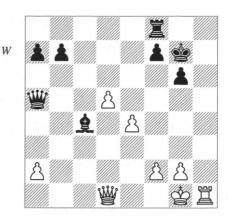

2) 22 ♕d4+! f6 23 ♕xc4 ♕e1+ 24 ♔f1 ♕xe4 25 ♕c1 ♕xd5 (after 25...g5 26 d6 the d-pawn becomes dangerous) 26 ♕h6+ ♔f7 27 ♕h7+ ♔e6 28 ♖h4 and Black still faces problems. White will regain his sacrificed pawn at g6 or b7, after which his safer king will give him at least a slight advantage.

18 ♖xc4 ♕a6?!

This loses at once, but even after 18...exd4 19 ♖xd4! (19 ♗xd4 ♗b5 20 ♗xg7 transposes into the previous note, which is just slightly better for White) 19...♕xa2 20 ♔g1 White is the exchange up for nothing.

19 ♕d3! exd4 20 ♗xd4 ♗b5 21 ♕h3!

White's thematic switch to the h-file.

21...♗xc4+ 22 ♔g1 f6 23 ♕h7+ ♔f7 24 ♖h6! *(D)*

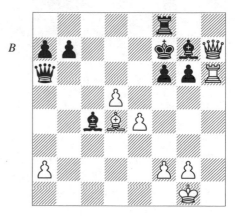

1-0

24...g5 25 ♖g6 wins, or 24...♖h8 25 ♕xg6+ ♔f8 26 ♖xh8+ ♗xh8 27 ♗c5+ mating.

Game 49

Vasily Ivanchuk – Istvan Csom

Erevan 1989

Nimzo-Indian Defence, 4 f3

1 d4 ♘f6 2 c4 e6 3 ♘c3 ♗b4 4 f3 c5 5 d5 ♗xc3+

If Black is going to play ...♘h5, he should do so straight away.

6 bxc3 ♘h5

An attempt to exploit the weakening created by f3.

7 g3

Cutting out the check on h4.

7...f5 8 e4 f4 9 dxe6

The sharpest line, but 9 ♘e2 is also playable.

9...fxg3? *(D)*

A tempting but incorrect move. 9...♕f6 10 ♘e2 fxg3 11 ♗g2 is better, although theory gives White the edge here too. It may well be that Black cannot justify his attempt to seize the initiative at such an early stage.

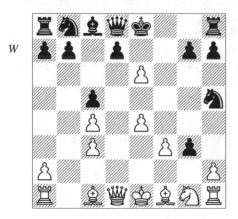

10 ♕d5! g2

10...♘f6 11 ♕xc5 g2 12 ♗xg2 dxe6 13 ♘e2 favours White, while 10...♕h4 11 ♗g5 g2+ 12 ♗xh4 gxh1♕ loses to 13 ♕xh5+ g6 14 ♕e5.

11 ♕xh5+!

11 ♗xg2 ♕h4+ 12 ♔f1 is also good for White, but the text-move is even stronger.

11...g6 12 ♕e5 ♕h4+ 13 ♔e2 gxh1♕ *(D)*

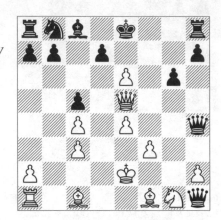

14 ♕xh8+ ♔e7 15 ♕g7+ ♔xe6

Or 15...♔d6 16 ♕f8+ ♔c6 (16...♔xe6 17 ♗h3+ ♕xh3 18 ♕g8+ ♔d6 19 ♗f4+ ♔e7 20 ♗g5+ ♔d6 21 ♖d1+ mates) 17 ♕xc8+ ♔d6 18 ♕f8+ ♔c6 19 ♗f4 and White wins.

16 ♗h3+ ♔d6

16...♕xh3 17 ♕g8+ transposes to the previous note.

17 ♕f8+ ♔c7 *(D)*

17...♔c6 18 ♕xc8+ ♔d6 19 ♕f8+ ♔c6 20 ♗f4 ♔b6 21 ♖b1+ ♔a6 22 ♕c8 and White mates.

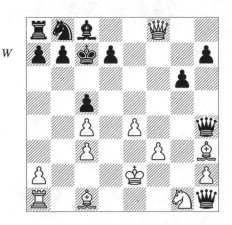

18 ♗f4+

Black must surrender a queen to avoid being mated, but this does not solve his problems.

18...♕xf4

18...♔b6 19 ♖b1+ ♔a6 20 ♕xc8 transposes into the note to Black's 17th.

19 ♕xf4+ d6

Material equality has been restored, but Black is dead lost.

20 ♖d1

First White goes for the king...

20...♘c6 21 ♕xd6+ ♔b6 22 ♕g3

...and now returns for the queen. There is no way to meet the threats of 23 ♗g2 and 23 ♗xc8 ♖xc8 24 ♘h3.

22...h5 23 ♗xc8 ♖xc8 24 ♘h3 h4 25 ♕f2 1-0

Game 50

Julian Hodgson – Zsuzsa Polgar

European Team Ch, Haifa 1989

Trompowsky Attack

1 d4 ♘f6 2 ♗g5

Although this opening is named after Trompowsky, Hodgson has done more than anyone else in modern times to advance the theory of 2 ♗g5.

2...e6 3 e4 h6 4 ♗xf6 ♕xf6

Black has gained the two bishops, but at the cost of considerable time.

5 ♘f3 d6 6 ♘c3 c6

6...♘d7 7 ♕d2 a6 is a solid line for Black, intending ...♕e7, ...g6 and ...♗g7.

7 ♕d2 e5 8 0-0-0 ♗e7 *(D)*

8...♘d7?! 9 dxe5 dxe5? is a classic opening blunder which has caught several victims: 10 ♘b5! gives White a decisive attack.

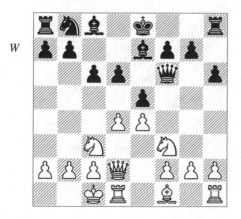

9 ♔b1

Preventing Black from forcing the queens off by ...♕g5.

9...♘d7?!

9...0-0 is more flexible.

10 h4 exd4

Now 10...0-0 11 ♗e2 is awkward for Black since the c8-bishop is blocked in and White has an automatic attack by g4, etc.

11 ♘xd4 ♘e5 *(D)*

11...♘c5 12 f4 ♗g4 13 ♗e2 ♗xe2 14 ♘dxe2 favours White, but is better for Black than the game.

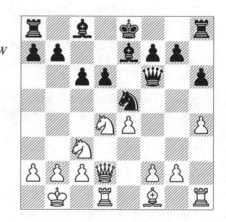

12 f4! ♘g4

Now 13 ♘db5 0-0 14 ♘xd6 ♗xd6 15 ♕xd6 ♘f2 is unclear, so further preparation is necessary.

13 h5

This threatens 14 g3 followed by 15 e5 dxe5 16 ♘e4.

13...♗d8

There was nothing better.

14 ♘db5! *(D)*

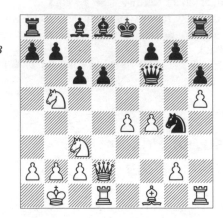

B

14...cxb5 15 ♗xb5+ ♗d7?!

Now White wins without difficulty. 15...♔f8 is better, even though 16 e5 ♕e6 (16...♕f5 17 ♕xd6+ ♗e7 18 ♕d8+ ♗xd8 19 ♖xd8+ ♔e7 20 ♖xh8 is also very good for White) 17 ♖he1! d5 18 ♘xd5 gives White two pawns and a very strong attack for the piece.

16 ♗xd7+ ♔xd7 17 ♕e2 ♕xf4

Thanks to White's earlier advance h5, Black's knight is insecure and this is the only way to save it.

18 ♖hf1 ♕g5

18...♕g3 19 ♕b5+ ♔c8 20 ♖xf7 mates.

19 ♖f5 *(D)*

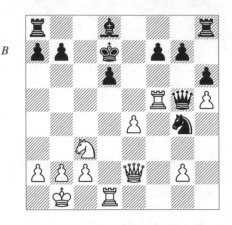

B

19...♕h4 20 ♕b5+ ♔c8 21 ♖xf7 ♗e7 22 ♘d5 1-0

Game 51
Kiril Georgiev – Gennadi Zaichik
Palma de Mallorca (GMA) 1989
Sicilian Defence, Najdorf Variation

1 e4 c5 2 ♘f3 d6 3 d4 cxd4 4 ♘xd4 ♘f6 5 ♘c3 a6 6 ♗c4 e6 7 0-0 b5 8 ♗b3 ♗e7 9 ♕f3 ♕b6 10 ♗e3

In recent years 10 ♗g5!? has been overwhelmingly the most popular move.

10...♕b7 11 ♕g3 ♘bd7

11...0-0, 11...b4 and 11...♘c6 are alternatives. The move played is more risky as it invites a possible sacrifice on f5.

12 ♖fe1

The immediate 12 ♘f5 is also possible.

12...♘c5 *(D)*

13 ♘f5 ♘xb3!

The best defence. 13...exf5 14 ♕xg7 ♖f8 15 ♗xc5 dxc5 16 exf5 leads to a decisive attack for White.

14 ♘xe7!?

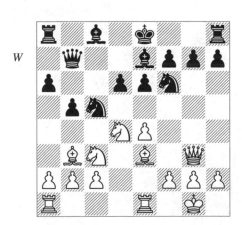

W

14 ♘xg7+ ♔f8 15 ♗h6 (15 axb3? h6 leaves the knight trapped and vulnerable to capture by ...♖h7) 15...♘xa1 16 e5! is also very unclear.

14...♘xa1 *(D)*

Not 14...♕xe7 15 axb3 ♗b7 16 ♗g5! with advantage to White.

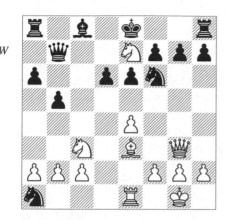

15 ♕xg7 ♖f8

Black could also try 15...♘xc2 and now:

1) 16 ♕xf6? ♘xe1 (not 16...♖f8? 17 ♗g5 ♘xe1 18 ♘f5 ♕c7 19 ♘d5 exd5 20 ♘xd6+ ♕xd6 21 ♕xd6 f6 22 ♗h6 ♖g8 23 ♕c6+ and White wins) 17 ♘xc8 ♕xc8 18 ♕xh8+ ♔d7 19 ♕f6 ♕g8 and White does not have enough for the exchange.

2) 16 ♗g5 ♕xe7 17 ♕xh8+ ♔d7 18 ♗xf6 ♗b7! 19 ♕g7 ♕f8 is approximately equal.

3) 16 ♘ed5! (the best chance since Black must defend very accurately to avoid defeat) 16...♘xd5 17 exd5 ♘xe1 (17...♕e7? 18 ♕xh8+ ♕f8 19 ♕xh7 ♘xe1 20 ♘e4! exd5 21 ♘f6+ ♔d8 22 ♗h6 ♗f5 23 ♕xf5 ♕e7 24 ♘xd5 ♕e6 25 ♕xe6 fxe6 26 ♗g5+ wins for White) 18 ♘e4 ♕b8 19 ♕xh8+ ♔d7 20 ♕f8 exd5 21 ♘f6+ ♔c6 (21...♔e6? 22 ♘g8! gives White a decisive attack) 22 ♕e8+ ♔b7 23 ♘xd5 ♖a7! (23...♘c2 24 ♕xf7+ ♔c6 25 ♘e7+ ♔c7 26 ♘xc8+ ♔xc8 27 ♕f5+ ♔d8 28 ♗g5+ ♔c7 29 ♕xc2+ ♔d7 30 ♕xh7+ is promising for White) 24 ♕xf7+ ♔a8 25 ♗xa7 ♕xa7 26 ♕f8 ♕c5 27 ♘b6+ ♕xb6 28 ♕xc8+ ♔a7 29 ♕c3 ♘xg2 30 ♔xg2 ♕b7+ 31 ♔g3 with just the faintest edge for White.

16 e5! *(D)*

This unexpected move causes Black most problems.

16...dxe5?

Other lines are:

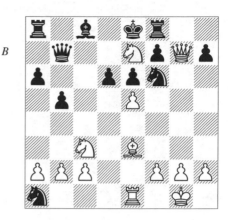

1) 16...b4? 17 ♗h6 bxc3 18 ♕xf8+ ♔d7 19 ♘xc8 cxb2 20 exf6 b1♕ 21 ♕xd6+ ♔xc8 22 ♕f8+ ♔d7 23 ♕xf7+ wins as the black king will be forced onto the b-file.

2) 16...♘d7? 17 ♗g5! d5 (or else ♘e4) 18 ♘f5 exf5 19 e6 with a winning attack.

3) 16...♘h5? 17 ♕xh7 ♕xe7 18 ♘e4 ♘xc2 19 ♘xd6+ ♕xd6 (19...♔d7 20 ♕xc2 favours White) 20 exd6 ♘xe1 21 ♕xh5 ♖g8 22 ♕h7 ♖g4 23 d7+ ♔xd7 24 ♕xf7+ ♔c6 (or 24...♔d6 25 ♗f4+ e5 26 ♕f6+ ♗e6 27 ♕xe5+ ♔e7 28 ♗g3 and Black is in trouble) 25 ♔f1 winning the knight, when White is better.

4) 16...♘xc2! 17 ♗h6 (17 exf6? ♘xe1 18 ♗h6 ♕xg2+ 19 ♕xg2 ♘xg2 wins for Black) and now:

4a) 17...♘d7?! 18 ♖d1! ♔xe7 19 ♖xd6 ♔d8 (19...♔e8 20 ♗g5! and Black has no satisfactory way to prevent the threat of 21 ♖xe6+) 20 ♕xf8+ ♔c7 21 ♕xf7 gives White good play for the piece.

4b) 17...♘xe1! 18 ♕xf8+ ♔d7 19 ♘ed5! ♘xd5 20 ♕xd6+ ♔e8 leads to a draw.

17 ♗c5 ♘d7 *(D)*

Or 17...♕c7 18 ♘ed5 ♕xc5 (or 18...♘xd5 19 ♕xf8+ ♔d7 20 ♘xd5 exd5 21 ♗d4!) 19 ♘xf6+ ♔e7 (19...♔d8 20 ♖d1+ ♔c7 21 ♘fe4 wins for White) 20 ♘ce4! with a winning attack.

18 ♘xc8

This is sufficient to win, but a more forcing line would have been 18 ♘f5!! exf5 (18...♘xc5 19 ♘d6+ ♔e7 20 ♘xb7 ♗xb7 21 ♕xe5 ♘d7 22 ♕g5+ f6 23 ♕h4 ♘xc2 24 ♕xh7+ is also winning for White) 19 ♖xe5+! ♔d8 (19...♘xe5 20 ♕xf8+ ♔d7 21 ♕e7+ ♔c6 22 ♕d6#) 20

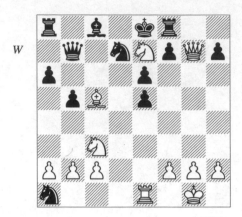

W

♘d5 ♕xd5 21 ♖xd5 ♖e8 22 ♕c3! and Black is helpless.

18...♖xc8

Or 18...♕xc8 19 ♘e4 ♕c6 20 ♘f6+ ♔d8 21 ♗xf8 and White wins.

19 ♗xf8

Not 19 ♘e4? ♕xe4 20 ♖xe4 ♖xc5, when Black turns the tables.

19...♘xf8 20 ♘e4 ♕b6 *(D)*

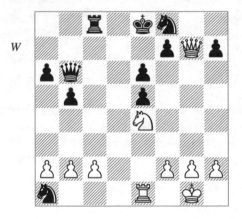

W

21 ♕xe5

21 ♘f6+ ♔e7 22 ♕g5! is simpler, since then Black is defenceless.

21...♖xc2

Best, as 21...♘xc2? 22 ♘f6+ ♔d8 23 ♖d1+ and 21...♖c6 22 c3 ♘c2 23 ♘f6+ ♔d8 24 ♖d1+ ♔c8 25 ♕e4 win for White.

22 ♖d1 ♘d7

The most resilient defence, because after 22...♘g6 23 ♕g5 (23 ♘f6+? ♔f8 24 ♘xh7+ ♔g8 25 ♘f6+ ♔g7 26 ♘h5++ ♔h6 wins for Black, while 23 ♕g7?! ♕c7 is not very clear) 23...h6 24 ♘f6+ ♔f8 25 ♕xh6+ ♔e7 26 ♘e4! Black is strangely helpless; for example, after 26...♕c7 27 ♕g5+ ♔e8 28 h4 Black's king and knights are all in trouble.

23 ♘d6+ *(D)*

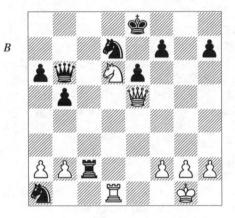

B

23...♔d8?

Losing at once. 23...♔e7 was a better try, but even in this case 24 ♕g5+ ♔f8 25 ♕f4 f6 (25...♘e5 26 ♘e4 wins for White) 26 ♕h6+ ♔g8 27 ♘e4 gives White a large advantage.

24 ♕h8+ 1-0

White forces mate in a few moves. An exciting if not flawless game.

Game 52
Efim Geller – Alexei Dreev
New York Open 1990
French Defence, Tarrasch Variation

1 e4 e6 2 d4 d5 3 ♘d2 a6 4 ♘gf3 c5 5 exd5 exd5 6 ♗e2 c4 *(D)*

An ambitious move. If Black manages to maintain the pawn at c4, White's minor pieces,

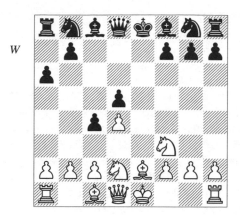

W

especially his light-squared bishop, will be se-‐ verely restricted in their mobility. Everything now depends on whether White can blow up Black's queenside pawn-chain. In the game White is ready to offer a piece to achieve this.

7 0-0 &d6 8 b3 b5 9 a4 &b7

The alternative is 9...c3, when again White must sacrifice a piece, by 10 axb5 cxd2 11 &xd2. Although White's practical results have been good in this position, the theoretical status is less clear. After 11...&f6 (11...&b7 12 bxa6 &xa6 13 &xa6 &xa6 14 We2+ We7 15 Wxa6! &xa6 16 &xa6 favoured White in Geller-Kekki, European Clubs Cup, Matynkylä 1986) 12 c4 dxc4! (12...0-0 13 c5 &c7 14 b6 &xb6 15 cxb6 Wxb6 16 &a5 is good for White) 13 bxc4 0-0 the position was unclear in Kr.Georgiev-Niko-lić, Burgas 1993.

10 bxc4 bxc4 (D)

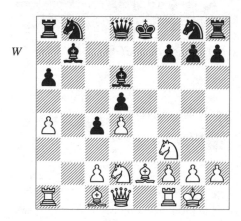

W

11 &xc4!

Once again, a piece sacrifice is necessary to break up the pawns.

11...dxc4 12 &xc4

Black will find it hard to castle, and in the centre his king comes under a prolonged assault.

12...&e7

12...&e7 13 &xd6+ Wxd6 14 &a3 Wc7 15 &e1 &c6 16 d5 0-0-0 gives White a tremendous initiative; e.g., 17 c4 (17 dxc6!? is also promising) 17...&f5 18 Wb1 &cd4 19 &xd4 &xd4 20 Wd3 and wins. Thus Black is forced into the retrograde text-move.

13 &e1 Wc7

Black dreams of castling queenside. 13...&f8 14 &b1 gives White strong long-term pressure; e.g., 14...Wc7 15 d5 &c5 16 d6 Wc8 17 &fe5 &f6 18 &xf7 &xf7 19 &e7+ &f8 20 &exb7 and Black is in serious trouble.

14 &b1

Threatening 15 &xb7.

14...Wxc4 15 &xb7 &c6 (D)

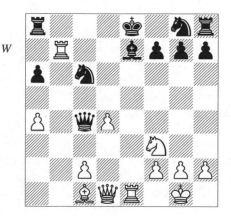

W

16 &d2

It would be a mistake to try to regain the material by 16 &a3?! 0-0-0 17 &xe7 &gxe7 18 &bxe7 &xe7 19 &xe7 as after 19...&he8 White's initiative would have totally disappeared and Black would be slightly better. However, 16 &c7! was even stronger than the move played. This prevents Black from moving his g8-knight because of &exe7+, and so he is virtually paralysed. After 16...&d8 17 &a3 Wxa4 18 &c5 &d7 19 &xd7 &xd7 20 d5, for example, White's attack crashes through.

16...♕xd4

Or 16...♕xa4 (16...♕d5 17 c4 only makes the situation worse) 17 d5 ♘a5 18 ♖c7 ♕f4 (18...♔d8 loses to 19 d6! ♗xd6 20 ♘e4) 19 ♖c3 ♔f8 20 ♘c4 ♕xc4 (20...♕f6 21 ♘e5) 21 ♖xc4 ♘xc4 22 ♕g4 ♘d6 23 c4 ♘f6 24 ♕d4 with a large advantage for White.

17 ♗b2 *(D)*

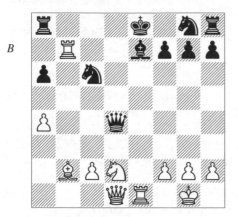

17...♕xa4

17...♕f4 is a slightly tougher defence, but White still has an excellent position after 18 ♘f3 (not 18 ♗xg7? 0-0-0!) 18...♖d8 (or 18...♔f8 19 ♕d7) 19 ♕e2 ♔f8 20 ♕xa6 ♖c8 (20...♘b4 21 ♕a5 ♘c6 22 ♕c3 and 20...♘b8 21 ♕b5 win for White) 21 ♖d7 ♕b8 22 ♘e5.

18 ♖e4?

A serious error endangering the win. Regaining the sacrificed material by 18 ♗xg7 0-0-0 19 ♖b3 is simple and good; for example, 19...♗f6 20 ♗xh8 ♗xh8 21 c4 ♕a5 (21...♖xd2 22 ♖b8+) 22 ♕f3 ♕c7 23 ♘e4 with overwhelming threats.

18...♕a2?

Black lets the chance slip by. 18...♕a5 is correct, and now:

1) 19 ♘c4? ♖d8 20 ♕g4 h5 21 ♕e2 ♕d5 is winning for Black.

2) 19 ♗xg7 0-0-0 20 ♖b1 ♖xd2! (20...♕xd2 21 ♕g4+ ♔c7 22 ♗xh8 ♕xc2 23 ♖ee1 favours White as Black's king remains very exposed) 21 ♕f3 ♕d5! (21...♕a2 22 ♖a1 ♕xc2 23 ♗xh8 favours White) and White is slightly worse.

3) 19 ♘f1 ♖d8 20 ♕g4 f5 21 ♕xg7 fxe4 22 ♕xh8 ♕g5 is at least equal for Black.

19 ♗xg7 0-0-0 20 ♖b3 *(D)*

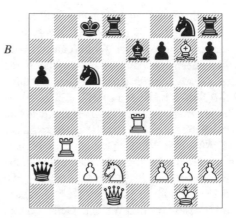

With the queen shut out on a2, Black has no chances at all.

20...♗f6

20...♘f6 21 ♖c4! ♖xd2 (or 21...♔c7 22 ♗xf6 ♗xf6 23 ♖xc6+! ♔xc6 24 ♕f3+) 22 ♖xc6+ ♔d7 23 ♕xd2+ ♔xc6 24 ♕c3+ and White wins.

21 ♕g4+ ♔c7 22 ♕f4+ ♔c8

22...♖d6 loses to 23 ♖d3.

23 ♗xf6 ♘xf6 24 ♕xf6 ♕xc2 25 ♕f5+ 1-0

Game 53

Michael Adams – Patrick Wolff

London (Watson, Farley & Williams) 1990

Pirc Defence

1 e4 d6 2 d4 g6 3 ♘c3 ♗g7 4 ♗e3 c6 5 ♕d2 b5 6 h4 ♘f6 7 f3 ♕c7

7...h5 has been the most popular choice, achieving reasonable results for Black.

8 ♗h6

White exploits the omission of ...h5 to exchange dark-squared bishops.

8...♗xh6 9 ♕xh6 ♗e6

After 9...♘bd7 10 ♘h3, White threatens 11 ♘g5 followed by 12 ♕g7. Therefore Black first develops his bishop, so as to be able to take on h3.

10 ♘h3 *(D)*

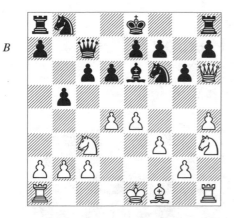

10...♗xh3

The drawback is that this capture now costs Black a tempo.

11 ♖xh3 ♘bd7 12 0-0-0 ♘b6 13 ♔b1 0-0-0 14 ♕e3

White's queen has done its duty in preventing ...0-0 and can return to the centre.

14...e5

If Black does not take action, then White will play g4 and h5.

15 a3 *(D)*

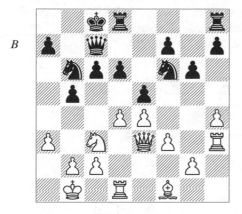

15...d5?

It is risky for Black to open the game while positionally inferior, especially as his king is insecure. 15...♖he8 would have restricted White to an edge.

16 dxe5

16 ♕g5 exd4 17 ♖xd4 is also promising for White.

16...♕xe5 17 f4 ♕e7 *(D)*

17...♕c7 18 e5 ♘fd7 19 ♗xb5 cxb5 20 ♘xb5 ♘c4 21 ♕xa7 gives White three pawns and an initiative for the piece.

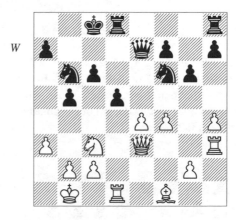

18 e5 ♘fd7

18...♘g4 19 ♕f3 h5 20 ♘e2 followed by ♘d4 is also good for White.

19 a4! a6? *(D)*

An error allowing White's attack to break through. 19...b4? is also bad, due to 20 ♘xd5! cxd5 21 a5. The best defence is 19...bxa4 20 ♘xa4 ♔b8 (20...♘xa4 loses to 21 ♕xa7 ♘ac5 22 ♖b3!, while 20...♕b4 is strongly met by 21 ♖d4), but after 21 ♘xb6 axb6 22 ♕c3 White retains a clear advantage.

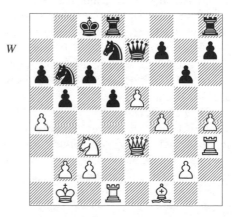

20 a5

Winning for White.

20...♘a8

20...♘c4 loses to 21 ♕a7.

21 ♘xd5!

An attractive final combination.

21...cxd5 22 ♕a7 ♘c7 23 ♖c3 ♘b8 24 g3!

1-0

Black cannot counter White's threat of 25 ♗h3+.

Game 54

Alexander Khalifman – Predrag Nikolić

Moscow (GMA) 1990

French Defence, Winawer Variation

1 e4 e6 2 d4 d5 3 ♘c3 ♗b4 4 e5 c5 5 a3 ♗xc3+ 6 bxc3 ♘e7 7 ♕g4 0-0 8 ♗d3 ♘bc6?!

8...f5 is the main line. The text-move is now considered inferior on account of the continuation played in this game.

9 ♕h5 *(D)*

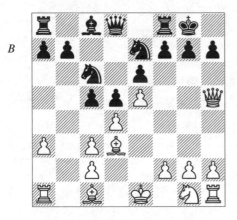

9...♘f5?!

9...♘g6 is a better idea, and has been the subject of detailed investigation; after 10 ♘f3 ♕c7 11 ♗e3 Black can choose between 11...c4 and 11...♘ce7. 9...h6? is a blunder which has claimed a number of victims: 10 ♗xh6! gxh6 11 ♕xh6 ♘f5 12 ♗xf5 exf5 13 0-0-0! gives White a decisive attack.

10 ♘f3 f6 11 g4! *(D)*

This direct approach gives White a very strong attack and more or less refutes Black's play. White's queen and minor pieces are already in good attacking positions and opening the g-file allows the rook to join in.

11...c4

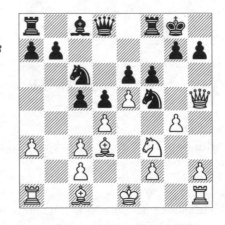

11...fxe5?! is bad in view of 12 gxf5 e4 13 ♘g5 h6 14 ♘xe4! dxe4 15 ♖g1!, while 11...g6 12 ♕h3 ♘g7 13 ♕h6! also favours White.

12 gxf5

This innovation, instead of the previously played 12 exf6 and 12 ♗e2, effectively put the whole line out of business for Black.

12...cxd3 13 ♖g1 *(D)*

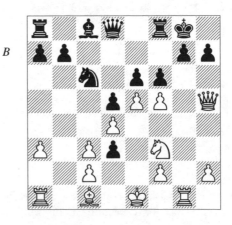

13...exf5

This is the critical position. Firstly, let's dispose of Black's inferior defences:

1) 13...♕e8 fails to 14 ♕xe8 ♖xe8 15 exf6 exf5+ 16 ♘e5! ♘xe5 17 ♖xg7+ with a large advantage to White.

2) 13...dxc2 14 ♗h6 ♖f7 15 ♔d2 ♗d7 led to catastrophe after 16 ♗xg7! ♖xg7 17 ♕h6 ♕f8 18 ♖xg7+ ♔xg7 19 ♖g1 ♕xg1 20 ♘xg1 fxe5 21 f6 1-0 in M.Palac-V.Kovačević, Vinkovci 1995.

3) 13...♕a5 14 ♖xg7+! ♔xg7 15 ♗h6+ ♔h8 16 ♗xf8 ♕xc3+ 17 ♔f1 ♕xa1+ 18 ♔g2 and Black cannot meet the threat of 19 ♕f7.

4) This leaves 13...♘e7, undoubtedly the most resilient of Black's defences. Although perhaps not a forced loss, there is nothing attractive about this position for Black. White continues 14 exf6 ♖xf6 15 ♖xg7+!! ♔xg7 16 ♕g5+ ♘g6 (16...♔f7 17 ♘e5+ wins for White) 17 fxg6 (D).

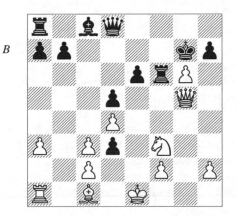

17...hxg6 (or 17...♕e7? 18 ♕h6+ and now both 18...♔h8 19 ♗g5 ♖xg6 20 ♕xg6 and 18...♔g8 19 ♗g5 hxg6 20 ♕h4 ♔g7 21 ♘e5 win for White) 18 ♗f4! ♗d7 (the lines 18...♔f7 19 ♗e5, 18...♖f8 19 ♕h6+ and 18...♕a5 19 ♗e5 ♕xc3+ 20 ♔f1 ♕xa1+ 21 ♔g2 are all lost for Black) 19 ♗e5 dxc2 (19...♖c8 20 cxd3 ♖xc3 21 ♔d2 and White wins after 21...♖b3 22 ♖g1 ♗e8 23 ♖g4) 20 h4! and then:

4a) 20...♕e7 21 h5 ♖f8 (21...♗e8 22 ♘h2 is similar) 22 ♘h2 and White wins.

4b) 20...♗a4 21 h5 ♔f7 22 ♗xf6 ♕xf6 23 ♘e5+ ♔e7 24 ♘xg6+ ♔f7 25 ♘e5+ ♔e7 26 f4

♖c8 27 ♔d2 leads to a winning ending for White.

4c) 20...♗e8 21 ♘h2! ♔f7 22 ♕h6! ♗e7 (22...g5 23 ♕h7+ ♔f8 24 ♕h8+ ♔f7 25 ♘g4 and 22...♗b5 23 ♘g4 ♖f5 24 ♕g7+ ♔e8 25 ♘f6+ ♖xf6 26 ♗xf6 ♕d6 27 ♕g8+ are also hopeless for Black) 23 ♗xf6+ ♔xf6 24 ♕f8+ ♗f7 25 ♘g4+ ♔f5 26 ♕xf7+! ♔xg4 27 ♔e2 (forcing mate) 1-0 Kruppa-Komarov, Kherson 1991.

14 ♗h6 ♖f7 15 ♔d2! *(D)*

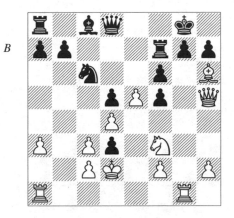

Clearing the first rank for White's last piece to join the attack.

15...♗e6 16 ♗xg7!

We have already seen this sacrifice in line '2' above; here, in a slightly different setting, it also proves decisive.

16...♖xg7 17 ♖xg7+ ♔xg7 18 ♖g1+ *(D)*

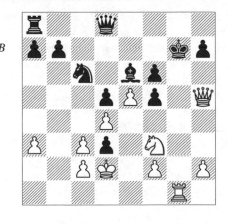

1-0

There is no defence; for example, 18...♔h8 (or 18...♔f8 19 ♕xh7 ♖c8 20 ♖g7) 19 ♘h4 ♘xd4 (19...♕d7 20 ♘g6+ ♔g7 21 ♘f4+ ♔h8 22 ♕h6 wins Black's queen at the very least) 20 ♘g6+ ♔g7 21 ♘f4+ ♔h8 22 cxd4 and White wins.

Game 55

Walter Arencibia – Yasser Seirawan

Manila Interzonal 1990

Modern Defence

1 d4 d6 2 ♘c3 g6 3 h4?!

Amazingly, in a database of more than 3.5 million games I could only find four other examples of this position.

3...♗g7

3...♘f6 4 e4 transposes into a line of the Pirc.

4 h5 ♘c6 5 ♘f3 e5! *(D)*

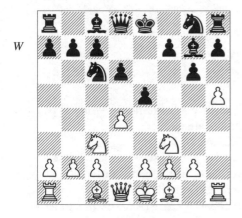

Seirawan reacts thematically to White's flank advance by counterattacking in the centre. Thanks to the time White has spent pushing his h-pawn, Black is not behind in development.

6 h6 ♗f6 7 d5

White closes the centre and drives the knight back to base.

7...♘b8 8 e4 ♗e7 *(D)*

Black intends to develop by ...♘f6 and ...0-0. Eventually, he might aim for counterplay by ...f5, but he will have to take care in view of the proximity of White's h-pawn to his king.

9 ♗b5+

9 ♗e2 ♘f6 10 ♘d2 followed by ♘c4 is approximately equal.

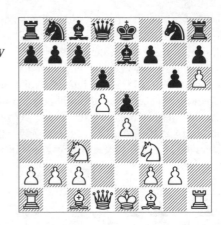

9...♘d7

Not 9...c6? 10 dxc6 bxc6 11 ♗c4 with a slight plus for White.

10 g4?

So far White has played ambitiously but has not taken too many risks. However, with this further pawn advance (aimed at preventing Black's kingside development) he goes too far. 10 ♗e3 ♘gf6 11 ♘d2 is safer, with equality.

10...♘gf6

Before g5 seals Black in.

11 ♘h4 *(D)*

11 g5 ♘h5 favours Black as f4 is a tempting square for the knight, while 11 ♖g1 0-0 followed by ...♘c5 will attack e4 and g4.

11...a6

Black is careful not to allow White to mix things up. 11...0-0 12 ♘f5!? gxf5 13 exf5 may not be objectively sound but it would certainly be troublesome in practice.

12 ♗d3 ♘c5

Attacking g4. As 13 f3 and 13 ♖g1 both run into 13...♘xg4, White is forced to push.

13 g5 ♘h5 14 ♖g1

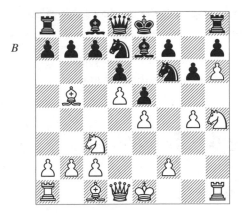

B

Far from giving attacking chances, White's early kingside advance has left him scrambling to hold on to his protruding pawns.

14...♘f4! 15 ♗xf4

15 ♘f3 0-0 followed by ...f6 is no better.

15...exf4 16 ♘f3 0-0 *(D)*

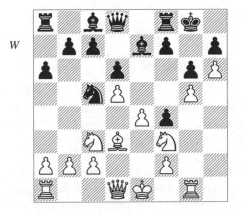

W

Black has a clear advantage. Thanks to all his pawn moves, White is well behind in development. In contrast, Black is safely castled and is ready to break open the position by ...f6, activating his dark-squared bishop and opening lines towards the white king.

17 ♗e2?

White seeks a tactical solution to his positional problems, even though this is almost always a bad idea. 17 ♕d2 f6 18 gxf6 ♗xf6 19 0-0-0 favours Black due to his extremely powerful dark-squared bishop, but at least it would still be a fight.

17...f6 18 ♘d4

After 18 ♕d4 ♘d7 19 0-0-0 ♘e5 White must take on f6, when Black has an even larger advantage than in the note to White's 17th move.

18...fxg5 19 b4

This is White's idea: he hopes to win material, because 19...♘d7 allows 20 ♘e6.

19...♗f6! *(D)*

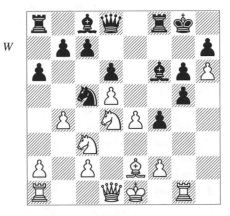

W

The long dark diagonal, on which three white pieces are conveniently lined up, proves the Achilles' Heel.

20 ♕d2

20 bxc5 dxc5 regains the piece with an overwhelming position.

20...♗e5

Clearing f6 for the queen.

21 ♖d1

21 bxc5 ♕f6! 22 0-0-0 dxc5 wins for Black, while 21 0-0-0 f3 followed by ...♗f4 is catastrophic. Thus the king must stay in the centre.

21...♕f6 *(D)*

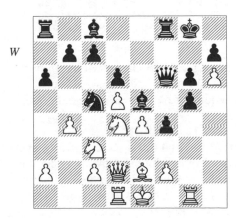

W

White's position is hopeless. His plan to gain material has backfired and he is a pawn down with his king trapped in the centre.

22 ♗g4

22 bxc5 dxc5 wins for Black.

22...♗xg4 23 ♖xg4 ♘d7 24 ♘ce2 f3 0-1

Since 25 ♘c1 ♗f4 26 ♕c3 ♘e5 27 ♖g1 ♗xc1 28 ♖xc1 ♕f4 leads to further material loss. This game provides a textbook example of the refutation of a premature attack.

Game 56

Sergei Smagin – Dragutin Šahović

Biel Open 1990

Nimzowitsch Defence

1 e4 ♘c6 2 d4 d5 3 e5

The position resembles a 3 e5 Caro-Kann in that Black can develop his light-squared bishop outside his central pawn-chain.

3...♗f5 4 c3 e6 5 ♘d2

An unusual move. 5 ♘e2, 5 ♗d3 and 5 ♘f3 are more common alternatives.

5...f6

5...♕d7 followed by ...0-0-0 is another possible plan.

6 f4 fxe5 7 fxe5 ♘h6 8 ♘df3 ♘f7 9 ♘e2 *(D)*

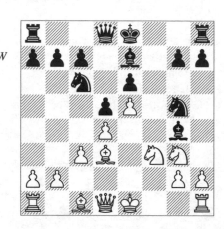

The point of Black's previous move was to exert pressure against the pinned knight, but it runs into an unexpected tactical riposte.

12 ♘xg5!

12 ♗xg5 ♗xg5 13 0-0 followed by ♕c2 would also be favourable for White because Black's bishops are awkwardly placed. However, the sacrificial text-move is even more forceful.

12...♗xd1 13 ♘xe6 ♕b8

13...♕d7 is refuted by 14 ♘xg7+ followed by 15 ♗f5, trapping Black's queen. After 13...♕c8, White continues 14 ♘xg7+ ♔f7 15 ♗h6 ♗g4 16 0-0+ ♔g8 17 ♘3f5 ♕b8 18 ♖f4! and Black's position collapses.

14 ♘xg7+ *(D)*

14...♔d8

14...♔f8 15 ♗h6 ♗g4 16 0-0+ ♔g8 17 ♖f4! is conclusive as Black has no reasonable square for his bishop.

After 14...♔f7, White wins by 15 ♗h6 ♗f8 (15...♗g4 16 0-0+ ♔g8 transposes to 14...♔f8)

White's idea is to hunt down the f5-bishop by ♘g3 and (after ...♗g6) h4. However, this plan requires several time-consuming knight moves.

9...♗e7 10 ♘g3 ♗g4?

10...♗g6 11 h4 0-0 is more logical, playing for a lead in development. After 12 h5 ♗e4, for example, White cannot play 13 ♘xe4 as 13...dxe4 followed by 14...♗h4+ wins for Black.

11 ♗d3 ♘g5 *(D)*

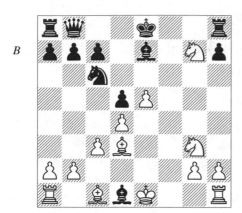

16 0-0+ ♔g8 17 ♘3f5! ♗g4 18 ♖f4 with overwhelming threats.

15 ♔xd1

Black has a miserable position. His slight material advantage in no way compensates for the fact that his three most powerful pieces are virtually impotent, and his king is permanently exposed.

15...b5

An attempt to extract Black's queen from its hiding place on b8.

16 ♘e6+ ♔c8 17 ♘f5 *(D)*

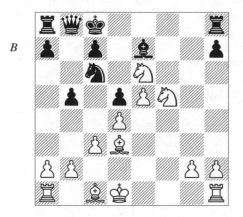

17...♗f8

The bishop returns to base, but there was no satisfactory move. 17...♕b6 18 ♘e3! wins the d5-pawn, while 17...♔b7 18 ♗xb5 strongly favours White.

18 ♖f1! ♔b7

18...♕b6 loses after 19 ♘e3. The move played aims to extract the queen along the first

rank, but the escape route is closed before Black can make use of it.

19 ♗h6! *(D)*

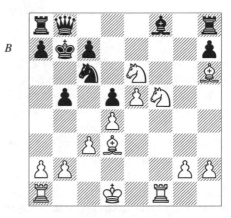

Another powerful blow, aiming to gain the c5-square for a white knight.

19...♗xh6

Or 19...♔b6 20 ♘e3! (20 ♘xf8 ♖xf8 21 ♗xf8 ♕xf8 22 ♘e3 ♕g8 23 ♖f6 also wins) 20...♗xh6 21 ♘xd5+ ♔a5 (or 21...♔b7 22 ♘c5+ ♔c8 23 ♖f7 winning) 22 b4+ ♔a4 23 a3! ♔b3 24 ♘c5+ ♔b2 25 ♖f2+! ♔xa1 26 ♘b3#.

20 ♘c5+ ♔c8 21 ♘xh6 ♘e7 22 ♗e2

The light-squared bishop reaches the h3-c8 diagonal after all, with devastating effect.

22...♘g6 23 ♘f7 *(D)*

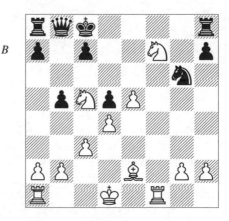

1-0

There is no defence to the twin threats of 24 ♘xh8 and 24 ♗g4#.

Game 57

Jan Timman – Viktor Korchnoi

Tilburg 1991

French Defence, 3...dxe4

1 e4 e6 2 d4 d5 3 ♘c3 dxe4 4 ♘xe4 ♘d7 5 ♘f3 ♘gf6 6 ♗g5 ♗e7 7 ♘xf6+ ♗xf6 8 h4

This line offers White chances of a slight advantage.

8...c5

The solid but boring 8...0-0 9 ♕d2 e5 gives Black better chances of equality.

9 ♕d2 cxd4

White can retain a faint edge after other moves too; e.g., 9...0-0 10 0-0-0 cxd4 11 ♘xd4 or 9...h6 10 ♗xf6 ♕xf6 11 0-0-0.

10 0-0-0 e5 *(D)*

This move looks greedy, but it is not a mistake. Korchnoi wants to make White work a bit to regain the pawn. 10...0-0 11 ♘xd4 transposes into the previous note.

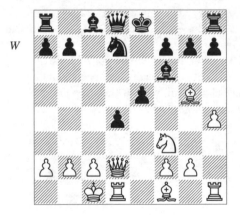

11 ♖e1 0-0

11...♕b6 12 ♗xf6 ♕xf6 13 ♕xd4 0-0 14 ♘xe5 ♘xe5 15 ♖xe5 gives White a useful extra tempo over the following note.

12 ♘xe5 ♖e8? *(D)*

A tactical error. Black could have justified his strategy by 12...♘xe5 13 ♖xe5 ♗e6 14 ♗xf6 ♕xf6 15 ♕xd4 ♖fd8! 16 ♕e3 ♖ac8, with enough play for the sacrificed pawn.

13 ♘xf7!

A devastating blow.

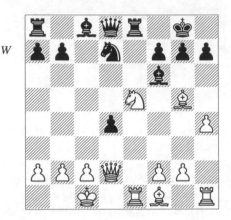

13...♖xe1+

Forced, because 13...♔xf7 14 ♗c4+ ♔f8 (14...♔g6 15 h5+ ♔f5 16 ♕f4#) 15 ♖xe8+ ♕xe8 16 ♖e1 ♘e5 (or else 17 ♕b4+) 17 ♗xf6 gxf6 18 ♕h6+ ♔e7 19 ♕g7+ wins for White.

14 ♕xe1 ♔xf7 15 ♗c4+ ♔f8 16 ♕e6 ♗xg5+

16...♘e5 17 ♕g8+ ♔e7 18 ♕xg7+ is winning for White.

17 hxg5 ♕xg5+ 18 ♔b1 ♘e5

Or 18...♕f6 19 ♕g8+ ♔e7 20 ♖e1+ ♘e5 21 ♕d5! and White wins.

19 ♕g8+ ♔e7 *(D)*

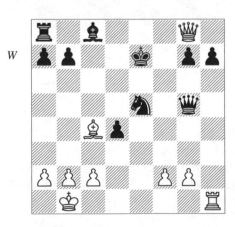

20 ♖e1!

Threatening 21 ♕d5.

20...♗d7

Black is forced to jettison material, because 20...h6 21 ♕d5 ♔f6 22 ♕d6+ leads to mate.

21 ♕xa8 ♕d2 22 ♖xe5+ ♔f6 23 a3

Simplest. White emerges a piece up.

23...♔xe5 24 ♕b8+ ♔f5

Both 24...♔e4 25 ♕xb7+ and 24...♔f6 25 ♕d8+ drop a piece.

25 ♕f8+ 1-0

As 25...♔g6 26 ♕f7+ again wins the enemy bishop.

Game 58
Evgeny Sveshnikov – Ruslan Scherbakov
USSR Ch, Moscow 1991
Sicilian Defence, Rossolimo Variation

1 e4 c5 2 ♘f3 ♘c6 3 ♗b5 e6 4 0-0 ♘ge7 5 c3 a6

5...d5 6 exd5 ♕xd5 is a playable alternative for Black.

6 ♗a4 b5 7 ♗c2 d5

7...♗b7 is a more popular continuation, but there is nothing wrong with the text-move.

8 e5 (D)

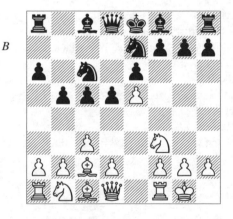

B

White threatens 9 d4, reaching a favourable type of French position in which d4 is absolutely secure and White's light-squared bishop is actively posted on the b1-h7 diagonal.

8...d4

Black prevents White's d4, but now the e4-square is available for White's bishop.

9 ♗e4 ♗b7

A normal developing move, but the combative 9...d3!? is probably stronger, sealing in White's queenside pieces.

10 a4

White has several routes to a slight advantage; for example, 10 d3 ♘g6 11 ♖e1 ♗e7 12 cxd4 cxd4 13 ♘bd2 0-0 14 ♘b3, Torre-Fedorowicz, San Francisco 1991 or 10 cxd4 cxd4 11 d3 ♕b6 12 ♖e1 ♖c8 13 a3 h6 14 h4 g6 15 ♗f4, Morozevich-J.Polgar, Amsterdam 1995.

10...♘g6 (D)

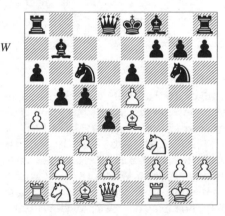

W

The e5-pawn exerts a cramping influence on Black's position, so Black starts to besiege it. However, thanks to White's pressure along the e4-a8 diagonal, actually capturing it will be far from easy.

11 axb5 axb5 12 ♖xa8 ♗xa8

12...♕xa8 13 ♕e2! (13 ♘a3 ♘cxe5 14 ♘xb5 ♘xf3+ 15 gxf3 ♕a5 is less clear) 13...b4 14 ♕b5 is awkward for Black as there is no easy escape from the pin.

13 ♘a3

White strikes at the weak b5-pawn.

13...♘a7?!

This is a little passive, since Black abandons his pressure against the e5-pawn. 13...♘cxe5 is better; for example, 14 ♗xa8 ♕xa8 15 ♘xe5 ♘xe5 16 cxd4 cxd4 17 ♘xb5 ♕c6 18 ♘xd4 ♕c4 19 ♘f3 ♘d3 and while White is freeing his pieces, Black will complete his development. The position is about equal, since the extra pawn is balanced by White's poor structure.

14 ♗xa8 ♕xa8 15 ♕b3?! *(D)*

15 cxd4 cxd4 16 ♕b3 is more accurate, cutting out the defence in the next note.

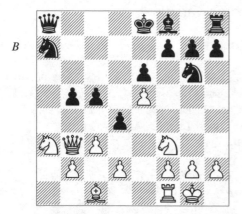

15...♕b7?

15...dxc3 16 dxc3 only makes it easier for White to develop his bishop, but Black could have played 15...c4! 16 ♘xc4!? bxc4 17 ♕a4+ ♕c6! (17...♔d8 18 ♘xd4 ♘f4 19 ♘f3 and 17...♔e7 18 ♘xd4 ♘xe5 19 ♘b5 ♘ec6 20 d3 are slightly better for White) 18 ♕xa7 ♗c5 19 ♕a2 d3; White cannot prevent castling, after which the cramping d3-pawn provides adequate compensation for the pawn.

16 cxd4 cxd4 17 ♘xd4

Opening the position is logical, as White is ahead in development. 17 d3 ♗c5 18 h4 is less effective because 18...h6 prevents the advance h5-h6.

17...♗xa3

17...b4 18 ♘c4 favours White.

18 bxa3

18 ♕xa3 ♘xe5 19 ♖e1 b4 is weaker as White has problems developing his bishop.

18...♘xe5

18...0-0 19 ♘f3 keeps the extra pawn.

19 ♗b2 *(D)*

Aiming for threats on the long diagonal. 19 a4 is a tempting line which fails, since after 19...0-0 20 ♘xb5 ♘xb5 White cannot retain the extra pawn.

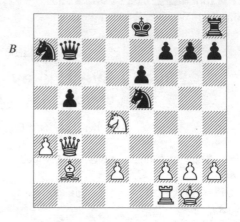

19...♘c4

19...0-0 20 ♘xe6 ♘f3+ 21 gxf3 fxe6 22 ♕xe6+ ♔h8 23 ♕e4 wins for White.

20 ♕g3

Sveshnikov thinks that White is already winning, but this is not correct, as we shall see. White has an advantage, but Black can still hope to defend.

20...0-0

20...♘xb2? loses at once to 21 ♕xg7 ♖f8 22 ♘xe6.

21 ♗c3 *(D)*

21 ♘f5? f6 22 ♘d6 ♕b6 lets Black off the hook.

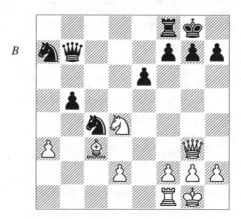

21...g6?

Only after this move is Black losing. 21...e5? is also bad due to 22 ♘f5 f6 23 ♗b4 ♖b8 (White also wins after 23...♖e8 24 d3 or 23...♖d8 24 ♗e7) 24 d3 ♘b6 25 ♗e7 and White wins.

21...♕b8! is the only chance; after 22 ♕g5! h6 (22...f6 23 ♕g4 e5 24 ♘f5 g6 25 d3 also gives White an edge) 23 ♕g4 ♘e5 24 ♕e4 White's active bishop gives him some advantage, but Black is still in the game.

22 d3 ♘b6

22...♘xa3 is impossible since 23 ♕d6! traps the knight.

23 ♕e5! ♘d7 *(D)*

23...f6 24 ♕xe6+ ♔g7 25 ♕d6 followed by ♘e6+ is also decisive.

24 ♕g7+!! 1-0

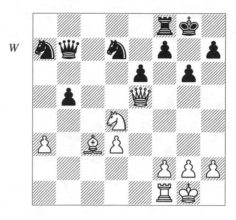

A beautiful finish. White forces mate after 24...♔xg7 25 ♘f5++ ♔g8 26 ♘h6#.

Game 59

William Watson – Eduard Meduna

Prague 1992

Caro-Kann Defence, 4...♘d7

1 e4 c6 2 d4 d5 3 ♘d2 dxe4 4 ♘xe4 ♘d7 5 ♘g5 ♘gf6 6 ♗d3 g6?

6...e6 is overwhelmingly the most popular move today.

7 ♘1f3 ♗g7 8 ♕e2!

A good reply, avoiding castling in order to retain the option of a direct kingside attack by h4-h5.

8...0-0

8...h6 9 ♘e6! fxe6 10 ♗xg6+ ♔f8 11 0-0 gives White strong long-term pressure for his sacrifice.

9 h4

The only way to cause real problems for Black.

9...h6 10 h5! *(D)*

Consistent play.

10...♘xh5

The only real test of White's idea is to take the piece, although with accurate play White can secure a clear advantage in any case: 10...hxg5 (10...gxh5 11 ♘h3 followed by ♘f4 is unpleasant for Black) 11 h6! ♗h8 12 ♘xg5 ♘b6! (12...♕a5+ 13 ♗d2 ♕d5 14 h7+ ♔g7 15 ♗c4 ♕xg2 16 0-0-0 gives White a crushing attack,

while 12...♘h7 13 ♗xg6! ♘xg5 14 h7+ ♔g7 15 ♗xg5 fxg6 16 ♕e6! ♕a5+ 17 ♗d2 ♘f6 18 ♕xe7+ ♖f7 19 ♕xf7+ ♔xf7 20 ♗xa5 leads to a favourable ending for White) 13 h7+ ♔g7 14 ♖h4! ♕d5 15 ♘e4 ♘g4 (15...♘xe4 16 ♗xe4 ♕e6 17 ♗h6+ is very good for White) 16 f3 ♕xd4 17 fxg4 ♕g1+ 18 ♔d2 and White has an enormous attack.

11 g4!

Black is already in serious trouble.

11...♘hf6

Or 11...hxg5 12 gxh5 g4 13 ♘g5 ♘f6 14 h6 ♗h8 15 h7+ ♔g7 16 ♕e3 with a decisive attack.

12 ♘e6! *(D)*

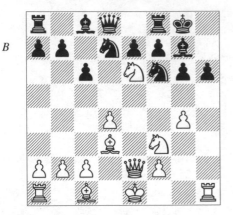

12...fxe6

Both 12...♕a5+ 13 ♗d2 ♕b6 14 ♘xg7 and 12...♕b6 13 ♘xg7 win for White.

13 ♕xe6+ ♖f7

13...♔h7 14 ♗xh6 ♗xh6 15 g5 wins for White; for example, 15...♘b6 16 ♖xh6+ ♔g7

17 ♖xg6+ ♔h8 18 ♖h6+ ♔g7 19 ♖h7+! ♘xh7 20 ♕g6+ ♔h8 21 ♕xh7#.

14 ♗xg6 ♕f8 15 g5 ♘d5

Or 15...♘b6 16 ♗xf7+ ♖xf7 17 ♕xf7+ ♔xf7 18 gxf6.

16 gxh6 ♘e5 *(D)*

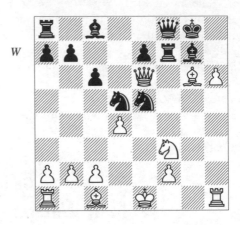

17 ♗h7+! 1-0

In view of 17...♔xh7 (17...♔h8 18 hxg7+ ♕xg7 19 ♗e4+! ♔g8 20 ♕xe5 winning) 18 hxg7+ ♔xg7 19 ♕h6+ ♔g8 20 ♕h8#.

Game 60

Jan Timman – Garry Kasparov

Linares 1992

King's Indian Defence, Sämisch Variation

1 d4 ♘f6 2 c4 g6 3 ♘c3 ♗g7 4 e4 d6 5 f3 0-0 6 ♗e3 e5 7 d5 ♘h5 8 ♕d2 f5 9 0-0-0 ♘d7 10 ♗d3 ♘c5

This is marked as a novelty in *Informator*, even though it had been played as long ago as Kotov-Szabo, Zurich Candidates 1953.

11 ♗c2 a6 12 ♘ge2 *(D)*

12 ♔b1 and 12 b4 are alternatives, but the move played appears most natural.

12...b5!?

Black must continue actively, or there is no point to his moves ...a6 and ...♘c5.

13 b4 ♘d7 14 cxb5

White decides to exchange pawns on the queenside. 14 exf5!? gxf5 15 ♘g3 and 14 c5 a5 are alternatives, with unclear play in both cases.

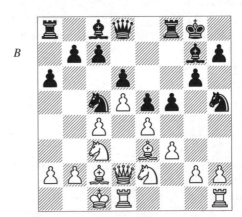

14...axb5 15 ♘xb5

15 ♔b2? ♘b6 favours Black.

15...罩xa2 16 ♘ec3 罩a8 *(D)*

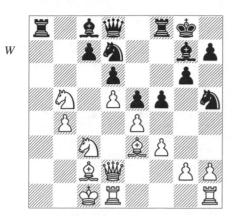

The exposure of White's king may appear hazardous, but the open a-file may well help him if he has time for ♔b2 and 罩a1. White's greater firepower on the queenside means that there is no immediate danger for White's king, always provided that the long dark-square diagonal remains closed.

17 ♔b2

Since White does not follow this up with 罩a1, there is surely an argument for playing 17 ♘a7 first.

17...♘df6

Clearing d7 for the bishop. The alternative 17...罩b8?! 18 ♔b3 ♗a6 19 ♘a7 ♘c5+ 20 ♔a3 favours White.

18 ♘a7

Now 18 罩a1?! could be met by 18...罩b8 19 ♔b3 ♗d7, so White aims to occupy c6 instead.

18...fxe4 19 ♘c6 ♕d7 *(D)*

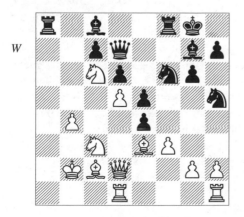

20 g4!?

White initiates a forcing sequence which leads to tremendous complications. 20 fxe4 ♘g4 is fine for Black, but 20 ♗xe4 is playable, again with a murky position.

20...♘f4 21 g5 ♘6xd5! *(D)*

Black has to go in for this, since 21...♘6h5 22 fxe4 would leave Black's kingside play stymied, and White would then be able to continue at his leisure on the queenside.

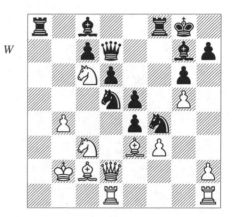

22 ♘xd5

22 ♗b3 is met by 22...♕xc6 23 ♘xd5 ♔h8 keeping the pawn.

22...♘d3+! *(D)*

Definitely best. 22...exf3 23 ♘xf4! exf4+ 24 ♗d4 ♕xc6 25 ♗b3+ d5 26 ♗xg7 ♔xg7 27 ♕d4+ and 22...♗b7 23 ♘ce7+ ♔h8 24 ♗xe4 c6 25 ♘b6 are winning for White, while 22...♔h8 23 ♘xf4 exf4+ 24 ♗d4 is clearly in White's favour.

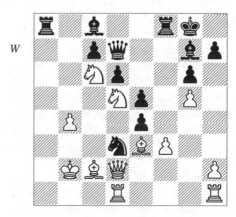

23 ♗xd3?

Timman goes wrong and allows the long diagonal to be opened – the one thing which he should avoid at all costs. Both Timman and Kasparov rejected 23 ♗b3 in their notes at the time because of 23...♛xc6, citing 24 ♘e7+ ♔h8 25 ♘xc6 ♗e6+ 26 ♔c3 ♜a3+ 27 ♗b3 ♜xb3+ 28 ♔c2 ♜b2+ with a massive advantage for Black after 29 ♔c3 ♜xd2 30 ♔xd2 ♜xf3. However, 24 fxe4 (D) is much stronger.

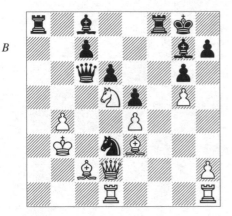

Then it is not clear if Black can achieve more than perpetual check by, for example, 24...♛a4+ 25 ♔c3 ♛c6+, etc. If 24...♘c5+, then 25 ♗xc5 (25 bxc5? ♛a4+ 26 ♔c3 ♛a5+ 27 ♘b4 ♜b8 28 ♛d5+ ♔h8 29 ♜b1 ♜f3 30 cxd6 c5! is very good for Black) 25...♛a4+ 26 ♔c3 ♛a3+ 27 ♗b3 dxc5 28 ♜a1 ♜f3+ 29 ♘e3+ ♗e6 30 ♜xa3 ♜xa3 31 ♜b1 c4 32 ♛c1 ♜xb3+ 33 ♜xb3 cxb3 34 ♔b2 leads to equality. Going back to an earlier point, Black should probably meet 23 ♔b3 by 23...♜xf3, since 24 ♗xd3 exd3 25 ♛xd3 ♔h8 gives him tremendous pressure for the piece.

It follows that the most critical line is 23 ♔b1. Timman believes it to be better for White, while Kasparov thinks it unclear. Both pieces of analysis are very lengthy and I shall not reproduce them in full here because my own analysis deviates at a very early stage. The critical position arises after 23...♜xf3 24 ♜hf1 (D) (but not 24 ♛c3 ♗b7 25 ♛c4 ♔h8 26 ♛xe4 ♜xe3 27 ♛xe3 e4! and Black wins).

Timman's main line continues 24...♜xf1 (this was also the only move considered by

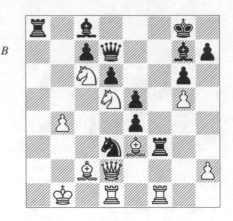

Kasparov) 25 ♜xf1 ♔h8 (25...♗b7 26 ♘f6+! ♗xf6 27 gxf6 ♛f7 28 ♘a5 ♗d5 29 ♗xd3 exd3 30 ♛xd3 and Black doesn't have enough for the piece) 26 ♗xd3 ♛xc6 27 ♗e2 ♗e6 28 ♜c1 and now he thinks White is better after 28...♗xd5 29 ♛xd5 ♗xd5 30 ♜xc7 because the b-pawn is very dangerous. However, 28...♛a4 seems safe enough for Black; e.g., 29 ♗c4 ♛a1+ 30 ♔c2 ♛a4+ 31 ♗b3 ♛a6 32 ♘xc7 ♗xb3+ 33 ♔xb3 ♛a4+ 34 ♔c3 ♛a3+ 35 ♔c2 ♛a4+ drawing by perpetual check.

However, all this may not be relevant because Black need not exchange rooks on f1, which gives White counterplay down the f-file. Instead 24...♔h8! looks better. In my view the only question then is whether White can hold the balance; e.g., 25 ♛c3 (25 ♜xf3 ♛xc6 and 25 ♘ce7 ♜xf1 26 ♜xf1 ♗b7 favour Black, while 25 ♗xd3 ♛xc6 26 ♗xe4 ♜xf1 27 ♜xf1 ♛c4 is lost for White) 25...♜xf1 (Black has gained half a tempo because ♛c3 is not an especially useful move, and now this exchange makes sense because Black can maintain his knight on d3) 26 ♜xf1 ♗a6! 27 ♜d1 ♗b5 28 ♘a5 ♜c8 and now that the c7-pawn has been defended, Black is ready to activate his queen with ...♛h3 or ...♛f7. He has three pawns for the piece and his advanced knight is like a bone in White's throat, so I would assess the position as somewhat in Black's favour.

23...exd3 (D)

Now White is in trouble. He cannot necessarily block the long diagonal by ♘f6+ since Black can reply ...♜xf6.

24 ♘ce7+?

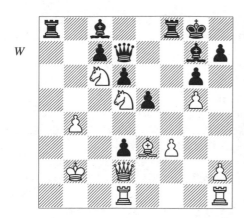

W

Total collapse, although White had a miserable choice in any case:

1) 24 ♔b3 ♗b7 gives Black a strong attack.

2) 24 ♖a1 ♗b7 25 b5 ♗xc6 26 bxc6 e4+ wins for Black.

3) 24 ♖c1 ♗b7 25 b5 ♗xc6 26 ♖xc6 e4+ 27 ♘f6+ ♖xf6 28 gxf6 ♗xf6+ 29 ♔b3 ♕e6+ 30 ♖c4 c6! 31 b6 d5 and White's position collapses.

4) 24 ♕c3 is best, but after 24...♕f7! 25 ♖xd3 e4 26 ♖d4 exf3 27 ♘ce7+ ♔h8 28 ♘xc8 ♖fxc8 White remains in serious difficulties.

24...♔h8

With a winning position for Black.

25 ♘xc8

25 ♕c3 ♗b7 26 ♖xd3 c5 is hopeless.

25...e4+ *(D)*

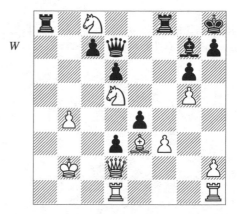

W

0-1

This thematic King's Indian move, activating the g7-bishop, ends the game. 26 ♘f6 ♖xf6 27 gxf6 ♗xf6+ 28 ♔b3 ♕e6# is mate, while 26 ♘c3 ♕a4 is hopeless.

Game 61

Alexander Beliavsky – Boris Gelfand

Linares 1992

Queen's Gambit, Slav Defence

1 d4 d5 2 c4 c6 3 ♘c3 e5 4 dxe5 d4 5 ♘e4 ♕a5+ 6 ♘d2 ♘h6

After White's success in this game, most players switched to 6...♘d7.

7 ♘f3 ♘f5 8 g3 ♘e3 9 fxe3 dxe3 10 a3! *(D)*

This novelty practically put 6...♘h6 out of business. 10 ♗g2 exd2+ 11 ♗xd2 ♗b4 had been played previously, with an equal position.

10...♗f5?!

Black seeks to develop his pieces actively, but this undefended bishop gives White a free tempo later on. Black should try either 10...♗e6!? or 10...♘a6 11 ♗g2 ♗e6 (but not 11...♗e7 12 b4! ♘xb4?, when 13 ♔f1! unexpectedly wins a piece).

11 ♗g2 ♗c5?

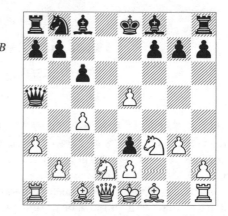

B

Consistent, but one risk too many. 11...♘d7 12 ♘d4! exd2+ 13 ♗xd2 ♕xe5 14 ♗c3 gives

White an initiative, but this would be much better than the game.

12 b4!

12 ♘h4 ♗e6 13 b4 ♗xb4 14 axb4 ♕xa1 15 ♘e4 is also good for White, but the text-move is more forceful.

12...♗xb4

Black is obliged to accept the sacrifice.

13 axb4 ♕xa1 14 0-0 exd2 15 ♕xd2 (D)

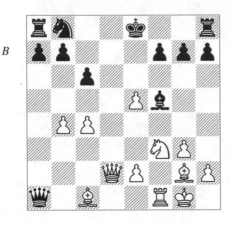

B

15...0-0 16 ♗b2

White can look forward to two free tempi, one from Black's queen and one from the loose bishop on f5.

16...♕a6

16...♕a4 17 ♘d4 followed by ♖a1 wins for White.

17 ♘g5 ♗g6

17...♗e6 18 ♕d3 g6 19 ♘xe6! fxe6 20 ♖xf8+ ♔xf8 21 ♕d8+ ♔f7 22 ♕f6+ is an easy win for White.

18 e6

White's attack is overwhelming.

18...f6

Or 18...♕xc4 19 exf7+ ♗xf7 20 ♖f4 ♕b5 21 ♖xf7 ♖xf7 22 ♕d8+ ♖f8 23 ♕e7 and wins.

19 e7 ♖e8 20 ♗h3! ♕b6+

20...fxg5 21 ♗e6+ ♔h8 22 ♖f8+ mates.

21 c5 ♕c7 22 ♗e6+ ♔h8 23 ♖xf6 (D)

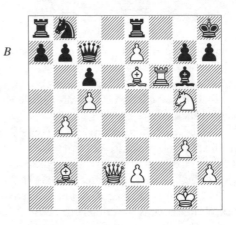

B

23...♘d7

23...♕xe7 24 ♖xg6 hxg6 25 ♕d4 mates quickly.

24 ♖xg6! 1-0

24...hxg6 25 ♕d4 ♘f6 26 ♕xf6! ♕xe7 27 ♕xg6 is an attractive finish.

Game 62

Yasser Seirawan – Nigel Short

Amsterdam (VSB) 1992

Queen's Gambit Declined, 5 ♗f4

1 d4 ♘f6 2 c4 e6 3 ♘f3 d5 4 ♘c3 ♗e7 5 ♗f4 0-0 6 e3 c5 7 dxc5 ♗xc5 8 ♕c2 ♘c6 9 a3 ♕a5 10 ♖d1 ♗e7 11 ♘d2 e5 12 ♘b3 ♕b6 13 ♗g5 ♗e6?! (D)

This was a new move at the time. Although it led to a brilliant win for Black on its first outing, later analysis showed it to be inferior to the alternatives and it has not been seen since. 13...d4 is playable, but perhaps the safest line for Black is 13...♗g4 14 f3 ♗e6. In this refinement of Short's idea, Black induces a weakness before playing the bishop to e6.

14 ♘a4

White can also secure an edge by 14 ♗xf6 (14 cxd5?! ♘xd5 15 ♘xd5 ♗xd5 16 ♖xd5 ♗xg5 is equal) 14...dxc4 and now either 15 ♘d2 ♗xf6 16 ♗xc4 or 15 ♗xe7 cxb3 16 ♕e4 ♘xe7 17 ♕xe5. The text-move is equally effective.

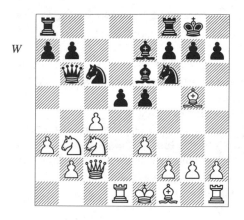

14...♕a6 *(D)*

Black could have kept his disadvantage to a minimum by 14...♕c7; e.g., 15 ♗xf6 dxc4 16 ♗xc4 ♗xc4 17 ♕xc4 ♗xf6 18 ♘c3, when the coming occupation of d5 gives White an edge but nothing more.

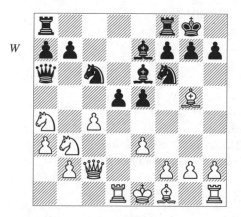

15 cxd5?

White starts a tactical sequence, but there is a flaw. 15 ♗xf6? is also bad due to 15...♕xa4 16 ♗xe7 (16 cxd5 transposes to the game) 16...♘xe7, with advantage to Black.

15 ♘ac5! ♗xc5 16 cxd5! is best, when Black cannot equalize: 16...♕a4 (or 16...♗b4+ 17 ♘d2 ♗xd2+ 18 ♖xd2 ♕a5 19 dxe6 ♖ad8 20 ♗xf6 gxf6 21 exf7+ ♔g7 22 ♗c4 and Black cannot prevent White from freeing himself with ♔e2) 17 dxe6 ♗b4+ 18 axb4 ♘xb4 19 exf7+ ♔h8 (19...♖xf7 20 ♕c4 b5 21 ♕xb5 ♕xb3 22 ♗c4 ♘c2+ 23 ♔e2 ♕xb5 24 ♗xb5 gives White every chance to win the ending) 20

♕f5 ♕xb3 21 ♗xf6 and now 21...♕xf7 22 ♗xg7+ ♕xg7 23 ♕e4 and 21...♖xf7 22 ♗xg7+ ♖xg7 23 ♕xe5 ♘c2+ 24 ♔e2 ♖c8 25 f4 both favour White.

15...♕xa4 *(D)*

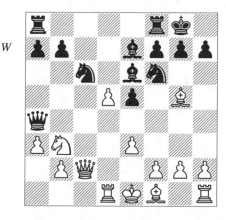

16 ♗xf6

Black is much better after 16 dxe6 ♘b4! 17 exf7+ ♔h8 18 axb4 ♗xb4+ 19 ♔e2 ♖ac8 20 ♕f5 (20 ♕d3 e4 21 ♕d4 ♕b5+ is winning for Black) 20...e4 21 ♘d2 ♖c5 22 ♕xf6 ♕b5+ 23 ♔e1 ♗xd2+ 24 ♖xd2 ♖c1+ 25 ♖d1 ♕a5+ 26 ♕c3 ♖xc3 27 bxc3 ♕xg5.

16...♘b4!! *(D)*

Throwing a spanner in the works of White's combination. Not 16...♗xd5? 17 ♖xd5 ♗xf6 18 ♗d3 g6 19 0-0, when White has a definite advantage on account of Black's vulnerable light squares.

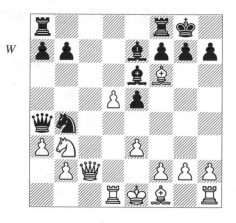

17 ♕e4

Running into a second surprise, but there was nothing better. 17 axb4 ♗xb4+ 18 ♔e2 ♖ac8 19 ♕d3 ♗d7! 20 ♖a1 (20 ♔f3 ♗d6 21 e4 gxf6 regains the piece with a massive positional advantage) 20...e4! 21 ♕xe4 ♕xb3 22 ♗d4 ♖fe8 gives Black a decisive attack.

17...♖ac8! *(D)*

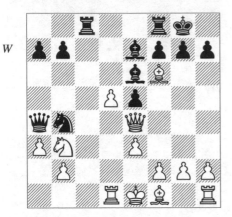

18 axb4?!

Hopeless, but other moves would also not have saved the game in the long run. The lines 18 ♗d3 ♘xd3+ 19 ♕xd3 ♗xf6 20 dxe6 ♖fd8, 18 f3 gxf6 19 dxe6 ♕xb3 20 exf7+ ♔h8 and 18 ♗xe7 ♘c2+ 19 ♕xc2 ♖xc2 20 ♘a1 ♗g4 21 ♘xc2 ♗xd1 22 ♗xf8 ♕xc2 23 ♗b4 ♕b1 all lose fairly simply. 18 ♗c4 ♘c2+ 19 ♕xc2 ♗xf6 is more complex, but the result is the

same after 20 ♕d3 (or 20 ♕e2 ♖xc4 21 ♘d2 ♗g4 22 f3 ♖c2 23 fxg4 ♖xb2 24 0-0 ♕xa3) 20...e4 21 ♗b5 (21 ♕e2 ♖xc4 22 ♘d2 ♖c2 23 dxe6 ♗xb2 24 exf7+ ♖xf7 25 0-0 ♖d7 is also winning for Black) 21...exd3 22 ♗xa4 ♗xd5 23 ♖xd3 ♗c4.

18...♗xb4+ 19 ♔e2 ♕xb3

White cannot take the piece, because after 20 dxe6 fxe6! the bishop cannot move owing to 21...♖c2+. Thus he is left with a shattered position and his king hopelessly exposed.

20 ♗xe5 *(D)*

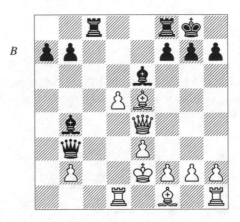

20...♖c4! 21 ♖d4

21 ♗d4 loses to 21...♖c2+ 22 ♔f3 ♗xd5.

21...♖xd4 22 ♕xd4 ♗xd5 0-1

White cannot avoid loss of the queen.

Game 63
Efim Geller – Maya Chiburdanidze
Aruba (Veterans vs Ladies) 1992
Owen's Defence

1 e4 b6

Chiburdanidze decides to steer the game into non-theoretical channels. There is clearly a gamble involved in this approach, which does not pay off here.

2 d4 ♗b7 3 ♗d3 e6 4 ♘f3 g6?! *(D)*

4...♘f6 is the most common move, but even this can hardly be recommended for Black. The text-move is still more dubious, as it weakens the kingside dark squares.

5 ♗g5!

The best move, because each reply has its defects.

5...♕c8

Losing time, but there was no really natural response; for example, 5...f6 (not 5...♘e7? 6 ♗f6) 6 ♗e3 ♗g7 7 ♕d2 and the g7-bishop is blocked in, or 5...♗e7 6 ♗e3 and the bishop is misplaced on e7.

6 ♘c3 ♗g7 7 0-0 d6 8 ♖e1

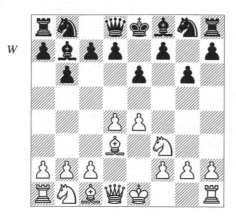

White wastes no time on unnecessary pawn moves but simply develops all his pieces to the centre.

8...♘d7 9 e5! (D)

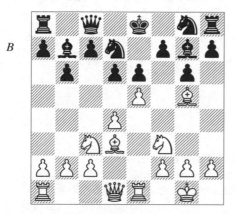

Clearing e4 for White's pieces. A knight arriving there would target the weak d6- and f6-squares.

9...d5

Black decides to prevent White from moving to e4, but now she has an inferior type of French Defence in which the kingside fianchetto is totally out of place. Other moves are also unsatisfactory because 9...dxe5 10 ♘xe5 ♘xe5 11 dxe5 renders Black's kingside development almost impossible, while 9...♗xf3? 10 ♕xf3 dxe5 11 ♗a6! ♕b8 12 ♗b7 costs Black material.

10 a4

White gains space on the queenside.

10...a6

10...♗a6 can be met by 11 ♘b5.

11 ♘e2 (D)

White has several ways to obtain a clear advantage. The straightforward 11 a5 is good, but Geller prefers to switch his knight to the kingside, while preparing to meet ...c5 by c3.

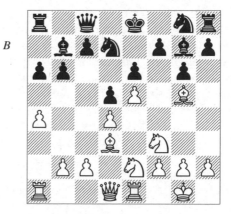

11...♘e7 12 ♘f4

12 ♗xe7? ♔xe7 would only make life easier for Black, since the dark-squared pressure would have disappeared.

12...♘c6

12...h6 13 ♗xe7 ♔xe7 14 ♗xg6!? fxg6 15 ♘xg6+ ♔f7 16 ♘xh8+ ♕xh8 17 ♘h4, followed by ♖a3, is very good for White. The theme of a sacrifice on g6 after that square has been weakened by ...h6 also arises in the game.

13 c3 a5

Black takes steps to prevent White's threatened 'big clamp' with b4, after which Black would be suffocating.

14 h4! (D)

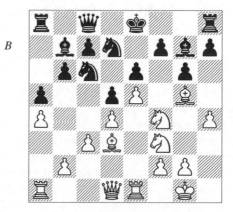

14...h6

Waiting would just allow White to improve his position with h5, etc., so it is understandable that Black tries to force White's hand. However, the attack proves to be too strong.

15 ♗f6 ♗xf6

15...0-0 16 h5 ♗xf6 17 exf6 g5 18 ♘xg5 ♘xf6 19 ♕d2 is not pretty for Black – 19...hxg5 loses to 20 ♘xd5 while otherwise Black has too many holes on the kingside. If 15...♘xf6 16 exf6 ♗xf6, then White breaks through by 17 ♗xg6! fxg6 18 ♖xe6+ ♔f7 (18...♗e7 19 ♕d3 ♖g8 20 ♖ae1 and White wins) 19 ♕d3 ♘e7 (if 19...♖g8, then 20 h5 is decisive) 20 ♖ae1 ♕g8 21 ♘e5+ ♗xe5 22 ♖1xe5 and Black's position collapses.

16 exf6 ♘xf6 *(D)*

16...0-0 17 h5 transposes to the previous note.

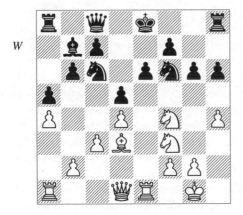

17 ♗xg6!

The thematic blow.

17...fxg6 18 ♖xe6+ ♔f7 19 ♕d3 ♖g8

19...♘e4 20 c4 and 19...♕g8 20 h5 g5 21 ♕f5 are lost for Black.

20 ♖ae1

20 ♖xc6 ♗xc6 21 ♘e5+ is also very strong.

20...♘e4? *(D)*

This loses at once, but even 20...♖g7 21 h5! g5 (21...♘xh5 22 ♘xh5 gxh5 23 ♕f5+ ♔g8 24 ♕xh5 gives White a decisive attack) 22 ♕f5 ♔g8 23 ♕xf6 gxf4 24 ♕xh6 only holds out a little longer.

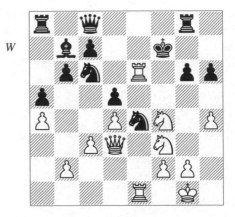

21 ♖1xe4! dxe4 22 ♕c4 1-0

There is no defence; for example, 22...♔g7 (or 22...♗a6 23 ♕d5) 23 ♖xg6+ ♔h8 24 ♖xh6+ ♔g7 25 ♖g6+ ♔h8 26 ♘g5 ♕f8 27 ♘f7+ ♔h7 28 ♕e6 mating.

Game 64

Mikhail Krasenkov – Evgeny Sveshnikov

Moscow 1992

Queen's Gambit, Semi-Slav Defence

1 ♘f3 d5 2 d4 ♘f6 3 c4 e6 4 ♘c3 c6 5 e3 ♘bd7 6 ♕c2 ♗d6 7 g4 *(D)*

This outrageous-looking move came into prominence during the 1990s and has remained popular right up to the present day. It is a typical example of the unfettered approach to the openings adopted by today's grandmasters – no matter what the appearance of a move, so long as it brings results they are prepared to try it. In my database White scored an above-average 61% with 7 g4, so its popularity is understandable.

7...♘xg4

In my view, Black does better to decline the sacrifice. One logical continuation is 7...dxc4 8 ♗xc4 b5, seeking to take advantage of the weak diagonal from b7 to h1 (see also Game 115).

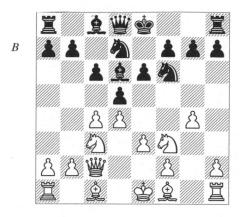

8 ♖g1 ♘h6

One of several possibilities.

9 e4

The preparatory 9 ♗d2!? has also achieved practical success.

9...dxe4 10 ♘xe4 ♗b4+ 11 ♗d2 ♗xd2+ 12 ♕xd2 ♘f5 13 0-0-0 (D)

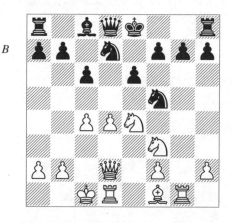

In return for the pawn White has a lead in development and pressure down the g-file. Objectively speaking White may not have an advantage, but Black's position is the more awkward to handle in practice.

13...♘f6 14 ♗d3

The most direct. 14 ♘c3 has also been tried, but this appears less effective.

14...0-0

Black should avoid 14...♘xe4 (and certainly not 14...♘xd4? 15 ♖xg7! ♘xf3 16 ♕f4 ♔f8 17 ♗e2 winning for White) 15 ♗xe4 ♕f6 16 ♗xf5 ♕xf5 (16...exf5 17 ♕e3+ ♔f8 18 ♖ge1 ♗e6 19

d5 cxd5 20 cxd5 ♗d7 21 ♕c5+ ♔g8 22 ♕e7 also favours White) 17 ♘e5 0-0 18 ♖g5 ♕f6 19 ♘g4 ♕e7 20 ♖xg7+ and White wins.

15 ♖g2 (D)

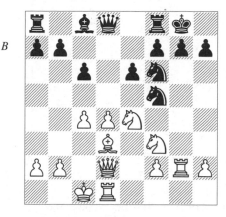

The plan of doubling rooks on the g-file is the most natural method of continuing the attack.

15...♘xe4 16 ♗xe4 ♕f6 17 ♘e5 ♖d8?

Up to here Black has defended calmly and accurately, but now he starts to falter. 17...♕h6 18 f4 ♖d8 is a better defence, aiming for counterplay against d4.

18 ♘g4! ♕e7?

This allows White a forced win, although by now Black is already in trouble. 18...♕xd4 is also dubious due to 19 ♘h6+! ♔h8 (19...♔f8? 20 ♕b4+ wins at once, while 19...♘xh6? 20 ♕xd4 ♖xd4 21 ♖xd4 is catastrophic as the rook penetrates to d8) 20 ♘xf7+ ♔g8 21 ♘xd8 ♕xe4 22 f3 ♕xc4+ 23 ♔b1 and White maintains a strong initiative.

Black's best try is 18...♕h4, when White must continue accurately to prove an advantage: 19 ♗xf5 exf5 20 ♘h6+ ♔f8 21 ♖xg7! ♔xg7 22 ♖g1+ (D).

22...♔f8 (22...♔f6 23 ♕e3 and White wins after 23...♕xd4 24 ♘g8+ or 23...♕e4 24 ♕g5+ ♔e6 25 ♕xd8) 23 ♕e3 and now:

1) 23...♕e4 24 ♖g8+ ♔e7 25 ♕g5+ ♔e6 26 ♖xd8 ♕e1+ 27 ♔c2 ♕xf2+ (27...♕e2+ 28 ♔c3 ♕f3+ 29 ♕e3+ ♕xe3+ 30 fxe3 gives White a winning ending) 28 ♔b3 ♕f3+ 29 ♔a4! ♗d7 (29...b5+ 30 ♔a5) 30 ♘g8! c5+ 31 ♔a5 b6+ 32 ♔a6 forcing mate.

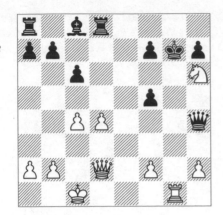

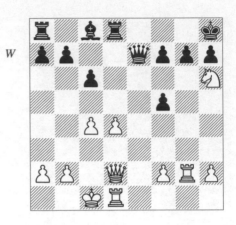

2) 23...♗e6 24 ♖g8+ ♔e7 25 ♘xf5+ ♔d7 26 ♘xh4 ♖xg8 27 ♘f3 with advantage to White, although Black can still fight.

19 ♗xf5 exf5 20 ♘h6+ ♔h8 *(D)*

If 20...♔f8, then 21 ♖xg7! leads to the same conclusion.

21 ♖xg7!

The start of an attractive finishing combination.

21...♔xg7

Or 21...♗e6 22 ♖dg1 ♕f6 (22...♕h4 23 ♕e3 f6 24 ♖e7! wins for White) 23 d5 cxd5 24 ♖xf7! ♗xf7 25 ♘xf7+ forcing mate.

22 ♖g1+ ♔h8 23 ♕e2! 1-0

White must have been very happy to finish with this queen sacrifice. After 23...♗e6 (or 23...♕f6 24 ♘xf7+ ♕xf7 25 ♕e5+ mating) 24 ♘xf7+! Black loses his queen (for a start).

Game 65

Bobby Fischer – Boris Spassky
Match (9), Sveti Stefan 1992
Ruy Lopez, Exchange Variation

1 e4 e5 2 ♘f3 ♘c6 3 ♗b5 a6 4 ♗xc6

The modern popularity of the Exchange Variation stems from three games Fischer played in the Havana Olympiad 1966. It has a small but loyal following amongst grandmasters.

4...dxc6 5 0-0 f6 6 d4 exd4 7 ♘xd4 c5 8 ♘b3 ♕xd1 9 ♖xd1 ♗g4 10 f3 ♗e6 *(D)*

Black chooses a line which is regarded as one of his most solid defences. The preliminary ...♗g4 induces White to weaken the a7-g1 diagonal, thereby giving Black the possibility of developing his bishop at c5 with gain of tempo.

11 ♘c3

11 ♗f4 c4! 12 ♘d4 0-0-0 13 ♘c3 ♖xd4 14 ♖xd4 ♗c5 is one line in which Black makes use of the weakening move f3.

11...♗d6 12 ♗e3 b6 13 a4 0-0-0?!

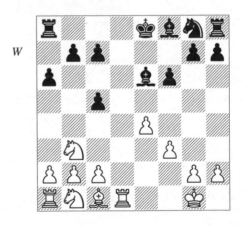

Although this has been played quite frequently, it seems far more risky than the two alternatives. These are the slightly passive 13...a5 and the solid 13...♔f7 14 a5 c4 15 ♘d4 b5.

14 a5 ♔b7 *(D)*

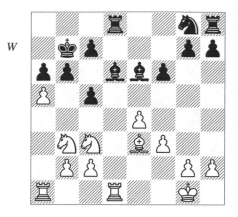

15 e5!

The most combative move. 15 axb6 cxb6 16 e5 is another variant of the e5 idea, which is also important for the game as there are transpositional possibilities. After 16...♗e7 17 ♖xd8 ♗xd8 18 ♗xc5 *(D)* (or 18 ♘e4 ♗xb3 19 ♘d6+ ♔c6 20 cxb3 ♘e7 21 ♖xa6 ♗c7 22 exf6 and White's chances of exploiting the extra pawn are minimal in view of his weak queenside pawns and Black's active king) Black can try:

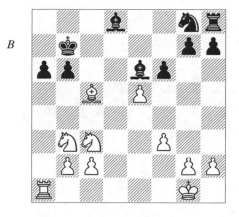

1) 18...♗xb3 19 ♗f8 ♘e7 20 ♗xg7 ♖g8 21 exf6 is very good for White.

2) 18...♘h6 19 ♘d4 ♗d7 20 ♗d6 ♖e8 (or 20...♘f7 21 e6!) 21 e6! ♗xe6 22 ♖e1 ♗d7 23 ♖xe8 ♗xe8 24 ♗f8 and White wins a pawn.

3) 18...fxe5! 19 ♗f8 (after 19 ♗d6 ♗f6 20 ♖e1 ♗xb3! 21 cxb3 ♘h6 22 ♗xe5 ♖e8 23 ♗g3 ♖xe1+ 24 ♗xe1 ♘f5 we again have the

situation where White's chances of exploiting the extra pawn are not all that great in view of his weakened queenside pawns and Black's active pieces) 19...♗f6 20 ♘e4 ♗xb3 21 ♘xf6 ♘xf6 22 ♗xg7 ♖g8 23 ♗xf6 ♗d5 and again White will have trouble making use of the extra pawn; e.g., 24 ♔f2 e4 25 ♖d1 ♗c6 26 f4 e3+ 27 ♔xe3 ♖xg2.

15...♗e7

15...fxe5 is bad; for example, 16 axb6 cxb6 17 ♘e4 ♗xb3 (17...♗e7 loses to 18 ♖xd8 ♗xd8 19 ♘bxc5+) 18 ♘xd6+ ♔c6 19 cxb3 ♖xd6 20 ♖xd6+ ♔xd6 21 ♖xa6 ♘f6 22 ♖xb6+ ♔d5 23 ♖b7 and White is clearly better. 15...♗xb3 is also inadequate after 16 exd6 ♗xc2 17 ♖dc1 ♗g6 18 dxc7.

16 ♖xd8 ♗xd8 17 ♘e4 *(D)*

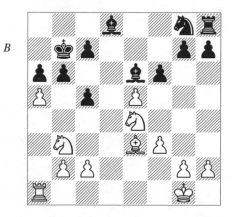

Intending 18 ♘bxc5+.

17...♔c6?

Spassky makes a serious mistake and loses quickly. The alternatives are:

1) 17...♗xb3 18 cxb3 ♘e7 19 axb6 cxb6 20 exf6 (20 ♘d6+ ♔c6 transposes into the 18 ♘e4 bracket in the note to White's 15th move) 20...gxf6 21 ♖d1 (both 21 ♘d6+ ♔c6 22 ♘f7 ♖f8 23 ♘xd8+ ♖xd8 24 ♖xa6 ♖d3 and 21 ♘xf6 ♘f5 22 ♘d5 ♘xe3 23 ♘xe3 ♗f6 are fine for Black) 21...♘f5 22 ♗f2 with just an edge for White.

2) 17...♗e7! 18 axb6 (18 ♗xc5 ♗xb3 19 ♗xe7 ♘xe7 20 cxb3 fxe5 21 axb6 ♔xb6 with equality) 18...♗xb3 19 cxb3 cxb6 20 ♖d1 (20 ♘d6+ ♗xd6 21 exd6 ♘h6 22 ♗xh6 gxh6 should be a draw) 20...fxe5 (20...♔c6 is also

playable) 21 ♖d7+ ♔c8 22 ♖a7 ♔b8 23 ♖d7 ♔c8 is equal.

18 axb6 cxb6 *(D)*

If 18...♗xb3, then 19 b7 ♔xb7 20 ♘xc5+ ♔b8 21 cxb3 fxe5 22 ♘xa6+ leaves White a pawn up with an excellent position.

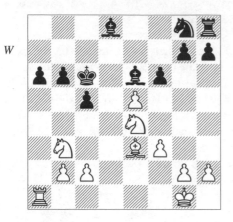

W

19 ♘bxc5
Crushing.

19...♗c8

Or 19...bxc5 20 ♖xa6+ ♔d5 21 ♘xc5 ♗f7 22 ♖d6+.

20 ♘xa6 fxe5 21 ♘b4+ *(D)*

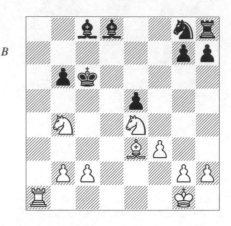

B

1-0

The end might be 21...♔b5 (21...♔c7 22 ♖a7+ ♔b7 23 ♖xb7+ ♔xb7 24 ♘d6+ wins for White) 22 ♘d6+! ♔xb4 23 ♖a3 and 24 c3#.

Game 66

Georgy Georgadze – Andras Adorjan

European Team Ch, Debrecen 1992

Grünfeld Defence, Exchange Variation

1 d4 ♘f6 2 c4 g6 3 ♘c3 d5 4 cxd5 ♘xd5 5 e4 ♘xc3 6 bxc3 ♗g7 7 ♗b5+

At the time this game was played, the slightly odd-looking text-move was giving Grünfeld players headaches.

7...c6 8 ♗a4 *(D)*

8...b5

These days 8...0-0 is considered sounder, but the text-move is a typically dynamic idea from Mr 'Black is OK'.

9 ♗b3 b4

It is of course thematic for Black to undermine the long dark diagonal in the Grünfeld, but it is very unusual for this to be achieved by ...b5-b4 rather than the traditional ...c5.

10 ♗e3

10 ♕f3 0-0 11 ♘e2 is now believed to favour White, but the move played is also not bad.

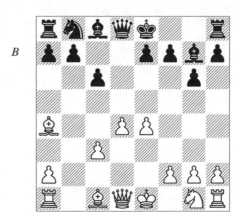

B

10...bxc3 11 ♖c1 ♘d7 12 ♘e2

The alternative 12 ♖xc3 c5 is indeed OK for Black.

12...♗a6 *(D)*

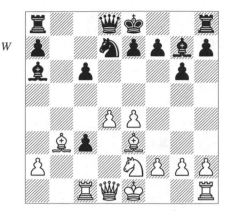

Black must put up a fight over the c3-pawn, because if White is allowed to take it without any concession, then the isolated c6-pawn will be exposed to attack along the c-file.

13 e5

13 ♘xc3 c5 is awkward as White cannot castle, while 13 ♖xc3 c5 affords Black equality.

13...♕a5

13...e6 is sometimes played to prevent the possibility of the next note, but this probably fails to equalize.

14 ♕c2

White can also play more aggressively by 14 e6!? fxe6 15 0-0, with a totally unclear position.

14...c5

Black proceeds with the undermining of White's centre.

15 ♕e4?

This move is based on a tactical trick that backfires. 15 f4! was correct, supporting the important e5-pawn and preparing simply to take on c3. In this case White could still count on a slight advantage, whereas after the move played his position goes downhill rapidly.

15...0-0 16 ♗xf7+ (D)

White was obviously pinning his hopes on this move, but it fails to have much impact. 16 e6? is bad in view of 16...cxd4! 17 exf7+ ♔h8 18 ♗xd4 c2! 19 ♔f1 (19 ♘c3 ♕xc3+! mates) 19...♕d2, when Black wins.

16...♔h8

16...♔xf7 is also promising; for example, 17 ♕d5+ (17 e6+ ♔g8 18 exd7 ♗xe2 19 ♔xe2 cxd4 20 ♗xd4 ♕xa2+ 21 ♔d3 ♖ad8! is winning

for Black) 17...e6 18 ♕xd7+ ♔g8 19 ♕xe6+ ♔h8 and it is hard to see how White will ever be able to castle.

17 ♘f4 (D)

Playing for ♘xg6+. White's attack may appear dangerous, but Black can defuse it by giving up a modest amount of material, whereupon White's own king will be subject to a deadly counter-attack. 17 f4 is also bad for White after 17...♖ab8 (heading for b2) 18 ♗b3 ♖b4 and Black is exerting pressure from all sides.

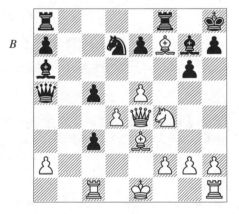

17...♖xf7!

Much stronger than 17...g5, when 18 ♗b3, intending 19 ♗c2, gives White dangerous kingside counterplay.

18 ♕xa8+ ♖f8 (D)

19 ♕d5

Other queen moves are no better: 19 ♕xa7 cxd4 20 ♕xd7 (20 ♕xd4 ♘xe5) 20...c2+! 21 ♗d2 ♕xe5+ 22 ♗e3 dxe3, 19 ♕c6 cxd4 20

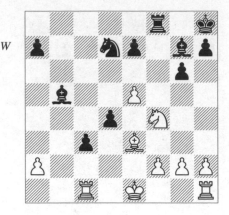

♗xd4 ♖xf4 21 ♕xc3 ♕b5 and 19 ♕e4 cxd4 20 ♕xd4 ♘xe5 all win for Black.

19...♕b5

Threatening 20...♖xf4.

20 ♕b3

20 ♖c2 cxd4 21 ♕xb5 ♗xb5 22 ♘e6 dxe3 23 ♘xf8 ♘xe5 wins as in the game.

20...cxd4!

The attack persists even without queens.

21 ♕xb5 ♗xb5 *(D)*

22 ♘e6

Or 22 ♗xd4 ♖xf4 23 ♗xc3 ♖e4+ 24 ♔d2 ♗h6+ and Black wins.

22...dxe3 23 ♘xf8 ♘xe5 0-1

The resignation looks a little early, but the attack is indeed decisive; for example, 24 ♘e6 (24 ♖xc3 ♘f3+ 25 gxf3 ♗xc3+ 26 ♔d1 e2+ wins, or 24 fxe3 ♘d3+ 25 ♔d1 ♘xc1 26 ♔xc1 ♗xf8) 24...♘d3+ 25 ♔d1 (25 ♔e2 fails to 25...♘xc1++ 26 ♔xe3 ♘xa2) 25...♘xc1 26 fxe3 (or 26 ♘xg7 exf2) 26...♘xa2 27 ♔c2 ♗a4+ 28 ♔b1 ♗b3 and White is finished.

Game 67

Jeroen Piket – Zurab Sturua

European Team Ch, Debrecen 1992

Queen's Gambit Declined

1 d4 d5 2 c4 e6 3 ♘c3 ♗e7 4 ♘f3 ♘f6 5 ♗g5 h6 6 ♗xf6 ♗xf6 7 e3 0-0 8 ♕c2

8 ♖c1 is the most common move in this position.

8...♘a6

An ambitious move instead of 8...c5, which gives excellent equalizing chances.

9 ♖d1 c5

A correct temporary pawn sacrifice.

10 dxc5

10 cxd5 ♘b4 11 ♕b3 ♘xd5 12 ♘xd5 exd5 is level.

10...♕a5 11 cxd5 ♘xc5 12 ♘d4!?

Returning the material in the hope of playing against an isolated d-pawn.

12...exd5 13 a3 *(D)*

13 ♗d3 ♘xd3+ 14 ♕xd3 ♗e6 15 0-0 ♖fd8 is equal.

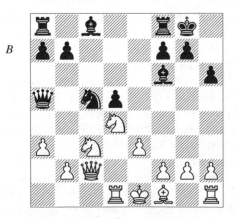

13...♘e6!

Fighting for control of the blockading square equalizes immediately.

14 ♘b5?

Too risky with his king in the centre. 14 ♗e2 or 14 ♘b3 would have been safe enough.

14...a6!

Once again Black offers a pawn.

15 b4 ♕d8 16 ♖xd5 ♗d7!

Now White pays a heavy price for his poor kingside development.

17 ♕d2 (D)

17 ♘d6 ♗c6 18 ♖d1 ♘d4! 19 exd4 ♕xd6 gives Black a winning attack.

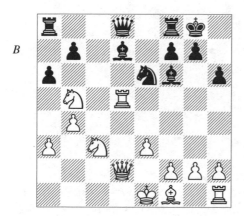

17...axb5 18 ♖xd7

Or 18 ♘e4 ♗d4! 19 exd4 (if 19 ♘c5 ♗xc5 20 ♖xd7, then 20...♕f6 21 bxc5 ♖xa3 wins for Black) 19...♖xa3 20 ♗e2 ♖a1+ 21 ♗d1 ♕h4

22 0-0 ♗c6 23 ♖e5 ♗xe4 24 g3 ♘g5! and Black wins.

18...♕xd7!

This spectacular sacrifice is the logical culmination of Black's play.

19 ♕xd7 ♗xc3+ 20 ♔e2

With only his queen in play, it is no surprise that White cannot defend.

20...♖fd8 21 ♕xb7

Or 21 ♕xb5 ♘g5! 22 e4 ♖xa3 23 f3 ♖d2+ 24 ♔e3 ♘e6!, followed by 25...♗xb4+, and wins.

21...♘g5! (D)

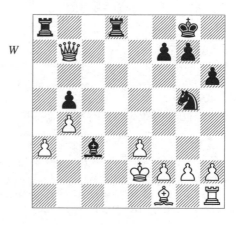

22 e4

A desperate attempt to give the king some air.

22...♖xa3 23 ♕xb5 ♖a2+ 24 ♔e3 ♗d2+ 0-1

25 ♔e2 ♗f4+ 26 ♔e1 ♖a1+ 27 ♔e2 ♖d2# is mate.

Game 68

Yuri Yakovich – Yuri Balashov

St Petersburg Zonal 1993

Sicilian Defence, Sozin Attack

1 e4 c5 2 ♘f3 ♘c6 3 d4 cxd4 4 ♘xd4 e6 5 ♘c3 d6 6 ♗e3 ♘f6 7 ♗c4 ♗e7 8 ♗b3 a6 9 f4 0-0 10 ♕f3 ♕a5?

An unusual and inferior move, which is drastically punished by White. The standard continuations for Black are 10...♘xd4 11 ♗xd4 b5 and 10...♕c7.

11 0-0-0 ♘xd4 12 ♖xd4 ♗d7

The problem with 10...♕a5 is that Black cannot now play 12...b5 because of 13 e5. Thus Black has to be content with the far slower text-move.

13 g4

White is quick to exploit Black's lagging development by launching an immediate kingside attack.

13...e5?! *(D)*

13...♗c6 14 g5 ♘d7 is a better chance, but still far from attractive after 15 h4.

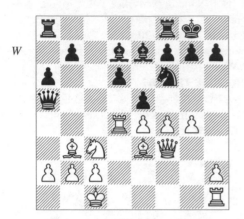

14 ♘d5!

A surprising and very strong exchange sacrifice.

14...exd4

14...♘xd5 15 ♖xd5 ♕c7 16 f5 gives White an automatic kingside attack, while 14...♗xg4 15 ♕g2 exd4 loses to 16 ♘xe7+ ♔h8 17 ♗xd4 ♕d8 18 ♘d5 ♘xd5 (or 18...♖g8 19 ♖g1) 19 ♗xd5.

15 ♘xe7+ ♔h8 16 ♗xd4 *(D)*

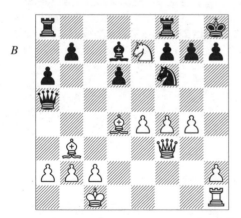

The threat is simply 17 g5 ♘g8 (17...♘e8 18 ♕h5) 18 ♘d5, with a huge attack for minimal material sacrifice.

16...♕d8

16...♗xg4 17 ♕g2 transposes into the analysis of 14...♗xg4 above.

17 g5! ♘e8

Forced, as 17...♕xe7 loses to 18 gxf6 gxf6 19 ♕c3.

18 ♘d5

At the cost of a very small sacrifice, White has gained an irresistible attack.

18...♗e6

Countering the effect of one white bishop, but the other is not so easy to neutralize.

19 ♕h5 *(D)*

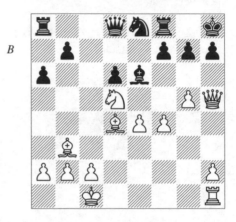

19...♖c8

19...♔g8 loses to 20 ♘f6+ gxf6 21 gxf6 ♔h8 22 ♕h6 ♖g8 23 ♗xe6 fxe6 24 f7+ ♘g7 25 ♖g1 e5 26 fxe5.

20 f5 ♗xd5 21 g6! *(D)*

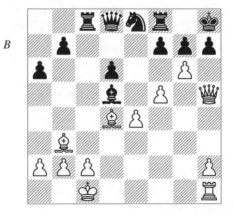

1-0

White wins after 21...♖xc2+ (or 21...fxg6 22 fxg6 ♘f6 23 ♗xf6) 22 ♔d1! ♖c1+ (22...fxg6 23 fxg6 is the same) 23 ♔xc1 ♕c7+ 24 ♔d2.

Game 69
Garry Kasparov – Boris Gelfand
Linares 1993
Sicilian Defence, Najdorf Variation

1 e4 c5 2 ♘f3 d6 3 d4 cxd4 4 ♘xd4 ♘f6 5 ♘c3 a6 6 ♗c4 e6 7 ♗b3 b5 8 0-0 ♗e7 9 ♕f3 ♕c7 10 ♕g3 0-0 11 ♗h6 ♘e8 *(D)*

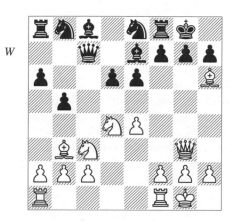

A topical variation. At first sight White appears to be having things all his own way, with five pieces already in play and his rooks about to arrive on the central files. However, Black's position is fairly solid and given time he will catch up with White in development, when Black's extra central pawn may be an important factor.

12 ♖ad1 ♗d7 *(D)*

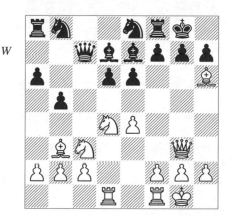

13 ♘f3!?

Other moves are possible, but Kasparov's continuation is regarded as the main line today.

13...b4

A somewhat risky move driving the knight towards the kingside, where there is already a dangerous accumulation of white pieces. 13...a5 and 13...♘c6 are sounder alternatives – indeed, Gelfand used the latter move to draw with Kasparov in a later game at the Moscow Olympiad 1994.

14 ♘e2 a5 *(D)*

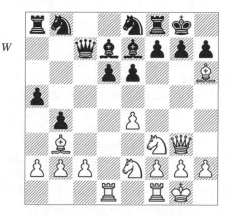

This is the point of Black's previous move – he just wants to trap the b3-bishop. Although this plan is certainly playable, Black is teetering on a knife-edge, never a comfortable position to be in, especially against Kasparov.

15 ♘f4! ♔h8

15...a4?? 16 ♗xg7 ♘xg7 17 ♘h5 ♗f6 18 ♘xf6+ ♔h8 19 ♕h4 mates.

16 ♗g5 ♘f6

16...♗xg5? 17 ♘xg5 a4 is bad after 18 ♕h4 and now both 18...h6 19 ♗xe6 fxe6 20 ♘fxe6 ♗xe6 21 ♘xe6 ♕f7 22 ♘xf8 ♕xf8 23 ♕d8 and 18...♘f6 19 ♗xe6 ♗xe6 20 ♘fxe6 fxe6 21 ♘xe6 ♕f7 22 ♘xf8 ♕xf8 23 ♕f4 ♖a6 24 ♖d4 are distinctly better for White. 16...f6?? is totally wrong and loses to 17 ♗xe6 fxg5 18 ♘g6+ hxg6 19 ♕h3#.

17 ♕h4! *(D)*

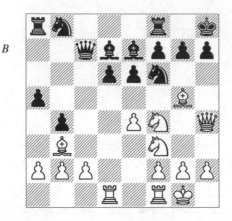

17...♗b5?

This decisively weakens e6. The alternatives are:

1) 17...a4 is critical but seems bad after a long, forcing line: 18 ♘h5 axb3 (not 18...♖a5? 19 e5 dxe5 20 ♘xf6 gxf6 21 ♗xf6+ ♗xf6 22 ♕xf6+ ♔g8 23 ♘g5 axb3 24 ♖d3 and White wins) 19 ♘xf6 ♗xf6 (19...h6? 20 ♗xh6 ♗xf6 21 ♗g5+ ♔g8 22 ♗xf6 gxf6 23 ♘g5! fxg5 24 ♕xg5+ ♔h8 25 ♖d3 forces mate) 20 ♗xf6 (threatening 21 ♘g5) 20...gxf6 (not 20...♖a5? 21 ♘g5 ♖xg5 22 ♕xg5 ♖g8 23 ♖d3, when White has a winning attack) 21 ♕xf6+ ♔g8 22 ♘g5 ♗b5 (Black must cover d3; 22...♗c8 23 ♖d3 ♖d8 24 ♘xh7 wins for White) 23 ♕h6 ♖e8 (23...f6 24 ♕xf8+! ♔xf8 25 ♘xe6+ and White wins) 24 ♕xh7+ ♔f8 25 ♖xd6! bxa2 26 ♖a1. The advanced a2-pawn looks dangerous, but Black seems unable to make use of it. Meanwhile White threatens to take on e6 or just to close the net around Black's king with e5. I don't see any way out for Black.

2) 17...♘c6! is a more practical move, when it is hard to prove any advantage for White; for example, 18 c3 bxc3 19 bxc3 h6 or 18 ♘h5 ♘xh5 19 ♗xe7 ♘xe7 20 ♕xe7 ♖ac8, intending ...a4 or ...♗b5, with an unclear position in both cases.

18 ♘d4! *(D)*

Now a decisive breakthrough is unavoidable.

18...♗e8

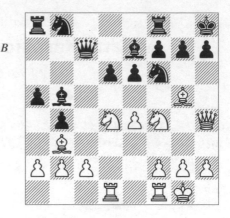

A desperate attempt to hold Black's position together. 18...♗xf1 loses to 19 ♘dxe6 fxe6 20 ♗xe6! (threatening mate in one) 20...h6 (20...g6 21 ♘xg6+ ♔g7 22 ♕h6#) 21 ♗xh6 gxh6 22 ♕xh6+ ♘h7 23 ♘g6#.

19 ♘dxe6! fxe6 20 ♘xe6 ♕a7

Or 20...♕b6 21 ♘xf8 ♗xf8 22 ♗xf6 gxf6 23 ♕xf6+ ♗g7 24 ♕e6, mating.

21 e5! *(D)*

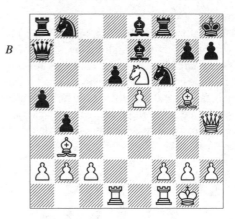

It's tough keeping Kasparov out in positions like this!

21...dxe5 22 ♘xf8 ♗xf8 23 ♗xf6 gxf6 24 ♖d8

The point of the preliminary 21 e5.

24...♘d7

White also wins after 24...♕e7 25 ♕g4! ♗g6 (or 25...♗g7 26 ♕e6 ♕xe6 27 ♗xe6) 26 ♕c4 ♕g7 27 ♕d5.

25 ♕g4 1-0

After 25...♗g7, 26 ♕e6 mates.

Game 70
Zsuzsa Polgar – Jon Speelman
Dutch Team Ch 1993
English Defence

1 d4 e6 2 c4 ♗b4+ 3 ♘c3 b6 4 e4 ♗b7

This slightly off-beat line is a favourite of Jon Speelman.

5 d5?!

Unusual. 5 ♕c2, 5 f3 and especially 5 ♗d3 are the main lines. The text-move aims to block out the b7-bishop, but it costs time and weakens the dark squares.

5...♕e7 *(D)*

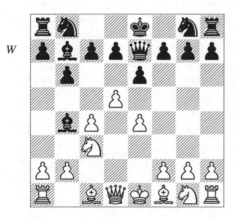

In my database this position has scored 61% for Black and, while such statistics can be deceptive, this time I think they are spot on – White should avoid this line.

6 ♗e2?!

6 ♘e2 exd5 7 exd5 ♘f6 leaves White in a tangle along the e-file, so 6 ♗e3!? may be relatively best, but here 'best' means equalizing for White.

6...♘f6 7 f3

Meeting the threat to e4, but it gives up another development tempo and further exposes the dark squares. If 7 ♗g5 h6 8 ♗h4, then 8...g5 (or 8...exd5 9 exd5 0-0 10 ♘f3 ♖e8 11 ♔f1 ♘a6) 9 ♗g3 ♘xe4 10 ♕d4 ♘f6 11 0-0-0 ♗c5 12 ♕d2 ♘a6 is fine for Black. 7 ♕d4 exd5 8 exd5 ♕e4 was quite safe for Black in Tartakower-Réti, Gothenburg 1920(!) – indeed, Black went on to win this game. 8...c6!? would be a

more dynamic alternative for those without Réti's endgame technique.

7...exd5 8 cxd5

White wants to keep the e-file closed, but Black has other ideas.

8...c6 *(D)*

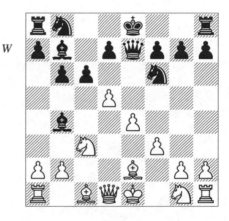

The rest of the game sees Black systematically opening line after line to exploit White's poor development and exposed king.

9 dxc6

It is evident that the plan of blocking out the b7-bishop has been a total failure.

9...♘xc6 10 ♘h3 d5!

The e-file didn't stay shut for long!

11 exd5 0-0-0 12 ♗g5

12 0-0 ♗xc3 13 bxc3 (13 dxc6 ♖xd1 14 cxb7+ ♔xb7 15 ♖xd1 ♗d4+ favours Black) 13...♖xd5 (13...♘xd5 is also good) 14 ♕c2 (14 ♕e1 ♖e5 is very bad for White) 14...♕c5+ 15 ♔h1 ♘d4 16 ♕b2 ♘xe2 17 ♕xe2 ♖e8 gives Black a large lead in development.

12...♖he8 *(D)*

Black completes his development.

13 ♗xf6

13 ♘f4 ♕e5 14 ♗xf6 gxf6! 15 g3 ♘d4 is also miserable for White.

13...gxf6!

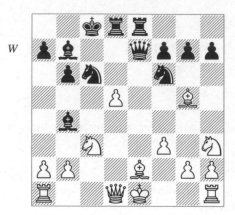

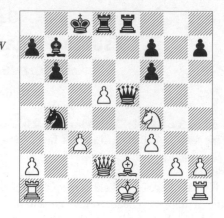

13...♕xf6 14 0-0 ♗xc3 15 bxc3 ♕xc3 16 ♘f2 lets White off lightly.

14 ♘f4

14 ♔f1 ♗xc3 15 bxc3 ♖xd5 16 ♕xd5 (16 ♕c2 ♕e3 is also dreadful) 16...♕xe2+ 17 ♔g1 ♘e5 18 ♕d4 ♘xf3+ 19 gxf3 ♖g8+ mates.

14...♕e5 (D)

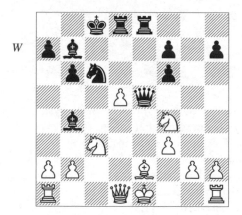

15 ♕d2

Or 15 ♕c1 ♖xd5! 16 0-0 ♗c5 17 ♘d3 ♕d4+ 18 ♘f2 ♖xe2 19 ♘xe2 ♖xc1 20 ♘xd4 ♖xa1 21 ♖xa1 ♘xd4 and again Black has a large advantage. After the text-move, accuracy is required, because Black must take into account the possibility of 0-0-0 as well as 0-0.

15...♗xc3!

Not 15...♘d4? 16 0-0-0! and White escapes.

16 bxc3 ♘b4 (D)

Black threatens to regain the pawn with crushing pressure along the central files.

17 ♔f2?

Loses at once, but there was no real defence:

1) 17 0-0-0 ♘xd5 18 ♘xd5 ♖xd5 19 ♗d3 ♖ed8 20 f4 (or 20 ♖he1 ♖xd3) 20...♕d6 21 ♔c2 (21 ♗f5+ ♔c7 22 ♕c2 ♕xf4+) 21...♗c6 and 22...♗a4+ wins for Black.

2) 17 ♖d1 ♘xd5 18 ♘d3 ♕f5 followed by 19...♘e3.

3) 17 ♖c1 ♘xd5 18 ♘d3 ♕e7 19 ♔f2 (19 c4 ♘f4!) 19...♘f4! 20 ♖he1 ♕c5+! 21 ♘xc5 ♖xd2 22 ♘e4 ♖xe2+ 23 ♖xe2 ♘xe2 24 ♘d6+ ♔d7 25 ♖d1 ♘xc3 26 ♖d2 ♖e2+ 27 ♖xe2 ♘xe2 and wins.

4) 17 ♔f1 ♘xd5 18 ♘xd5 ♖xd5 19 ♕c2 ♕e3 20 ♖d1 ♖xd1+ 21 ♕xd1 ♖d8 22 ♕e1 ♖d2 and again Black wins.

17...♘xd5 18 ♘d3 ♘xc3 (D)

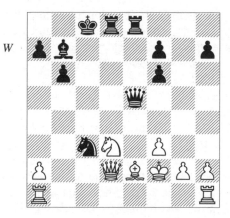

0-1

In view of 19 ♗f1 ♕d4+ 20 ♔g3 ♖g8+ 21 ♔h3 ♗xf3! 22 gxf3 ♖d5 or 19 ♖he1 ♕d4+ 20 ♔f1 ♖xe2 21 ♖xe2 ♘xe2.

Game 71
Mihai Suba – Gyula Sax
Budapest Zonal 1993
Nimzo-Indian Defence, Rubinstein Variation

1 d4 ♘f6 2 c4 e6 3 ♘c3 ♗b4 4 e3 0-0 5 ♗d3 d5 6 ♘e2

A popular system for White.

6...dxc4 7 ♗xc4 e5

This is a relatively uncommon response. Black usually plays ...c5, either here or without exchanging on c4.

8 ♕b3?! *(D)*

The normal moves here are 8 a3 and 8 0-0, but not 8 dxe5?! ♕xd1+ 9 ♔xd1 ♘g4 regaining the pawn and displacing White's king. The text-move appears tempting, attacking the bishop and exerting pressure along the newly opened diagonal from b3 to f7, but the queen turns out to be misplaced and soon has to move again.

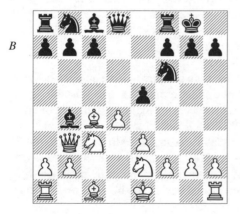

8...exd4

8...♘c6 is also playable.

9 ♘xd4

Black also equalizes after the other captures; e.g., 9 exd4 ♘c6 or 9 ♕xb4 ♘c6 10 ♕c5 dxc3 11 ♘xc3 ♕d7 12 ♕h5 ♘de5.

9...c5 10 ♘f3

After 10 ♘c2 ♘c6 both 11 ♗e2 ♗e6 12 ♕a4 a6 and 11 ♘xb4 ♘a5! favour Black.

10...♘c6 *(D)*

White must lose a tempo to meet the threat of 11...♘a5.

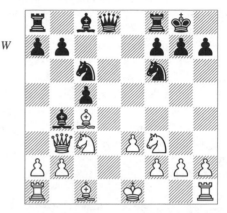

11 ♕c2 ♗g4 12 ♗d2 ♕d7

White's position is already slightly uncomfortable. He cannot castle kingside, because ...♗xf3 would expose his king too much, but castling queenside in the face of Black's pawn-majority also poses some risk.

13 a3 ♗a5 14 0-0-0

14 0-0? ♗xf3 15 gxf3 ♘e5 16 ♗e2 ♕h3, for example, clearly favours Black.

14...♗f5 *(D)*

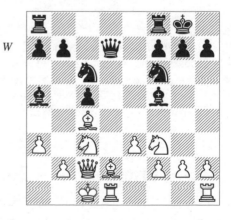

Now that White has castled queenside, the bishop serves little purpose on g4, so Black repositions it with gain of time.

15 ♕b3?

Leaving Black's bishop undisputed master of the diagonal from f5 to b1 poses a permanent danger to White's king. It would have been better to play 15 e4, which should hold the balance; e.g., 15...♘d4!? (15...♗g6 16 ♗g5 ♕g4 17 ♗xf6 ♕f4+ 18 ♔b1 ♕xf6 19 ♘d5 is unclear) 16 ♘xd4 and now Black should probably prefer safe equality by 16...♕xd4 17 ♗xf7+ ♖xf7 18 exf5 ♕xf2 to the double-edged 16...cxd4 17 exf5 ♖ac8 18 ♘d5 (18 ♗b5? dxc3! 19 ♗xd7 cxd2+ and 18 ♕b3? dxc3 19 ♗xc3 ♕xf5 are very good for Black, while 18 ♘b5 ♖xc4 19 ♕xc4 ♖c8 20 b3 and 18 b3 dxc3 19 ♗xc3 ♕e7 are unclear) 18...♘xd5 19 ♗xa5 ♖xc4 20 ♕xc4 ♖c8 21 ♖xd4, when White may have a slight advantage.

15...♕e7 *(D)*

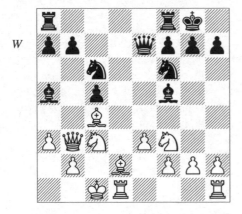

16 ♘d5?!

Black is slightly better after both 16 ♖he1 ♘e4 17 ♘d5 ♕d6 and 16 ♘h4 ♗g4 17 f3 ♗xc3 18 ♕xc3 (or 18 ♗xc3 ♕xe3+ 19 ♔b1 ♗e6) 18...♘e4! 19 fxe4 ♕xh4 20 ♖df1 ♕e7. However, the text-move is even worse for White.

16...♘xd5 17 ♗xd5 *(D)*

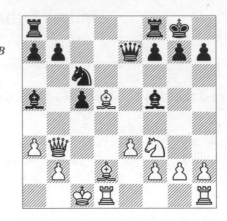

17...c4!

If the c-file were to be opened, then the white king's situation would be really serious.

18 ♕a4

Allowing Black a forced win, but the alternatives were dismal: 18 ♕xc4 and 18 ♗xc4 both lose to 18...♖ac8, while 18 ♕a2 ♗xd2+ 19 ♘xd2 (19 ♖xd2 ♘a5 20 ♘d4 ♕c5! 21 ♘xf5 ♘b3+ wins for Black) 19...♘e5 gives Black a large advantage.

18...b5!

Black is also happy to have an open b-file! It is White's misfortune that Black is able to advance his queenside majority with gain of time.

19 ♕xb5 ♖ab8 20 ♕xc6

20 ♕a4 loses to 20...♕f6 21 ♘d4 ♘xd4 22 exd4 ♗xd2+ 23 ♖xd2 c3, while 20 ♕xc4 ♕xa3! 21 ♕a2 gives Black a choice of attractive wins: either 21...♖xb2! 22 ♕xb2 ♖b8 or 21...♘d4! 22 ♘xd4 ♖fc8+.

20...♕xa3 0-1

It is mate in a few moves; e.g., 21 bxa3 ♖b1# or 21 ♗c3 ♗xc3.

Game 72

Eric Lobron – Zurab Azmaiparashvili

Groningen PCA Qualifier 1993

Modern Defence

1 d4 d6 2 e4 g6 3 ♘c3 ♗g7 4 f4 ♘c6

Quite a popular line for Black; he avoids 4...♘f6, which would transpose to the Pirc, and steers the game into independent channels.

5 ♗b5!? *(D)*

An interesting alternative to the usual 5 ♗e3. White solves the problem of the attack on d4, albeit at the cost of surrendering the two bishops.

B

5...a6

With 5...♗d7 Black can avoid the doubling of his c-pawns, but at the cost of losing time.

6 ♗xc6+ bxc6 7 ♘f3 ♗g4

Black is willing to surrender the two bishops in order to exert pressure against d4. White also has an edge after other moves; e.g., 7...♘f6 8 0-0 or 7...f5 8 e5 ♘h6 9 ♕e2.

8 0-0 ♕b8

8...♘f6 9 h3 ♗xf3 10 ♕xf3 is clearly better for White.

9 h3 ♗xf3 10 ♖xf3 ♕b6 11 ♗e3!

The critical move, offering the b-pawn. 11 ♘e2 c5 is equal.

11...♕xb2 *(D)*

If White is allowed to complete his development then he will have the advantage thanks to his pawn-centre, so this is the consistent move. 11...♘f6 12 ♗f2 0-0 13 ♕d2 gives White an edge; e.g., 13...♕xb2 14 ♖b1 ♕a3 15 e5 ♘d7 16 ♘d5 ♕xa2 17 ♘xe7+ ♔h8 18 ♖b7.

12 ♗f2 ♕b7

Not 12...♘f6? 13 ♖b1 ♕a3 14 ♘d5 ♕a5 15 ♗e1 and wins, while 12...♕b4 13 ♖b1 ♕c4 14 ♖b7 gives White a strong initiative.

13 f5! c5?!

Freeing the d5-square for the knight makes White's attack even stronger. 13...♘f6?! is also dubious after 14 e5 ♘d7 15 f6! exf6 16 exf6 ♗xf6 (16...♘xf6 17 ♗h4 ♘g8 18 ♕e2+ ♔f8

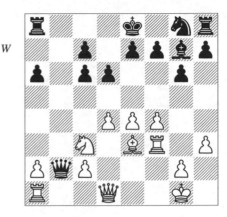

W

19 ♖af1 and White wins) 17 ♕e2+ ♔f8 18 ♖f1 with terrible pressure along the f-file. However, 13...♘h6 is better. After 14 g4 the knight is out of play, but 14...f6 15 ♘e2 ♘f7 offers Black some defensive chances.

14 ♖b1 ♕c6 15 ♘d5 *(D)*

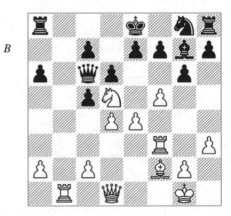

B

15...♘f6

After 15...gxf5 (15...e6 16 fxe6 fxe6 17 ♘f4 ♕e4 18 d5 and White wins) 16 ♖xf5! e6 17 ♖xf7!! ♔xf7 18 ♕h5+ ♔f8 19 ♖f1 White has a very promising attack. The main line runs 19...exd5 20 ♗h4+ ♘f6 21 ♗xf6 ♗xf6 22 ♕h6+! ♔e8 (22...♔g8? loses to 23 ♖xf6 ♕e8 24 ♕g5+ ♕g6 25 ♖xg6+ hxg6 26 ♕xg6+) 23 ♕xf6 ♔d7 24 ♕g7+ ♔c8 25 ♕xh8+ ♔b7 26 ♖b1+ ♔a7 27 ♕xh7 and White is much better.

16 c4! ♔f8

16...♘xd5 (16...♘d7 17 ♘xe7! ♔xe7 18 d5 traps the queen) 17 exd5 ♕d7 18 dxc5 dxc5 19 ♗xc5 0-0 20 ♕e2 also favours White.

17 e5! *(D)*

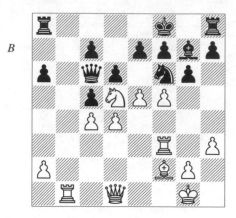

This second pawn sacrifice aims to trap Black's king on the back rank.

17...♘xd5 18 cxd5 ♕xd5 19 f6 ♗h6

19...exf6 20 exf6 ♗h6 21 ♖fb3 transposes to the following note.

20 ♖fb3 ♖d8?

Losing immediately, but with such a bad king position it is hard to see Black surviving. The key line is 20...exf6 (20...♖e8 21 ♖b8 ♕c6 22 d5 ♕d7 23 exd6 and White wins after 23...exd6 24 ♕e2 or 23...cxd6 24 ♖1b7) 21 exf6 ♔g8 (21...♖e8 22 ♖b8 ♕e6 23 ♕g4 ♖g8 24 ♖xe8+ ♕xe8 25 ♕h4 ♗d2 26 ♖b2 ♗c1 27 ♖c2 traps the bishop) 22 ♖b8+ ♗f8 23 ♕e2 and now:

1) 23...h6 24 ♕e7 ♔h7 25 ♖xa8! ♗xe7 26 ♖xh8+ ♔xh8 27 fxe7 ♕a8 28 dxc5 ♕e8 29 cxd6 cxd6 and White should win in the long run, e.g. by 30 ♖b7, followed by playing the bishop to d6 and the rook to b8.

2) 23...♖xb8 24 ♖xb8 ♕e6 25 ♕f3 d5 (after 25...h6? 26 ♕a8 White wins at once) 26 dxc5 h5 (26...♕e5 27 ♗g3 ♕d4+ 28 ♔f2 ♕d1+ 29 ♔h2 and now either 29...h5 30 ♗xc7 ♔h7 31 ♖b7, taking aim at f7, or 29...♕h5 30 ♖xf8+ ♔xf8 31 ♕b2 mating) 27 ♖d8 ♔h7 (27...c6? loses to 28 ♕f4) 28 ♕xd5! ♕xd5 29 ♖xd5 g5 30 ♖d7 ♔g6 31 ♖xc7 with a winning endgame for White.

21 ♖b8 dxe5 22 ♕f3! *(D)*

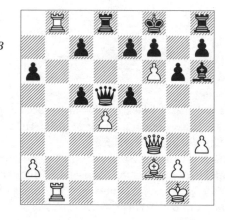

1-0

This finishes the game; e.g., 22...e4 23 ♕xe4 or 22...♕d7 23 ♕a8 ♔e8 24 ♖xd8+ ♕xd8 25 ♖b8.

Game 73
Andrei Sokolov – Alexei Shirov
French Team Ch 1994
Modern Defence

1 e4 g6 2 ♘c3 ♗g7 3 f4

A very unusual move. Black can, of course, transpose to the Sicilian with 3...c5, but Shirov pursues an independent course.

3...c6 4 ♕f3?! *(D)*

This is inaccurate; the aim is to prevent ...d5, but it turns out that Black can play it in any case. In return for the pawn, Black obtains a dangerous lead in development. 4 ♗c4 d5 5 exd5 b5 6 ♗b3 b4 7 ♘ce2 cxd5 is also good for Black, but 4 g3 d5 5 ♗g2 would have been a better chance.

4...d5!

Equalizing immediately.

5 d3

5 exd5 ♘f6 6 dxc6 (6 ♗c4 0-0 7 ♘ge2 ♗g4 8 ♕g3 b5 9 ♗b3 b4 is awkward for White) 6...♘xc6 7 ♗b5 ♗d7 8 ♗xc6 ♗xc6 gives Black excellent play for the pawn.

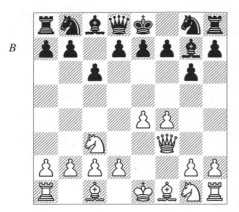

5...♘f6 6 h3

This non-developing move is perhaps a little slow. 6 e5 ♘g4 7 h3 ♘h6 8 g4 f6, with an unclear position, would have been more active.

6...e5! *(D)*

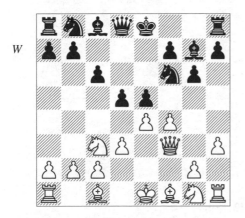

Black opens the position to exploit his lead in development.

7 f5

A double-edged move, which allows Black to take command of the centre. 7 fxe5 is safer, and after 7...dxe4 (7...♘fd7 8 d4 c5 9 ♗e3 is less clear, since 9...cxd4 10 ♗xd4 ♘c6? fails to 11 e6) 8 ♘xe4 (8 dxe4 ♘fd7 slightly favours Black) 8...♘xe4 9 ♕xe4 ♗f5 10 ♕e2 ♕a5+ 11 ♗d2 ♕xe5 an equal endgame arises.

7...gxf5 8 exf5 0-0

If White had time, the advance of his g-pawn would give him a crushing attack, but his own king is exposed.

9 ♘ge2?

Too casual. Having committed himself to the kingside attack, White should have pushed ahead without delay. 9 g4 e4 10 ♕g2 is unclear after 10...♖e8 11 d4 c5 12 g5 ♘fd7 13 ♘xd5 or 10...exd3 11 ♗xd3 ♖e8+ 12 ♘ge2 d4 13 ♘d1.

9...e4! *(D)*

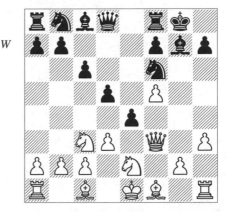

Seizing the initiative.

10 ♕f2

10 dxe4 dxe4 11 ♘xe4 ♘xe4 12 ♕xe4 ♖e8 13 ♕f3 ♘d7 is very good for Black.

10...exd3 11 cxd3 ♖e8

Threatening 12...d4.

12 ♔d1

White is in trouble whatever he plays. There is now no time for 12 g4 in view of 12...d4 13 ♘d1 ♘d5 14 g5 ♕a5+ 15 ♗d2 ♘b4 winning for Black. Also after 12 d4 c5! 13 ♗e3 cxd4 14 ♗xd4 ♘c6 15 0-0-0 ♘xd4 16 ♘xd4 ♘e4 17 ♘xe4 ♖xe4 White's position is crumbling. Finally, 12 ♗e3 ♗xf5 wins a pawn while retaining the initiative.

12...♘bd7? *(D)*

This lets White back into the game. Shirov points out that 12...c5! is stronger; for example, 13 ♕xc5 (or else 13...d4) 13...♗xf5 14 ♘d4 (14 ♗g5? ♘fd7! 15 ♗xd8 ♘xc5 wins material) 14...♗g6 with a large advantage for Black.

13 g4 ♘e5 14 ♘g3

Now White has managed to glue his position back together, and threatens to resume his kingside pawn advance.

14...d4 15 ♘ce4 ♘d5 16 ♖h2?

Too slow. 16 ♘h5! was the only chance. After 16...♘c4! 17 ♗g5 (17 dxc4? ♘e3+ 18 ♔d2

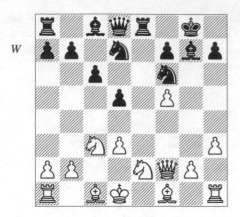

W

ℤxe4 is good for Black) 17...♘ce3+ 18 ♔c1 ♕a5 the position is roughly balanced.

16...b6

Preparing to take aim at White's weak d3-pawn.

17 ♘h5 ♗a6 *(D)*

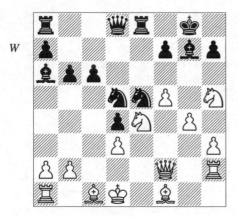

W

18 ♕xd4

18 ♗g5 loses to 18...f6 19 ♗h4 ♘xd3, while 18 ♘xg7 ♔xg7 19 ♕xd4 c5 leads to disaster along the d-file.

18...ℤh8!

Quite suddenly White is lost. His king is trapped by the crossfire of Black's bishops and the pressure along the central files.

19 f6

Or 19 ♗g5 ♘f3! 20 ♗xd8 ♗xd4 winning material.

19...c5 20 ♕f2 ♘xd3 21 ♕h4 ♘f2+

21...ℤxe4 also wins.

22 ♔c2 *(D)*

Allows mate, but it no longer matters since 22 ♔e1 (or 22 ♘xf2 ♘e3++ 23 ♔e1 ♘c2#) 22...♘xe4 23 ♗xa6 ♘b4 24 ♗e2 ♘c2+ 25 ♔f1 ♘xa1 picks up a rook.

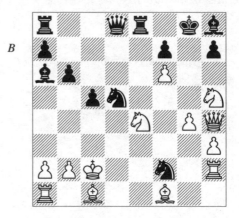

B

22...♘b4+ 0-1

Mate is forced in a few moves; one line runs 23 ♔b3 ♕d1+ 24 ♔a3 ♘c2+ 25 ♔b3 c4+ 26 ♗xc4 ♗xc4+ 27 ♔xc4 ♕d3#.

Game 74

Michael Adams – Sergei Tiviakov

PCA Candidates (2), New York 1994

Sicilian Defence, Moscow Variation

1 e4 c5 2 ♘f3 d6 3 ♗b5+ ♘c6 4 0-0 ♗g4?!

4...♗d7 is the most common alternative.

5 h3 ♗h5 6 c3 ♕b6 7 ♘a3 a6 8 ♗a4

8 ♗e2 is also promising.

8...♕c7 9 d4 b5?! *(D)*

Consistent, but the sacrifice that this invites turns out to be good for White.

10 ♘xb5! axb5 11 ♗xb5 0-0-0

11...♕b6 12 a4 does not help as Black is forced to castle in any case.

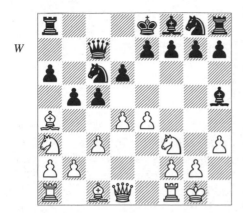

12 b4!

A powerful novelty. 12 ♕a4 ♘b8 13 dxc5 ♗xf3 14 gxf3 dxc5 led to a draw in Iskov-Larsen, Copenhagen 1979. Adams's move is stronger since it opens more lines on the queenside.

12...♗xf3 13 gxf3! *(D)*

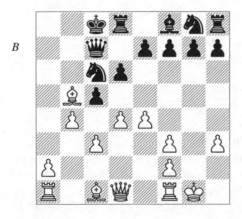

The queen is heading for a4.

13...♘b8

Not 13...cxb4? 14 cxb4 ♘xb4 15 ♕a4 ♕c3 16 ♕a8+ ♔c7 17 ♕a7+ ♔c8 18 ♗d2 and White wins.

14 ♕a4

White delays exchanging pawns on c5, in order to cut out the defensive resource ...♖d6.

14...c4

A desperate attempt to keep the queenside files closed. 14...e6 loses to 15 bxc5 dxc5 16 ♖b1 ♖d6 (or else 17 ♗a6+ wins) 17 ♗f4.

15 d5! ♘f6

Or 15...e5 16 ♗c6 ♘xc6 (16...♘e7 17 b5) 17 dxc6 ♘e7 18 b5 with a winning attack.

16 ♗e3 ♘fd7 *(D)*

16...e6 17 ♗c6 is similar.

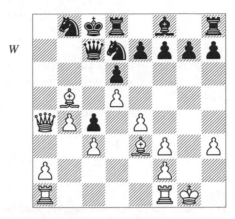

17 ♗c6 e6 18 b5 exd5 19 exd5 ♘b6

19...♘c5 20 ♕a8 h5 21 ♖fb1 ♕b6 22 a4 and 19...♘xc6 20 bxc6 ♘b8 21 ♖ab1 are hopeless for Black.

20 ♕b4 *(D)*

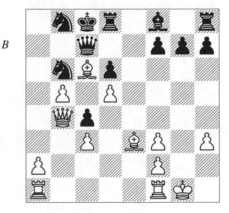

With the simple threat of a4-a5.

20...♗e7

20...♘xc6 21 bxc6 ♘xd5 loses to 22 ♕a4.

21 a4 ♗f6 22 a5 ♘xc6 23 bxc6 ♘xd5 24 ♕b5 ♖dc8

24...♘xc3 25 ♕a6+ ♔b8 26 ♖ab1+ mates.

25 ♗b6 1-0

As 25...♘xb6 (25...♕e7 26 ♕a6+ ♔b8 27 ♗c7+! mates in a few moves) 26 axb6 ♕b8 27 ♕a6+ is decisive.

Game 75

Vladimir Akopian – Igor Khenkin

Tilburg 1994

Sicilian Defence

1 e4 c5 2 ᐃf3 e6 3 b3

Black should not underestimate this unusual line, since it contains a certain amount of venom.

3...a6 4 ᐃb2 ᐃc6 5 c4

5 g3 and 5 d4 are other possibilities.

5...f6

After this game, 5...f6 does not seem to have been repeated. 5...d6 is a more solid and popular option.

6 ᐃe2

6 d4 cxd4 7 ᐃxd4 ᐃb4+ 8 ᐃd2 ᐃge7 is equal.

6...ᐃh6 (D)

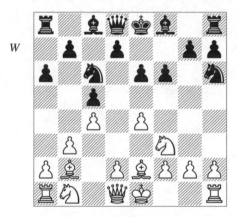

7 0-0

Now that White has castled, 8 d4 is a threat, reaching a favourable type of Hedgehog position in which Black's pieces are on very odd squares.

7...e5

Hence this move, despite the loss of time involved.

8 ᐃh4

White seeks to exploit Black's languid development by playing for a quick attack.

8...ᐃd6

Aimed against f4, but blocking in Black's queenside.

9 ᐃh5+

9 ᐃf5!? ᐃxf5 10 exf5 0-0 11 ᐃc3 gives White a safe edge in view of Black's vulnerable central light squares. The text-move is more ambitious, but also more risky.

9...g6 (D)

9...ᐃf7 10 ᐃc3 0-0 11 ᐃd5, with ideas of ᐃf5, ᐃg4 and f4 to come, gives White a clear advantage.

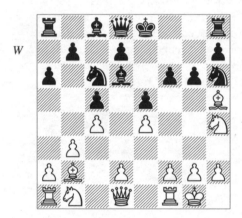

10 ᐃxg6+!?

The point of the check on h5. White obtains two pawns and an enduring attack for the piece.

10...hxg6 11 ᐃxg6 ᐃg8

11...ᐃf7 12 ᐃh5 ᐃg7 13 ᐃxh8 ᐃxh8 14 ᐃc3, followed by ᐃd5 and f4, is also unpleasant for Black.

12 ᐃh5 ᐃf7 13 f4!

Preventing the defence ...ᐃe7, which meets other attacking ideas; e.g., 13 ᐃh7? ᐃe7 14 ᐃxe7 ᐃh8 15 ᐃg7 ᐃxe7 or 13 ᐃc3?! ᐃe7! 14 ᐃxe7 ᐃxe7 15 f4 d6 and Black has some advantage in either case.

13...exf4

Best, as 13...ᐃe7 14 ᐃxe5! ᐃxe5 15 fxe5 ᐃh8 16 ᐃf3 ᐃc7 17 ᐃf4 clearly favours White, while 13...ᐃg7 14 ᐃc3 followed by ᐃd5 is awkward for Black.

14 ᐃc3 (D)

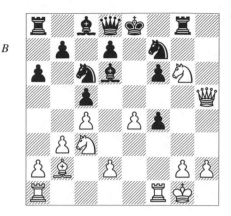

14...♗e5!

At first sight this is a complete answer to White's attack, since it nullifies the dangerous b2-bishop. Black's problems are not solved by 14...♘e7 15 ♘xe7 ♗xe7 16 ♘d5, followed by 17 ♖xf4, nor by 14...♘ce5 15 ♘xf4 (not 15 ♘d5? ♖xg6 16 ♗xe5 ♖g5 and Black wins) 15...♖h8 (15...♖g5 16 ♕h7) 16 ♕e2 b5 17 ♘h5 ♗b7 18 ♘xf6+ ♔f8 19 ♘cd5 and White has the advantage thanks to the three pawns for the piece and the continuing threats against Black's king.

15 ♖xf4!! (D)

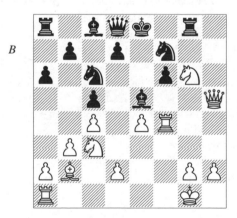

A brilliant answer, reviving White's threats. White must conquer the key square f6, regardless of material loss.

15...♗xf4

Or 15...♖xg6 (15...d6 16 ♖af1 ♗xf4 17 ♘d5 ♘ce5 18 ♘dxf4 transposes to the game, while 15...♗d4+ 16 ♔h1 ♘ce5 is met by 17 ♘xe5

♗xe5 18 ♖af1! with a strong attack) 16 ♕xg6 ♘e7 (16...♗xf4 17 ♘d5 wins for White after 17...♘e7 18 ♘xf6+ ♔f8 19 ♘h7+ ♔e8 20 ♕g7! or 17...♗h6 18 ♕g8+ ♗f8 19 ♗xf6) 17 ♕g7! ♗xf4 (17...f5 18 ♕g3 d6 19 ♖af1 favours White) 18 ♘d5 ♘xd5 (18...♗e5 19 ♗xe5 ♘xd5 20 ♗d6 ♘xd6 21 exd5 wins for White) 19 exd5 ♕e7 (19...d6 20 ♗xf6 and 19...♗e5 20 d6! ♘xd6 21 ♗xe5 fxe5 22 ♖f1 are lost for Black) 20 ♗xf6 and now:

1) 20...♗e5 21 ♖e1 ♕f8 (21...d6 22 ♖xe5 and 21...♗d4+ 22 ♔f1 are winning for White) 22 ♕g6 d6 23 ♗xe5 dxe5 24 ♖xe5+ ♔d7 25 ♕f6 wins as Black is paralysed.

2) 20...♕f8 21 ♖e1+ ♘e5 22 ♕g6+ ♕f7 23 ♕f5 ♗xh2+ 24 ♔xh2 d6 25 ♕g5 and after the capture on e5 White will have three pawns and a strong attack for the piece.

16 ♘d5 (D)

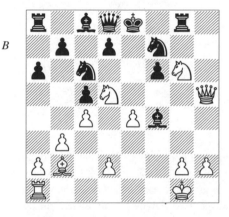

16...♘ce5!

The best chance. 16...♗g5? just loses after 17 h4! d6 18 hxg5 ♗g4 19 ♕h7, while after 16...♗e5? 17 ♗xe5 ♘cxe5 (17...fxe5 18 ♕h7 ♖xg6 19 ♖f1 and White wins) 18 ♘xe5 fxe5 19 ♖f1 ♖f8 (19...♕g5 20 ♕xf7+ ♔d8 21 ♕f8+ mates, while 19...♖xg2+ 20 ♔xg2 ♕g5+ 21 ♕xg5 ♘xg5 22 ♘c7+ gains material) 20 ♖xf7 ♖xf7 21 ♖xe5+ ♕e7 (21...♔f8 22 ♕h8#) 22 ♘xe7 ♖xe7 23 ♕h8+ ♔f7 24 ♕h5+ ♔f8 25 ♕xc5 White has the advantage. It will cost Black another pawn to liberate his queenside, and the armada of white pawns will be hard to resist.

17 ♘dxf4

Threatening 18 ♗xe5 fxe5 19 ♕h7, trapping the rook on g8. The alternatives are inferior, since 17 ♘gxf4?! ♖h8! 18 ♕f5 d6 19 ♘xf6+ ♔f8 offers White a draw at best, while after 17 ♗xe5?! fxe5 18 ♕h7 ♖xg6 19 ♕xg6 ♕g5 20 ♘c7+ ♔f8 21 ♕xg5 ♗xg5 22 ♘xa8 ♗d8 Black traps the knight and secures a material advantage.

17...d6

17...♖g7 18 ♖f1 d6 transposes to the game, while 17...♘xg6?! 18 ♘xg6 ♖g7 19 ♖f1 gives White a distinct advantage.

18 ♖f1 (D)

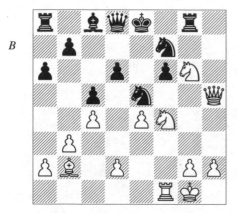

18...♖g7

This is a perfectly good move if followed up accurately, but 18...♖xg6 19 ♘xg6 ♗e6 was a simpler alternative, with a very unclear position. White has two pawns for the piece, but he has not yet conquered the f6-square, so Black can hope to defend. On the other hand, 18...♗d7? loses to 19 ♗xe5 dxe5 20 ♘d5.

19 ♗xe5 fxe5

White wins after 19...dxe5? 20 ♘d5 f5 21 exf5.

20 ♘d5 (D)

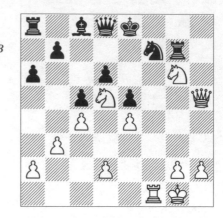

20...♔d7??

The unrelenting pressure finally takes its toll and Black collapses totally. He could still have held on by 20...♕g5! 21 ♕xg5 ♘xg5 22 ♖f8+ ♔d7 23 ♘b6+ and now:

1) 23...♔c6? 24 ♘xa8 ♗d7 (24...♗e6 25 ♖f6) 25 ♖g8! ♘h3+ (25...♖xg8? 26 ♘e7#; 25...♖f7 26 ♘xe5+ dxe5 27 ♖xg5 should win as Black is a long way from rounding up the knight) 26 ♔f1 ♖f7+ 27 ♔e1 ♘f4 (27...♘f2 28 ♘xe5+ dxe5 29 ♖g6+ wins for White) 28 ♘xf4 ♖xf4 29 d3 and the two connected passed pawns should decide, despite the oddly-placed knight on a8.

2) 23...♔e6! 24 ♘h4 (24 ♘xa8 ♖xg6 25 ♖xc8 ♘f3+ 26 ♔h1 ♘xd2 is unclear) 24...♖b8 (24...♔e7 is also satisfactory for Black) 25 ♘f5 ♖g6 26 ♖e8+ ♔f7 27 ♖xc8 ♖xc8 28 ♘xc8 ♘xe4 29 d3 ♘g5 30 ♘cxd6+ ♔e6 with a complicated and unclear ending.

21 ♕f5+ ♔e8

21...♔c6 22 ♘ge7+ wins the queen.

22 ♘f6+ 1-0

Game 76

Hugo Spangenberg – Lubomir Ftačnik

Moscow Olympiad 1994

Sicilian Defence, Grand Prix Attack

1 e4 c5 2 ♘c3 d6 3 f4 g6 4 ♘f3 ♗g7 5 ♗c4 e6 6 0-0 ♘e7 7 d3 ♘bc6 8 f5

8 ♕e1 is more popular, and has been used by players such as Anand, Short, Macieja and

Sutovsky. Anand-Gelfand, Wijk aan Zee 1996 is a fine example of White's strategy.

8...d5 9 ♗b3 dxe4 (D)

9...gxf5 10 exd5 exd5 is also very unclear.

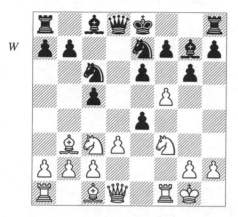

10 fxg6!?

This extremely dangerous piece sacrifice was an innovation. Many players would have collapsed quickly when confronted by such a surprise, but Ftačnik reacts calmly. White has various alternatives:

1) 10 fxe6? exf3 11 exf7+ ♔f8 12 ♕xf3 ♘d4 is clearly better for Black.

2) 10 dxe4?! ♕xd1 11 ♖xd1 gxf5 gives Black an edge.

3) 10 f6!? is an interesting pawn sacrifice; after either 10...exf3 11 fxg7 ♕d4+ 12 ♖f2 ♕xg7 13 ♕xf3 or 10...♗xf6 11 ♘xe4 ♗g7 12 ♗g5 White obtains considerable dark-squared pressure in return for the pawn.

10...exf3

Black must accept the piece as 10...hxg6 11 ♘xe4 b6 12 ♗g5 and 10...fxg6 11 ♘xe4 give White an excellent position without any material sacrifice.

11 gxf7+

11 ♕xf3? f5 defends.

11...♔f8

Not 11...♔xf7? 12 ♕xf3+ and White wins.

12 ♕xf3 (D)

White has good compensation for the piece in the form of two pawns and a dangerous attack.

12...♕d4+

Black intends to reinforce his defence by swinging his queen to the kingside. 12...♘d4

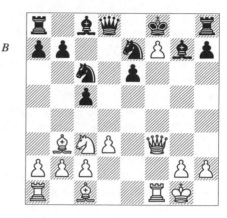

13 ♕h5 ♘ef5 14 ♘e4 looks dangerous for Black, but 12...♘f5!? is a possible alternative.

13 ♔h1

After 13 ♗e3 ♕xe3+! 14 ♕xe3 ♗d4 15 ♖ae1 ♗xe3+ (15...♔g7 16 ♘b5! ♗xe3+ 17 ♖xe3 is a little better for White) 16 ♖xe3 ♘d4 17 ♘e4 the position is unclear.

13...♘e5 14 ♕e2

14 ♕h5 ♕g4 15 ♕xg4 ♘xg4 16 ♘e4 b6 is slightly better for Black, but 14 ♕g3!? is playable, with a totally unclear position after 14...c4 (but not 14...♘f5? losing to 15 ♖xf5! exf5 16 ♗e3).

14...♕g4 (D)

14...♘f5?! (not 14...♘xf7? 15 ♗xe6 and wins) 15 ♘b5! ♕h4 16 ♗f4 is dangerous for Black.

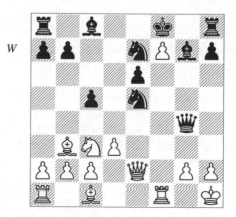

15 ♕f2

15 ♕xg4 ♘xg4 16 ♘e4 b6 transposes into the note to White's 14th move.

15...b6

Not 15...♘f5?, losing to 16 ♕xc5+ ♔xf7 17 d4. The text-move not only saves the c5-pawn, but also offers the prospect of eventual counterplay on the long diagonal.

16 h3!

16 ♗f4? ♗b7 (now h3 is no longer possible) 17 ♖ae1 ♘f3! 18 gxf3 ♕xf4 19 ♗xe6 ♖d8 is good for Black.

16...♕g6 17 ♗f4 ♗b7 (D)

The best move, since this bishop belongs on the long diagonal to provide counterplay against the white king. After 17...♘7c6?! (17...♘xf7? loses to 18 ♕f3!) 18 ♖ae1 ♗d7 (18...♘xf7 19 ♕f3 ♗d7 20 ♗xe6! ♗xe6 21 ♕xc6 wins for White) 19 ♖e3! h6 20 ♖g3 ♕h5 21 ♘e4 all White's pieces are in play and it is impossible to imagine Black surviving for long.

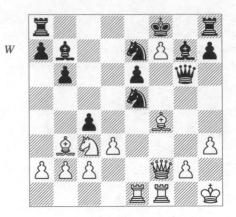

2) 19 ♗xc4?! ♘xc4 20 dxc4 ♔xf7 is also doubtful for White – although this looks dangerous for Black, in reality the discovered checks are ineffective.

3) 19 ♗xe5 (this leads to a safe endgame advantage) 19...♗xe5 (19...cxb3 20 ♗xg7+ ♕xg7 21 axb3 ♘f5 22 ♔h2 is better for White) 20 ♖xe5 cxb3 21 ♘e2! ♖c8 22 ♘f4 (22 c3 is met by 22...♖c5) 22...♗xg2+ 23 ♕xg2 ♕xg2+ 24 ♔xg2 ♖xc2+ 25 ♔g3 ♔xf7 26 ♘xe6+ ♔e8 27 ♘g7+ ♔d7 28 axb3 with a favourable ending for White, although Black retains some drawing chances.

19...♘xf7 (D)

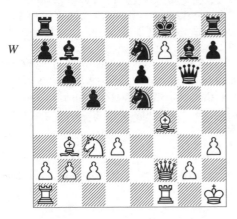

18 ♖ae1

White's pressure threatens to become overwhelming, hence Black's next move.

18...c4 (D)

Offering a pawn in order to neutralize White's dangerous light-squared bishop, at least temporarily. After 18...♘7c6 (not 18...♘xf7? 19 ♖xe6, winning) 19 ♖e3, heading for g3, White has very dangerous threats.

19 dxc4

Up to here White has conducted his attack accurately and indeed had a choice of good continuations at this point. The alternatives were:

1) 19 ♖xe5?! is wrong as 19...cxb3 20 ♖g5 ♕f6! offers Black good defensive chances.

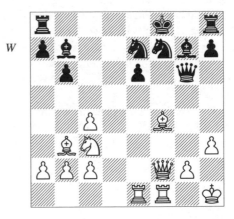

Black must have breathed a sigh of relief as this pawn vanished from the board.

20 ♘b5?

A critical turning point; this move wins material, but loses the initiative. White should have played 20 c5!, bringing the b3-bishop back to life. After 20...♗d4 21 ♕d2! ♗xc3 22 bxc3 ♘d5 23 ♗e5 Black faces serious difficulties.

20...♘f5 21 ♘c7 ♖e8! *(D)*

This sacrifice is the start of a beautiful counterattack. 21...e5 is less accurate as 22 ♔h2 ♖c8 23 ♘d5 favours White.

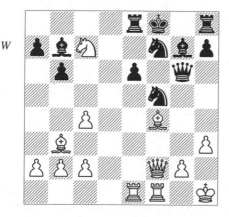

W

22 ♘xe8

There is nothing better than to accept, as 22 c3 ♖e7 and 22 c5 ♗d4 23 ♕d2 e5 clearly favour Black.

22...♗d4! 23 ♕d2?

By this point White has clearly lost the thread, and now makes a further error which meets with a stunning refutation. He could still have held the game with 23 ♕e2 ♖g8 24 ♘c7 ♗xg2+ (24...e5 25 ♖f3! is fine for White) 25

♔h2, when Black has nothing better than 25...♗xf1! 26 ♘xe6+ ♕xe6 27 ♕xe6 ♖g2+ 28 ♔h1 ♖g1+ with a draw by perpetual check.

23...♖g8 24 ♖e2 ♕g3!! *(D)*

A stunning blow which leaves White helpless. 24...♘g3+ would be less accurate due to 25 ♗xg3 ♕xg3 26 ♖xf7+! ♔xf7 27 ♘d6+! ♕xd6 28 c3 ♗c5 (28...♗f3 29 ♖f2!) 29 ♕xd6 ♗xd6 30 c5, when White is out of trouble.

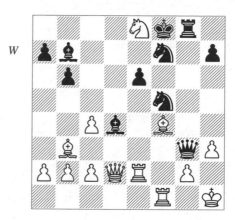

W

0-1

White is quite defenceless, e.g.:

1) 25 ♕xd4 ♕xh3+ 26 ♔h2 ♗xg2+.

2) 25 ♗h6+ ♔xe8 26 ♗a4+ ♔e7.

3) 25 ♗xg3 ♘xg3+ 26 ♔h2 ♘xf1+ 27 ♔h1 ♘xd2 28 ♖xd2 ♗e3 29 ♖e2 ♖g3.

4) 25 ♕b4+ ♔xe8 26 ♖xe6+ ♔d8 27 ♗xg3 ♘xg3+ 28 ♔h2 ♘xf1+ 29 ♔h1 ♗xg2#.

Game 77

Ilia Smirin – Boris Alterman

Haifa 1995

Petroff Defence

1 e4 e5 2 ♘f3 ♘f6 3 d4 ♘xe4 4 dxe5

This unusual alternative to 4 ♗d3 is normally thought to be harmless.

4...d5 5 ♘bd2 ♗e7

5...♘c5 is generally reckoned to equalize.

6 ♗b5+

An interesting idea, although objectively speaking White should probably play 6 ♘xe4 dxe4 7 ♕xd8+ ♗xd8 8 ♘g5 with an edge.

6...c6 7 ♗d3 ♘c5 8 ♗e2 ♗g4?! *(D)*

A slightly unwise move. Black should have played either 8...0-0 9 0-0 ♘bd7 or 8...♗e6 followed by ...c5 and ...♘c6, with excellent equalizing chances in either case.

9 ♘d4! ♗xe2 10 ♕xe2

White has gained time, and freed his f-pawn for a possible kingside attack.

10...♘bd7 11 0-0 ♘e6

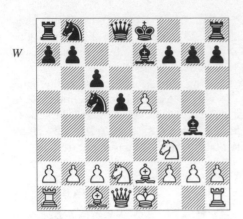

11...0-0 12 f4 ♘e6 13 ♘4b3, followed by f5, favours White.

12 ♘xe6 fxe6 13 ♕g4

White forces the pace before Black has time to castle.

13...♘xe5 14 ♕xg7 ♘g6 15 ♘f3 ♔d7!? (D)

15...♕d6 16 ♘g5 ♗xg5 17 ♗xg5 ♕d7 18 ♕h6 is slightly better for White as Black's king is pinned down in the centre.

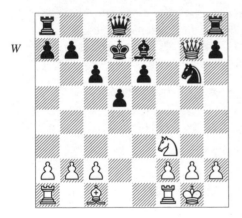

16 c4

If Black is given time, he will develop an attack along the open kingside files, so White must act quickly.

16...♕g8?!

It's really the h8-rook and not the queen which belongs on g8, so Black should have played 16...♕f8 17 ♕c3 ♖g8. After 18 cxd5 (18 ♖e1? ♗b4 19 ♕b3 dxc4! is fine for Black) 18...exd5 19 ♘d4 White has an edge but certainly not more.

17 ♕d4 (D)

17 ♕c3 ♖f8 18 ♗h6 ♖f7 19 cxd5 exd5 20 ♖ae1 is also favourable for White.

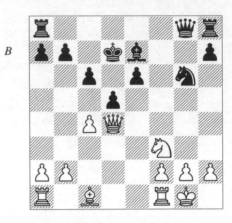

17...♖f8

17...♗d6 is a better chance, although White retains the advantage by 18 cxd5 exd5 19 ♗h6.

18 ♕xa7?!

White takes up the challenge, but although the play now becomes very complicated, it is not necessarily favourable for White. The simple 18 cxd5 exd5 19 ♗h6 ♖f5 20 ♖fe1 would have left White with a safe positional advantage in view of Black's exposed king and the blocked-in rook on h8.

18...♖xf3 19 ♕xb7+ ♔d6

19...♔d8 loses to 20 ♕b8+ ♔d7 21 ♕xg8 ♖xg8 22 gxf3.

20 ♖e1! (D)

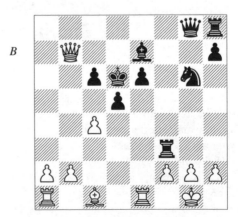

Cutting off the king's escape route.

20...e5!

Freeing e6 for the king. After 20...罝d3 21 c5+ 含xc5 22 兔d2! or 20...兔h4 21 c5+ 含xc5 22 兔e3+ 罝xe3 23 罝ac1+ 含d6 24 罝xc6+ White wins easily.

21 b3 *(D)*

21 c5+ 含e6 22 豐xc6+ 含f5 23 豐d7+ 含f6 is unclear.

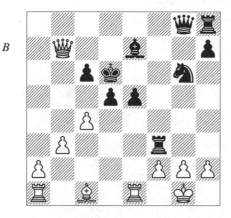

21...罝d3!

A good defence. The alternatives are:

1) 21...含e6? 22 豐xc6+ 含f5 23 cxd5 罝d3 (23...ᴺh4 loses to 24 罝xe5+! 含xe5 25 兔b2+) 24 d6! 罝xd6 25 豐e4+ 含f6 26 f4! 豐d5 27 fxe5+ ᴺxe5 28 豐f4+ 含e6 29 罝xe5+ 豐xe5 30 豐xe5+ 含xe5 31 兔b2+ and White wins.

2) 21...ᴺf4? 22 兔a3+ c5 23 兔xc5+ 含xc5 24 豐c7+ 含b4 25 a3+ 含xb3 26 豐b6+ with a quick mate.

3) 21...罝f6! is also possible and, just as after the text-move, it is hard for White to prove an advantage.

22 兔a3+ c5? *(D)*

After this White wins by force. 22...含e6 is the correct defence and after 23 cxd5+ 罝xd5 (not 23...cxd5? 24 豐a6+) 24 豐xc6+ 兔d6 (24...含f5?! 25 罝xe7 ᴺxe7 26 豐c3 with three pawns and a continuing attack for the piece) 25 罝ad1 ᴺf4! (25...豐a8 26 豐xd5+ 豐xd5 27 罝xd5 兔xa3 28 罝a5 and White wins) 26 g3 ᴺc2! 27 含h1! ᴺd4 28 罝xe5+ 含xe5 29 兔xd6+ 含f5 30 g4+! Black has two possibilities:

1) 30...含f6 31 罝xd4 (31 兔e5++ 含xe5 32 罝e1+ 含f4 33 豐f6+ ᴺf5 34 gxf5 looks like a draw) 31...罝xd4 32 兔c5+ 含g5 33 兔xd4 豐a8

and, although White is better, Black has defensive chances in view of his active king position.

2) 30...含xg4! 31 豐d7+ (31 罝g1+ 含f5 is a draw) 31...含h5 32 豐h3+ 含g6 33 罝g1+ 罝g5 34 罝xg5+ 含xg5 35 豐e3+ 含h5 36 豐xd4 豐a8+ 37 含g1 罝g8+ 38 兔g3 豐xa2 and a draw is very likely.

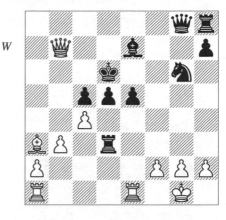

23 兔xc5+!

This sacrifice signals the start of a spectacular finish.

23...含xc5 *(D)*

23...含e6 24 兔xe7 ᴺxe7 25 罝xe5+ 含xe5 26 豐xe7+ gives White a winning attack after 26...含d4 27 豐f6+ 含c5 28 b4+ or 26...含f5 27 罝e1.

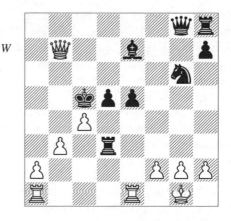

24 罝ac1!

There are other wins, but this is one of the most convincing.

24...dxc4

Everything loses: 24...♔d6 25 c5+ ♔e6 26 ♕a6+ ♔f7 27 ♕xd3, 24...♗g5 25 cxd5+! ♗xc1 26 ♖xc1+, 24...d4 25 ♕c7+ ♔b4 26 ♕b6+ ♔a3 27 ♕a5+ ♔b2 28 ♖b1+ ♔c2 29 ♖ec1# or

24...♔d4 25 cxd5 ♕xd5 26 ♕a7+ ♗c5 27 ♕a4+ mating.

25 ♖xc4+ 1-0

As 25...♕xc4 26 ♕c7+ wins the queen and the rook.

Game 78
Judit Polgar – Alexei Shirov
Amsterdam (Donner Memorial) 1995
Modern Defence

1 e4 g6 2 d4 ♗g7 3 ♘c3 c6 4 ♗c4 d6 5 ♕f3

This primitive-looking continuation is actually quite dangerous for Black.

5...e6 6 ♘ge2 b5 7 ♗b3 a5 *(D)*

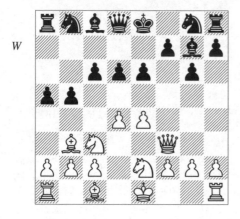

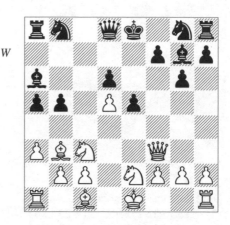

The critical line, in which Black attempts to inconvenience the light-squared bishop. The danger is that Black delays his development and if White can open the position, then Black may easily find himself in trouble.

8 a3 ♗a6 9 d5!?

Typically, Judit plays for a direct attack to exploit Black's lagging development. 9 0-0 is a reasonable alternative which has been used in some more recent games.

9...cxd5

9...exd5 10 exd5 c5 has received little attention, but it appears playable for Black.

10 exd5 e5 *(D)*

The position betrays a familiar story – Black has been willing to fall behind in development in order to gain strategic assets (here the better

pawn-structure). If he can complete his development then he will probably gain the advantage, but first he must survive the next few moves.

11 ♘e4 ♕c7?

Not 11...f5? 12 ♘g5 heading for e6, nor 11...♘f6? 12 ♗g5 winning material, but the move played is also poor since it does nothing to advance the development of Black's kingside. The correct line is 11...h6 preparing ...♘f6; after 12 g4 ♘f6 13 ♘2g3 ♘xe4 14 ♘xe4 0-0 15 ♕h3 f5!? a very unclear and double-edged position arises.

12 c4! *(D)*

White wastes no time with her attack. This move aims to gain a4 for the b3-bishop.

12...bxc4

12...♘d7 13 ♘2c3 bxc4 14 ♗a4 transposes to the game, while 12...♘e7 13 c5 and 12...a4 13 cxb5 ♗xb5 14 ♘2c3! ♗d7 15 ♗c4 favour White.

13 ♗a4+ ♘d7

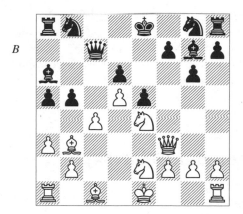

13...♔e7 14 ♘2c3 is similar to the game.

14 ♘2c3 ♔e7?

A serious error, overlooking the tactical refutation. 14...♘e7? is also bad due to 15 ♗xd7+ ♕xd7 16 ♗h6 ♔f8 17 ♗xg7+ ♔xg7 18 ♕f6+ ♔g8 19 ♘xd6 and White wins, while 14...♔f8 15 ♗c6 ♖b8 16 a4, creating an outpost at b5, gives White some advantage. 14...h6!? was the best chance. After 15 ♘b5 ♗xb5 16 ♗xb5 f5 17 ♘d2 White has some advantage, but Black is not without counterplay.

15 ♘xd6! *(D)*

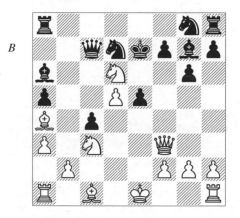

An unexpected tactical blow.

15...♕xd6

Forced, since the alternatives 15...♔xd6? 16 ♘e4+ ♔xd5 (16...♔e7 17 d6+) 17 ♕xf7+ ♔xe4 18 ♗c2+ ♔d4 19 ♗e3# and 15...f5 16 ♘xf5+ gxf5 17 d6+ ♕xd6 18 ♕xa8 ♘gf6 19 ♕a7 are even less appealing.

16 ♘e4 ♕xd5

White wins after 16...♕b8 17 ♗xd7 f5 18 ♗xf5 gxf5 19 ♕xf5 or 16...♕b6 17 d6+ ♔f8 18 ♘g5, attacking a8 and f7.

17 ♗g5+ *(D)*

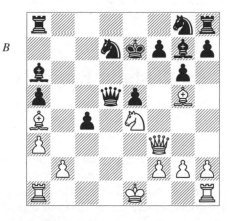

17...♘df6

The only move, as 17...f6 loses to 18 ♖d1 ♗b7 (18...♕xd1+ 19 ♕xd1) 19 ♖xd5 ♗xd5 20 ♕d1! ♘b6 21 ♗e3 when, in addition to his material disadvantage, Black's king is fatally exposed.

18 ♖d1 ♕b7

18...♕e6 19 ♘c5 ♕c8 20 ♕d5 gives White a winning attack.

19 ♖d7+ ♕xd7 20 ♗xd7 *(D)*

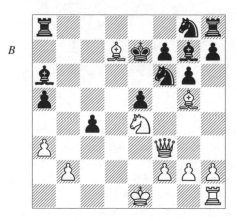

20...h6?

Black collapses. The only chance to fight on lay in 20...♗b7, after which 21 ♗a4 ♔f8 (21...h6 22 ♗e3! hxg5 23 ♕c5+ ♔e6 24 ♕b6+ ♔f5 25 ♘d6+ leads to a quick mate) 22 ♗c2 gives White a large advantage, due not so much to his small material plus but rather to the very awkward position of Black's king. In fact 21 a4! may be even stronger, as 21...h6 loses to 22 ♗b5! hxg5 23 ♕a3+ ♔d8 24 ♕d6+ ♔c8 25 ♘c5 ♖a7 26 ♘d7! forcing mate.

21 ♕d1! 1-0

Black cannot defend d6, and so loses after 21...hxg5 22 ♕d6+ ♔d8 23 ♗b5+ ♔c8 24 ♕c6+ ♔b8 (24...♔d8 25 ♕b6+ ♔c8 26 ♘d6#) 25 ♕b6+ ♗b7 (25...♔c8 26 ♘d6#) 26 ♘d6 ♖a7 27 ♕d8+ ♗c8 28 ♕xc8#.

Game 79
Vladimir Kramnik – Alexander Beliavsky
Belgrade 1995
Réti Opening

1 ♘f3 d5 2 g3 c6 3 ♗g2 ♗g4 4 0-0 ♘d7 5 d4

An interesting system in which White departs from pure King's Indian Attack strategy (which would involve d3 and e4) and tries to turn the game into a kind of reversed Torre Attack.

5...e6 6 ♘bd2 (D)

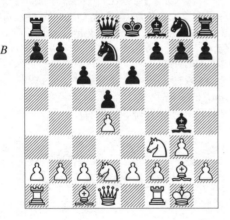

6...f5

An ambitious attempt to clamp down on White's e4, exploiting the fact that Black has not yet played ...♘gf6. After 6...♘gf6 we would indeed have a reversed Torre.

7 c4 ♗d6 8 ♕b3 ♖b8

8...♕b6? 9 ♕e3! wins a pawn.

9 ♖e1 (D)

Black has gone to great lengths to prevent White's e4, but this plan has cost him time, created weaknesses and left his king in the centre. If White were now to play slowly, Black would catch up in development and castle with a fine

position. However, Kramnik has no intention of playing slowly! 9 cxd5 exd5 10 ♕d3!? is another interesting attempt to disrupt Black's development.

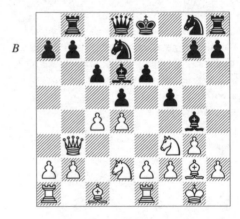

9...♘h6

9...♕e7 is the alternative, when White can play for the advantage with either 10 h3 ♗h5 11 cxd5 cxd5 12 g4! or 10 ♘e5! ♘xe5 (10...♗h5 may be better) 11 dxe5 ♗xe5 12 cxd5 exd5 13 e4! fxe4 14 ♘xe4 dxe4 15 ♖xe4 ♘f6 16 ♗g5, when Black faces difficulties, Tkachev-Tregubov, Wijk aan Zee 1995. Note that 9...♘gf6 10 ♘g5 ♕e7 11 f3 ♗h5 12 e4 is clearly unfavourable for Black.

10 cxd5 cxd5

10...exd5 11 e4 certainly favours White.

11 h3!

An innovation. 11 ♘e5 ♘xe5 12 dxe5 ♗c7 led to nothing in Hug-Speelman, Altensteig 1994.

11...♗h5 (D)

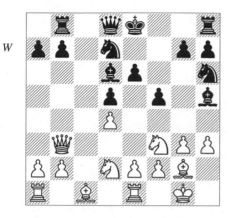

W

12 e4!!

If you spend a lot of time trying to stop your opponent doing something, and then he manages to do it anyway, then you are almost always in trouble. The text-move is the first in a series of hammer-blows shattering Black's position.

12...fxe4

12...dxe4 13 ♘g5 ♗f7 14 ♘dxe4 fxe4 15 ♘xe6 transposes to the game, while 12...♗xf3 13 ♗xf3 fxe4 14 ♘xe4 dxe4 15 ♕xe6+ ♕e7 (15...♗e7 loses to 16 ♗xh6 exf3 17 ♗xg7) 16 ♖xe4 ♔d8 17 ♕d5 is clearly better for White.

13 ♘g5! (D)

13 ♘xe4 dxe4 14 ♗xh6 gxh6 15 ♕xe6+ ♕e7 16 ♖xe4 ♔d8 is less convincing.

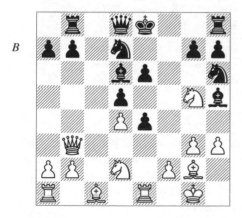

B

13...♗f7

Other moves are even worse; for example, 13...♕xg5 14 ♘xe4 ♕e7 15 ♗g5 ♘f6 (15...♕f8

16 ♕xd5! exd5 17 ♘xd6#) 16 ♘xd6+ ♕xd6 17 ♗f4 ♕d8 18 ♖xe6+ ♔f7 19 ♖d6 or 13...♕e7 14 ♘xe6! ♕xe6 (14...♘f6 15 ♗xe4 dxe4 16 ♘xe4 ♘xe4 17 ♖xe4 and 14...♗f7 15 ♘xe4 dxe4 16 ♖xe4 are also lost) 15 ♖xe4 ♗e5 16 ♖e1, and Black's position is hopeless in both cases.

14 ♘dxe4! dxe4

14...♗e7 15 ♘xf7 ♘xf7 16 ♘c3 ♘f8 17 ♗f4 is winning.

15 ♘xe6 (D)

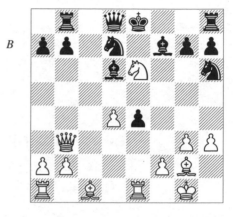

B

15...♗xe6

There are several other moves, but none offers a way out for Black: 15...♕e7 16 ♖xe4 ♗e5 17 ♘xg7+ ♔f8 (or 17...♔d8 18 ♕a4) 18 ♗xh6! ♗xb3 19 ♘f5+, 15...♘g8 16 ♖xe4 ♗xe6 17 ♖xe6+ ♗e7 18 ♗f4, 15...♘f5 16 ♖xe4 ♗e7 17 ♗f4 ♖c8 18 ♖ae1 or finally 15...♕f6 16 ♖xe4 ♗e7 17 ♗f4.

16 ♕xe6+ (D)

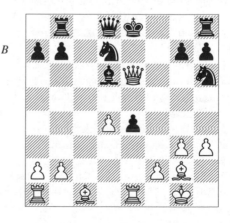

B

16...♕e7

16...♗e7 17 ♗f4 ♖c8 18 ♗xe4 ♘f8 19 ♕b3 gives White a decisive attack.

17 ♖xe4 ♔d8

After 17...♕xe6 18 ♖xe6+ ♗e7 19 ♗xh6 ♔f7 20 ♖xe7+ ♔xe7 21 ♗xg7 White has three pawns and a large positional advantage for the exchange.

18 ♕d5 (D)

In fact 18 ♕b3 would be a more accurate finish, when Black cannot even reach an ending.

1-0

Black's resignation comes slightly early, although he is in fact lost: 18...♘f6 (18...♕f8 19 ♗g5+ ♘f6 20 ♖ae1 is crushing) 19 ♖xe7 ♘xd5 20 ♖e6 ♘f5 21 ♗xd5 ♘xd4 22 ♖xd6+ ♔e7 23

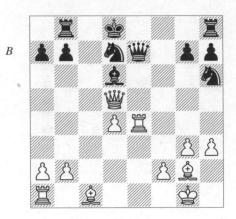

♗g2 ♔xd6 24 ♗f4+ ♔e6 25 ♖e1+ ♔f7 26 ♗d5+ ♔g6 27 ♗xb8 ♖xb8 26 ♖e7 gives White an easily winning ending.

Game 80

Vladimir Kramnik – Jaan Ehlvest

Riga (Tal Memorial) 1995

Queen's Gambit, Semi-Slav Defence

1 ♘f3 d5 2 d4 ♘f6 3 c4 c6 4 ♘c3 e6 5 ♗g5 dxc4 6 e4 b5 7 e5 h6 8 ♗h4 g5 9 ♘xg5 hxg5 10 ♗xg5 ♘bd7

This is the notorious Botvinnik System, one of the sharpest and most complex lines in modern-day opening praxis. Only the very bravest venture down these paths, especially when confronting a noted expert such as Kramnik.

11 g3

11 exf6 is the most common move. Playing g3 first is an attempted finesse of move-order; White hopes to restrict Black's options, but there are both pros and cons to this sequence.

11...♕a5 (D)

11...♗b7 is more to the point if Black hopes to transpose into the main line, while 11...♖g8 attempts to exploit White's unusual move-order.

12 exf6 ♗a6

12...b4 is now considered the correct response, with a very unclear position.

13 ♕f3

13 a3 is also promising, stifling Black's queenside play. However, Kramnik prefers to play directly for the attack.

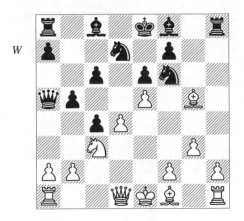

13...♖c8?!

An attempt to steer the game into uncharted territory. 13...b4 is the main line, but according to current theory this is less effective than a move earlier and does not equalize.

14 ♗e2 (D)

14...b4

14...c5 15 d5 ♗b7 16 0-0 b4 17 ♕e3! is very good for White.

15 ♘e4 c5 16 d5!

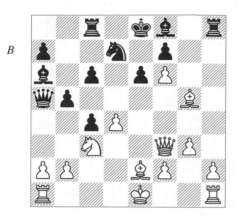

Kramnik's improvement on 16 dxc5 ♘xc5 17 ♘xc5 ♗xc5 18 0-0 ♗d4, which led to a draw in I.Sokolov-Kamsky, Belgrade 1991.

16...exd5 17 ♕f5! *(D)*

17 0-0!? was also successful in Oskulski-Tombette, corr. 1995, but Kramnik's move appears more forcing.

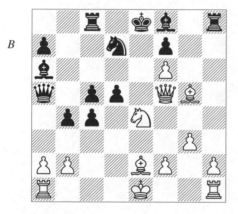

17...dxe4

17...d4? 18 ♗g4 followed by 0-0 and ♖fe1 gives White an enormous attack, while after 17...c3 White can gain a clear advantage by either 18 ♕xd5 ♗e2 (18...cxb2 19 ♖d1 b3+ 20 ♗d2 ♕b6 21 ♘g5 ♕xf6 22 ♗xa6 and White wins) 19 ♔xe2 cxb2 20 ♖ae1 or 18 ♗g4 ♕b5 (18...♗b5 19 ♕xd5 cxb2 20 ♖d1 is also very good for White) 19 ♕xd5 cxb2 (19...♗b7 20 ♘d6+ wins for White) 20 ♖d1.

18 0-0-0

In return for the piece White has an extremely dangerous attack.

18...♖c7

18...♕c7 loses to 19 ♖he1! ♗b7 20 ♗xc4 ♗c6 21 ♖xe4+ ♗xe4 22 ♕xe4+ ♕e5 23 ♕b7 ♕c7 24 ♗xf7+ ♔d8 25 ♕e4 and Black is defenceless.

19 ♗g4! *(D)*

Increasing the pressure against d7 is even stronger than 19 ♕xe4+ ♔d8.

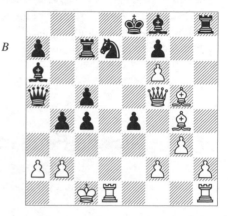

19...♗b5

There is no defence; for example, 19...♕xa2 20 ♖xd7 ♕a1+ 21 ♔d2 ♕xb2+ 22 ♔e3 ♕c3+ (22...♕d4+ 23 ♖xd4 cxd4+ 24 ♔d2 c3+ 25 ♔c1 and Black is too slow with his pawns) 23 ♔f4 ♗b7 24 ♖hd1 and White wins.

20 ♕xe4+ ♔d8 *(D)*

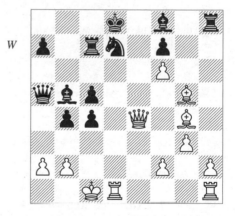

21 ♗xd7 ♗xd7

The alternative 21...♖xd7 fails to 22 ♗f4! ♕a6 (White also wins after 22...♖d3 23 ♕a8+ ♔d7 24 ♖he1) 23 ♕a8+ ♕c8 24 ♕xa7 ♖xd1+

25 ♖xd1+ ♗d7 26 ♕b6+ ♔e8 27 ♗c7! and there is no answer to the threat of 28 ♖e1+ ♗e6 29 ♕c6+ ♕d7 30 ♕a8+.

22 ♖he1 ♗h6

22...♗d6 (22...♔c8 23 ♕a8#) 23 ♖xd6 ♕xa2 24 ♕a8+ ♖c8 25 ♖xd7+ mates.

23 ♕a8+ ♖c8 (D)

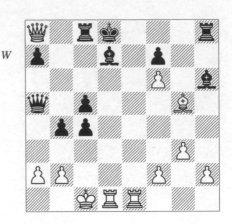

24 ♖xd7+! ♔xd7 25 ♕d5+ 1-0

As mate follows after 25...♔c7 26 ♖e7+ ♔b6 27 ♕b7#. This game is a good example of modern 'power chess'. Kramnik combined excellent opening preparation with dynamic and incisive play. Although Ehlvest is a strong grandmaster, he lost this game without really having a chance.

Game 81

Nick de Firmian – Robert Hübner

Polanica Zdroj 1995
French Defence, Classical Variation

1 e4 e6 2 d4 d5 3 ♘c3 ♘f6 4 e5 ♘fd7 5 f4 c5 6 ♘f3 ♘c6 7 ♗e3 cxd4 8 ♘xd4 ♕b6 9 ♕d2 ♕xb2

This line is similar to the Sicilian Poisoned Pawn: Black grabs a pawn and some dark squares, but faces an enduring attack.

10 ♖b1 ♕a3 11 ♗b5 ♘xd4 12 ♗xd4 ♗b4

Now White must choose between two continuations.

13 ♖b3

13 0-0 is the current preference, although the text-move is still seen occasionally.

13...♕a5 14 a3 ♗e7

Not 14...♗xa3? 15 ♘xd5 ♕xd2+ 16 ♔xd2 exd5 17 ♖xa3, when White has strong pressure for the pawn.

15 f5!?

15 ♕e3 0-0 16 0-0 is slower, but also quite dangerous.

15...exf5 16 ♘xd5 (D)

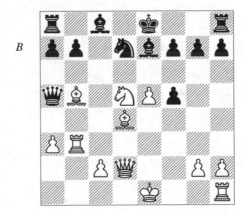

16...♗h4+!?

16...♕xd2+ 17 ♔xd2 ♗d8 transposes into the note to Black's 17th move.

17 ♔d1

17 g3 ♕xd2+ 18 ♔xd2 ♗d8 is fine for Black as ♖g3 is no longer possible.

17...♕d8?

This loses by force. 17...♕xd2+ 18 ♔xd2 ♗d8! 19 ♖g3 (19 c4 was tried in Nijboer-Porat, Cappelle la Grande 2006, but although White won this game, Nijboer's innovation was very unconvincing) 19...a6 20 ♗xd7+ ♗xd7 21 ♖xg7 offers White only a faint edge. In attempting to avoid this, Hübner makes a fatal error.

18 ♘f6+! (D)

This sacrifice wins by force. White even had a second very strong continuation in 18 ♗c5.

18...gxf6

Or 18...♗xf6 19 exf6 0-0 (19...gxf6 20 ♖e1+ ♔f8 21 ♕h6+ and White wins) 20 ♗xd7 ♕xd7

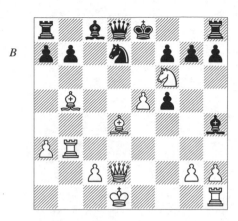

B

21 Rg3 Rd8 (21...g6 22 ♔c1 f4 23 ♕xf4 ♔h8 24 ♕h6 Rg8 25 Rh3 is also decisive) 22 Rxg7+ ♔h8 23 Re1 with a winning attack for White.

19 exf6 0-0

Now White has a forced mate in six, but there was nothing better; e.g., 19...♗xf6 20 Re1+ ♗e7 21 ♗xh8, 19...h6 20 ♕b4 f4 21 g3 or 19...a6 20 Re1+ ♗xe1 21 ♕xe1+ ♔f8 22 ♕b4+.

20 Rg3+! ♔h8 21 ♕h6 *(D)*

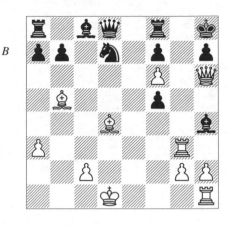

B

21...Rg8

Or 21...♗xf6 22 ♕g7+! ♗xg7 23 ♗xg7+ ♔g8 24 ♗f6#.

22 Rg7 ♘f8 1-0

In view of mate in two by 23 Rxg8+ ♔xg8 24 ♕g7#.

Game 82

Leonid Yurtaev – Yuri Shulman

Vladivostok 1995

King's Indian Defence

1 d4 ♘f6 2 c4 g6 3 ♘c3 ♗g7 4 e4 d6 5 ♘f3 0-0 6 ♗e2 e5 7 d5 a5 8 h3 ♘a6 9 g4!?

An unusual and ambitious move instead of the standard 9 ♗g5.

9...♘c5 10 ♕c2 c6 11 ♗e3 a4!?

An innovation. Previously, 11...cxd5 had been played.

12 0-0-0 *(D)*

12 dxc6 bxc6 13 0-0-0 ♕c7 14 ♗xc5 dxc5 15 g5 ♘h5 16 ♘xa4 wins a pawn, but after 16...♘f4 Black has good compensation.

12...cxd5 13 cxd5

13 ♗xc5 dxc5 14 cxd5 ♘e8 is unclear.

13...♕a5 14 ♘d2 ♗d7

White must act quickly, or else ...b5-b4 will be very strong.

15 g5?

15 ♘c4 is better. After 15...♕c7 16 g5 ♘h5 17 ♗xh5 gxh5 the position is double-edged.

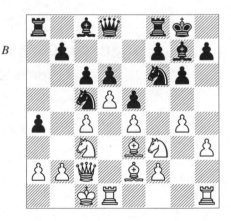

B

15...♘fxe4! *(D)*

A well-calculated and unexpected sacrifice. The opening of the diagonals leading to White's king turns out to give Black a near-decisive attack.

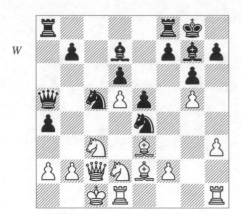

16 ⎔dxe4

Of course, anything is better than a forced loss, but the alternatives are also fairly bad for White:

1) 16 ⎔c4 ⎔xc3 17 ⎔xa5 ⎔xa2+ 18 ⎔d2 ⎔xa5 gives Black excellent compensation for the queen.

2) 16 ⎔cxe4 ⎔xe4 17 ⎔c4 ⎔d8! 18 ⎔xe4 ⎔f5 19 ⎔h4 b5 20 ⎔b6 ⎔c8+ 21 ⎔d2 (21 ⎔xc8 ⎔c7+ 22 ⎔c4 ⎔xc8 favours Black) 21...⎔b8 22 ⎔g4 (22 ⎔c1 ⎔xb6 23 ⎔xb6 ⎔xb6 24 ⎔c6 ⎔a5+ is also good for Black) 22...⎔xb6 23 ⎔xf5 gxf5 24 ⎔xb6 ⎔xb6 gives Black excellent compensation.

16...⎔xe4 17 ⎔xe4

17 ⎔xe4 ⎔fc8 18 ⎔c3 a3 wins for Black.

17...⎔f5 18 ⎔h4

Or 18 ⎔c4 ⎔fc8 19 ⎔b5 ⎔xc3+! mating.

18...⎔fc8 19 ⎔d2 *(D)*

19 ⎔d2 a3 20 b4 ⎔a4 mates.

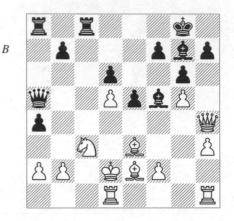

19...⎔xc3!

Crushing.

20 bxc3 ⎔xd5+ 21 ⎔d3

21 ⎔c1 ⎔xa2 22 ⎔d3 ⎔xd3 23 ⎔xd3 ⎔a1+ wins for Black.

21...⎔xd3 22 ⎔b4

Or 22 ⎔c1 ⎔xa2.

22...⎔f1+ 23 ⎔c1 ⎔xh1 24 ⎔xd6 ⎔xh3

0-1

Game 83

Miguel Illescas – Matthew Sadler

Linares Zonal 1995

Queen's Gambit Accepted

1 d4 d5 2 c4 dxc4 3 e4 ⎔c6 4 ⎔e3 ⎔f6 5 ⎔c3

5 f3 is an alternative.

5...e5 6 d5 ⎔a5!

The critical line, making White fight to regain the c4-pawn.

7 ⎔f3 ⎔d6!?

An innovation; hitherto, 7...a6 and 7...⎔g4 had been played.

8 ⎔a4+ ⎔d7!

The remarkable point of Black's previous move, offering a piece as early as move eight.

9 ⎔xa5 a6 *(D)*

Black threatens to win the queen by 10...b6. In order to extract her majesty, White must make a major concession.

10 ⎔b1??

Shocked by the sacrifice, White immediately goes wrong. The alternatives are:

1) 10 b4 keeps the piece, but at a heavy cost: 10...b6 11 ⎔a3 a5 12 ⎔c1 axb4 13 ⎔e2 ⎔xe4!? (13...b5 14 ⎔g3 ⎔g4 also looks uncomfortable for White) 14 ⎔xc4 f5 15 ⎔g3 (15 ⎔d2 ⎔f6 16 ⎔g5 h6 17 ⎔xf6 ⎔xf6 18 ⎔g3 e4

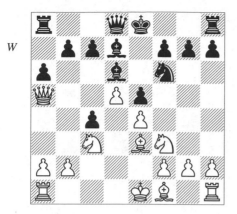

19 ℤb1 0-0 is unclear) 15...⊘c3 16 ♗g5 ♛c8 leads to a position in which it is not easy for White to complete his development.

2) 10 ⊘a4 ♛e7 (10...ℤb8!? 11 ⊘d2 b6 12 ⊘xb6 cxb6 13 ♛xa6 ⊘g4 is unclear) 11 a3 ⊘xe4 12 ♗xc4 b5 and now both 13 ♗b3 bxa4 14 ♗xa4 0-0 and 13 ♗d3 ⊘f6 14 ⊘c3 e4 15 ⊘xe4 ⊘xe4 16 0-0 0-0 17 ℤfe1 f5 are equal.

10...⊘xe4

Covering the queen's retreat.

11 ♚d1?

Another error, but even 11 b4 ♛e7 12 ⊘bd2 b6 13 ♛a3 ♗xb4 14 ♛c1 b5 gives Black three pawns and strong pressure for the piece.

11...c3! (D)

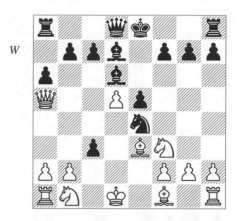

The queen is not to be allowed back.

0-1

12 b4 is the only chance, but even this fails to 12...b6 13 ♛a3 a5 14 ♗d3 (14 ♛c1 ♗a4+ 15 ♚e1 axb4 is just as bad) 14...axb4 15 ♛c1 ⊘c5 16 ♗xc5 ♗xc5, when White is dead lost.

Game 84
Georgy Timoshenko – Leonid Yudasin
St Petersburg 1996
Sicilian Defence, Scheveningen Variation

1 e4 c5 2 ⊘f3 d6 3 d4 cxd4 4 ⊘xd4 ⊘f6 5 ⊘c3 a6 6 ♗e2 e6 7 0-0 ♗e7 8 f4 0-0 9 ♚h1 ♛c7 10 a4 b6 11 ♗f3 ♗b7 12 f5

An unusual alternative to the main lines of 12 ♛e1 and 12 e5.

12...e5 13 ⊘de2 (D)

13 ⊘b3 has also been played, but without much success. The text-move appears more logical in that it is not obvious what the knight is doing on b3, while on e2 it has a future on the kingside.

13...⊘bd7 14 g4 h6

Slowing down the pawn advance but giving White the chance to open lines on the kingside. 14...d5 is the thematic central response to White's flank advance, but after 15 exd5 e4 16

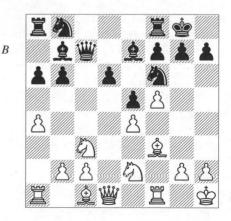

♗f4! (16 ⊘xe4 ⊘xd5 17 ♗g2 ℤad8 and 16 ♗g2 ⊘xg4 17 ⊘g3 ⊘df6 18 ⊘cxe4 ⊘xe4 19

♗xe4 ♘f6 give Black active play for the pawn) 16...♗d6 17 ♗xd6 ♕xd6 18 ♘xe4 ♘xe4 19 ♗xe4 Black was struggling to show compensation in A.Kovaliov-Navara, Krakow 2004.

15 g5

The conditions are particularly favourable for this advance. The bishop comes to g5 without a preliminary stop on e3, and the move ♔h1 makes it easy for White to occupy the g-file. 15 h4? ♘h7 16 ♕e1 ♕d8 is completely wrong as White must either sacrifice a pawn or see his kingside pawns totally blockaded.

15...hxg5 16 ♗xg5 (D)

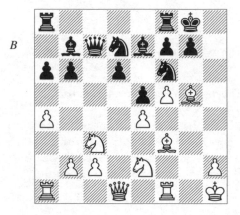

16...♖fe8

16...♖fc8 17 ♖g1 ♔f8 18 ♕e1 ♔e8 19 ♕h4 ♗f8 20 ♕h8 favoured White in Glek-Rodriguez Lopez, Budapest 1998.

17 ♘g3 ♖ad8?

Black realizes that he must generate counterplay quickly, or else White's kingside attack will become overwhelming. However, his plan of aiming for ...d5 is simply too slow. 17...b5!? is a quicker method of creating play; after 18 ♕d2 (or 18 axb5 axb5 19 ♖xa8 ♖xa8 20 ♘xb5 ♕c5 21 ♘c3 ♕b4 22 ♗c1 ♖a1 and Black has good play for the pawn) 18...b4 19 ♘d5 ♗xd5 20 exd5 ♖ac8 21 ♕f2 ♕c4! Black has sufficient counterplay to hold the balance.

18 ♕d2 d5 19 exd5 (D)

19...e4

A typical method of generating counterplay in the Sicilian, but it fails in this position because White's pieces are no less active than Black's. 19...♗b4 20 ♕g2! is good for White

since 20...♗xc3 21 bxc3 ♕xc3 loses to 22 ♘e4 ♘xe4 23 ♗xe4 f6 24 ♖g1!.

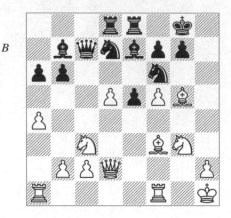

20 ♘gxe4 ♘xe4

20...♕e5 is refuted by 21 ♖ae1! ♘xe4 (White also wins after 21...♕xf5 22 ♗h5 ♕h7 23 ♗xf7+! ♔xf7 24 ♗xf6 or 21...♘xd5 22 ♗xe7 ♖xe7 23 ♘g3) 22 ♖xe4 ♗xg5 23 ♕xg5 and White remains two pawns up.

21 ♘xe4

21 ♗xe4 ♗xg5 22 ♕xg5 ♖xe4 23 ♖g1 g6 24 ♘xe4 ♗xd5 25 ♕e7 is also promising.

21...♘e5 (D)

Black attempts to solve his problems tactically, but runs foul of a mating attack. However, even after the superior 21...♗xg5 22 ♕xg5 (22 ♘xg5? ♘f6 23 ♖ae1 ♖f8 is less clear) 22...f6 (22...♕xc2 23 f6 and 22...♘e5 23 ♖g1 g6 24 ♕h6 win for White) 23 ♕g2 ♗xd5 24 ♖ad1 ♗xe4 25 ♗xe4, White has both an extra pawn and an attack.

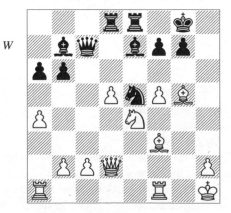

22 ♗xe7 ♘xf3

22...♕xe7 23 f6 gxf6 (23...♘xf3 24 fxe7) 24 ♕h6 and 22...♖xe7 23 f6! ♘xf3 24 ♕g2 g6 25 fxe7 ♕xe7 26 c4 are hopeless for Black.

23 ♘f6+! *(D)*

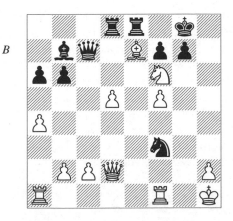

A killer blow.
23...gxf6

23...♔h8 24 ♖xf3 ♗xd5 25 ♕xd5 mates.

24 ♖xf3 ♗xd5

Or 24...♖xe7 25 ♕h6.

25 ♕g2+ *(D)*

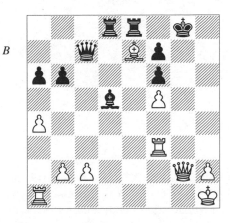

1-0

An attractive finish. The queen unpins the rook to deliver mate next move.

Game 85

Oleg Romanishin – Jaan Ehlvest

Biel 1996

Queen's Gambit Declined, Orthodox Defence

1 ♘f3 d5 2 d4 ♘f6 3 c4 e6 4 ♘c3 ♗e7 5 ♗g5 0-0 6 e3 ♘bd7 7 ♖c1 c6 8 ♗d3 a6 9 c5 *(D)*

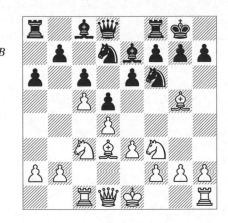

This position more often arises from the move-order 7...a6 8 c5 c6 9 ♗d3.

9...e5 10 dxe5 ♘e8 11 h4

The alternatives are 11 ♗f4 and 11 ♗xe7, with all three moves occurring about equally often.

11...♘xc5 12 ♗b1 ♘e6

12...f6 13 ♕c2 g6 14 ♗h6 ♘g7 15 h5 ♗f5 16 ♕e2 ♗xb1 17 ♖xb1 gives White a slight advantage, while 12...f5? loses to 13 ♘xd5! cxd5 14 ♖xc5.

13 ♕c2!? *(D)*

13 ♘d4 g6 gave White no advantage in Korchnoi-Agdestein, Tilburg 1989.

13...♘xg5

This is certainly risky, as it gives White the possibility of breaking open Black's kingside with a sacrifice. Although this sacrifice is not clearly correct, it is of a type which often succeeds in practice. 13...g6 (not 13...f5? 14 exf6 ♘xf6 15 ♗xf6) 14 ♗h6 ♘8g7 (14...♘6g7?! 15

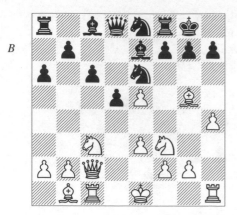

h5 &xf5 16 e4 dxe4 17 ⑤xe4 ♛a5+ 18 &d2 ♛d5 19 hxg6 &xg6 20 &c3 was slightly better for White in Izeta-Sulskis, Erevan Olympiad 1996) is a relatively safer defence for Black, after which 15 h5 ♖e8 16 hxg6 fxg6 17 ♖d1 ♛a5 was unclear in Lipinsky-Kharitonov, Berlin 1997. Even though Kharitonov eventually won this game, I would be very nervous playing this line with Black – White gets a strong attack without any sacrifice and Black's counterplay is rather slow to materialize.

14 ⑤xg5 g6 *(D)*

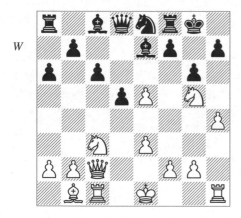

15 ⑤xh7!

At the very least, this poses many practical problems for Black.

15...&xh7

15...&f5? is worse because 16 e4 &xe4 17 ⑤xe4 &xh7 18 h5 dxe4 19 hxg6++ gives White an enormous attack; for example, 19...&g8 20 ♛xe4 ♛d5 (20...f5 21 ♛e3! and White wins)

21 ♛f5 ♖d8 22 0-0, with the deadly threat of 23 g7, or 19...&g7 20 ♖h7+ &g8 21 ♛xe4 ♛d5 (21...♛a5+ 22 ♖c3 wins for White) 22 ♛f5 ♖d8 23 &f1! and Black cannot meet the many threats (e.g. 24 ♛h5).

16 h5 &g7?

After this the attack breaks through quickly. However, it was not easy to choose the right defence from the various options. 16...&g8?! is also inferior because 17 hxg6 f5 18 ♛e2 ⑤g7 19 ♛f3 f4 (to prevent 20 ♛h3) 20 exf4 gives White three pawns for the piece and there is still the threat of transferring the queen to the h-file by ♛g3-h2. The best defence is 16...f5! and after 17 exf6 *(D)* (17 hxg6++ &xg6! is less dangerous for Black) there is a choice:

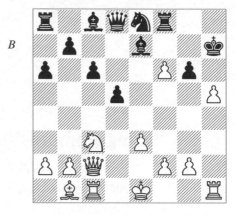

1) 17...⑤xf6 18 ♛xg6+ &h8 19 g4 &b4 (both 19...&xg4 20 ♖g1 ♛d7 21 ♛h6+ &g8 22 f3 and 19...d4 20 ♖d1 are good for White) 20 g5 ⑤e4 and it is doubtful if White has more than perpetual check.

2) 17...♖xf6 18 hxg6++ &g8 results in a position where White only needs to bring his queen to the h-file to finish the game. However, this is far from easy because Black's pieces cover the direct routes, so the position must be assessed as unclear.

17 hxg6

White has at least two deadly threats: 18 gxf7 and 18 ♖h7+ &g8 19 g7.

17...f5 18 ♛e2! *(D)*

Threatening both 19 ♛h5 and 19 ♖h7+ &g8 20 ♛h5. There is no reasonable defence.

18...&h4 19 g3 ♖h8 20 gxh4 ♖xh4 21 ♛f3

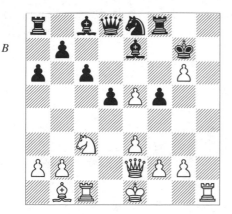

Black's king is too exposed to survive for long.

21...♘c7

21...♖xh1+ 22 ♕xh1 ♔xg6 23 ♔d2 is crushing.

22 ♔e2

The arrival of the other rook seals Black's fate.

22...♘e6

Or 22...d4 23 ♖xh4 ♕xh4 24 ♖h1 ♕g4 25 ♕xg4 fxg4 26 ♖h7+ ♔g8 27 ♘e4 and White wins.

23 ♖xh4 ♕xh4 24 ♖h1 *(D)*

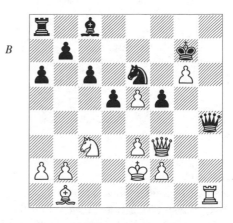

1-0

As 24...♕g4 25 ♖h7+ ♔g8 (25...♔xg6 26 ♕xg4+) 26 ♕xg4 fxg4 27 ♘a4 followed by ♘b6 ends any resistance.

Game 86

Tony Miles – Suat Atalik

Beijing 1996

Queen's Pawn

1 d4 ♘f6 2 c4 e6 3 ♘f3 c5 4 e3 g6 5 dxc5

5 ♘c3 is more common.

5...♘a6 6 ♘c3 ♘xc5

6...♗g7 7 ♕d6 ♕a5 (7...♗f8? 8 ♕e5!) 8 ♗d2 ♕xc5 9 ♘b5 gives White just an edge.

7 ♕d4!? d6 8 b4 e5 9 ♕d1

9 ♘xe5?? loses to 9...♘e6.

9...♘ce4 10 ♘xe4 ♘xe4 11 ♗b2 *(D)*

Given time, White will gain the advantage due to the vulnerable d6-pawn, so Black must act quickly.

11...a5 12 a3?!

Now Black equalizes. 12 ♕c2 ♘f6 (not 12...♕b6? 13 a3 ♘f6 14 c5! dxc5 15 ♘xe5, which is very good for White) 13 ♖d1 ♕c7 14 b5! ♗f5 15 ♗d3 ♗xd3 16 ♕xd3 would have given White a slight positional advantage.

12...axb4 13 axb4 ♖xa1 14 ♗xa1?!

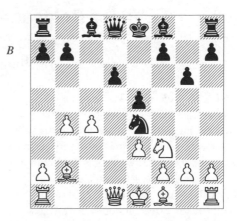

White should have played 14 ♕xa1 ♕b6 15 ♕a4+ ♗d7 16 ♕a8+ ♔e7 17 ♕a3 ♗h6 18 c5!?, maintaining the balance.

14...♕b6! *(D)*

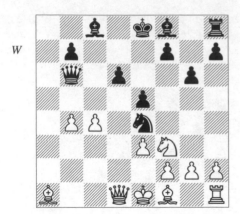

Suddenly Black takes over the initiative.

15 ♕a4+?

The start of a misguided manoeuvre which displaces Black's king but leaves White dangerously behind in development. 15 ♕b1 is better.

15...♗d7 16 ♕a8+ ♔e7

Black's king is relatively safe on e7.

17 ♕a3

After 17 ♕a5 ♕xa5 18 bxa5 ♗g7 White's queenside pawns are in trouble.

17...♗h6! 18 ♗e2?!

Allows a forced win, but the alternatives were uninviting: 18 ♗d3? ♘xf2 19 ♔xf2 ♕xe3+ 20

♔f1 ♖a8 21 ♕xa8 ♕xd3+ wins easily, or 18 ♘d2 ♘xd2! 19 ♔xd2 ♗e6! with a clear plus for Black.

18...♖a8! 19 ♕b2 (D)

19 ♕xa8 ♕xb4+ 20 ♔f1 ♕b1+ leads to a quick mate.

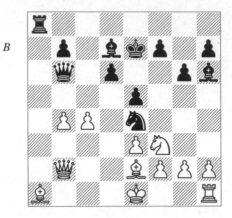

19...♗xe3! 20 fxe3 ♕xe3 21 c5

There is no defence: 21 ♘xe5 (21 ♖f1 ♕a7 is a neat win, trapping the bishop) 21...♕f2+ 22 ♔d1 ♗a4+ 23 ♔c1 ♕e3+ 24 ♔b1 ♘d2+ wins White's queen.

21...♗b5 22 ♘g1 ♕f2+ 23 ♔d1 ♗a4+ 0-1

Mate follows shortly.

Game 87
Viktor Bologan – Raj Tischbierek
Vienna Open 1996
Alekhine Defence

1 e4 ♘f6 2 e5 ♘d5 3 d4 d6 4 ♘f3 ♗g4 5 ♗e2 e6 6 h3 ♗h5 7 c4 ♘b6 8 exd6

This exchange is far more popular than the main alternative 8 ♘c3; the popularity seems to be justified because White's score with this move is the well above-average 69%.

8...cxd6 9 ♘c3 ♗e7 10 d5!? (D)

White takes direct action before Black can castle. This forthright approach has proved very troublesome for Black, who has yet to come up with a satisfactory answer; indeed, this continuation poses problems for the whole 5...e6 system in the Alekhine.

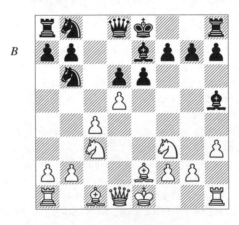

10...e5 11 ♗e3

11 g4 ♗g6 12 h4 has proved even more awkward for Black.

11...♗xf3

Another idea is 11...♘8d7 12 g4 ♗g6 13 h4 h5 14 g5, with just a slight advantage for White.

12 ♗xf3 ♘8d7 13 ♕e2 ♖c8 14 b3 f5?

A serious error because although ...f5 is Black's main plan, it is risky to play it before castling. 14...0-0 would have left White with just an edge.

15 g4! *(D)*

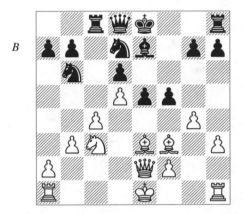

White exposes the flaw in Black's last move.

15...e4

Or 15...f4 (15...g6? loses to 16 gxf5 gxf5 17 ♗h5+ ♔f8 18 ♗h6+, while 15...0-0 16 gxf5 ♖xf5 17 ♗g4 ♖f8 18 ♖g1 prevents ...♗g5 and gives White the advantage) 16 ♗d2 ♘c5 17 ♘e4 ♘bd7 18 ♘xc5 ♘xc5 19 b4 ♘d7 20 ♖c1 and Black's light squares are permanently weak.

16 ♗g2 ♗f6

Black cannot prevent the collapse of his central pawn-chain, so he aims to exploit the tactical weakness of the long dark diagonal.

17 ♘b5!! *(D)*

White's response is to sacrifice a whole rook. 17 ♖c1? is bad in view of 17...♗xc3+ 18 ♖xc3 ♘xd5.

17...♗xa1

17...♘c5 18 ♗xc5 ♖xc5 19 ♖d1 leaves Black with no compensation for his crumbling centre.

18 ♘xd6+ ♔f8

18...♔e7 19 ♘xf5+ ♔f8 20 0-0 is even worse than the game; e.g., 20...♗f6 21 g5 ♗xg5 22

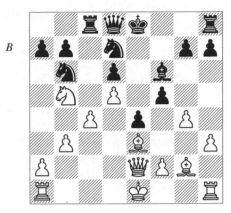

♘d4 ♘c5 23 b4 ♘bd7 24 bxc5 ♘xc5 25 ♕g4 with a crushing attack.

19 0-0 ♗e5

After 19...♗f6 20 g5! ♗xg5 (or 20...♗e5 21 ♘xf5 g6 22 f4!, again with a very strong attack) 21 ♕h5 g6 22 ♕xg5 ♕xg5 23 ♗xg5 ♖b8 24 f3 exf3 25 ♗xf3 White has more than enough for the exchange; e.g., 25...♘c8 (25...♘e5 26 ♗f6 ♘xf3+ 27 ♖xf3 ♖g8 28 ♖e3 and Black is helpless) 26 ♗f4 g5 27 ♖e1! ♘cb6 28 ♗e3 with c5 to come.

20 ♘xf5 *(D)*

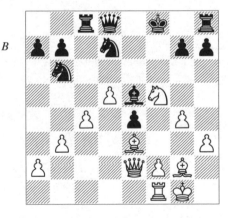

Demolishing Black's centre is more important than taking the exchange. In return for the rook White has only two pawns, but Black's defensive task is very difficult. His king is permanently exposed, the extra rook on h8 is playing no part in the game and White's pieces are extremely active.

20...h5?

Trying to bring the rook into the game, but there is no time for this. However, after 20...g6 (20...♖g8 21 f4 exf3 22 ♕xf3 h6 23 d6 ♗f6 24 ♘e7+ ♔f8 25 ♕xb7 and White wins) 21 ♘d4 ♗xd4 (21...♕f6 22 f3!? ♔e8 23 fxe4 ♕e7 24 ♘e6 ♘f8 25 ♗g5 ♕d7 26 ♗f4 removes the blockade of e5, when the central pawns can be set in motion) 22 ♗xd4 ♔f7 (22...♖g8 23 ♕xe4 ♕e7 24 ♕f4+ ♔e8 25 d6 ♖f8 26 ♕g3 ♕e2 27 ♗c3 is winning for White) 23 ♕e3! (guaranteeing that f3 will open the f-file) 23...♘f6 24 f3 ♖f8 25 fxe4 ♔g8 26 e5 the position speaks for itself.

21 f4! *(D)*

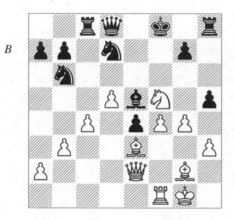

21...exf3

Now the f-file is opened, but there is nothing better; e.g., 21...♗f6 22 g5 ♗e7 (22...g6 23 ♘d6) 23 d6 or 21...♗b8 22 ♗d4 ♖g8 23 ♕b2 ♘f6 24 g5 ♘e8 25 ♕a3+.

22 ♕xf3 ♔g8

22...♘f6 23 g5 and 22...♕f6 23 g5 ♕f7 24 ♕e2 are winning.

23 d6 ♘f6

Or 23...♗f6 (23...hxg4 24 ♕xg4 ♗f6 25 ♘e7+ ♔f7 26 ♕g6+ ♔f8 27 ♗d4 and White crashes through on f6) 24 g5 ♗xg5 25 ♗xg5 ♕xg5 26 ♘e7+ ♔h7 27 ♕e4+ g6 28 ♖f7+ ♔h6 29 h4 ♕c5+ 30 ♔h1 leading to a quick mate.

24 g5 *(D)*

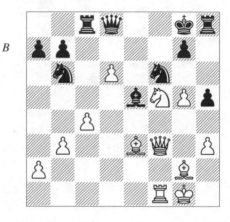

1-0

As 24...♘bd7 25 ♘e7+ ♔f7 (25...♔h7 26 g6#; 25...♔f8 26 ♘g6+) 26 ♕d5+ finishes Black off.

Game 88

Ilia Smirin – Pablo Ricardi

Erevan Olympiad 1996

Scandinavian Defence

1 e4 d5 2 exd5 ♕xd5 3 ♘c3 ♕a5 4 d4 ♘f6 5 ♘f3 ♗f5

5...c6 is the more common move-order, but 5...♗f5 has little independent significance as play almost always transposes back to normal lines. This game, however, is an exception.

6 ♘e5

6 ♗d2 c6 7 ♗c4 reaches another main line of the Scandinavian.

6...c6 7 ♗c4 e6 8 g4 ♗g6 9 ♕e2 *(D)*

Slightly unusual; 9 h4 is by far the most common move. It seems to me that White is unlikely to gain an advantage after the modest text-move.

9...♗b4 10 ♗d2 ♘bd7

10...♗xc2 11 ♘xf7! 0-0 12 ♘g5 favours White.

11 f4

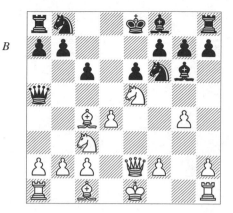

B

An aggressive attempt to inconvenience the g6-bishop, but this plan is double-edged. If it doesn't work, then the advance of the f-pawn will merely weaken White's position. 11 0-0-0 ♘xe5 12 dxe5 ♘d5 is safer, but the resulting exchanges are likely to lead to dull equality. White was hoping for more, but ends up with less.

11...0-0-0 12 0-0-0

After 12 0-0 (12 f5? exf5 13 gxf5 ♗h5 is disastrous for White) 12...♘xe5 13 fxe5 (13 dxe5? ♖xd2! 14 ♕xd2 ♕c5+) 13...♘d5 Black has some advantage as White's king position is insecure.

12...♘b6!? (D)

Ambitious play by Black, especially as he could have equalized easily by 12...♘xe5 13 fxe5 ♘d5 14 ♘xd5 ♗xd2+ 15 ♕xd2 ♕xd2+ 16 ♖xd2 cxd5.

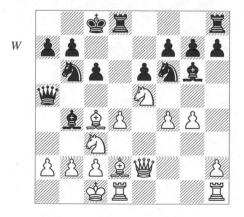

W

13 f5?

13 ♗b3? ♖xd4 14 a3 ♖xd2! 15 ♕xd2 ♘e4 is also bad, so the best chance was 13 a3. After 13...♗xa3 14 ♘a2! (not 14 ♘d5? ♗xb2+ 15 ♔xb2 ♘xc4+ and Black wins) 14...♕a4 15 ♗b3 ♕xd4! 16 c3 the position is very unclear.

13...exf5 14 a3?!

14 ♘xf7 ♘xc4! 15 ♕e6+ ♔d7 16 ♘xh8 ♘xd2 17 ♖xd2 ♗xc3 18 bxc3 ♕xc3 gives Black a dangerous initiative, but this was probably better than the text-move.

14...♖he8! (D)

A correct piece sacrifice. 14...♗xa3 15 ♘a2 is unclear, but 14...♖xd4! is also very strong; e.g., 15 ♗xf7 (15 axb4 ♕a1+ 16 ♘b1 ♖e4 wins for Black) 15...♖xd2 16 ♕xd2 (White loses after both 16 ♗e6+ ♔b8 17 ♘xc6+ bxc6 18 ♕xd2 ♗xc3 19 ♕d6+ ♔b7 20 bxc3 ♕xc3 and 16 ♖xd2 ♗xc3 17 ♗e6+ ♔b8) 16...♕xe5 17 ♗xg6 ♗xc3 18 ♗xf5+ ♕xf5 19 gxf5 ♗xd2+ 20 ♖xd2 ♖e8 21 ♖g1 ♖e7 with a winning ending for Black.

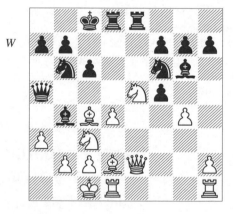

W

15 axb4

Acceptance is forced, since 15 gxf5 ♗h5 and 15 ♕f1 ♖xd4 are hopeless.

15...♕a1+ 16 ♘b1 ♘a4 17 ♗c3

The only way to defend b2.

17...♘e4 (D)

All Black's pieces are in excellent attacking positions, and White is under tremendous pressure both on the queenside and down the central files.

18 ♖d3

There is no real defence; for example, 18 ♕e1 ♘exc3 19 bxc3 f6 or 18 ♕e3 ♘exc3 19

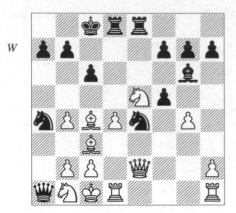

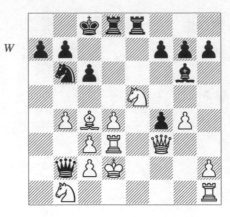

bxc3 f4 20 ♕xf4 ♘xc3 and Black wins in both cases.

18...f4

18...♘exc3 19 bxc3 f6 is another effective line.

19 ♕f3

Removing the queen from the gaze of the e8-rook. 19 ♘xg6 ♘exc3 20 ♘e7+ ♖xe7 21 ♕xe7 ♕xb1+ 22 ♔d2 ♕xh1 23 bxc3 ♘b2 is catastrophic.

19...♘exc3 20 bxc3 ♕b2+ 21 ♔d2 ♘b6! *(D)*

White's curious pawn-structure has left c4 vulnerable.

22 ♗a6

The alternatives 22 ♗xf7 ♖xe5! 23 dxe5 ♖xd3+, 22 ♗b3 ♖xe5 23 ♕xf4 ♗xd3 24 ♕xe5 ♗xc2 and 22 ♖e1 ♖xe5! are all winning for Black.

22...bxa6 23 ♕xc6+ ♔b8 24 ♘c4

24 ♘xg6 is refuted by 24...♖c8! 25 ♕d6+ (25 ♘e5 is met by 25...♖xe5!) 25...♔a8 26 ♘e5 ♖xe5 27 dxe5 ♘c4+ 28 ♔e2 ♘xd6 29 ♖xd6 ♕xc2+.

24...♘xc4+ 25 ♕xc4 ♖e3! 0-1

A surprising and neat finish. The pins from b2 to d2 and g6 to c2 mean that the d3-rook is oddly trapped. Of course 26 ♖xe3 ♕xc2+ 27 ♔e1 fxe3 is not worth continuing.

Game 89
Garry Kasparov – Zbynek Hraček
Erevan Olympiad 1996
Sicilian Defence, Richter-Rauzer Attack

1 e4 c5 2 ♘f3 d6 3 d4 cxd4 4 ♘xd4 ♘f6 5 ♘c3 ♘c6 6 ♗g5 e6 7 ♕d2 a6 8 0-0-0 ♘xd4

8...h6 and 8...♗d7 are by far the most popular moves, but this alternative is seen occasionally.

9 ♕xd4 ♗e7 10 f4 b5 11 ♗xf6 gxf6 12 e5! *(D)*

Before this game, White had tried a whole range of other possibilities, but thanks to Kasparov's spectacular success here, 12 e5 instantly became the main line and is still the most common move today.

12...d5

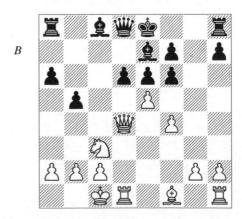

Forced, as the two captures on e5 are bad: 12...dxe5 13 ♕e4 ♗d7 14 ♖xd7 ♔xd7 15 ♗xb5+ axb5 16 ♖d1+ ♗d6 17 ♘xb5 favours White, while 12...fxe5 13 fxe5 dxe5 14 ♕xe5 ♗g5+ 15 ♔b1 ♕f6 16 ♕e4 followed by ♕c6+ even wins for White.

13 ♔b1 b4?

A definite error which has never been repeated; Black drives the white knight over to the kingside, where it proves even more dangerous. In later games Black tried 13...♗b7, 13...♗d7 or 13...♖g8 – for more details consult your database!

14 ♘e2

Grabbing a pawn by 14 exf6?! ♗xf6 15 ♕xb4 ♕c7 only activates Black's pieces.

14...a5 *(D)*

Black cannot castle in view of his shattered kingside, so he hopes to create counterplay with his king in the centre. It is important for White's plan that 14...♖b8 15 f5 ♕b6 does not force the exchange of queens; White can continue 16 ♕g4 fxe5 17 ♕g7 ♖f8 18 ♕xe5 ♕d6 19 ♕g7 with an advantage.

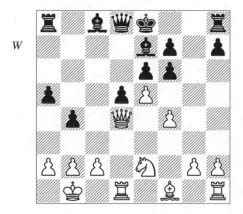

15 ♘g3

Heading for h5.

15...f5

15...♗a6 16 ♘h5 f5 17 ♗xa6 ♖xa6 18 h3 followed by g4 favours White, while 15...h5 16 ♗e2 h4 17 ♘h5 does nothing to help Black's position.

16 ♘h5 ♖b8 *(D)*

After 16...♖g8 17 h3 a4 18 g4 fxg4 19 hxg4 ♖xg4 20 ♗e2 ♖g8 21 ♘f6+ ♗xf6 22 exf6

White has a very strong attack for the sacrificed pawn.

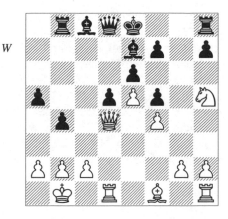

17 g4!

This is the start of an impressive sacrificial breakthrough.

17...fxg4 18 f5 ♖g8

18...exf5 fails to 19 e6 ♖g8 (19...f6 20 ♕f4 ♖b6? loses to 21 ♘g7+ ♔f8 22 ♕h6) 20 exf7+ ♔xf7 21 ♗g2 ♗b7 (21...♗e6 22 ♘f4 is decisive) 22 ♖hf1 ♖g5 23 ♘g3 ♔g6 (23...♗f6 24 ♕f4 is very pleasant for White) 24 ♕d3 ♕d7 25 h4 gxh3 26 ♗xh3 ♖f8 27 ♖xf5 ♖fxf5 28 ♘xf5 ♖xf5 29 ♖f1 and the pin proves fatal for Black.

19 ♘f6+!

19 f6 ♗f8 20 ♘g7+ ♖xg7 21 fxg7 ♗xg7 is less clear.

19...♗xf6 20 exf6 *(D)*

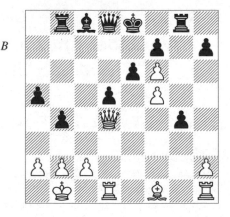

20...♕d6

20...exf5 21 ♕e5+ ♗e6 22 ♖xd5! ♕xd5 23 ♕xb8+ ♔d7 24 ♗b5+ wins Black's queen.

21 ♗g2

21 fxe6 fxe6 22 ♗e2 is also very promising.

21...♖g5?

Black collapses and allows White to break through in the centre. The lines 21...exf5 22 ♗xd5 ♗e6 23 ♕a7, 21...e5 22 ♖he1 ♗xf5 23 ♖xe5+ ♗e6 24 ♗xd5 and 21...♔f8 22 ♕e3 a4 23 ♕h6+ ♔e8 24 ♕xh7 ♖f8 25 ♖he1 also offer Black no defensive chances. The only way to continue the fight was by 21...♖b7!, although White retains a clear advantage after 22 ♕e3 ♔d8 23 ♕h6.

22 ♗xd5! (D)

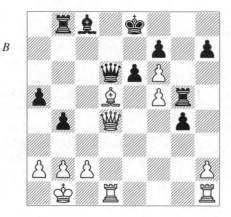

The capture of Black's bastion in the centre opens more lines for White's pieces to penetrate towards the enemy king.

22...♗d7

The alternatives are equally bad; for example, 22...♕xd5 23 ♕f4 ♕xf5 24 ♕xb8, 22...♗b7 23 ♗xb7 ♕xd4 24 ♗c6+ or 22...♔f8 23 ♕e3.

23 ♖he1

The last piece joins the attack.

23...h6

With such an array of force in the centre, it is not surprising that Black cannot defend. The variations run 23...♖xf5 24 ♗xe6 ♕xd4 25 ♗xf5+ ♔f8 26 ♖xd4 ♗xf5 27 ♖e5, 23...b3 24 axb3 ♖b4 25 ♕a7 ♕b6 26 fxe6 ♕xa7 27 exd7++ ♔d8 28 ♖e8+ ♔xd7 29 ♖e7+ ♔d6 30 ♗c4+ and 23...♖c8 24 fxe6 fxe6 25 ♕e4, with a win for White in all cases.

24 fxe6 fxe6 25 ♕a7 (D)

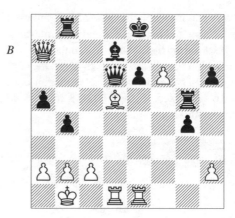

1-0

The threat of 26 ♗xe6 is unanswerable.

Game 90

Alexander Khuzman – Artashes Minasian

European Team Ch, Pula 1997

Schmid Benoni

1 d4 ♘f6 2 ♘f3 c5 3 d5 g6 4 ♘c3 ♗g7 5 e4 0-0

For many years this was an accepted move-order for Black (instead of 5...d6), but in the mid-1990s a new idea for White suddenly appeared, targeted at precisely this move-order. Practical results with this new idea have so far been substantially in White's favour, although not so heavily as to put 5...0-0 totally out of action.

6 e5!? ♘g4

The most natural move. Black's only real alternative is 6...♘e8 but after 7 h4 d6 8 e6 fxe6 9 h5 exd5 10 hxg6 hxg6 11 ♕xd5+ e6 12 ♕d3 White has good play for the pawn.

7 ♘g5! (D)

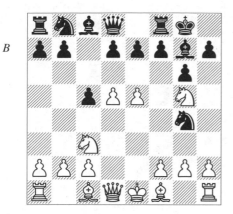

This is the point of White's idea.

7...♘h6

A critical moment. The alternatives are:

1) 7...♘xe5? is definitely bad after 8 f4 f6 (8...h6? loses a piece to 9 ♘h3) 9 ♘xh7! ♔xh7 10 fxe5 fxe5 11 ♗d3 with a massive attack.

2) 7...h5 8 f4 d6 9 h3 ♘h6 10 e6 looks good for White.

3) 7...d6 8 e6 f5 9 h3 ♘f6 10 g4 is less clear, but White is probably better here too.

8 h4 *(D)*

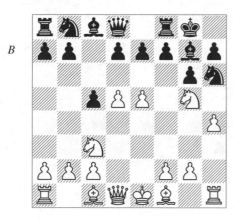

White is prepared to give up the e5-pawn to open the h-file against the enemy king.

8...f6

8...♗xe5 9 h5 ♘f5 (or 9...♗g7 10 ♘xh7! ♔xh7 11 hxg6+ fxg6 12 ♗xh6 ♗xh6 13 ♕d2 and White wins) loses to 10 ♘xh7! ♔xh7 11 hxg6++ ♔g7 12 ♖h7+ ♔g8 13 ♕h5 fxg6 14 ♕xg6+ ♔g7 15 ♗h6 ♖f7 16 ♗d3 with a winning attack.

9 ♘ge4! *(D)*

Stronger than 9 ♘f3, as played before this game.

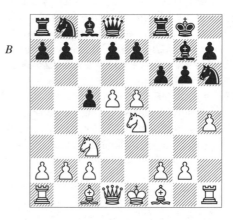

9...♘f7

9...fxe5 10 h5 ♘f5 11 hxg6 hxg6 12 ♕g4 ♕b6 13 ♘a4! drives the queen off the third rank and wins.

10 h5!

Consistently pursuing the attack. 10 exf6 exf6 11 ♘xc5 wins a pawn but allows some counterplay after 11...♕e7+ 12 ♗e3 d6 13 ♘b3 f5.

10...f5

10...♘xe5 11 hxg6 hxg6 12 f4 ♘f7 13 ♕g4 is clearly better for White.

11 ♘g5 *(D)*

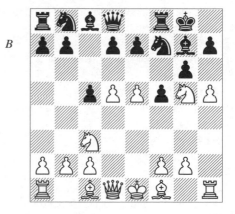

11...♘xg5

Or:

1) 11...♘xe5 12 ♘xh7! ♔xh7 13 hxg6++ ♔g8 14 ♕h5 ♖e8 15 ♕h7+ ♔f8 16 ♗h6 mates.

2) 11...♗xe5 fails to 12 ♘xh7! ♗xc3+ (the alternative 12...♔xh7 13 hxg6++ ♔xg6 leads to a forced mate after 14 ♕h5+ ♔f6 15 ♕h4+ ♔g6 16 ♕h7+ ♔f6 17 ♗g5+! ♔xg5 18 ♖h5+) 13 bxc3 ♔xh7 14 hxg6++ ♔xg6 15 ♕h5+ ♔f6 16 ♕h4+ ♔e5 (16...♔g6 17 ♕g3+ ♔f6 18 ♗g5+ ♘xg5 19 ♖h6+ ♔f7 20 ♕xg5 mates) 17 ♗c4! ♔d6 18 ♗f4+ ♘e5 19 ♗xe5+ ♔xe5 20 0-0-0 and White wins.

12 ♗xg5 ♗xe5

Black finally removes the cramping e5-pawn, but White's initiative is too strong. If 12...h6, then 13 hxg6! hxg5 14 ♖h8+!! ♗xh8 15 ♕h5 ♖f7 16 gxf7+ ♔g7 17 ♗d3 e6 18 0-0-0 followed by ♖h1 wins.

13 hxg6 hxg6 14 d6! (D)

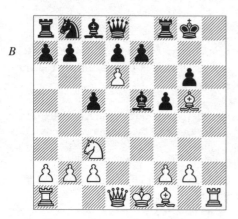

Burying the c8-bishop and opening the diagonal from c4 to g8.

14...♗f6

14...♗xd6 15 ♗c4+ ♔g7 16 ♗h6+ ♔f6 17 ♘d5+ is decisive.

15 ♗xf6 ♖xf6

After 15...exf6 White wins by 16 ♕d2 ♕e8+ 17 ♔d1 g5 18 ♘d5.

16 ♗c4+ e6

16...♔g7 loses to 17 ♕d2.

17 ♕d2 ♕f8

17...♖f7 leads to very much the same type of finish after 18 ♘d5! exd5 19 ♗xd5 ♕f6 (19...♕f8 transposes into the note to Black's 19th) 20 ♕e3 ♔f8 21 ♗xf7 ♔xf7 (21...♕xf7 22 ♖h8+ ♔g7 23 ♕h6+ ♔f6 24 ♖f8) 22 ♖h7+ ♔g8 23 ♕e7! ♕xe7+ 24 dxe7 and White wins.

18 ♘d5! (D)

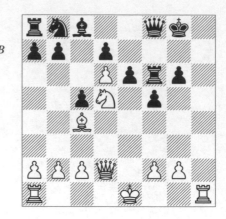

Forcing open the diagonal from c4 to g8.

18...exd5

18...♖f7 is met by 19 ♘c7.

19 ♗xd5+ ♖e6+

White wins after 19...♖f7 20 ♕g5 ♔g7 (or 20...♕xd6 21 ♕d8+ ♕f8 22 ♕f6) 21 ♗xf7 ♔xf7 22 ♖h7+ ♔e6 23 ♕e7+!.

20 ♗xe6+ dxe6 21 ♕g5

Only Black's queen is trying to defend the kingside.

21...♗d7

21...♔g7 22 ♕h6+ ♔f7 23 ♕xf8+ ♔xf8 24 ♖h8+ and White wins.

22 0-0-0 ♗e8

22...♘c6 loses to 23 ♖h6 ♗e8 (23...♘e5 24 f4) 24 d7 ♗f7 25 ♕h4! ♕g7 26 d8♕+.

23 ♕d8! (D)

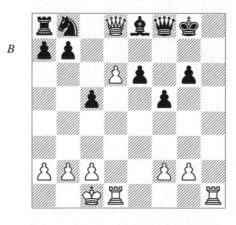

1-0

White wins after 23...♔g7 24 d7 ♗xd7 25 ♖h7+ or 23...♕f7 24 d7 ♘xd7 25 ♕xa8.

Game 91
Rafael Vaganian – Alexei Fedorov
European Team Ch, Pula 1997
Modern Defence

1 ♘f3 g6 2 e4 ♗g7 3 d4 d6 4 c3 ♘f6 5 ♗d3 0-0 6 0-0 ♘bd7

6...♘c6 is another popular continuation.

7 ♖e1 e5 8 ♘bd2 b6 9 ♘f1 ♗b7 10 ♘g3 ♖e8 *(D)*

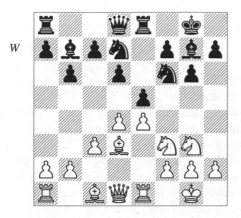

Black's pieces are all quite well placed and he has saved time in comparison with a Closed Spanish because the typical Spanish manoeuvres ...♘c6-b8-d7 and ...♗e7-f8-g7 have been avoided. It is true that White has also saved some time with his light-squared bishop, but Black is definitely ahead in tempi.

11 ♗d2

11 d5 c6 12 c4 ♘c5 13 ♗f1 a5 14 b3 b5 was fine for Black in Miles-Bologan, Wijk aan Zee 1996.

11...d5!?

Black takes advantage of White's slow play to liquidate the central pawns. However, opening up the position can be double-edged as it tends to amplify the effect of a lead in development.

12 exd5

12 dxe5 ♘xe4 13 ♘xe4 dxe4 14 ♗g5 ♕c8 15 ♗xe4 ♘xe5 is equal.

12...♘xd5 13 ♗g5!? *(D)*

13 c4 ♘5f6 14 d5 c6 gives White nothing.

13...♕c8

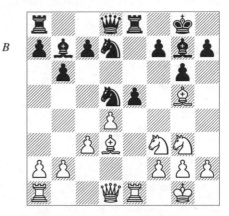

Now that the position is starting to open up, Black must take care. 13...♗f6 is inaccurate as 14 ♗xf6 ♕xf6 15 ♕a4 ♗c6 16 ♗b5 ♗xb5 17 ♕xb5 c6 18 ♕e2 is very awkward. However, 13...f6!? 14 ♗d2 exd4 is the simplest; after 15 cxd4 (or 15 ♘xd4 ♘e5) 15...♖xe1+ 16 ♕xe1 ♕f8 the position is equal.

14 ♕d2 exd4 15 ♘xd4 ♖xe1+?!

This casual move effectively gives White an extra development tempo (Black exchanges the developed rook on e8 for the undeveloped one on a1). 15...♘e5! is correct, with excellent prospects of safe equality.

16 ♖xe1 ♘e5 17 ♗f5!? *(D)*

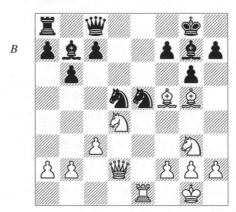

An imaginative and surprising sacrifice. Black faces considerable practical difficulties, even if objectively the sacrifice may only be good enough for a draw.

17...gxf5

Acceptance is forced as 17...♕f8 18 ♘e6 and 17...♕b8 18 ♘e6 ♗h8 19 ♘f4 favour White.

18 ♘dxf5 *(D)*

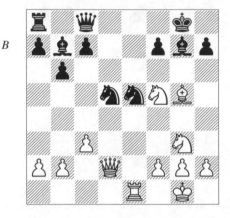

18...f6!

Not 18...♗h8? 19 ♗e7 h6 20 ♘xh6+ ♔h7 21 ♘xf7! ♗xf7 22 ♕d3+ ♔g7 23 ♘f5+ and White wins. However, 18...♘c4 19 ♕d1 f6 (not 19...♘d6 20 ♘xg7 ♔xg7 21 c4!, when Black has no good defence; for example, 21...♘xc4 22 ♕d4+ f6 23 ♘h5+ ♔g8 24 ♕xc4 fxg5 25 ♘f6+ or 21...f6 22 cxd5 fxg5 23 ♖e7+ ♘f7 24 ♕d4+ ♔f8 25 ♕f6 ♗xd5 26 ♘f5 with a clear plus for White in both cases) offers some defensive chances. Then 20 ♘xg7 fxg5 21 ♘3f5 ♘d6 is unclear, while 20 ♗h6 ♗xh6 21 ♘xh6+ ♔h8 22 ♘f7+ ♔g8! 23 ♕h5 ♘d6 24 ♘xd6 cxd6 25 ♘f5 ♔h8 leaves White running out of steam. 20 ♗h4! looks best; White preserves his attacking formation and threatens 21 ♕g4.

19 ♘xg7 ♔xg7 20 c4?

Offering a pawn in order to gain time, but taking what could have been one risk too many. 20 ♗xf6+! ♘xf6 21 ♕g5+ ♔f7 22 ♘f5 ♕e6 23 ♘h6+ ♔f8 24 ♖xe5 ♖d8 25 h4 would have been roughly balanced; White has enough for the piece but not more.

20...♘xc4 *(D)*

20...♘f7? 21 ♗h4 traps the d5-knight.

21 ♕d4

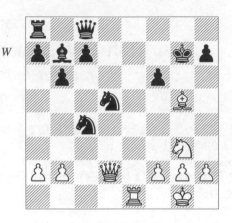

After 21 ♗xf6+ ♔f7! (21...♘xf6? 22 ♕g5+ ♔f7 23 ♘f5 is at least a draw for White) White's attack collapses, since now 22 ♕g5 can be met by 22...♕g8!.

21...♔g6?

White's decision is rewarded by a serious mistake from Black. There were several promising defensive lines, such as 21...♕d7!? or 21...♕f8 22 ♘f5+ ♔h8 23 ♖e7 ♘d6!, or perhaps best of all 21...♘d6! 22 ♗xf6+ ♔g8. This last continuation in particular would have left White in considerable difficulties, whereas now he wins by force.

22 ♕e4+! *(D)*

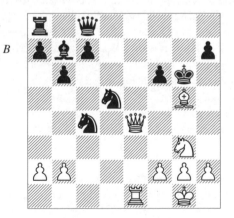

Very strong, as 22...♔xg5 23 ♕xh7 mates.

22...f5?!

22...♔g7 was the only chance, but 23 ♘h5+ ♔g8 24 ♕xc4 fxg5 25 ♘f6+ ♔g7 26 ♘xd5 is clearly very bad for Black.

23 ♕h4 ♕g8 24 ♕h6+ ♔f7 25 ♖e7+ 1-0

Game 92
Hugo Spangenberg – Vladislav Tkachev
Villa Martelli 1997
Four Knights Opening

1 e4 e5 2 ♘c3 ♘f6 3 ♘f3 ♘c6 4 ♗b5 ♘d4 5 ♗c4

5 ♗a4 is the main line.

5...♗c5 6 ♘xe5 d5!? *(D)*

It is unusual for an innovation to occur as early as move six in the Open Games. Hitherto, theory gave 6...♕e7, a move going back to Bernstein-Rubinstein, Vilna 1912.

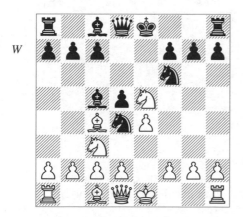

7 ♘xd5?

This is already a serious error – in fact, it is by far the worst of the three captures on d5. 7 exd5 0-0 8 0-0 gives Black reasonable play for the pawns after 8...♖e8 9 ♘f3 ♗g4 or 8...♕d6, so 7 ♗xd5 is probably best. Then 7...♘xd5 8 ♘xd5 0-0 (8...♕g5 9 ♘xc7+ ♔f8 10 ♔f1 ♕xe5 11 ♘xa8 ♕xe4 is too optimistic; e.g., 12 d3 ♕c6 13 ♗e3 b6 14 b4! ♗b7 15 ♖g1 and White is much better) 9 c3 ♖e8 10 cxd4 ♗xd4 11 0-0 ♖xe5 12 d3 left White with an edge in Shirov-Kramnik, WCC Match (6), Cazorla 1998.

7...♘xd5 8 ♕h5 *(D)*

White tries to solve his problems tactically, but as I have commented before, initiating tactics in a bad position usually only makes matters worse. However, even 8 ♗xd5 (8 ♘xf7 ♕h4! 9 d3 ♘b4 10 0-0 ♗g4 11 ♕d2 ♘e2+ 12 ♔h1 ♗xf2 wins for Black) 8...♕g5 9 ♗xf7+

♔e7 10 ♗h5 ♕xe5 11 d3 ♘xc2+! 12 ♕xc2 ♕xh5 is very good for Black, since White has only two pawns for the piece.

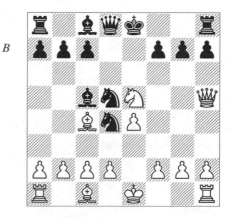

8...g6 9 ♘xg6 ♘xc2+

9...fxg6 10 ♕e5+ is the point of White's play, but Black need not fall in with White's plans.

10 ♔f1

A sad necessity because 10 ♔d1 loses to 10...♗g4+! 11 ♕xg4 ♘de3+ 12 fxe3 ♘xe3+ 13 ♔e1 ♘xg4 14 ♘xh8 ♕d4 and Black wins more material.

10...♕f6! *(D)*

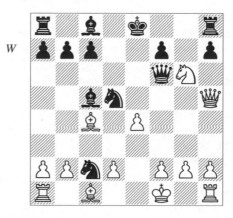

White's position collapses: a1 and g6 are under attack, and mate is threatened on f2.

11 f3

11 ♕e5+ ♕xe5 12 ♘xe5 ♘xa1 and 11 ♕e2 hxg6 12 exd5+ ♔f8 are also hopeless.

11...hxg6 12 ♕xd5 ♖h5 0-1

Game 93
Ferdinand Hellers – Curt Hansen
Malmö 1997
French Defence, Winawer Variation

1 e4 e6 2 d4 d5 3 ♘c3 ♗b4 4 e5 c5 5 a3 ♗xc3+ 6 bxc3 ♕c7 7 ♘f3 ♘e7 8 a4 h6

This move (instead of the usual 8...♘bc6 or 8...b6) looks rather slow, but White has no real way to exploit it and play often transposes into other lines.

9 ♗d3 b6

The point of Black's move-order is to cut out lines involving ♗b5+ by White.

10 0-0 ♗a6 (D)

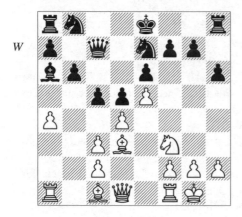

11 ♗xa6 ♘xa6 12 ♕d3 ♘b8 13 ♘h4

The objective merits of this ambitious plan are open to question, but in practice it is not so easy for Black. 13 a5 would be a more positional continuation.

13...♘bc6

13...♘d7 also looks good; after 14 f4 cxd4 15 cxd4 ♖c8 it is hard for White to proceed with his attack.

14 f4 0-0 15 ♗a3

15 f5 exf5 16 ♘xf5 ♘xf5 17 ♖xf5 ♖ae8! is fine for Black.

15...♘a5 (D)

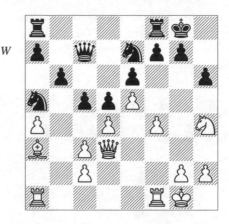

16 ♖ae1

16 g4 ♘c4 17 f5 f6 rebounds on White as he is tied down to defending the a3-bishop.

16...♕c6!

Better than 16...♘c4 17 ♗c1 threatening 18 f5.

17 g4 ♕xa4 18 ♗c1 cxd4 19 f5

White is totally committed on the kingside and cannot afford the time to recapture mere pawns.

19...♖ac8?! (D)

Black has several playable moves and it must have been hard to decide which one to adopt. The text-move may still allow Black to defend, but it requires an extremely precise follow-up. There were two safer possibilities:

1) 19...dxc3 20 ♖f4 ♘c4 21 f6 ♘c6 22 fxg7 (22 g5 ♘6xe5 looks good for Black) 22...♔xg7 23 ♘f5+ exf5 24 ♕xf5 ♖ae8 and White has enough compensation to draw, but surely no more than that.

2) 19...♘c4 20 ♕g3 ♕xc3 21 ♖f3 ♕xc2 22 f6 ♘g6 and again White might be able to force a draw, for example by 23 fxg7 ♔xg7 24 ♘xg6

fxg6 25 ♗xh6+ ♔xh6 26 ♕h4+ ♔g7 27 ♕e7+ ♔g8 28 ♕xe6+, but cannot hope to do better.

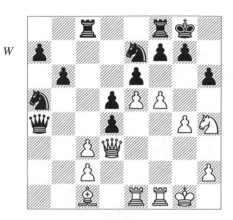

20 ♗xh6!

This sacrifice creates serious problems for Black, although it is by no means clear that White is already winning.

20...gxh6

20...♖xc3 21 ♕d2 gxh6 (21...♖e3 22 f6! also favours White) 22 ♕xh6 ♕xc2 is bad in view of 23 ♕g5+ ♘g6 24 fxg6 fxg6 25 ♖xf8+ ♔xf8 26 ♘xg6+ and wins.

21 f6 *(D)*

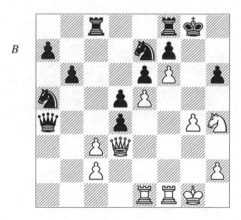

21...♘ec6?

Moving the last defensive piece away from the kingside is asking to be mated and White duly obliges. Black also cannot survive after 21...♖fe8?, because of 22 ♕d2! dxc3 (22...♔h7 23 fxe7 ♖xe7 24 ♖f6) 23 ♕xh6 ♕xg4+ 24 ♔h1 winning. Another tempting possibility is

21...♘ac6?!, but after 22 ♕d2 ♔h7 23 fxe7 ♘xe7 24 ♖f6 ♘g8 25 ♖ef1! White has dangerous threats.

21...♖xc3 is the best chance and may draw, but Black is certainly on a knife-edge. The analysis runs 22 ♕d2 and now:

1) 22...♕xc2 23 ♕xh6 ♕h7 24 ♕xh7+ ♔xh7 25 fxe7 ♖e8 26 ♖xf7+ *(D)*.

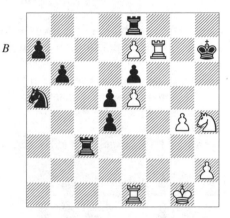

26...♔g8! (26...♔h6 27 ♖ef1 ♔g5 28 ♘f3+ and White wins after 28...♔xg4 29 ♔h1! or 28...♖xf3 29 ♖1xf3 ♘c6 30 ♖f8 ♖xe7 31 ♖g8+) 27 ♖ef1 ♖cc8 28 ♘g6 d3! 29 ♖f8+ ♔h7! (29...♔g7 loses to 30 ♘f4) 30 h4 d2! (30...♔xg6 31 ♖8f7 ♖c1 32 h5+ ♔g5 33 ♖xc1 ♘c4 34 ♖g7+ wins for White) 31 h5 ♖c1 (31...♔h6 32 ♔f2 ♘c4 33 ♔e2 favours White) 32 ♖xe8 ♖xf1+ 33 ♔g2 ♖g1+ (not 33...d1♕?? 34 ♖h8+ ♔g7 35 e8♘+ ♔f7 36 ♖f8#) 34 ♔f2 ♖f1+ 35 ♔g3 ♖g1+ 36 ♔h4 ♖xg4+ 37 ♔xg4 (37 ♔h3? ♔h6! 38 ♖h8+ ♔g5 39 e8♕ d1♕ favours Black) 37...d1♕+ 38 ♔g5 ♕g1+ 39 ♔f6 ♕f1+ 40 ♔xe6 ♕h3+ 41 ♔d6 ♕a3+ is a draw.

2) 22...♖e3 23 fxe7 ♖e8 24 g5 (24 ♘g6!? should also lead to a draw) is dismissed by Hellers in *Informator* as winning for White, but this is probably also a draw after 24...♖xe1 25 ♖xe1 (25 ♕xe1 ♕xc2 26 gxh6 ♕c3 appears OK for Black) 25...d3! 26 gxh6 ♕g4+ 27 ♔h1 ♘c4 28 ♕f2 d2 29 ♖g1 d1♕ 30 h7+ ♔xh7 31 ♕xf7+ ♔h6 32 ♕f8+ ♔h7 with perpetual check.

22 ♕d2! ♔h7

22...d3 23 h3 changes nothing.

23 ♖f5!

A beautiful finish.

23...dxc3

23...exf5 24 ♘xf5 forces mate.

24 ♕xh6+! ♔xh6 25 ♖h5# (1-0)

Game 94

John Emms – Aaron Summerscale

London (Drury Lane) 1997

Philidor Defence

1 e4 d6 2 d4 e5 3 ♘f3 exd4 4 ♘xd4 g6 5 ♘c3 ♗g7 6 ♗e3 ♘f6 7 ♕d2 0-0 8 0-0-0 ♖e8 9 f3 ♘c6

This interesting position can arise from a number of different openings (e.g. the Pirc and the line 1 e4 e5 2 ♘f3 ♘c6 3 ♘c3 g6).

10 h4 *(D)*

10 g4 ♘e5 11 ♗e2 is the main alternative.

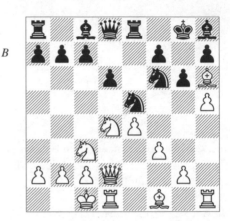

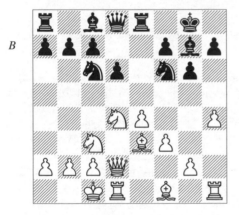

10...♘e5

Probably best; exchanging on d4 only helps White by bringing his bishop to the long diagonal.

11 ♗h6 ♗h8

This looks like a Dragon except that Black has no counterplay on the c-file. However, the missing e7-pawn gives Black some extra space to defend his kingside (for example, along the second rank).

12 h5! *(D)*

Surprisingly, this move was an innovation. Hitherto, the less energetic 12 ♗g5 and 12 ♗e2 had been played. It is surprising no one had tried sacrificing the h-pawn before, since it is such a familiar theme in the Dragon.

12...♘xh5 13 g4 ♘g3

13...♘f6 looks a more critical test. White has plenty of dangerous attacking ideas, but nothing clear-cut.

14 ♖h3 ♘xf1 15 ♖xf1 *(D)*

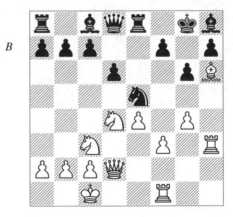

The exchange of Black's developed knight for White's unmoved bishop has favoured White. Black has lost an important defensive unit while White has gained time – indeed, he is already threatening to double on the h-file.

15...c5

Black tries to solve his problems by force, but as usual forcing play tends only to expose the weaknesses of one's own position.

16 ♘f5! *(D)*

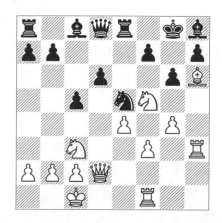

16...♘c4

16...gxf5 17 gxf5 and White wins after 17...♘g6 18 ♖hh1 (or 18 ♕g2 transposing into the following note after 20 ♕g2) 18...♕a5 19 ♗g5 ♗xc3 20 bxc3 ♕xa2 21 ♕h2 or 17...♗f6 18 ♖g1+ ♔h8 19 ♗g7+!! ♗xg7 20 ♖xg7 ♔xg7 21 ♕h6+ ♔g8 22 ♘d5, when mate is inevitable.

17 ♕d3 ♗e6

Or 17...♘e5 18 ♕e2, when it is still very risky for Black to take the piece; e.g., 18...gxf5 19 gxf5 ♘g6 20 ♕g2 ♕a5 21 ♖g3 ♗xc3 22 bxc3 ♖xc3 (22...♔h8 23 fxg6 fxg6 24 ♖xg6 hxg6 25 ♕xg6 wins for White) 23 fxg6 ♕a1+ 24 ♔d2 ♕d4+ 25 ♔e2 ♕c4+ 26 ♔e1 and White wins.

18 ♗f4 ♕b6

Once again 18...gxf5 19 gxf5 ♗e5 20 ♖g1+ ♔h8 21 ♗xe5+ ♘xe5 22 ♕d2 gives White an extremely strong attack; one variation runs 22...♗xf5 23 exf5 ♕f6 24 f4 ♘d7 25 ♕h2 ♕xf5 26 ♖h5 and wins.

19 b3 ♘e5 20 ♕d2 *(D)*

White is now ready to double or even triple on the h-file.

20...♗xf5?!

This makes life easy for White, but 20...gxf5 21 gxf5 ♘g6 22 ♖fh1 is again very strong. One attractive continuation is 22...♕a5 23 fxg6

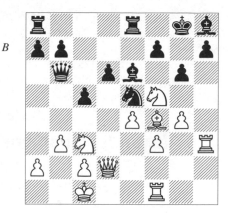

♗xc3 24 gxf7+ ♗xf7 25 ♖g3+ ♗g6 26 ♕d5+ ♔g7 27 ♖xg6+ hxg6 28 ♗h6+ ♔f6 29 ♗g5+ ♔g7 30 ♕xb7+ with mate to follow, while 22...♗xc3 23 ♕xc3 ♘xf4 24 ♖xh7 ♘e2+ 25 ♔b2 ♘xc3 26 f6 mating is another nice line.

21 gxf5

White's attacking chances are enhanced by his grip on the light squares.

21...♕b4 *(D)*

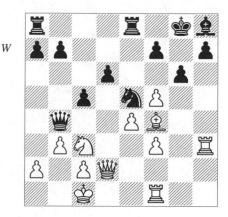

22 ♖xh7!

A spectacular finish.

22...♔xh7

22...♕a3+ 23 ♔b1 ♔xh7 doesn't help much, since White wins by 24 ♖h1+ ♔g7 (24...♔g8 25 ♖xh8+ ♔xh8 26 ♗xe5+ mates) 25 ♗xe5+ ♖xe5 26 f6+ ♔xf6 27 ♕xd6+ ♖e6 28 ♕f4+ ♔g7 (Black is also mated after 28...♔e7 29 ♘d5+) 29 ♕h6+ ♔f6 30 ♘d5+ ♔e5 31 ♕f4+ ♔d4 32 ♖d1#.

23 ♖h1+ ♔g8

23...♔g7 24 ♗xe5+ ♖xe5 25 f6+ ♔xf6 26 ♕xd6+ wins as in the previous note.

24 ♖xh8+! 1-0

The other rook is sacrificed in order to eliminate Black's main defensive piece. The finish

would be 24...♔xh8 (24...♔g7 25 f6+ ♔xf6 26 ♕xd6+ ♔g7 27 ♗h6+ ♔xh8 28 ♕f6+ mates) 25 ♗xe5+ and now taking back on e5 loses to 26 ♕h6+ ♔g8 27 f6, while 25...♔g8 26 ♕h6 mates in any case.

Game 95
Alexander Shabalov – Hannes Stefansson
Winnipeg 1997
Nimzo-Indian Defence, Rubinstein Variation

1 d4 ♘f6 2 c4 e6 3 ♘c3 ♗b4 4 e3 0-0 5 ♗d3 d5 6 ♘f3 c5 7 0-0 ♘c6 8 a3 ♗xc3 9 bxc3 ♕c7

If Black delays ...dxc4, White usually tries to take advantage of it by playing 10 cxd5. However, in this game White decides to continue as in the normal lines.

10 h3 dxc4 11 ♗xc4 b6 *(D)*

11...e5 12 ♗a2 transposes to a main line, but Black pursues an independent course.

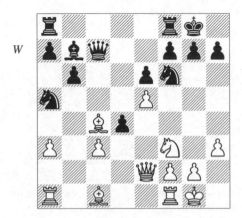

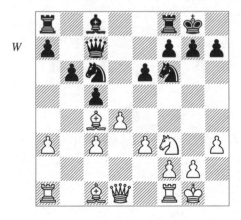

12 ♕e2!?

Removing the queen from the potentially dangerous d-file and preparing e4.

12...♗b7

12...♖d8 13 e4 cxd4 14 e5 ♘e8 15 ♗g5 gives White a dangerous initiative for the pawn.

13 e4 cxd4

13...e5 14 ♗g5 is awkward.

14 e5 ♘a5 *(D)*

This is obviously hazardous, but the real mistake only comes later.

15 exf6 ♕xc4 16 ♕e5 ♕d3

Black is taking rather a lot of risks. 16...♕d5 17 ♕g3 g6 is safer; e.g., 18 ♕h4 (18 ♕f4 ♕h5) 18...♕h5 19 ♕xh5 gxh5 20 ♘xd4 ♖fc8 with an unclear position.

17 ♘h4 ♗e4? *(D)*

Now Black is really entering the danger zone. 17...g6 is still satisfactory for Black, since he can defend g7 by ...♔h8 and ...♖g8 if necessary.

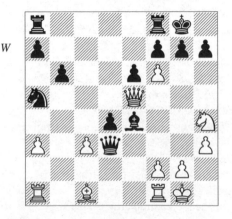

18 ♗h6!! *(D)*

It is not often that a piece is developed in such spectacular style. White threatens 19 ♗xg7 and cuts out the defence 18...g6. Not 18 fxg7?! ♖fc8, when the kingside attack is blocked.

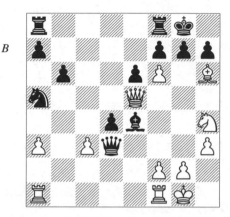

18...gxh6

18...♖fd8 19 ♖ad1 ♖d5 20 ♕f4 ♕xc3 21 ♕xe4 gxh6 22 ♘f5! favours White.

19 ♖fd1 ♕c4?!

This allows White to bring his rooks into the attack with gain of tempo. 19...♕c2 was the best chance, although then 20 ♖ac1 ♕e2 21 ♖e1 ♕d2 22 ♕xe4 ♕g5 23 cxd4 ♕xf6 24 ♖e3 leaves White with a clear advantage thanks to Black's offside knight.

20 ♖xd4 ♕xc3

20...♕c5 21 ♕xe4! ♔h8 22 ♖ad1 is similar to the game.

21 ♖ad1! *(D)*

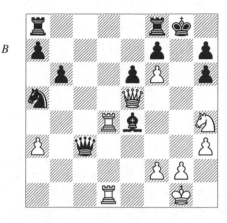

21...♔h8

Or 21...♗g6 22 ♕f4 ♔h8 23 ♕xh6 ♖g8 24 ♘xg6+, mating after 24...♖xg6 25 ♖d8+ or 24...fxg6 25 ♕xh7+.

22 ♕xe4

Threatening 23 ♕xa8.

22...♕xa3 23 ♘f3 ♘b3

Or 23...♖ac8 24 ♕f4.

24 ♖4d3 1-0

Black cannot prevent 25 ♕e3, attacking both b3 and h6.

Game 96

Alexander Onishchuk – Gerald Hertneck

Biel 1997

French Defence

1 e4 e6 2 d4 d5 3 ♘d2 ♘f6 4 e5 ♘e4

An unusual line with a poor theoretical reputation.

5 ♘xe4 dxe4 6 ♗c4

6 ♗e3 is the main alternative.

6...c5 7 d5 ♕b6?!

A risky idea. Black threatens 8...♗b4+, but this is easily met and then the queen is badly placed on b6. 7...♘d7 is a better chance, although White has an advantage in any case.

8 c3 ♘d7 9 f4! *(D)*

An excellent move. If Black exchanges on f3, White's development is accelerated, while otherwise White secures his e5-pawn and leaves Black with a weakling on e4.

9...exd5

9...exf3 10 ♘xf3 cxd5 11 ♕xd5 ♕e6 12 ♕xe6+ fxe6 13 0-0 ♘b6 14 ♗d3 favours White.

10 ♕xd5 ♕g6 11 ♘e2

On g3, the knight will both shield g2 and attack the e4-pawn.

11...♗e7

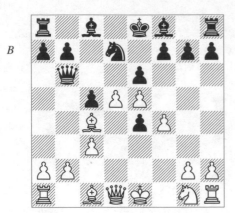

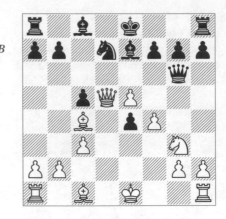

White wins a pawn after 11...♘b6 12 ♗b5+ ♗d7 13 ♗xd7+♘xd7 14 ♘g3, while 11...♕xg2 12 ♕xf7+ ♔d8 13 ♖g1 ♕xh2 14 ♗e3 gives him a decisive attack.

12 ♘g3 (D)

Not bad, but it was probably even better to play 12 f5! ♕xf5 13 ♖f1 ♕e6 (or 13...♕h5 14 ♕xf7+ ♕xf7 15 ♗xf7+ ♔d8 16 ♗f4 and Black is paralysed) 14 ♕xe4 ♕xe5 15 ♗xf7+ ♔d8 16 ♕g4, followed by ♗f4 and 0-0-0, with a crushing position for White.

12...♗h4?!

12...f5 is slightly better, but after 13 exf6 (13 ♗b5 a6 14 ♗a4 is also strong, since 14...♖a7 15 e6 b5 can be met by 16 0-0! bxa4 17 ♘xf5 ♘b8 18 ♘xe7 ♖xe7 19 f5, followed by ♗f4, with tremendous compensation for the piece) 13...♘xf6 14 ♕e5 White has a clear advantage as Black has trouble castling.

13 0-0 ♗xg3 14 hxg3 0-0 15 f5 ♕xg3

15...♕c6 16 e6 ♕xd5 17 ♗xd5 and White wins.

16 ♗f4 ♕g4

The decisive combination is unusually attractive.

17 e6! fxe6

17...♘b6 18 exf7+ ♔h8 19 ♕xc5 ♗xf5 20 ♗d6 wins for White.

18 fxe6 ♘b6 (D)

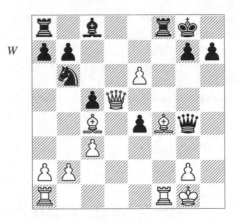

19 e7+! ♘xd5 20 exf8♕+ ♔xf8 21 ♗d6++ ♔e8 22 ♗b5+ ♗d7 23 ♖f8# (1-0)

Game 97
Rafael Leitão – Alexander Baburin
Europe vs Americas, Bermuda 1998
Queen's Gambit Accepted

1 d4 d5 2 c4 dxc4 3 e3 e6 4 ♗xc4 c5 5 ♘f3 a6 6 0-0 ♘f6 7 ♘c3

A somewhat unusual move, although it often transposes back into normal lines. 7 a4, 7 ♕e2, 7 ♗b3 and 7 dxc5 are the most popular moves. The last is suitable for those wishing to test their endgame skills.

7...b5 8 ♗b3 ♗b7 9 ♕e2 ♘bd7 10 e4

10 Rd1 reaches a standard position, but White prefers an immediate central advance.

10...cxd4

10...b4 11 e5!? Ng4 (11...bxc3 12 exf6 Qxf6 13 d5 is good for White) 12 Ne4 cxd4 13 Ba4 is unclear.

11 Nxd4 Bc5 12 Be3 Qb6 13 Rfd1 Ne5 *(D)*

It is sounder to play the simple 13...0-0, but Black has not yet overstepped the mark.

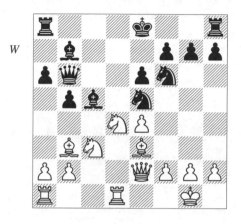

14 Rac1

14 a4 is another possibility, when Black can reply 14...Neg4 or even 14...0-0.

14...Rc8?

Now, however, Black delays castling one move too long. 14...0-0 15 f3 Rfd8 would have been equal.

15 Na4!! *(D)*

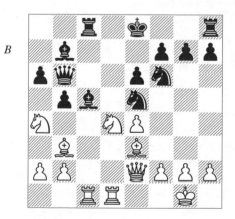

A stunning and completely sound sacrifice. Acceptance is forced.

15...bxa4 16 Bxa4+ Ke7

This move was given a question mark by Leitão in *Informator*, but so far as I can see there is nothing better. 16...Kf8 loses to 17 Rxc5 Rxc5 18 Nb3, while 16...Ned7 17 Rxc5 Rxc5 (17...Qxc5 18 Nxe6 will transpose to the analysis of 16...Nfd7) 18 Nb3 Bc6 19 Nxc5 Bxa4 (19...Qxc5 loses to 20 Rd6!) 20 Nxa4 leaves White a pawn up.

The only other defence is 16...Nfd7 *(D)*, and now White has two promising lines:

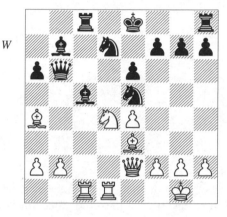

1) 17 Rxc5 Qxc5 (17...Rxc5 18 Nb3 Bc6 19 Bxc6 Qxc6 20 Bxc5 Nxc5 21 Rc1 Ned3 22 Qxd3 Nxd3 23 Rxc6 Ke7 24 Rxa6 and White has a clear extra pawn in the ending) 18 Nxe6 Qc4 (18...Qb4 19 Bxd7+ Nxd7 20 Nxg7+ Kd8 21 Bg5+! Kc7 22 Bf4+ Kd8 23 Qg4! gives White a winning attack, while 18...Qa5 19 Bxd7+ Nxd7 20 Nxg7+ Kd8 21 Qf3 is clearly better for White) 19 Bxd7+ Nxd7 20 Nxg7+ Kf8 21 Qxc4 Rxc4 22 Bh6! Rc6 (the alternatives 22...Rxe4 23 Nf5+ Ke8 24 Nd6+ Ke7 25 Nxe4 Bxe4 26 Re1 and 22...Ke7 23 Nf5+ Kd8 24 Nd6 Rc6 25 Nxb7+ Kc7 26 Bf4+ are also very good for White) 23 Rxd7 Rxh6 24 Nf5 Re6 25 Rxb7 Rxe4 26 g3 Re6 27 Ra7 and White wins the a-pawn as well, with a large endgame advantage.

2) 17 b4 Qxb4 (Black is also worse after 17...Rxd4 18 Bxd4 Qxb4 19 Bxd7+ Nxd7 20 Rb1 or 17...Bxb4 18 Nc6!) 18 Bxd7+ Nxd7 19 Rb1 Qa4 (19...Qxb1 20 Rxb1 Bxe4 21 Rd1 favours White) 20 Rxb7 Nf6 21 Nxe6! Bxe3 22 Rc7! Bxf2+ 23 Kxf2 Rxc7 24 Nxc7+ Ke7

25 ♘d5+! ♘xd5 26 exd5+ and Black is in trouble.

17 ♖xc5! ♖xc5

Not 17...♕xc5 18 ♘f5+ exf5 19 ♗xc5+ ♖xc5 20 exf5 and further material drops off.

18 ♘b3 *(D)*

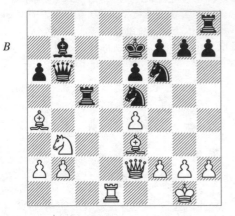

The critical position.

18...♖hc8?!

18...♘xe4 is the only possible defence, but even after this Black is in considerable trouble: 19 ♘xc5 ♘xc5 and now:

1) 20 ♕d2 ♗d5! (the alternatives 20...♘e4 21 ♕d7+! ♘xd7 22 ♖xd7+ ♔f6 23 ♗xb6 ♖c8 24 h4, 20...♘g4 21 ♕d7+ ♘xd7 22 ♖xd7+ ♔f6 23 ♗xb6, 20...♘ed3 21 ♗xc5+ ♕xc5 22 ♕xd3 ♗d5 23 ♕g3 g6 24 ♕h4+ f6 25 ♕h6 and 20...♘c4 21 ♗xc5+ ♕xc5 22 ♕d7+ ♔f6 23 ♕xb7 ♘b6 24 ♗b3 all favour White in varying

degrees) 21 b4 (21 ♖c1 ♘e4 22 ♕xd5 exd5 23 ♗xb6 ♖b8 is unclear) 21...♘e4 22 ♗xb6 ♘xd2 23 ♗c5+ ♔f6 24 ♖xd2 and, although White has the two bishops, Black's pieces are firmly entrenched in the centre. While White retains an edge, the odds are on a draw.

2) 20 f4! ♘g6 21 f5 ♕a5 22 ♕c4 ♖c8 23 fxg6 ♘xa4 (23...hxg6 24 ♕h4+ f6 25 ♕h7 ♔f8 26 ♗c2 gives White a winning position) 24 ♕h4+ f6 25 ♕xh7 ♗d5 26 ♕xg7+ ♔d6 27 ♕xf6 and White has three pawns for the piece, including the dangerous g6-pawn, plus an attack. Black is in trouble.

19 ♘xc5 ♖xc5 20 b4! *(D)*

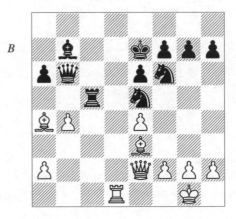

Baburin must have overlooked this neat finish.

20...♕xb4 21 ♕d2 1-0

White wins material.

Game 98

Jan Timman – Loek van Wely

Match (6), Breda 1998

Sicilian Defence, Scheveningen Variation

1 e4 c5 2 ♘f3 d6 3 d4 cxd4 4 ♘xd4 ♘f6 5 ♘c3 a6 6 ♗e3 ♘c6 7 h3 e6 8 g4 ♗e7 9 ♗g2 h6 *(D)*

A tricky decision. Black would like to prevent g5 by White, but the danger is that if Black castles kingside, then White might eventually play g5 in any case, when lines will be opened against Black's king. 9...0-0 10 f4 is the alternative.

10 f4 ♕c7 11 0-0 ♘xd4?!

It may be better to delay this capture, because if White plays, for example, ♕d2, then Black may gain a tempo. In fact, after 11...♗d7 White has no good waiting move and should probably continue 12 ♘b3, ruling out the exchange on d4 for good.

12 ♕xd4 e5 13 ♕d2 exf4 14 ♖xf4 ♗e6

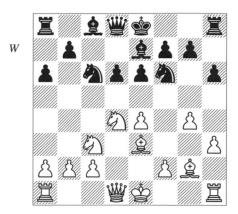

Black's plan has given White extra time – he has gained the moves ♕d2 and ♖xf4 almost for free – and Timman uses this time to bring up the reserves.

15 ♖af1 0-0?! *(D)*

This move invites a very dangerous sacrifice, but 15...♘d7 also fails to equalize after 16 ♘d5 ♗xd5 17 ♕xd5 ♗f6 (not 17...♘e5? 18 ♖xf7) 18 e5! ♘xe5 (18...dxe5 19 ♖c4 ♕d8 20 ♕xb7 ♖b8 21 ♕xa6 also favours White) 19 ♕xb7 ♕xb7 20 ♗xb7 ♖b8 21 ♖b4 ♔d7 22 ♖b3, when White has a slight endgame advantage.

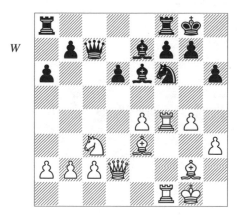

16 ♖xf6!

This double exchange sacrifice is remarkable because it does not result in instant threats – it is just that Black is unable to prevent White's queen and minor pieces from converging slowly on the black king.

16...♗xf6 17 ♖xf6 gxf6 18 ♕f2 *(D)*
18...♔g7?

This is a serious error which loses quickly. Of the alternatives, 18...♕d8 19 ♕h4 ♖c8 20 ♕xh6 ♖c4 (trying to prevent ♗d4) 21 ♘e2!, heading for h5, and 18...♖fe8 19 ♗d4 ♕d8 20 ♗xf6 ♕a5 21 ♕h4 ♕b6+ 22 ♔h2 ♕e3 23 g5 are both winning for White. 18...♕a5 is slightly better, but after 19 ♗xh6 (19 e5 fxe5 20 ♘e4 f5 defends) 19...♕c5 (19...♖fc8 loses to 20 ♘d5 ♗xd5 21 ♕xf6) 20 ♗e3 ♕a5 21 ♗d4 ♕g5 22 ♗xf6 Black is still in difficulties.

Curiously enough, the position after 18 ♕f2 occurred a few months later in a game from the Elista Olympiad. In this game Black found the best defence, 18...♕e7, aiming to transfer the queen to f8. Play continued 19 ♗d4 ♖fc8 20 ♗xf6 ♕f8 21 ♕g3 ♖c5 22 h4 *(D)* with the deadly threat of g5.

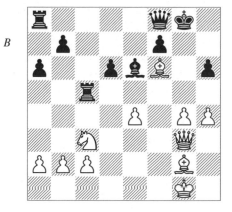

Now Black can try:

1) 22...♖e5 23 g5 is dangerous for Black; for example, 23...♔h7 24 ♘e2 ♖c8 25 ♘f4

♕g8 26 c3 ♖c4 27 ♕f3 ♕f8 28 ♕h5 ♗f5 29
exf5 ♖xf4 30 g6+ ♔g8 31 g7 ♕c8 32 ♕xh6
♕c5+ 33 ♔h2 ♖xh4+ 34 ♕xh4 1-0 Nguyen
Anh Dung-Mohd, Elista Olympiad 1998.

2) 22...♔h7 may be a better chance, since
neither 23 ♘d5 ♖xc2 24 e5 ♖xg2+ 25 ♕xg2
♗xd5 26 ♕xd5 dxe5 nor 23 e5 ♖xe5 24 ♗xe5
dxe5 25 ♕xe5 ♕g7 is adequate for White. However, in this case too 23 g5! is the correct reply,
the immediate threat being 24 ♘d5; if Black
then exchanges on d5, the e4-square becomes
available for White's light-squared bishop. The
most obvious reply is 23...♖e5, but this just
transposes to line '1'. Although it is not clear
that White's attack is truly winning, Black certainly has to endure great defensive difficulties.

19 e5! (D)

Clearing the e4-square for the light-squared
bishop enhances White's attack. 19 ♗xh6+?
♔xh6 20 ♕xf6+ ♔h7 is only a draw.

19...fxe5

Or 19...♖h8 20 ♕xf6+ ♔g8 21 exd6 ♕xd6
22 ♗d4 ♖h7 23 ♘e4 and Black cannot hope to

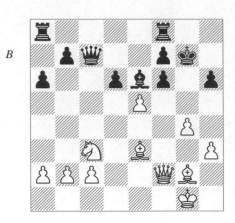

B

survive; e.g., 23...♕c7 24 ♕f2 ♔f8 25 ♘f6
♖h8 26 ♗c5+ ♔g7 27 ♕d4! and wins.

20 ♗xh6+! ♔g6

After 20...♔xh6 White forces mate by 21
♕f6+ ♔h7 22 ♗e4+ ♔g8 23 ♕g5+ ♔h8 24
♕h6+ ♔g8 25 ♕h7#.

21 ♕h4 1-0

Since after 21...f6 22 ♕h5+ ♔h7 23 ♗xf8+
♔g8 24 ♗h6 White wins easily.

Game 99

Vladimir Kramnik – Joël Lautier

Tilburg 1998

Queen's Gambit, Semi-Slav Defence

1 d4 d5 2 ♘f3 c6 3 c4 e6 4 ♕c2

Avoiding the main variations of the Semi-
Slav.

4...dxc4

It is a little unusual to exchange on c4 so
soon. 4...♘f6 is more common.

**5 ♕xc4 ♘f6 6 ♗g5 ♗e7 7 e3 0-0 8 ♗d3 h6 9
♗xf6**

9 ♗h4 is also playable, but Kramnik prefers
to depend on a lead in development.

9...♗xf6 10 ♘c3 ♘d7 11 ♖d1 ♕e7 12 ♗b1

White cannot prevent ...e5; for example, 12
♘e4 e5 13 d5 cxd5 14 ♕xd5 ♕b4+ 15 ♖d2
♘b6! only leads to equality.

12...e5 13 0-0 (D)

13 d5 ♘b6 14 ♕d3 e4!? 15 ♘xe4 ♘xd5 is
safe for Black.

13...exd4

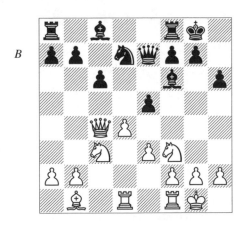

B

Now Black will inevitably lose a tempo along
the e-file. 13...g6 is probably best, when 14
♕b3 (not 14 ♗xg6? ♘b6 15 ♕b3 ♗e6 and
Black wins a piece) 14...exd4 15 exd4 ♘b6 is

better for Black than the game since White's queen is less actively placed.

14 exd4 ♘b6 15 ♕d3 g6 16 ♖fe1 *(D)*

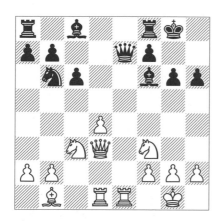

16...♕b4?!

The start of a faulty plan which takes too many pieces away from the kingside. 16...♕d8 17 ♕e3 would be only slightly better for White.

17 ♕d2

Attacking h6 and threatening 18 ♘e4.

17...♘c4?

It is too risky to allow White's queen so near to the black king. 17...♗g7 is better, although White has some advantage after 18 a3 ♕d6 19 ♘e5 ♗e6 20 ♘e4 ♕c7 21 ♘c5 or 18 ♘e5 ♘c4

19 ♘xc4 ♕xc4 20 a3 ♗g4 21 ♗a2 ♕a6 22 f3 ♗d7 23 ♖e7.

18 ♕xh6 ♘xb2 *(D)*

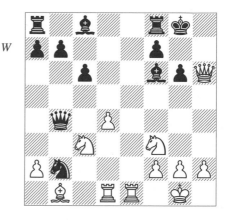

Attacking c3 and d1.

19 ♗xg6! fxg6 20 ♘g5!

This is the point. Not 20 ♕xg6+? ♗g7 followed by ...♗f5.

20...♗xg5 21 ♕xg6+ ♔h8 22 ♕h5+ ♔g7 23 ♕xg5+ ♔f7

Or 23...♔h8 24 ♖e4 and White wins.

24 ♖e3! 1-0

Since 24...♗e6 (or 24...♘xd1 25 ♕f4+ ♔g7 26 ♖g3+ ♔h7 27 ♕h4#) 25 ♖de1 ♖ae8 allows mate by 26 ♖f3+.

Game 100

Alexei Shirov – Zbynek Hraček

Match (2), Ostrava 1998

Caro-Kann Defence, Advance Variation

1 e4 c6 2 d4 d5 3 e5 ♗f5 4 ♘c3

One of the most aggressive systems against the Caro-Kann.

4...♕b6

A perfectly reasonable alternative to the more common 4...e6. This early queen sortie became popular after the game Velimirović–Kasparov, Moscow Interzonal 1982.

5 ♘f3

One point of delaying ...e6 is to meet 5 g4 by 5...♗d7.

5...e6 6 ♗e2 ♘d7 7 0-0 ♘e7 8 b3 *(D)*

A direct method of solving the problem of the queen's attack on b2.

8...c5!?

8...♗g4 and 8...a6 have also been played, but Hraček prefers to seek immediate counterplay.

9 dxc5 ♘xc5 10 ♘d4

10 ♗c3 ♘c6 11 ♘b5!? may give White some advantage, but not 11 ♘a4?, which achieves nothing after 11...♕a5.

10...a6 11 ♗e3 ♕d8

Black moves the queen out of the bishop's line of fire, perhaps fearing the line 11...♗g6 12

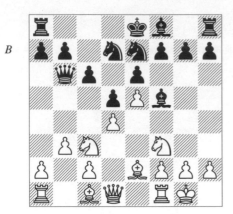

B

♘xe6 fxe6 13 ♘a4 ♘xa4 14 ♗xb6 ♘xb6 15 c4, which looks good for White.

12 g4?!

Rather too ambitious. 12 f4!? is sounder, with an edge for White.

12...♗g6 13 f4 *(D)*

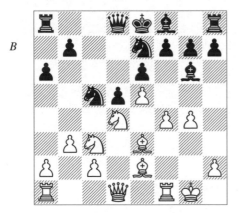

B

Typically, Shirov gives little thought to the safety of his own king, but plays directly for the attack.

13...♘e4! 14 ♘a4 h5!

Hraček defends by counter-attack; this move involves a possible piece sacrifice.

15 f5! *(D)*

15 gxh5 ♘f5 is good for Black.

15...hxg4 16 fxe6!

It is more important to demolish Black's pawn-structure than to grab material. After 16 fxg6 ♘xg6 17 ♗xg4 ♕h4 18 ♕e2 ♘xe5 Black has a very strong attack; e.g., 19 ♗f3 ♗d6 20 ♗xe4 ♘c4! and White is in trouble.

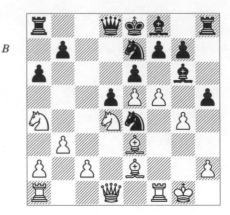

B

16...g3?

Once again Black chooses the most active move, but this time it is probably a mistake. 16...f5 is better, cementing his kingside pawns together. After 17 exf6 (17 c4!? is another interesting try) 17...gxf6 18 ♗f4! (18 ♗xg4 f5 is excellent for Black after 19 ♘xf5 ♘xf5 20 ♗xf5 ♗xf5 21 ♖xf5 ♕h4 or 19 ♗f3 b5 20 ♘b2 ♕c7 21 ♕e2 ♗g7) 18...♗g7 19 c4 the position is very double-edged.

17 exf7+ ♗xf7 *(D)*

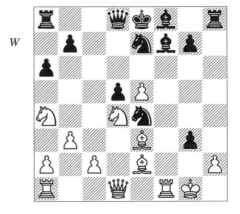

W

18 h3!

Slowing down Black's counter-attack. 18 hxg3? ♘xg3 is good for Black, while 18 ♗g4? gxh2+ 19 ♔g2 ♘g6 20 e6 ♘h4+ 21 ♔xh2 ♕c7+ 22 ♗f4 ♘g6+ 23 ♔g1 ♘xf4 24 exf7+ ♕xf7 even wins for Black.

18...g2 *(D)*

Shirov considers this a mistake, but in my view Black is already in a very bad way. Shirov suggests 18...♘f2 (18...♖xh3? 19 ♗g4 followed by ♕f3 clearly favours White) 19 ♗xf2 gxf2+ 20 ♖xf2 ♘c6 and indicates in *Informator* that Black has compensation for the pawn. However, so far as I can see Black is lost after 21 ♗g4!; for example, 21...♕c7 (21...♘xe5 22 ♕e1 ♗d6 23 ♘f3 ♕c7 24 ♘xe5 ♗xe5 25 ♖f5 and 21...♘xd4 22 ♕xd4 ♕c7 23 ♖af1 ♗g6 24 ♕xd5 are also winning for White) 22 ♘xc6 ♕xc6 (or 22...bxc6 23 ♕d3 with an extra pawn and a crushing attack) 23 e6 ♗g6 24 ♕d4 ♗e4 (24...b5 25 e7! and White wins) 25 e7 ♔xe7 26 ♘c3 and White must win.

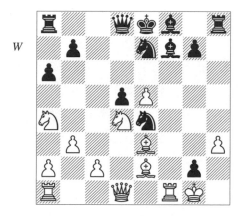

19 ♖xf7!

Black's pawn-thrust has only encouraged White to make this sacrifice.

19...♔xf7 20 ♗g4!

The weakness of e6 provides the motivation for White's combination.

20...♕c7

Black has nothing better.

21 ♕f3+ ♔e8 22 ♗e6 *(D)*

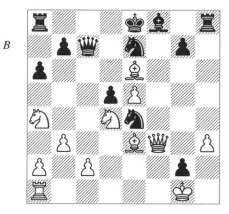

22...♘c6

Black cannot stave off White's attack; for example, 22...♕xe5 23 ♗f7+! ♔d8 24 ♘e6+ ♔d7 25 ♖d1 or 22...♘g6 23 ♗xd5 ♘c5 24 ♕xg2! ♘h4 (24...♘e7 25 ♖f1) 25 ♕g4 ♕xe5 26 ♖e1 and Black's king, trapped in the centre, has no escape.

23 ♗xd5 ♘xd4 24 ♕xe4 1-0

Because 24...♘e2+ 25 ♔xg2 and 24...♕xc2 25 ♗xd4 are hopeless.

Game 101
Veselin Topalov – Vasily Ivanchuk
Linares 1999
English Opening

1 ♘f3 c5 2 c4 ♘c6 3 d4 cxd4 4 ♘xd4 e6 5 g3

A slightly unusual move-order (instead of 5 ♘c3 ♘f6 6 g3). Ivanchuk immediately takes advantage of it by delaying ...♘f6.

5...♗b4+ 6 ♘c3 ♕a5 7 ♘b5 d5! 8 a3 ♗xc3+ 9 bxc3?!

A dubious novelty. 9 ♘xc3 d4 10 b4 ♘xb4 11 axb4 ♕xa1 12 ♘b5 ♘f6 was unclear in Lerner-Khuzman, Kuibyshev 1986.

9...♘f6 10 ♗g2 0-0

White is losing the initiative. He has yet to castle, while Black is already well developed.

11 ♕b3 dxc4 12 ♕xc4 e5

Freeing the light-squared bishop for action.

13 ♘d6?!

13 ♕b3 is the best chance, although Black retains an advantage after 13...♗e6 14 ♕b2 ♖fd8.

13...♗e6 14 ♕d3 *(D)*

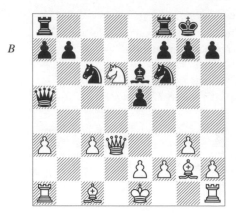

B

14...e4!

Ivanchuk exploits White's doubtful opening play with great energy.

15 ♘xe4

White may as well accept, as there is no good square for his queen; e.g., 15 ♕e3 ♘g4 16 ♕d2 ♖ad8! 17 ♘xb7 ♕a4 18 ♘xd8 ♖xd8 and Black wins.

15...♘xe4 16 ♗xe4 ♖ad8 (D)

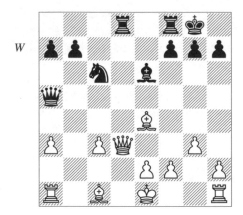

W

17 ♕c2

After 17 ♕e3 ♖fe8 White has no good way to disentangle his e-file pieces.

17...♘d4! 18 ♕b2 ♘xe2!

This sacrifice is far more incisive than the alternatives.

19 ♔xe2

19 ♕b4 is met by 19...♘xc3!.

19...♖fe8! 20 ♕b4

There is only a choice of evils; for example, 20 f3 f5 21 ♗xb7 ♕xc3!! 22 ♕xc3 (22 ♔f1 ♗c4+ 23 ♔f2 ♕xb2+ 24 ♗xb2 ♖e2+ also wins for Black) 22...♗c4++ 23 ♔f2 ♖e2+ 24 ♔g1 ♖d1+ leads to mate.

20...♕h5+! 21 f3 f5 (D)

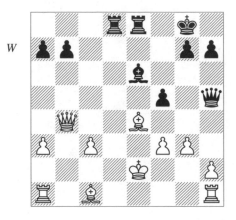

W

22 g4

22 ♕c5 ♗d5! is also decisive.

22...♕h3 23 gxf5

Or 23 ♔f2 fxe4 24 ♕xe4 ♗d5 and Black wins.

23...♗xf5 24 ♕c4+ ♔h8 25 ♖e1 ♖xe4+!

An attractive conclusion.

0-1

26 fxe4 leads to mate after 26...♗g4+ 27 ♔f2 ♕xh2+ 28 ♔e3 (or 28 ♔f1 ♗h3#) 28...♕g3#.

Game 102

Garry Kasparov – Loek van Wely

Wijk aan Zee 2000

Sicilian Defence, English Attack

1 e4 c5 2 ♘f3 d6 3 d4 cxd4 4 ♘xd4 ♘f6 5 ♘c3 a6 6 ♗e3

During the 1990s, 6 ♗e3 increased in popularity to such an extent that it can now be considered White's main line against the Najdorf.

6...e6

A big decision for Black. 6...e5 is more in keeping with the strategy behind the Najdorf, but many players prefer to switch to a Scheveningen pawn-structure when confronted by 6 ♗e3.

7 f3 b5 8 g4

White adopts the English Attack, so called because it was largely developed by Chandler, Nunn and Short in the 1980s. The theory of this line is now rather extensive and both players continue down one of the critical continuations.

8...h6 9 ♕d2 ♘bd7 10 0-0-0 ♗b7

The latest twist is 10...b4 11 ♘a4 ♘e5, which came into prominence as a result of the game Kramnik-Topalov, Wijk aan Zee 2005, which was won by Black in a mere 20 moves.

11 h4 b4 12 ♘a4 (D)

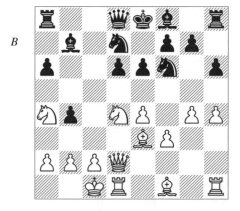

12...d5

The most popular move has been 12...♕a5 but the immediate pawn-push has also attracted considerable attention. However, this line is risky for Black. The rule that a flank attack should be met by a central thrust is only a guide and may not apply in every situation. Here White has a lead in development and Black's king is stuck in the centre, so opening up the position may only provide White with extra avenues of attack.

13 ♗h3

A typical move for White in this line, taking aim at the e6-square. If White manages to play g5, then Black has to worry about both g6 and a possible sacrifice on e6.

13...g5 (D)

Black has also tried 13...♕a5 and 13...♘e5, but the practical results after these moves have been heavily in White's favour. 13...dxe4 is also dubious in view of the surprising reply 14 g5 hxg5 15 hxg5 exf3 16 ♘xe6 fxe6 17 ♗f5! exf5 18 ♖xh8 and White has a very dangerous attack.

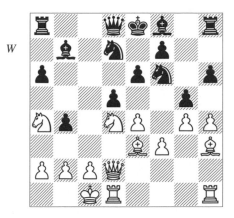

14 ♗g2

In a later game Kasparov-Wojtkiewicz, Kopavogur (rapid) 2000, Kasparov switched to 14 hxg5 hxg5 15 e5!? ♘xe5 16 ♗xg5 and won convincingly after 16...♖g8 17 ♘b6 ♘c4 18 ♘xc4 dxc4 19 ♗xf6 ♕xf6 20 ♘xe6 ♗h6 21 g5 fxe6 22 ♕d7+ ♔f8 23 gxh6 ♗d5 24 ♕d6+ ♕e7 25 ♕f4+ ♕f7 26 ♕e5 1-0. Doubtless Black could have played better, but the general impression is that his position is not really strong enough to support 12...d5.

14...gxh4?!

This looks wrong on general principles since Black destroys his own kingside pawn-structure. 14...dxe4?! is also bad since 15 hxg5 exf3 16 ♗xf3 ♗xf3 17 ♘xf3 ♘g4 18 ♗d4 gives a wide-open position in which Black has no safe place for his king. Kasparov suggested 14...♖g8 in *Informator*, and it may be that this is why he switched to 14 hxg5 against Wojtkiewicz. However, to this day the move remains untested in over-the-board play, and the only example I could find was Walsh-Diaz, corr. 2002, which continued 15 hxg5 hxg5 16 ♗xg5 ♘xe4 17 fxe4 ♕xg5 18 exd5 ♗xd5 and Black had a comfortable position.

15 ♖xh4 *(D)*

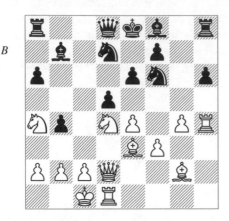

Now Black once again has to contend with the threat of g5.

15...dxe4

The greedy 15...♘xe4 16 fxe4 ♕xh4 is punished by 17 exd5 exd5 (17...e5 18 d6! is also very bad for Black) 18 ♗xd5! ♗xd5 19 ♘f5 ♕f6 20 ♕xd5 ♖d8 21 ♗d4 and White wins.

16 g5 ♘d5

16...exf3 17 ♘xf3 ♘d5 18 ♗d4 ♖h7 19 ♕d3 costs Black material.

17 ♖xe4

White's rook has reached the e-file by an unusual route and a sacrifice on e6 is not far off.

17...hxg5

The alternatives allow White to crash through straight away:

1) 17...♘xe3 18 ♘xe6! fxe6 19 ♖xe6+ ♔f7 20 ♕xe3 with a winning attack.

2) 17...♕a5 18 ♘xe6 fxe6 19 ♖xe6+ ♗e7 (after 19...♔f7 20 ♕d3! ♔xe6 21 ♕e4+ ♘e5 22 ♗h3+ ♔d6 23 ♗c5+ Black must give up his queen) 20 ♘b6! ♘7xb6 21 ♗xb6 ♕xa2 22 ♕d4 ♖g8 23 g6 and Black cannot meet the various threats, such as 24 ♖xe7+ and 24 ♕e5.

18 ♗xg5 ♕a5

18...♕xg5 19 ♕xg5 ♗h6 20 ♘xe6! ♗xg5+ 21 ♘xg5+ leaves White a clear pawn up in the ending. While this is hardly an attractive option, it is probably objectively better than the line played.

19 f4! *(D)*

The most clear-cut continuation of the attack. White takes time out to bring his light-squared bishop into the fray, so that when he does finally sacrifice on e6 it will be truly decisive. Many players would have rushed in with 19 ♘xe6 fxe6 20 ♖xe6+ but, although dangerous, this is less clear after 20...♔f7 21 ♕e2 ♖c8 22 f4 ♖h2!.

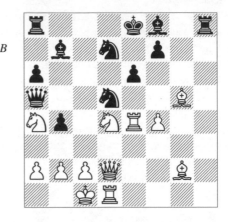

19...♖h2

Other moves are no better, since 19...♕xa4 20 ♘xe6 fxe6 21 ♖xe6+ wins after 21...♔f7 22 ♗xd5 or 21...♘e7 22 ♗xb7, while 19...♘7f6 20 ♗xf6 ♘xf6 21 ♘xe6 ♗xe4 22 ♗xe4 ♖c8 23 ♘xf8 gives White a winning attack.

20 ♘xe6 *(D)*

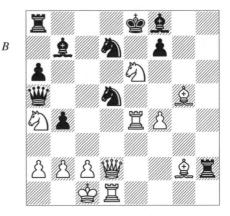

The inevitable blow falls.

20...fxe6

Or 20...♗e7 21 ♘g7+ ♔f8 22 ♗xe7+ ♔xg7 23 ♖g1 and White wins.

21 ♖xe6+ ♔f7

21...♗e7 22 ♖xe7+ ♔f8 23 ♕d4 wins at once for White.

22 ♕d3!

Black has no hope once the white queen joins the attack.

22...♗g7

Black also loses after 22...♔xe6 23 ♗xd5+ ♗xd5 24 ♕g6+ ♘f6 25 ♕xf6+ ♔d7 26 ♖xd5+ ♕xd5 27 ♘b6+ or 22...♔g8 23 ♕g6+ ♔h8 24 ♖ee1, followed by ♖h1.

23 ♕f5+ ♔g8 24 ♖xd5 ♕xa4 25 ♖e7 1-0

Game 103
Alexei Fedorov – Alexei Shirov
Polanica Zdroj 2000
King's Gambit

1 e4 e5 2 f4

You won't find many grandmasters willing to play the King's Gambit, especially against such a feared tactician as Alexei Shirov. In this game Fedorov pays the price for his bravery. Indeed, in his *Informator* notes, Shirov already gives this move a '?!' mark – a bit harsh, perhaps, but it indicates how far the King's Gambit has fallen in the estimation of top players.

2...exf4 3 ♘f3 g5

There are many different ways to meet the King's Gambit. These days this move is played not to hang on to the extra pawn at all costs, but more to hand back the pawn after extracting some concessions from White.

4 h4 g4 5 ♘e5

5 ♘g5 h6 6 ♘xf7 ♔xf7 7 d4 is the Allgaier Gambit, which is virtually refuted by 7...f3!.

5...d6

Attacking the knight limits White's choice. The alternative is 5...♘f6, which may transpose to the game after 6 ♘xg4 d6 but which gives White a range of alternatives. Note that old lines which aim to hang on to Black's material, such as 5...h5, are no longer played. Instead, Black returns the pawn to catch up with, or even overtake, White in development.

6 ♘xg4 ♘f6 *(D)*

7 ♘f2?!

White plays to avoid exchanges and continue his development with d4 and ♘c3. However, this move is very slow and Black is able to get his pieces out quickly. 7 ♘xf6+ ♕xf6 8 ♘c3 is a more solid line which leads to a roughly equal position.

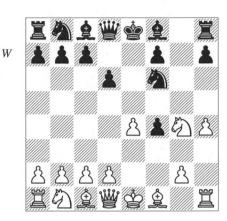

7...♖g8!

Occupying the half-open file is best. White's score after this move in MegaBase 2007 is a meagre 26%. Even in 2000, when this game was played, White's score was miserable, which makes you wonder why anyone should want to adopt this line for White.

8 d4 ♗h6

The f4-pawn remains a thorn in White's flesh and makes it awkward for White to develop his queenside and castle to safety on that side.

9 ♘c3 ♘c6!

Stronger than 9...♕e7 10 ♘d3 ♗g4 11 ♗e2 ♗xe2 12 ♕xe2 ♘c6, which was played in Planinc-Korchnoi, Moscow 1975. In that game White blundered here with 13 ♗xf4?, when instead 13 e5! would have given him a good game.

10 ♘d5?

This allows Black to open the e-file, after which White's king comes under direct assault. The alternatives are:

1) 10 ♗b5 a6 11 ♗xc6+ bxc6 doesn't help White as he must now deal with the problem of his hanging g2-pawn.

2) 10 ♘d3 ♗g4 11 ♗e2 ♗xe2 12 ♘xe2 ♘xe4 13 ♗xf4 ♖g4 14 ♗xh6 ♖xh4 15 0-0 ♖xh6 is at least slightly better for Black.

3) 10 ♕d3 is White's best chance, intending ♗d2 and 0-0-0, although even here the best White can hope for after 10...♘h5 is equality.

10...♘xd5 11 exd5 (D)

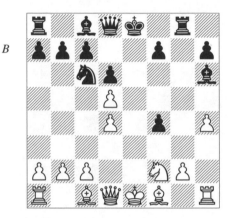

11...♕e7+!

A strong novelty. Hitherto Black had played 11...♘e7, with rather unclear consequences.

12 ♗e2

Forced, since 12 ♕e2 loses to 12...♘xd4.

12...♘b4 13 c4 ♗f5!

This piece sacrifice is the point behind Black's innovation. White is forced to accept the sacrifice, but then all Black's pieces can join in the attack against White's king.

14 ♕a4+ ♔f8!

The most accurate, since 14...♔d8 15 ♕xb4 ♖e8 16 ♕d2 f3 17 ♕d1 ♕xe2+ 18 ♕xe2 ♖xe2+ 19 ♔f1 ♗g7 (19...♗xc1 20 ♖xc1 ♖xb2 21 g4 followed by ♖h3 is not clear) 20 gxf3 ♖c2 21 ♗e3 still offers White a slight hope of saving the game.

15 ♕xb4 ♖e8 16 ♕d2 ♖xg2 (D)

In return for the piece, Black has a pawn and an immense attack. The immediate threats are 17...f3, 17...♗g4 and 17...♕xh4!.

17 ♔f1
Forced.
17...♖g3

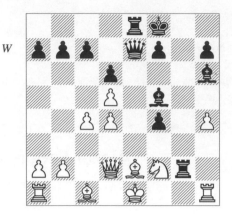

With the deadly threat of 18...♖e3, so White must move his queen.

18 ♕d1

18 ♕e1 loses more quickly after 18...♗e4 19 ♖h2 (19 ♘xe4 ♕xe4 20 ♖h2 ♗g7! followed by ...♗xd4 wins) 19...♗f3 20 ♘h1 ♗xh1 21 ♖xh1 ♕e4.

18...♗e4 19 ♖h2 f5

Creating a new threat of 20...♕g7.

20 ♘xe4

White must remove the dangerous bishop, since 20 ♘h1 loses to 20...♗xh1 21 ♖xh1 ♕e4.

20...fxe4

20...♕xe4? would be a serious mistake, since after 21 a4! followed by ♖a3 White would have defensive chances. The move played gives Black two connected passed pawns in the centre.

21 ♗g4 (D)

Or 21 ♗h5 ♕g7 22 ♖h1 ♖g2 (threatening 23...e3) 23 ♗xe8 ♕g3 and Black wins because now he can meet ♕e1 by ...♕f3+.

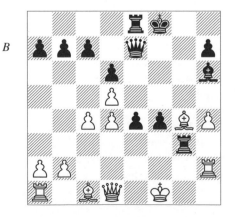

21...e3! 22 ♗f3

There is no defence; for example, 22 ♗h5 f3 23 ♗xf3 ♕f6, 22 ♖g2 ♕xh4 23 ♖xg3 fxg3, 22 ♗e6 ♕g7, 22 ♕e2 f3 23 ♗xf3 ♕f7 or 22 ♕d3 e2+ 23 ♕xe2 ♕g7 – Black wins in every case.

22...♕g7 23 ♖h1

23 ♔e2 ♖xf3! 24 ♔xf3 ♕g3+ is also decisive.

23...♖g2! 0-1

A neat finish. After 24 ♗xg2 e2+ White faces catastrophic material loss.

Game 104

Nikola Mitkov – Sergei Rublevsky

European Clubs Cup, Neum 2000

Sicilian Defence, Paulsen Variation

1 e4 c5 2 ♘f3 e6 3 d4 cxd4 4 ♘xd4 a6

The Kan Variation of the Sicilian has remained popular for several decades. At one time 5 ♗d3 was the most highly regarded reply, but Black's successes with 5...♗c5 have led some players to switch to 5 ♘c3.

5 ♘c3 ♕c7 6 ♗d3 ♘c6 7 ♗e3

The other main line is 7 ♘xc6.

7...♘f6

This very common position is often reached via a Taimanov/Paulsen move-order (4...♘c6 5 ♘c3 ♕c7 6 ♗e3 a6 7 ♗d3 ♘f6, for example).

8 0-0 ♘e5 (D)

Black has tried a wide range of moves here, including 8...♗d6, 8...b5 and 8...♘xd4, but playing the knight to e5 is the most popular continuation.

W

9 h3

This is the most natural method of meeting the threat of 9...♘eg4, but some players have

preferred 9 ♘f3 ♘fg4 10 ♘xe5 ♘xe3 11 ♕h5 g6 12 ♕f3 ♕xe5 13 fxe3 f6 14 ♕xf6 ♕xf6 15 ♖xf6 ♗g7, which wins a pawn for White at the cost of doubled isolated pawns and weak dark squares.

9...♗c5 10 ♔h1

10 f4 d6 11 ♔h1 transposes.

10...d6 11 f4 ♘g6

The most common move. 11...♘xd3 12 cxd3 b5 is also playable, although the exchange on d3 does reinforce White's centre.

12 ♕e1 (D)

B

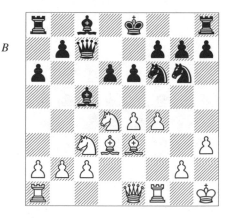

From here the queen can switch to g3 or (after f5) to h4.

12...0-0

While this may not objectively be a bad move, it does present White with an obvious target to aim at. 12...♗d7 is a more cautious continuation, leaving the king in the centre for the moment. For example, after 13 f5 ♘e5 14

♕h4 ♕b6 15 ♘ce2 0-0-0 Black makes use of the possibility of castling queenside, with a satisfactory position. This shows how in modern openings the decision to castle is far from automatic.

13 f5 ♘e5 14 ♕h4

White should attack with pieces rather than pawns in order to keep his own king safe. After 14 g4 d5 15 exd5 b5!? 16 fxe6 ♘xd3 17 cxd3 ♘xd5! 18 ♘xd5 ♗b7 Black had good play for the pawn in Tischbierek-Lazarev, Meisdorf 1996.

14...♗d7

14...b5 may also be met by 15 ♖f3!? but after 15...♘xf3 16 gxf3 ♔h8 17 ♖g1 ♖g8 the situation is less clear than in the game (see the note to Black's 17th).

15 ♖f3!? *(D)*

This extraordinary move was played for the first time in the current game. White's kingside attack in the Sicilian generally follows a typical pattern, at least in its early stages, and it is astonishing to see a completely new idea in such a familiar situation. Whether Black takes the rook or not, White gets one of his rooks to the g-file. Hitherto, White had played 15 g4 ♕b6 16 g5 ♘h5 17 ♕xh5 ♗xd4 18 ♗xd4 ♕xd4 19 f6 ♗c6 20 fxg7 ♔xg7, but without demonstrating any advantage.

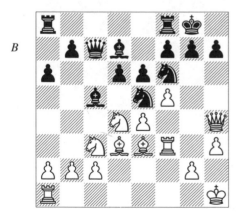

15...♘xf3?

Accepting the sacrifice is wrong. White also gets a strong attack after 15...♕b6 16 ♖g3 ♗xd4 17 ♕xf6 g6 18 ♗xd4 ♕xd4 19 ♖f1, but the correct line was 15...exf5! when matters are not so

clear; for example, after 16 ♘xf5 (16 exf5 is probably better) 16...♗xf5 17 ♖xf5 ♗xe3 18 ♖xf6 gxf6 19 ♘d5 ♗g5 20 ♕g3 ♕d8 21 h4 ♔h8 Black can defend.

16 gxf3

The attacking chances along the g-file more than compensate for the exchange.

16...♔h8

The alternatives are not encouraging for Black:

1) It is now too late for 16...exf5? since 17 ♖g1 ♕d8 18 exf5 gives White a crushing attack.

2) 16...♕d8 17 ♖g1 ♘e8 18 ♖xg7+! ♔xg7 (18...♘xg7 loses to 19 f6) 19 ♕h6+ ♔g8 20 e5 dxe5 21 f6 ♘xf6 22 ♗g5 e4 23 ♗xf6 ♕xf6 24 ♕xf6 ♗xd4 25 ♕xd4 exd3 26 ♕xd7 ♖fd8 27 ♕e7 d2 28 ♘d1 should be winning for White.

3) 16...♕b6 17 ♖g1 ♗xd4 18 e5! ♗xe3 19 ♖xg7+! ♔xg7 (19...♔h8 20 fxe6 also mates) 20 exf6+ ♔h8 21 fxe6 forces mate in a few moves.

4) 16...♘e8 17 ♖g1 g6 (17...♕d8 transposes to line '2' above) 18 ♕h6 threatens 19 e5 followed by a breakthrough on g6. Black cannot hope to defend his kingside when so many white pieces are participating in the attack.

17 ♖g1 *(D)*

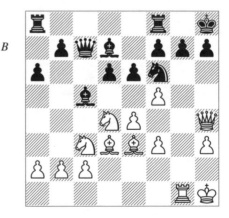

17...♕d8

The alternative is 17...♖g8, but after 18 fxe6 fxe6 (18...♗xe6 19 ♘d5! ♕d8 20 ♘xe6 fxe6 21 e5 exd5 22 exf6 g6 23 ♗xg6 wins for White) 19 e5 dxe5 20 ♗g5! (20 ♘e4 ♘xe4 21 ♗xe4 g6 22 ♖xg6 ♖xg6 23 ♗xg6 ♗c8 is far less clear)

20...♗c6 21 ♗xf6 gxf6 22 ♕xf6+ ♖g7 23 ♖xg7 ♕xg7 24 ♕xg7+ ♔xg7 25 ♘xe6+ ♔h6 26 ♘xc5 ♗xf3+ 27 ♔g1 the ending should be a win for White. However, had Black played 14...b5 rather than 14...♗d7 then this line would be unclear as the Black's queen's guard of h7 would not be blocked by the bishop on d7.

18 e5!

We have already seen how opening the d3-h7 diagonal is often a key element in the attack.

18...dxe5

18...♗xd4 19 ♗xd4 ♘e8 20 f6 g6 21 ♕h6 ♖g8 22 ♘e4 followed by ♘g5 wins easily.

19 ♖xg7! *(D)*

Black's defences are blasted away as White gives up his other rook.

19...♖g8

There is nothing better, since 19...exf5 20 ♗g5 and 19...♔xg7 20 ♗h6+ ♔h8 21 ♗g5 ♗e7 22 fxe6 win for White, while 19...♗xd4 20 ♖xh7+ ♘xh7 21 f6 leads to mate.

20 ♖xg8+ ♔xg8

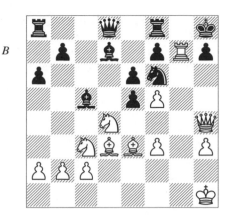

Or 20...♘xg8 21 f6! ♘xf6 22 ♗g5 and White wins.

21 ♗g5 ♗e7 22 ♘e4 ♘d5 23 f6

White's forces rush in to murder the defenceless king.

23...♕b6 24 ♘c5

One of many quick wins.

24...♕xc5 25 ♕xh7+ 1-0

Game 105
Judit Polgar – Ilia Smirin
Istanbul Olympiad 2000
Pirc Defence, Austrian Attack

1 e4 g6 2 d4 ♗g7 3 ♘c3 d6 4 f4 ♘f6 5 ♘f3 0-0 6 ♗e3

White has tried a wide range of moves here. 6 ♗d3 and 6 ♗e3 are the most popular at present, but you also sometimes see the older moves 6 ♗e2 and 6 e5.

6...b6

The most common reply, preparing both ...♗b7 and ...c5.

7 ♕d2 *(D)*

This is the modern way of playing the ♗e3 system. Previously, White had continued 7 e5 (7 ♗d3 c5 is fine for Black) 7...♘g4 8 ♗g1 c5 9 h3 ♘h6 10 d5, but this is now thought fully satisfactory for Black.

The idea behind 7 ♕d2 is to continue with queenside castling and reach a position rather similar to a Sicilian Dragon.

7...c5?!

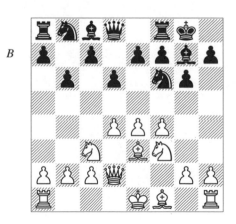

The key alternative is 7...♗b7 8 e5 ♘g4 9 0-0-0 (this line differs from 7 e5 in that White makes no attempt to preserve his dark-squared bishop) 9...c5 10 dxc5 bxc5 (10...♘xe3 11 ♕xe3 bxc5 12 h4 gives White a dangerous attack against the poorly defended kingside) 11 ♗xc5 ♕a5 12 ♗a3 dxe5 13 h3 ♗h6 with unclear complications. Such was the impact of the current game that 7...c5 all but disappeared, and current practice is almost entirely focused on 7...♗b7.

8 0-0-0

The most natural follow-up to White's previous move, but 8 d5 is also playable.

8...cxd4 9 ♗xd4!

An interesting move, very much in the modern style of play in which each position is treated on its individual merits. The alternative 9 ♘xd4 ♗b7 10 e5 ♘g4 is unclear, but at first sight Polgar's move looks no better since after the obvious reply 9...♘c6 White will either have to retreat the bishop with loss of time or allow it to be exchanged. At one time, players would have reacted with horror to the idea of exchanging their dark-squared bishop for a knight in a Dragon structure – think of all those lines in the Dragon in which White is reluctant to part with this bishop even in return for a rook. However, the point of 9 ♗xd4 is to gain time to launch a direct kingside attack. If Black never gets time to organize some play on the long diagonal, then the lack of a dark-squared bishop won't be of much concern for White. However, this move does commit White to rapid kingside action; any delay, and the missing bishop will prove a serious problem.

9...♘c6 10 ♗xf6

This is the idea; a key defender of Black's kingside is removed.

10...♗xf6 11 h4 (D)

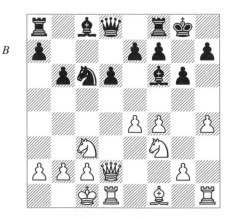

A quick follow-up is essential. As MegaBase curiously puts it (notes by Finkel), "Polgar's play is fantastic: she simply doesn't give Smirin time to breeze!". Certainly Smirin was quickly wafted out of the tournament hall.

11...♗g4

It is clear that once White plays h5 and hxg6, Black will be facing a dangerous attack, and the text-move is the obvious way to try to prevent this. However, White's brilliant reply essentially refutes the idea. Perhaps Black should already have resorted to a desperate move such as 11...b5 (11...h5 is strongly answered by 12 f5).

12 h5!

White crashes through in any case.

12...♗xh5 (D)

Alternatives such as 12...♘b4 13 hxg6 hxg6 14 f5 and 12...gxh5 13 ♘d5 ♗g7 14 ♗b5 ♘a5 15 ♘e3 also look grim for Black.

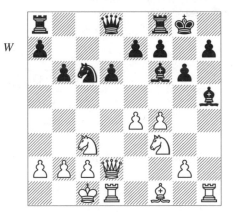

13 ♖xh5! gxh5 14 ♕d5

This is the point; the attack on c6 gives White a tempo to transfer her queen to the kingside.

14...♖c8

Judit Polgar's notes give this as dubious, but in fact Black doesn't have a satisfactory continuation. After 14...♗xc3 15 bxc3 ♘a5 (or 15...♕c8 16 ♕xh5 ♕e6 17 ♗b5 ♘a5 18 ♖h1 ♕g6 19 ♕h4 with the crushing threat of 20 ♖h3) 16 ♕xh5 f6 17 e5 ♕e8 18 ♕h4, for example, White has a massive attack. The continuation might be 18...♕f7 19 ♗d3 dxe5 20 fxe5 ♖fc8 21 exf6 exf6 22 ♗e4 ♖d8 23 ♘d4 ♕g7 24

♔b1 ♖ac8 25 ♖h1 ♖d7 26 ♗f5 ♖e8 27 ♘e6 with overwhelming threats.

15 ♕xh5 ♗g7

15...♗xc3? 16 ♘g5 results in a quick mate, while 15...♘b4 16 e5 ♗g7 17 a3 ♘c6 18 ♗d3 h6 19 ♕f5 ♖e8 20 e6 leads to a slightly slower mate.

16 e5 ♕e8

16...h6 is no better since it weakens the kingside; after 17 ♗a6 ♖c7 18 g4 ♕e8 (or else g5 wins) 19 ♘d5 White gains too much material.

17 ♕h3!

17 ♗b5 f5 18 ♕xe8 ♖fxe8 19 exd6 exd6 20 ♖xd6 ♗xc3 21 bxc3 ♘a5 22 ♗xe8 ♖xe8 23 ♘e5 also looks very good, but Polgar correctly plays to settle matters in the middlegame.

17...h6

White also wins after 17...dxe5 18 ♘g5 h6 19 ♕f5! hxg5 20 ♗d3 f6 21 ♕h7+ ♔f7 22 ♗g6+ ♔e6 23 f5# and 17...♘b4 18 ♗b5 ♘xa2+ 19 ♔d2 ♕d8 20 ♗d3 h6 21 ♕f5.

18 ♗d3

Threatening 19 ♕f5.

18...♘b4

18...e6 19 ♘e4 ♕e7 20 ♘f6+ ♗xf6 21 ♕xh6 mates.

19 ♗e4 e6 *(D)*

19...d5 20 ♘xd5 ♘xd5 21 ♕f5 also leads to mate.

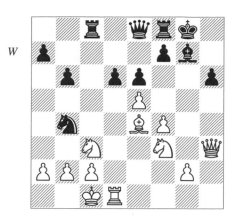

20 f5!

Polgar conducts the final breakthrough with the same energy as the rest of the game.

20...♖xc3

20...♘xa2+ 21 ♘xa2 ♕a4 22 ♖d4 ♕xa2 23 f6 wins, while 20...dxe5 21 f6 ♗xf6 22 ♕xh6 is another mating line.

21 f6 ♕b5

21...♕a4 22 bxc3 ♘xa2+ 23 ♔b2 ♘xc3 (or 23...♕xe4 24 ♕g3 ♕g6 25 ♕xg6 fxg6 26 fxg7) 24 ♖d4 ♘d1+ 25 ♖xd1 ♕b4+ 26 ♔c1 ♕xe4 27 ♕g3 will leave White a piece ahead.

22 ♕g3! 1-0

White forces mate after 22...♖xc2+ 23 ♗xc2 ♘xa2+ 24 ♔d2 ♕b4+ 25 ♔e3 ♕c5+ 26 ♖d4.

Game 106
Alexei Shirov – Veselin Topalov
Wijk aan Zee 2001
Sicilian Defence, Perenyi Attack

1 e4 c5 2 ♘f3 d6 3 d4 cxd4 4 ♘xd4 ♘f6 5 ♘c3 a6 6 ♗e3 e6 7 g4!? *(D)*

This is surely one of the sharpest variations in the whole of opening theory. As early as move seven, White commits himself to sacrificing a piece. Theory in these very sharp variations often tends to stabilize with a forced drawing variation, but the odd thing about this line is that although it has always been considered satisfactory for Black in theory, most top-level encounters have ended in wins for White. Apparently the practical difficulties involved in

defending are so great that even leading grandmasters often go wrong.

7...e5

Black takes up the challenge. If he wants to back down, then 7...h6 is an acceptable continuation.

8 ♘f5 g6

Here, too, Black can decline the sacrifice with the interesting idea 8...h5.

9 g5

Although White is now committed to giving up a piece, he at least has a choice about how to

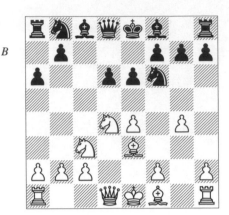

surrender it. The alternative is 9 &g2 gxf5 (9...d5!? is also playable) 10 exf5 h6, which is another very unclear line.

9...gxf5 10 exf5 d5 11 ♕f3

At one time this was the main move, before being superseded by 11 gxf6 d4 12 &c4. However, when this latter line appeared to be analysed out to a forced draw, attention reverted to 11 ♕f3 and most recent games have featured this move.

11...d4 12 0-0-0 ♘bd7 13 &d2!? (D)

The modern revival of 11 ♕f3 has been based on this idea. The 'old' theory explored lines such as 13 &xd4 exd4 14 ♖xd4 &c5 15 ♖d2 ♕c7 and 13 gxf6 dxc3 14 &c4 ♕xf6 15 ♖hg1, but without finding anything especially convincing for White.

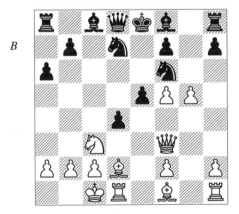

It is perhaps surprising that a move such as 13 &d2 can be dangerous for Black; when you are a piece down, it always looks wrong to play

a quiet retreating move. However, Black has had some difficulties in countering this idea, at least in practice.

13...♕c7

Black has tried various moves here; perhaps the other key continuation is 13...dxc3 14 &xc3 ♕c7, when White has a choice between 15 gxf6, transposing to the game, or the unclear 15 &d3.

14 gxf6 dxc3 15 &xc3 ♕c6

It looks very risky to play 15...♘xf6; for example, 16 &h3 &e7 17 ♖he1 e4 18 ♖xe4 ♘xe4 19 ♕xe4 f6 20 &xf6 ♖f8 21 &h4 gives White a decisive attack.

16 ♕g3

Threatening simply 17 &xe5, so Black must react quickly.

16...&h6+

You get two miniatures for the price of one in this game, because Shirov-Van Wely, Istanbul Olympiad 2000 concluded 16...♕xh1?! (an experiment which Black did not care to repeat in subsequent games) 17 &g2 &h6+ 18 &d2 &xd2+ 19 &xd2 ♕xg2? (19...♕xd1+ 20 &xd1 ♖f8 is better, but Black's position still looks uncomfortable; for example, 21 f4 ♘xf6 22 ♕c3! ♘d7 23 fxe5 ♖g8 24 &f3 with unpleasant pressure for White) 20 ♕xg2 a5 21 f4! (Black is doomed by his total lack of development) 21...exf4 22 ♕g7 ♖f8 23 ♖e1+ &d8 24 ♖e7 (there is no real defence to the threat of 25 ♖xd7+) 24...&c7? 25 ♕xf8 1-0.

17 &b1 &f4 18 ♕d3 (D)

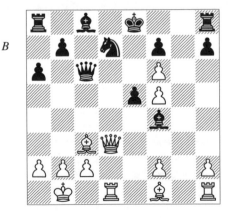

18...♖g8

Black has had more success with 18...0-0 19 ♖g1+ ♔h8 20 ♗b4 ♘c5 (20...♖g8?! was played in another Shirov-Van Wely game, from Polanica Zdroj 2000, but after 21 ♖xg8+ ♔xg8 22 ♗e7 White had a very strong attack), with a position which can only be described as double-edged. The move played, leaving the king in the centre, is riskier but not actually bad, provided Black follows it up correctly. However, as we have noted so often in this book, putting pressure on yourself to find 'only moves' is a dangerous business.

19 ♗h3 *(D)*

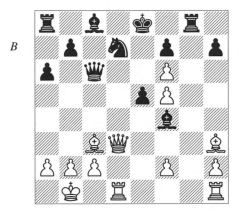

B

19...♔d8?

This move leads to disaster. 19...♕xf6?! 20 ♖he1 is not totally clear, but looks dangerous for Black. Therefore 19...b6! appears best, as it prepares simply to develop Black's remaining pieces. After 20 ♖hg1 ♖xg1 21 ♖xg1 ♗b7 22 ♖g8+ (22 ♗g2 e4 23 ♗xe4 ♕xe4 24 ♖e1 ♕xe1+ 25 ♗xe1 0-0-0 and Black consolidates with a slight advantage) 22...♘f8 23 ♗g2 e4 24 ♗b4 ♗h6 White still has some pressure, but there is no obvious continuation of the attack. Note that 19...b5? would have been wrong, because at the end of the above line White would be able to play 25 ♗xf8 ♗xf8 26 ♕a3 and Black would lack the defence 26...♕c5. Of course, it would be very hard to appreciate this finesse in over-the-board play.

20 ♗b4

The threatened transfer of the bishop to e7 creates awkward problems for Black.

20...♕xf6

If Black does not take this pawn then he runs into trouble due to the weakness of the f7-pawn: 20...♔c7 21 ♕b3! e4 22 ♕xf7 ♖d8 23 ♖he1 with three pawns and a very strong attack for the piece, or 20...e4 21 ♕b3 ♕xf6 (21...♔e8 22 ♖he1 ♘xf6 23 ♗c3 and Black's king is defenceless) 22 ♖he1 ♖e8 23 ♕c4 with very strong pressure for White.

21 ♕c4

Threatening 22 ♖d6.

21...♖g5

There is no escape:

1) 21...b5 22 ♗a5+ ♔e8 23 ♕c7 ♖g5 24 ♖hg1 ♔f8 25 ♗g2 and White wins.

2) 21...♕c6 22 ♕xf7 and Black collapses at once.

3) 21...a5 22 ♖d6 ♕g5 23 f6 axb4 24 ♖hd1 ♔e8 (24...♕g1 25 ♗xd7 ♕xd1+ 26 ♖xd1 ♗xd7 27 ♕xf7 wins for White) 25 ♕c7 and Black can resign.

22 ♖d6! *(D)*

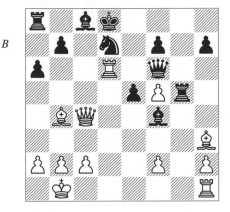

B

Decisive.

22...♕g7

After 22...♕e7 23 f6 White wins at once, but the text-move doesn't last much longer.

23 f6 ♖g1+

Or 23...♕g6 24 ♗a5+ b6 25 ♖xb6 ♔e8 26 ♖e6+ fxe6 27 ♕xe6+ ♔f8 28 ♗b4+ and White forces mate next move.

24 ♗f1! 1-0

After 24...♕g4 (24...♕g2 25 ♗a5+ ♔e8 26 ♖e6+ mates one move more quickly) 25 ♖xg1 ♕xg1 26 ♗a5+ ♔e8 27 ♖e6+! White mates shortly.

Game 107
Vladimir Kramnik – Darmen Sadvakasov
Astana 2001
Queen's Gambit Accepted

1 d4 d5 2 c4 dxc4 3 ♘f3 ♘f6 4 e3 e6 5 ♗xc4 c5 6 0-0 a6 7 a4

White has a wide choice of moves here, ranging from the tedious 7 dxc5 to the ambitious 7 e4. The text-move, which aims to prevent Black's queenside expansion by ...b5, lies somewhere in the middle of the scale.

7...♘c6 8 ♕e2 ♕c7

8...cxd4 9 ♖d1 ♗e7 10 exd4 0-0 has been the most popular line, immediately heading for an isolated queen's pawn position, but the text-move is a close second.

9 ♖d1 (D)

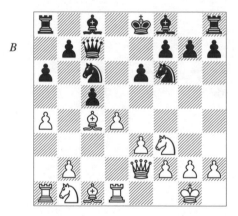

Kramnik adopts a slightly unusual continuation which involves delaying ♘c3. At the time this game was played, White had scored 90% with this idea, which perhaps explains why Kramnik chose it. White's score has since dropped somewhat to 78%, but even this indicates that Black has been struggling to find a good reply.

9...♗d6 10 dxc5 ♗xc5 11 b3 0-0 12 ♗b2 e5?!

Black attempts to solve the problem of developing his queen's bishop by clearing a path to g4; however, this has the defects of opening the a2-g8 diagonal and weakening the d5-square.

Kramnik's reply shows that Black's plan is risky. Instead, Black should develop his bishop by 12...b6, in which case White has only a slight advantage.

13 ♘c3!

Rather surprisingly, this natural developing move was a novelty. Worried by the possibility of ...e4 followed by ...♗g4, White had hitherto taken time out for 13 h3, but Kramnik convincingly demonstrates that this preparatory move is unnecessary. Three players since have allowed their opponents to repeat Kramnik's move, and all lost.

13...e4?!

13...♗g4?! is also doubtful after 14 ♘d5 ♘xd5 15 ♗xd5 (threatening 16 ♕c4) 15...♗d6 16 ♖ac1 with strong pressure, so Black's best chance is probably 13...♘b4, keeping White's advantage to a minimum.

14 ♘g5 (D)

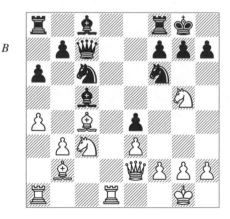

14...♗d6?!

Black switches plans and plays to attack the h2-pawn, but White is able to sacrifice this pawn to launch a direct attack on Black's king. 14...♗f5? is also wrong as 15 ♘d5 ♘xd5 16 ♖xd5 ♘e7 17 ♖xf5! ♘xf5 18 ♕h5 ♘h6 19 ♘xe4 gives White a large advantage.

Having played ...e5-e4, Black should at least have continued with the consistent 14...♗g4, although after 15 ♘d5 ♗xe2 16 ♘xc7 ♗xd1 17 ♘xa8 White retains an advantage in every line:

1) 17...♗h5 18 ♗xf6 ♗g6 (White wins after 18...gxf6 19 ♘xe4 ♗e7 20 ♘b6) 19 ♗b2 ♖xa8 20 ♖d1 ♗e7 21 ♘h3 ♗f5 22 ♘f4 favours White since his bishops are more active than Black's.

2) 17...♗c2 18 ♖c1 ♘b4 19 ♗c3! (19 ♘c7 ♗e7 20 ♗c3 ♗d3 21 ♗xb4 ♗xb4 22 ♘d5 ♗a3 gives White no more than an edge) 19...♖xa8 20 ♗xb4 ♗xb4 21 ♖xc2 ♖f8 22 ♘xf7 ♖xf7 23 ♗xf7+ ♔xf7 24 ♖c7+ ♔g6 25 ♖xb7 a5 26 f3 and the endgame is clearly better for White.

15 ♘d5!

The simple 15 h3 is also very promising, but Kramnik's move is more incisive.

15...♘xd5 16 ♖xd5

Best, preventing Black from transferring his bishop to the threatened kingside by ...♗f5.

16...♗xh2+ 17 ♔h1 ♗e5

Forced, since 17...h6 loses to 18 g3 hxg5 19 ♖xg5.

18 ♕h5 ♗f5? *(D)*

This final error allows White a quick and attractive kill. Rather surprisingly, there is no simple route to victory after 18...h6 although White secures excellent winning chances by 19 ♖xe5 ♘xe5 20 ♘xf7 ♖xf7 (20...♘xf7 21 ♕g6

mates, while 20...♘xc4 21 ♘xh6+ ♔h7 22 ♘f7+ ♔g8 23 ♕h8+ ♔xf7 24 ♕xg7+ wins Black's queen) 21 ♖xe5 ♕e7 22 ♕xf7+ ♕xf7 23 ♗xf7+ ♔xf7 24 ♖c1 since Black has weak pawns on b7, e4 and g7, while White's pieces are very active.

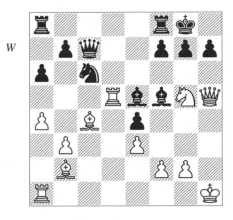

19 ♘xf7! ♖xf7

There is no escape; for example, 19...♗xb2 20 ♖xf5 g6 21 ♕h6 gxf5 22 ♘d8+ or 19...♕xf7 20 ♖xe5.

20 ♕xf5 g6

20...♖xf5 21 ♖d8# is mate, while 20...♔h8 21 ♗xe5 and 20...♗xb2 21 ♖d7 ♔h8 22 ♕xf7 ♕e5 23 ♖ad1 lead to a decisive material advantage for White.

21 ♗xe5 1-0

Game 108

Alexander Morozevich – Loek van Wely

Wijk aan Zee 2002

French Defence, 3...dxe4

1 e4 e6 2 d4 d5 3 ♘c3 dxe4 4 ♘xe4 ♘d7 5 ♗d3 ♘gf6 6 ♕e2

The most accurate move-order, because it prevents the natural 6...♘xe4 7 ♗xe4 ♘f6 on account of 8 ♗xb7!, a trap which has claimed no fewer than 60 victims in my database.

6...c5

The most natural reply, since playing 6...♗e7 may lose time if the bishop later has to recapture on c5.

7 ♘xf6+ ♘xf6 8 dxc5 ♗xc5 9 ♗d2

This is one of the two main lines for White here, the other being 9 ♘f3 0-0 10 ♗g5. With the text-move, White aims for queenside castling, but must be prepared to sacrifice a pawn.

9...0-0

Such a natural move cannot really be wrong, but there is a strong argument in favour of 9...♕b6 10 0-0-0 ♗d7! (10...♗xf2 11 ♘f3 is risky because White gains a serious lead in development) 11 ♘f3 ♘g4 and the weakness of the f2-pawn troubles White. If this line indeed proves fine for Black, then 9 ♗d2 is effectively put out of business.

10 0-0-0 ♛d5?! *(D)*

A rather greedy attempt to win a pawn or two. While this is a critical test of White's system, the dangers involved in losing time and opening lines on the kingside are clear. The safer moves 10...♛c7 and 10...♛b6 are preferable.

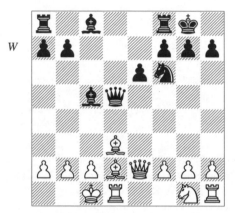

11 ♔b1

The only winning try, because after 11 ♗c3 ♛xa2 White has nothing better than perpetual check, which he can force in many ways, such as 12 ♗xf6 gxf6 13 ♗xh7+ ♔xh7 14 ♛h5+.

11...♛xg2?!

This was played several times in the years 2001-3, but Black's score with it was so miserable that the line has now disappeared. If Black wants to back out, then he can play 11...e5 here, retaining some equalizing chances.

12 ♘f3 ♛xf2

Black may as well take the second pawn, since he will have to move his queen in any case when a rook arrives on the g-file.

13 ♛e5 *(D)*

13...♘d7

Black had a real choice to make, but none of the available moves appears satisfactory:

1) 13...♛xf3 14 ♛xc5 b6 15 ♛g5 h6 16 ♛h4 ♛h5 17 ♛g3 ♔h8 18 ♖hg1 ♖g8 19 ♖df1 gives White a decisive attack, Ivanišević-Supatashvili, Panormo Zonal 1998.

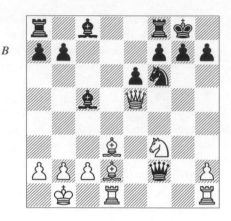

2) 13...♗e7 14 ♖df1 ♛c5 15 ♛g3 (in four attempts, Black failed to make a single half-point from this position) 15...♘h5 16 ♛h3 g6 17 ♖hg1 ♘g7 (17...♘f4?? 18 ♗xf4 e5 19 ♛h6 exf4 20 ♖g5 1-0 Khalifman-Bareev, Wijk aan Zee 2002 is another miniature played the round before our main game) 18 ♘g5 ♗xg5 19 ♖xg5 e5 20 ♛h6 and White has good compensation for the two pawns, Kazhgaleev-Pushkov, Cappelle la Grande 2002.

The text-move had been played in an earlier game by Van Wely (see White's 17th move) but his faith in the move proved misplaced since he lasts one move less than Bareev did.

14 ♗xh7+!

This piece sacrifice is the critical move; White must maintain the momentum of his attack and that means moving the queen with gain of tempo.

14...♔xh7

Black must accept, since 14...♔h8 15 ♛g3! ♘f6 (after 15...♔xh7 16 ♛h3+ ♔g8 17 ♖df1 ♛e2 18 ♘g5 White wins at once) 16 ♛h3 e5 17 ♗f5+ ♔g8 18 ♗h6! ♗xf5 19 ♛xf5 e4 20 ♖hg1 ♛xf3 21 ♛xc5 gives White a decisive attack.

15 ♛h5+ ♔g8 16 ♖hg1 *(D)*

16...♗e3

The alternatives are also miserable for Black:

1) 16...♘f6 17 ♖xg7+ ♔xg7 18 ♛h6+ ♔g8 19 ♛xf6 ♗d4 20 ♛g5+ ♗g7 21 ♖g1 ♛xg1+ 22 ♛xg1 ♘h8 23 ♗b4 ♖d8 24 ♘g5 ♔g8 25 ♘e4 with a large advantage for White as he still has a strong attack.

2) 16...e5 17 ♗h6 (the more adventurous 17 ♖xg7+ ♔xg7 18 ♗h6+ ♔f6 19 ♖xd7 is also

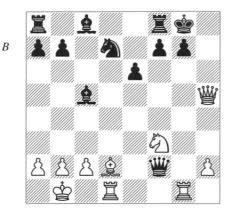

very promising for White) 17...♛xg1 18 ♖xg1 ♝xg1 19 ♕g5 g6 20 ♝xf8 ♘xf8 21 ♕xg1 with excellent winning chances for White.

17 ♝xe3!

17 ♝c3 was played in Anand-Van Wely, Monaco (Amber blindfold) 2001 and now 17...e5 would have been unclear, although White has an immediate draw if he wants by perpetually attacking the black queen. Unfortunately for Van Wely, Morozevich improves on the earlier game.

17...♕xe3 18 ♖g3 *(D)*

18...♕c5??

A terrible blunder losing at once, but Black is in trouble whatever he plays:

1) 18...g6? 19 ♖xg6+ fxg6 20 ♕xg6+ ♚h8 21 ♘g5 ♘f6 22 ♘f7+! ♖xf7 23 ♖d8+ mates.

2) 18...♘f6 19 ♕h4 ♘e4 20 ♘g5 ♕xg5 21 ♖xg5 ♘xg5 22 ♕xg5 and White's advantage should be sufficient to win.

3) 18...♕f4 19 ♖dg1 ♖d8 20 ♘d2! ♚f8 (after 20...g6 21 ♖f3 Black must give up his queen to avoid mate, while 20...♘e5 21 ♖xg7+ ♚f8 22 ♖f1 ♘f3 23 ♖xf7+ ♕xf7 24 ♖xf3 ♕xf3 25 ♕xf3+ ♚e7 26 ♚c1 gives White a winning position in view of his continuing attack and passed h-pawn) 21 ♖f3 ♘f6 22 ♕h8+ ♚e7 23 ♕xd8+ ♚xd8 24 ♖xf4 ♚e7 25 ♖xg7 with a clear extra exchange for White in the endgame.

19 ♕h6 1-0

After 19...g6 20 ♖h3 it is mate in a few moves.

Game 109
Alexander Riazantsev – Vladimir Nevostruev
Russian Ch, Krasnodar 2002
King's Indian Defence, 4 ♝g5

1 d4 ♘f6 2 c4 g6 3 ♘c3 ♝g7 4 ♝g5

This is a somewhat unusual system against the King's Indian. It is related to the Smyslov System 4 ♘f3 d6 5 ♝g5, but offers Black more options since he is not yet committed to playing ...d6.

4...c5

The most direct reply.

5 d5

After 5 e3 0-0 6 ♘f3 Black can exploit his omission of ...d6 to continue 6...cxd4 7 exd4

d5! with equality. The move played attempts to reach a standard type of position, but with this move-order Black can attempt to seize the initiative straight away.

5...b5!? *(D)*

A bold move, but it is double-edged to play so aggressively with Black as early as move five.

6 cxb5?!

The wrong choice, since in the resulting Benko Gambit type of position, White's early

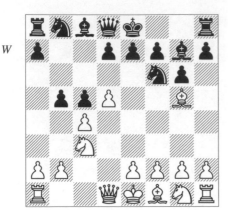

♗g5 may turn out to be an ineffective way to spend a tempo. 6 ♘xb5?! is also wrong due to 6...♘e4 7 d6 (7 ♗c1 a6) 7...♘xg5 8 ♘c7+ ♔f8 9 f3 (9 ♕d5 ♘c6 10 ♘xa8 ♗xb2 wins for Black) 9...♗b7 and Black is better. White should have played to exploit Black's omission of ...d6 with 6 d6! bxc4 7 e4, reaching a very sharp and unclear position. Curiously, in the seven games I could trace reaching the position after 5...b5, White played 6 cxb5?! in every one.

6...a6 7 e3

The alternatives are:

1) 7 bxa6 ♗xa6 8 e4 ♗xf1 9 ♔xf1 d6 reaches a Benko Gambit position in which White has spent a tempo on the inferior move ♗g5, which leaves b2 weak.

2) 7 e4 axb5 8 e5 b4 9 exf6 exf6 10 ♕e2+ ♔f8 11 ♗d2 bxc3 12 ♗xc3 is very comfortable for Black.

3) 7 a4 ♕a5 is unclear.

The text-move furthers White's development, but leaves the bishop isolated on g5.

7...♕a5 8 ♕d2 0-0 9 bxa6

9 ♘f3 was safer; after 9...d6 (9...axb5 10 ♗xb5 plays into White's hands) 10 a4 ♘bd7 Black has sufficient play for the pawn, but not more.

9...e6

Black plays consistently for the initiative. He leaves open the option of recapturing on a6 with bishop or knight, and spends the tempo undermining White's centre.

10 dxe6

10 ♗c4?! only encourages Black to play 10...♗xa6 since now the exchange on a6 costs

White a tempo, while after 10 ♗xf6?! ♗xf6 11 ♘e4 ♕xd2+ 12 ♔xd2 ♗xb2 13 ♖b1 ♗g7 Black's two bishops and good development give him the advantage.

10...dxe6 11 ♘e4 (D)

Hoping to force the exchange of queens. 11 ♗xf6 ♗xf6 12 ♘e4 ♕xd2+ 13 ♔xd2 ♗xb2 is clearly better for Black.

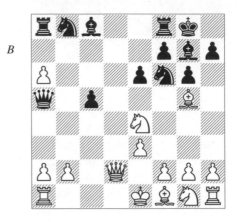

11...♘xe4?!

A remarkable queen sacrifice, which is particularly brave given that Black had a safe option in 11...♕xd2+ 12 ♘xd2 ♗xa6, with sufficient play for the pawn. Although the sacrifice succeeds admirably in the game, objectively speaking the safe line was better since by precise play White could have exposed the queen sacrifice as unsound.

12 ♕xa5 ♗xb2 (D)

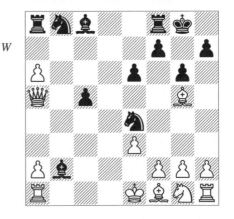

13 ♘e2!

Preventing the check on c3 at the cost of surrendering the a1-rook. 13 ♗f6?! is an amazing computer move which deflects the b2-bishop so that White can play ♖c1. After 13...♗xf6 14 ♖c1 ♗xa6 White has a choice:

1) 15 ♕a4 ♗c3+ 16 ♖xc3 ♘xc3 17 ♕c2 ♘d5 gives Black sufficient play for the sacrifice.

2) 15 ♘f3 ♗d8 16 ♕a3 ♗b7 17 ♕b2 ♗a5+ 18 ♔d1 ♖d8+ 19 ♔c2 ♗b4! with a tremendous attack for Black.

3) 15 ♗d3 ♘c6 16 ♕a3 ♗b7 17 ♕b3 ♘b4 favours Black.

4) 15 ♕a3! ♗b7 16 ♕b3 ♘d6 with a very unclear position.

White could also have considered the safe line 13 ♗d3 ♗c3+ 14 ♕xc3 ♘xc3, with a roughly level ending, although one can understand his desire to refute Black's sacrifice.

13...♗xa1 14 ♗h6

This is what White was playing for; after the obvious reply 14...♖e8 White continues 15 a7 ♘d7 (15...♘c6 loses material to 16 ♕a4) 16 f3 and Black's pieces are retreating in confusion. Black, therefore, decides to add the f8-rook to his sacrifices and the critical moment of the game arrives.

14...♗xa6

14...♘c6 is wrong due to 15 ♕b6 ♖b8 16 ♕xb8! ♘xb8 17 a7 ♗b7 18 ♗xf8 ♘c6 19 ♗h6, followed by f3, and Black does not have enough for the sacrificed exchange.

15 ♗xf8

After 15 ♕a4?! ♗b7 16 ♕d1 ♖xa2! (16...♗g7 is well met by 17 ♗xg7 ♔xg7 18 f3 ♘f6 19 ♘c3) 17 ♗xf8 ♗b2 18 ♗d6 ♗a3 (18...♗d5 19 ♗c7! is less clear) 19 ♗xc5 ♗xc5 20 ♕b1 ♗b4+ 21 ♕xb4 ♖a1+ 22 ♘c1 ♖xc1+ 23 ♔e2 ♖b1 Black has enough compensation.

15...♘c6 *(D)*

16 ♕c7?

There was only one good square for the queen, but this isn't it. 16 ♕a3? is also bad since 16...♗xf8 17 f3 ♘b4 wins for Black, but after the correct choice 16 ♕b6! Black would have been in trouble. One line runs 16...♘b4 (or 16...♖b8 17 ♕xb8 ♘xb8 18 ♗h6 followed by f3 and White consolidates his extra exchange) 17 f3 ♘d3+ (after 17...♘c2+ 18 ♔d1 ♘xe3+ 19 ♔c1 ♗xe2 20 fxe4 ♘xf1 21 ♗d6 Black's

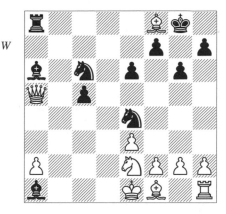

attack peters out) 18 ♔d1 ♘ef2+ 19 ♔d2 ♘b2 20 ♘d4 ♗xf1 21 ♕b7 ♖xa2 22 ♗h6 and White wins since despite Black's apparently ominous collection of checks, none of them leads anywhere and sooner or later Black is doomed by his back rank.

16...♘b4! *(D)*

Now, however, the situation is completely different and Black has an extremely dangerous attack. Only by the most precise defence can White defend.

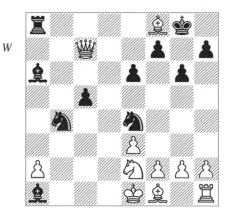

17 ♗h6

When faced by an unpleasant turn of events, it is easy to stumble and make further mistakes. 17 ♗d6! is best, and now:

1) 17...♘d3+?! 18 ♔d1 leaves Black with no fully satisfactory reply:

1a) 18...♘dxf2+ 19 ♔c1 ♘xd6 20 ♕xd6 ♘xh1 21 ♕c6 ♖a7 22 ♕a4 is clearly better for White.

1b) 18...♗b5 19 ♘c1 ♘dxf2+ 20 ♔c2 ♗a4+ 21 ♔b1 (21 ♘b3? ♗xb3+ 22 axb3 ♖a2+ 23 ♔b1 ♘c3+ 24 ♔c1 ♗b2+ 25 ♔c2 ♗a1+ is a draw) 21...♗f6 22 ♗e5 ♘d2+ 23 ♔b2 ♗xe5+ 24 ♕xe5 ♘xh1 25 ♗e2 and Black's forces are too scattered.

1c) 18...♘exf2+ 19 ♔c2 (19 ♔d2?! ♘e4+ 20 ♔c2 ♘b4+ is a draw) 19...♘b4+ 20 ♔b3 ♘e4 21 ♗xc5 ♘d5 22 ♕a7 ♖xa7 23 ♗xa7 can only be better for White.

2) 17...♗b5! 18 ♘d4 ♗c3+ 19 ♔d1 ♘xf2+ 20 ♔c1 ♖xa2+ 21 ♔b1 ♘b4 22 ♘c2 ♘fd3 23 ♗xc5 (23 ♕b7 ♗c6 24 ♕xa8+ ♖xa8 25 ♘xb4 ♘xb4 26 ♗xc5 ♗d2 is also a likely draw) 23...♗c4 24 ♗xd3 ♗xd3 25 ♔c1 ♘xc2 26 ♗a7 ♘b4 and the position is roughly level.

The key difference between 16 ♕b6! and 16 ♕c7? is revealed in the line 17 f3? ♗b5!, which is only possible now that b5 is unguarded; Black wins by force after 18 fxe4 ♘d3+ 19 ♔d1 ♖xa2 20 ♘d4 ♗a4+ 21 ♘c2 ♗xc2+ 22 ♔e2 ♗e5 23 ♕c8 ♗a4+ 24 ♔xd3 (or 24 ♔f3 ♗d1+) 24...♗b5#.

17...♗e5

Now White is in trouble.

18 ♕d7?

18 ♕b6! was White's only chance. After 18...♘d3+ 19 ♔d1 ♖b8 20 ♕xb8+ ♗xb8 21 ♘g3 ♘dxf2+ 22 ♔c2 Black has various ways to win material, but in all cases White gets some counterplay thanks to his passed a-pawn: 22...♗b7! (22...♘xh1 23 ♗xa6 ♘hxg3 24 hxg3

♗xg3 25 a4 is also not clear due to the dangerous a-pawn and Black's confined king) 23 ♖g1 ♘g4 24 ♗f4 e5 25 ♘xe4 ♗xe4+ 26 ♗d3 ♗xd3+ 27 ♔xd3 exf4 28 ♖b1 ♗d6 29 exf4 ♗xf4 30 a4 and it is not clear if Black can put his material advantage to good use.

18...♘d3+ 19 ♔d1?!

After 19 ♕xd3 ♗xd3 20 f3 ♘c3 21 ♗f4 ♗f6 Black is a pawn ahead with the better position.

19...♖b8 (D)

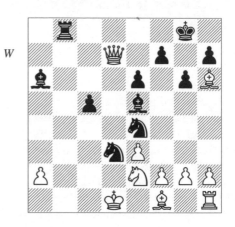

Now Black's attack is irresistible.

20 ♘d4 ♖b1+ 21 ♔e2 ♘e1+ 22 ♘b5 ♘c3+ 0-1

It's mate next move. Black's sacrifice wasn't objectively correct, but the practical problems proved too much for White, and Black was rewarded by a spectacular victory.

Game 110

Loek van Wely – Peter Acs

Hoogeveen 2002

Nimzo-Indian Defence, Rubinstein System

1 d4 ♘f6 2 c4 e6 3 ♘c3 ♗b4 4 e3 0-0 5 ♗d3 d5 6 cxd5

The most popular continuation here has always been 6 ♘f3, but the line played, which intends to develop the knight at e2, has also been employed quite often.

6...exd5 7 ♘e2 ♖e8 8 0-0

There is an argument for delaying this, because it gives Black a target to aim at. After 8

♗d2 ♗d6 9 ♖c1, for example, Black must spend a tempo meeting the threat of ♘b5.

8...♗d6

At the time this game was played, White had scored a lowly 43% from this position. Such statistics can be misleading and one should not conclude that Black is already better, but it is a sign that White must take care.

9 a3

White prepares queenside play, but this looks a little slow. Developing the knight at e2 gives White the option to play f3, keeping Black's pieces out of e4 and g4, and White should have made use of this opportunity. After 9 f3 c5 10 ♕e1, for example, White has an edge.

9...♘g4!? *(D)*

Black at once takes advantage of White's omission and launches a direct attack against the white king. Even though White's play has been rather passive, Black must take care when committing himself to an attack while his queenside is still at home. The sacrifice 9...♗xh2+? 10 ♔xh2 ♘g4+ is unsound due to 11 ♔g3.

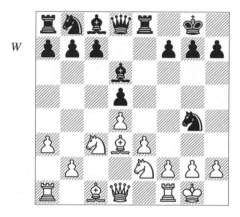

10 h3?

This casual move justifies Black's play – perhaps White could not believe that after only ten moves he was already at the point of making life-or-death decisions. 10 g3?! avoids immediate problems, but it is not the move White wants to play since it weakens the kingside. 10 ♘f4! is best, although this move is only justified thanks to a surprising tactical resource. After 10...g5?! 11 ♘fxd5! ♗xh2+ 12 ♔h1 ♕d6 it seems that White is in trouble, but by 13 ♗e2! ♗g1 14 ♘f6+! ♘xf6 15 ♔xg1 he not only saves the day but even gains the advantage thanks to his central control and two bishops. Therefore Black must meet 10 ♘f4! more quietly, but in this case it is harder for him to justify his aggressive knight sortie.

10...♘h2!

Black's gamble has paid off and now the storm breaks over White's position.

11 ♖e1 ♘f3+!

Not 11...♗xh3? 12 gxh3 ♘f3+ 13 ♔g2 ♘xe1+ 14 ♕xe1 and White has a large advantage.

12 gxf3 ♕g5+ 13 ♔h1

13 ♘g3? ♗xg3 14 fxg3 (14 ♔f1 ♗xh3+ 15 ♔e2 ♗xf2 led to a quick win for Black in the later game Tkeshelashvili-Xu Yuhua, FIDE Women's Knockout, Elista 2004) 14...♕xg3+ 15 ♔h1 ♕xh3+ 16 ♔g1 ♕g3+ 17 ♔h1 ♖e6! 18 e4 ♖g6 and Black mates in a few moves.

13...♕h4! *(D)*

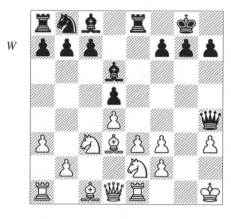

14 ♘f4?

This loses quickly, but Black has a clear advantage even against the best defence:

1) 14 f4? ♕xh3+ 15 ♔g1 ♗g4! and Black wins since 16 ♕a4 fails to 16...♗f3!! 17 ♕xe8+ ♗f8 followed by mate.

2) 14 ♔g1 (White's most resilient defence) 14...♗xh3 (14...♕g5+ 15 ♔h1 ♕h4 is a draw, but Black can play for more) and now:

2a) 15 f4 ♗g4 16 ♕a4 (16 f3 ♖e6! 17 fxg4 ♖h6 18 ♔f1 ♕h3+ 19 ♔f2 ♕h2+ 20 ♔f1 ♖h3 21 ♘g1 ♖g3 leads to mate, while after 16 ♕b3 ♗f3 17 ♘g3 ♗xf4! 18 ♘ce2 ♗d6 19 ♕xb7 ♘d7 20 ♗f5 ♘f6 followed by ...g6 White's bishop has no safe square on the h3-c8 diagonal) 16...♖e6! (with the queen on h4 rather than h3, White survives after 16...♗f3 17 ♕xe8+ ♗f8 18 ♘g3 ♕h3 19 ♗f1) 17 ♘g3 (after 17 ♘xd5 ♗f3 18 ♘g3 c6 White must immediately return his extra piece to meet the threat of ...♖h6) 17...♖h6 18 ♕e8+ ♗f8 (threatening ...♗f3 followed by mate at h1) 19 ♘xd5 (19

♗e4 dxe4 20 ♕xe4 ♕h2+ 21 ♔f1 ♘c6 gives Black a very strong attack without any material sacrifice) 19...♘c6! (19...♗f3 20 ♘e7+! forces the exchange of queens) 20 ♕e4 (20 ♕xa8 ♗f3 leads to mate) 20...♕h2+! 21 ♔f1 ♖e8! and White must give up his queen.

2b) 15 e4 ♗h2+ 16 ♔xh2 ♗g4+ 17 ♔g1 ♗xf3 18 ♘g3 ♗xd1 19 ♖xd1 dxe4 20 ♘cxe4 ♘c6 favours Black, but White is not without defensive chances.

14...♗xh3 *(D)*

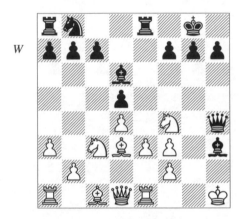

15 ♘cxd5

There is nothing better:

1) 15 ♘xh3 ♕xh3+ 16 ♔g1 ♗h2+ forces mate.

2) 15 ♘g2 ♕xf2 16 ♗f1 (16 ♖g1 loses to 16...♖e6) 16...♘c6 (threatening both 17...♖e6

and 17...♘xd4) 17 ♖e2 ♕xf3 (now Black is threatening 18...♗g4) 18 ♘b5 ♗g3, with a winning position for Black.

3) 15 e4 ♘c6 16 e5 ♘xd4 17 ♗xh7+ ♔xh7 18 ♕xd4 c5 19 ♕e3 ♖xe5 20 ♕xe5 ♖e8! 21 ♕xe8 ♗xf4 22 ♗xf4 ♗g4+ 23 ♔g1 ♗xf3 and Black mates.

15...♖e6! *(D)*

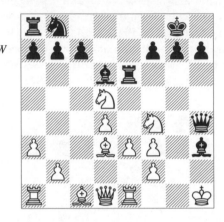

Black's rook joins in the attack and creates the immediate threats of 16...♖h6 and 16...♕xf2. Black does not need his two queenside pieces to press his attack home.

16 ♘xe6

Now it's a forced mate in seven.

16...♗f5+! 17 ♔g1 ♕h2+ 18 ♔f1 ♗g3 0-1

The end might be 19 ♘e7+ ♔h8 20 ♕d2 (20 fxg3 ♗h3#) 20...♗xd3+ 21 ♖e2 ♕h1#.

Game 111
Alexei Shirov – Loek van Wely
Bundesliga 2002/3
Sicilian Defence, ♘c3

1 e4 c5 2 ♘f3 ♘c6 3 ♘c3 ♘f6

White has been increasingly turning to 3 ♘c3 as a means of avoiding the Sveshnikov. Perhaps the most logical reply is 3...g6, but of course Black then has to learn some lines of the Dragon as well. If Black plays 3...e6, then 4 d4 cxd4 5 ♘xd4 ♘f6 6 ♘xc6 bxc6 7 e5 leads to a dangerous line which many Sveshnikov players prefer to avoid. Some players have responded with

3...e5, which is at least logical in that it attempts to 'punish' White for not playing d4 straight away. However, it isn't clear if weakening d5 is really justified (see Games 113 and 117 for more about this line). That leaves the text-move.

4 ♗b5

Of course 4 d4 cxd4 5 ♘xd4 e5 is just what Black wants, so when White adopts this move-order he almost always goes for 4 ♗b5. The result is a transposition to the Rossolimo system, but with Black having played an unusually early ...♘f6.

4...♕c7

This may be regarded as the current main line. Although 4...♘d4 has been played more often, the continuation 5 e5 ♘xb5 6 ♘xb5 ♘d5 7 ♘g5! gives White a dangerous initiative and this line is probably best avoided by Black.

5 0-0 e6 (D)

Perhaps I am being prejudiced, but I just don't like this move for Black. White can develop quickly and easily, putting all his pieces on natural squares, while Black's king has to stay in the centre for several moves. It seems particularly risky against Shirov, who is likely to take advantage of any attacking possibilities offered. In recent years 5...♘d4, which offers Black reasonable equalizing chances, has become established as the main line. See Game 120 for more on this variation.

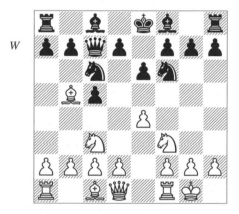

6 ♖e1

White's 84% from this position speaks for itself. Black already has to worry about the threat of e5.

6...♘g4

Attempting to maintain a grip on e5 looks best, although playing a non-developing move involves an obvious risk. The alternative 6...d6 is also unattractive after 7 d4 cxd4 8 ♘d5! exd5 (8...♕d8 9 ♘xd4 ♗d7 10 ♗g5 gives White strong pressure) 9 exd5+ ♗e7 10 ♘xd4 ♘xd5 11 ♘xc6 bxc6 12 ♕xd5 with a definite advantage for White.

7 ♗xc6

By exchanging on c6 White forces through e5 in any case.

7...bxc6

7...dxc6 8 e5 b6 9 d3 ♗b7 10 h3 was very good for White in Kr.Georgiev-Lerch, Selestat 2000.

8 e5

The e5-pawn cuts Black's position in half and prevents development of the c8-bishop. White threatens to improve his position with 9 h3 followed by 10 ♘e4, or simply 9 d4, so Black tries to remove the pawn by force.

8...f6 9 d4

Curiously, this natural move was an innovation; the insipid 9 d3 had been played in a previous game.

9...cxd4 10 ♕xd4 ♘xe5 11 ♘xe5 fxe5 12 ♖xe5 (D)

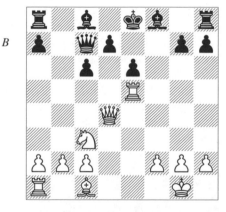

Black has the two bishops and a 2-0 central majority, but White's lead in development and Black's difficulty in castling are equally important factors. The rook on e5 may appear exposed to attack, but White is quite happy to sacrifice the exchange to gain total domination of the dark squares.

12...♗e7?

Black's play up to now has been rather risky, but not actually wrong. However, the defect of such play is that it usually requires an accurate follow-up, which places a serious burden on Black. Amongst the wide range of possible moves, there was only one good one, and this wasn't it. The alternatives are:

1) 12...♗d6? 13 ♗f4 transposes to the position after White's 14th move in the game.

2) 12...♖b8?! 13 ♗f4 ♕b6 (13...♖b4 costs Black a pawn after 14 ♕xb4! ♗xb4 15 ♖xe6+ dxe6 16 ♗xc7, while 13...d6 14 ♖ee1 e5 15 ♗xe5! dxe5 16 ♖xe5+ ♔f7 17 ♕c4+ ♔g6 18 ♖ae1 gives White a crushing attack) 14 ♕d1 d6! (14...♗e7 15 ♖e3 ♖b7 16 ♘e4 is also very promising for White) 15 ♖e3 with strong pressure.

3) 12...♕b6?! 13 ♕g4 doesn't solve Black's development problems.

4) 12...d6?! 13 ♖e1 e5 14 f4 ♕b6 15 ♕xb6 axb6 16 fxe5 is not very attractive, but Black has some chances of holding the ending a pawn down.

5) 12...d5! is the best move, keeping White's knight out of e4 and preparing ...♗d6 followed by ...0-0. After 13 ♗f4 Black can try 13...♗d6 (13...♕b6 14 ♕a4 ♗d7 15 ♖ae1 0-0-0 is also not very clear) 14 ♖e4 0-0 (not 14...dxe4? 15 ♗xd6 followed by ♘xe4) 15 ♗xd6 ♕xd6, when it isn't easy for White to keep a grip on the position and prevent Black from advancing his central pawns; e.g., 16 ♘a4 ♗f5 17 ♖ae1 ♕f8! 18 ♖4e2?! ♗a6 19 ♖xe6 ♖f4 20 ♕c5 ♖c4 (20...♖xa4? 21 ♕xc6 will leave White a pawn up) 21 ♕xf8+ ♖xf8 22 ♘c3 d4 and only Black can be better.

13 ♗g5! *(D)*

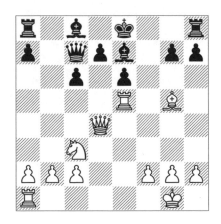

This strong move is awkward for Black. He cannot now castle, and the exchange of dark-squared bishops is bound to favour White, especially if his knight reaches e4.

13...♗d6?!

This further slip puts Black in a critical situation. 13...♗f6? is also bad since 14 ♗xf6 gxf6 15 ♖f5! picks up the f6-pawn (note that 15...exf5? 16 ♕xf6 wins at once). However, there were two better alternatives. The first is 13...d6 14 ♗xe7 ♕xe7 (not 14...dxe5? 15 ♕c5 ♖b8 16 ♗d6 ♕b6 17 ♕xe5 and White has a large advantage; e.g., 17...♕xb2 18 ♖d1 ♖b7 19 ♕h5+ ♖f7 20 ♘e4 ♕xc2 21 ♖e1 with a decisive attack) 15 ♖e3 0-0 16 ♘e4 and White has an advantage, but much less than in the game. The second possibility is 13...♕b6 14 ♕d2 ♗xg5 15 ♖xg5 0-0 16 b3 which, although somewhat better for White, is also preferable to the game.

14 ♗f4!

Now Black is in serious trouble. 14...0-0 15 ♖g5 costs Black a pawn, while 14...♗xe5 15 ♗xe5 ♕b6 16 ♕g4 is disastrous for Black. Therefore he declines the offer, but now his d-pawn is blocked and this obstructs his development.

14...c5 15 ♕e3

The most energetic reply.

15...a6

Another non-developing move, but it hardly matters by this stage since the alternatives are also bad:

1) 15...♗xe5? 16 ♗xe5 ♕c6 17 ♘e4 with a winning attack since 17...0-0 loses to 18 ♕g5 ♖f7 19 ♘d6 h6 20 ♕g6 ♖e7 21 ♖d1! followed by ♗f6.

2) 15...♕b7 16 ♖xe6+ dxe6 17 ♗xd6 offers no hope for Black.

3) 15...0-0 16 ♘b5 ♕c6 17 ♘xd6 ♕xd6 18 ♖f5 ♕e7 19 ♗g5 and White wins a pawn while retaining a positional advantage.

4) 15...♕b8 16 ♖f5! ♕xb2 (16...♗xf4 17 ♖xf4 is also very bad for Black) 17 ♖d1! ♕xc2 18 g4 ♗e7 19 ♖c1 ♕b2 (19...♕xc1+ 20 ♕xc1 exf5 21 ♘d5 ♗d8 22 ♕xc5 wins for White) 20 ♘d5 with an enormous attack for White.

5) 15...♖b8 16 ♘d5 ♕c6 (16...♕b7 17 ♖xe6+ dxe6 18 ♗xd6 ♕xb2 19 ♖e1 is very good for White) 17 ♕g3! ♗xe5 18 ♗xe5 ♕xd5 19 ♕xg7 ♖f8 20 ♗xb8 and Black is a pawn down with a bad position.

After the text-move, Shirov wraps the game up in typically forceful style.

16 ♘d5 ♛c6

16...♛b7 17 ♖f5 ♗xf4 18 ♕xf4 exd5 (or 18...exf5 19 ♖e1+ mating) 19 ♕g5 wins for White.

17 ♖g5

17 ♖f5? allows Black to limp on by 17...♗xf4 18 ♕xf4 d6.

17...h6

After 17...0-0 18 ♕g3! White wins at once, while 17...♗xf4 18 ♘xf4 0-0 19 ♘h5 ♖f7 20 ♕c3 is also not a pretty sight.

18 ♗xd6

An exchange sacrifice comes in any case.

18...hxg5

18...♕xd6 19 ♖d1 is crushing.

19 ♖d1 *(D)*

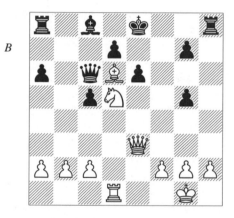

White brings his last piece into play, while Black's only piece not on its original square is his queen. The threat is 20 ♕xg5.

19...♖h6

19...♕xd6 loses to 20 ♘f6+ ♚e7 21 ♘g8+! ♖xg8 22 ♕xg5+. The text-move prevents 20 ♕xg5 due to 20...♕xd6 21 ♘f6+ gxf6 and there is no check on g6. However, Shirov finds another way into Black's position.

20 ♘e7 ♕a4

20...♛b7 loses to 21 ♕xg5 ♚f7 22 ♗e5.

21 ♕f3 ♗b7

21...♕xc2 22 ♘g8 finishes Black.

22 ♕xb7

22 ♘d5 would have won even more quickly, but this is not important.

22...♖d8 23 ♘g8 *(D)*

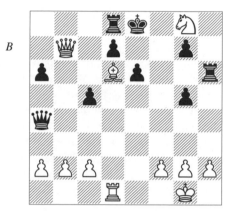

An unusual circumstance: a white knight moves (without capturing) to the original square of one of Black's knights as early as move 23!

23...♖h8

Or 23...♖g6 24 ♕f3.

24 ♕f3! ♖xg8 25 ♕h5+ 1-0

25...g6 26 ♕h7 leads to mate.

Game 112
Judit Polgar – Shakhriyar Mamedyarov
Bled Olympiad 2002
Ruy Lopez, Open

1 e4 e5 2 ♘f3 ♘c6 3 ♗b5 a6 4 ♗a4 ♘f6 5 0-0 ♘xe4 6 d4 b5 7 ♗b3 d5 8 dxe5 ♗e6 9 ♘bd2 ♘c5 10 c3 d4 11 ♘g5!? *(D)*

This spectacular move has proved controversial ever since its introduction in Karpov-Korchnoi, World Ch (10), Baguio City 1978. It was one of the most stunning novelties ever played in a world championship match, but in the prototype game Korchnoi, to his credit, held on to a draw by grim defence. Since then its theoretical evaluation has changed several times – the current view being that White can

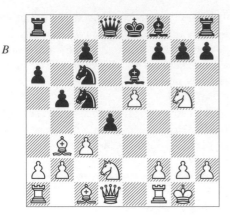

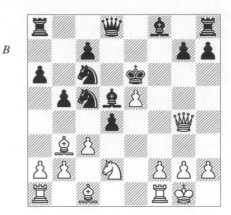

gain little or no advantage against accurate play.

11...♗d5?!

This ambitious move was introduced by Ivan Sokolov, who used it to beat Anand in 1994. However, according to current theory, it is too risky. The two other main continuations are:

1) 11...dxc3 12 ♘xe6 fxe6 13 bxc3 ♕d3 14 ♗c2! (14 ♘f3 was played in the original Karpov-Korchnoi game) 14...♕xc3 15 ♘b3 led to a spectacular win for White in the famous game Kasparov-Anand, PCA World Ch (10), New York 1995.

2) 11...♕xg5 12 ♕f3 0-0-0 13 ♗xe6+ fxe6 14 ♕xc6 ♕xe5 15 b4 ♕d5 16 ♕xd5 exd5 17 bxc5 dxc3 18 ♘b3 d4 is now established as the critical variation. In this complex position, Black has two dangerous connected passed pawns in return for a knight. Recent practical results have indicated that Black has satisfactory chances.

12 ♘xf7!

This piece sacrifice is the only dangerous continuation.

12...♔xf7

12...♗xf7? 13 ♗xf7+ ♔xf7 14 ♕f3+ followed by ♕xc6 leaves White a pawn up and Black with an exposed king.

13 ♕f3+ ♔e6 14 ♕g4+ (D)

The only real alternative is 14 ♘e4, although this is hardly a winning attempt since after 14...♘xb3 15 ♕g4+ ♔f7 16 ♕f5+ ♔g8 17 e6 h6 White has nothing better than 18 ♕f7+ ♔h7 19 ♘g5+ hxg5 20 ♕h5+ ♔g8 21 ♕f7+ with perpetual check (Kalod-Virostko, Czech Team Ch 2001).

14...♔f7?

After this, Polgar demonstrates a forced win. 14...♔e7 is Black's only chance, as played in the game Svidler-Anand, Dos Hermanas 1999. That game continued 15 e6 ♗xe6 (15...♘xb3 16 ♘xb3 ♗xe6 17 ♖e1 ♕d5 18 ♘c5 ♘d8 19 cxd4 gives White a crushing attack) 16 ♖e1 ♕d7 (16...♕d6?! is wrong as White can play ♘e4 with gain of tempo; for example, 17 ♗xe6 ♘xe6 18 ♘e4 ♕d5 19 ♘c5 ♘e5 20 ♕f5 g6 21 ♕xe5 ♕xe5 22 ♖xe5 ♔d6 23 ♖xe6+ ♔xc5 24 cxd4+ and White will emerge a pawn ahead since 24...♔d5 25 ♖e5+ ♔xd4? 26 ♗f4 ♖g8 27 ♖d1+ ♔c4 28 ♗e3 gives White a crushing attack) 17 ♗xe6 ♘xe6 18 ♘f3 (18 ♘b3 is also promising; for example, 18...♔f7 19 ♕f5+ ♔g8 20 ♕xe6+ ♕xe6 21 ♖xe6 ♘d8 22 ♖e4 dxc3 23 bxc3 ♔f7 24 a4 with an endgame advantage for White) 18...♖e8 19 ♘g5 ♘cd8 20 ♗d2 with a dangerous attack for White. Thus the knight sacrifice on f7 gives White an advantage even against the best defence.

15 ♕f5+!

This innovation gives White a winning attack. Previously 15 e6+ had been played, but after 15...♗xe6 16 ♕f3+ ♕f6 17 ♕xc6 ♘xb3 18 axb3 ♗d6 19 ♘e4 ♕e5 20 ♘xd6+ cxd6 White has only a very slight advantage. Polgar's improvement effectively put this whole line out of business.

15...♔e7

15...♔g8 16 e6 ♘e5 17 ♕xe5 ♘xb3 18 axb3 dxc3 19 bxc3 and 15...♔e8 16 e6 ♗xe6 17 ♗xe6 ♕f6 18 ♕xf6 gxf6 19 ♗d5 both leave Black a pawn down with a miserable position.

16 e6! (D)

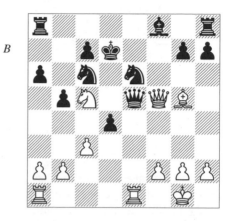

This move is much stronger thanks to the preliminary check on f5.

16...♗xe6

The alternatives are hopeless:

1) 16...♘xb3 17 ♘xb3 ♗xe6 18 ♖e1 ♕c8 19 ♗g5+ ♔d6 20 ♘f4+ ♔e7 21 ♘c5 wins.

2) 16...♘xe6 17 ♗xd5 followed by ♖e1 also wins.

3) 16...♗xb3 17 ♘xb3 ♘xe6 18 ♖e1 ♕c8 19 ♘c5 ♘cd8 20 cxd4 with a decisive attack.

17 ♖e1!

This ruthlessly accurate move is even stronger than the obvious 17 ♕xc5+.

17...♕d6

After 17...♕d7 18 ♗xe6 ♘xe6 19 ♘b3 Black cannot counter the threats of 20 ♘c5 and 20

♗g5+, but the move played gives White a free tempo with her knight.

18 ♗xe6 ♘xe6 19 ♘e4 ♕e5 20 ♗g5+ ♔d7

20...♘xg5 21 ♘xg5 and 20...♔e8 21 ♘f6+ are easily winning for White.

21 ♘c5+! (D)

An attractive finish.

21...♗xc5 22 ♕f7+

Better than 22 ♖xe5 ♘xe5 23 ♕xe5 ♗d6, when Black could limp on for a time.

22...♔d6

22...♔c8 23 ♖xe5 ♘xe5 24 ♕xe6+ ♘d7 25 cxd4 ♗xd4 26 ♖d1 and White wins.

23 ♗e7+ 1-0

Black is mated after 23...♘xe7 24 ♖xe5 ♔xe5 25 ♖e1+ or 23...♔d5 24 ♕f3+ ♔c4 25 b3#.

Game 113

Emil Sutovsky – Ilia Smirin

Israeli Ch, Tel Aviv 2002

Sicilian Defence, ♘c3

1 e4 c5 2 ♘c3 ♘c6 3 ♘f3

The same anti-Sveshnikov system as in Games 111 and 117.

3...e5 4 ♗c4 d6 5 d3 ♗e7 6 0-0

The alternative is 6 ♘d2, which aims to increase White's control of d5 by playing ♘f1-e3. See Game 117 for more information on this line.

6...♘f6 7 ♘g5 (D)

If Black is allowed simply to complete his development, it will be very hard for White to show any advantage. Therefore, he gains a tempo to clear the way for f4 in order to start a direct attack. Launching an attack before completing your development is often risky, but here the static central structure makes it hard for Black to generate counterplay.

7...0-0 8 f4 exf4

Black has several options at this point, but it is worth noting that if Black intends to play ...♗g4, he should do so before exchanging on f4, since otherwise the white queen can move directly to d2. After 8...♗g4 9 ♕e1 exf4 10 ♗xf4 ♘d4 11 ♕d2 ♕d7 White maintains an edge, but nevertheless this is probably Black's safest line.

9 ♗xf4 h6

By far the most popular move, driving away the aggressively-posted knight, but it involves an element of risk as it weakens Black's kingside.

10 ♘f3 ♗e6 11 ♘d5! (D)

The only dangerous continuation since 11 ♕d2 d5 allows Black to free his position.

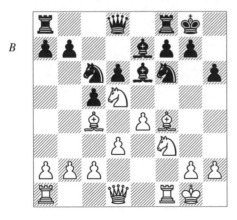

11...♗xd5

This immediate exchange leaves White with a pawn on d5, which should reduce his attacking chances.

12 exd5

Even though White blocks the c4-bishop in, it is the only try for an advantage since 12 ♗xd5 ♘xd5 13 exd5 ♘e5 leads to immediate equality.

12...♘a5

It looks odd to play the knight to the edge of the board, but after 12...♘b4 13 ♗d2! ♘bxd5 14 ♘h4, followed by ♘f5, White gets a dangerous attack in return for the pawn. Here, as in many of the subsequent lines, Black has cause to regret the move ...h6, which makes it impossible to dislodge the knight from f5.

13 ♘h4 (D)

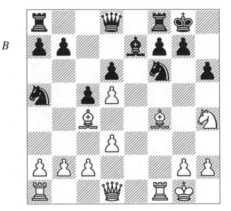

Also in this case the knight heads for the tempting f5-square. Black cannot prevent this because ...g6 leaves the h6-pawn hanging.

13...b5?

Black tries to solve his problems by forcibly eliminating the d5-pawn, but he runs into a vicious sacrificial attack. He should have played 13...♘xc4 14 dxc4 ♘xd5 15 ♕xd5 ♗xh4 16 ♗xd6 (16 ♖ad1 ♗e7 is also close to equality) 16...♗e7 17 ♗g3 ♕b6 18 b3 and here a draw was agreed in Smirin-Wang Yue, FIDE World Cup, Khanty-Mansiisk 2005.

14 ♘f5!

This is an example of a sacrifice so complicated that not all the consequences could have been worked out over the board. White sacrifices two pieces to expose Black's king, but White's threats build up rather slowly and Black has many ways to attempt a defence. However, it turns out that the traffic jam in

Black's position prevents him from feeding his extra material across to the kingside where it is really needed.

14...bxc4 15 ♗xh6! *(D)*

Giving up the second piece is a brave decision, especially as White could have regained the first sacrificed piece by 15 ♕e1 ♘xd5! (15...♖e8 16 ♕g3 gives White a very strong attack) 16 ♕e4 cxd3 17 cxd3. However, in this line Black's pieces start to emerge after 17...♖b8 18 ♕xd5 ♗f6 and it is not clear if White has much of an advantage.

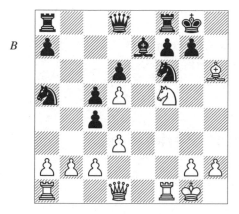

15...gxh6

Black could have declined the second piece by 15...♘e8, but after 16 ♕e1! White obtains a raging attack in any case; for example, 16...♗f6 17 ♗d2 ♘b7 18 ♗c3 ♗xc3 (Black has nothing better than to give up his queen) 19 ♘e7+ ♕xe7 20 ♕xe7 ♗d4+ 21 ♔h1 ♖b8 22 c3 ♗e5 23 ♕h4 with a large advantage to White due to the possibility of playing a rook to h3.

16 ♘xh6+

Eliminating an important defensive pawn, albeit at the cost of some time since the knight has to return to f5 next move.

16...♔h7

16...♔h8 requires a different method of attack by White: 17 ♖xf6! ♗xf6 18 ♕h5 ♗d4+ 19 ♔h1 ♕c7 20 ♘f5+ ♔g8 21 ♕g5+ ♔h7 (21...♔h8 22 ♘e7 ♕xe7 23 ♕xe7 cxd3 24 cxd3 is much better for White as Black's knight is still totally out of play and his king remains exposed) 22 ♖f1 (Black cannot organize a defence despite his large material advantage) 22...♖fe8

23 c3 f6 24 ♕h4+ ♔g8 25 ♘h6+ ♔h8 26 ♘f7++ ♔g7 27 ♕h6+ ♔xf7 28 ♕h7+ ♔f8 29 ♕xc7 and White wins.

17 ♘f5 *(D)*

Now 17 ♖xf6? ♗xf6 18 ♕h5 fails after 18...♖h8.

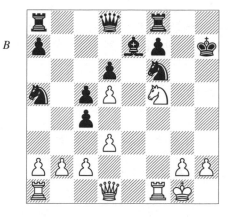

17...cxd3?

This is a clear mistake, because now the white queen can join the attack with gain of tempo. However, Black is struggling in any case:

1) 17...♔h8 18 ♖f3! ♘h7 19 ♖h3 ♗h4 20 ♖xh4 ♕g5 21 ♕f3 cxd3 22 ♕xd3 f6 23 ♕h3 ♖f7 24 ♘xd6 ♕xd5 25 ♘xf7+ ♔xf7 26 ♖f1 with a winning position for White.

2) 17...♖e8 18 ♖f3 ♗f8 19 ♖h3+ ♔g8 20 ♕f3 with a decisive attack.

3) 17...♖h8 18 ♕e1 ♘xd5 (18...♘g8 19 ♕e2 ♕f8 20 ♕e4 ♗f6 21 ♘xd6+ ♔g7 22 ♘f5+ ♔g6 23 ♖f3 gives White a massive attack) 19 ♕e4 ♗f6 20 ♕xd5 ♔g8 21 ♖f4 ♖h7 22 ♘xd6 ♗d4+ 23 ♔h1 ♖b8 24 ♖af1 and White's attack is worth more than the sacrificed piece.

4) 17...♔g8! (the best chance for Black) 18 ♕e2 ♖e8 (18...♘xd5 19 dxc4 ♘c6 20 ♕g4+ ♗g5 21 ♖ad1! ♘e5 22 ♕g3 and Black is in trouble) 19 ♕e3 ♗f8 20 ♕g3+ ♔h8 21 ♖f4 is dangerous for Black, but he has more defensive chances than in other lines; e.g., 21...cxd3 (21...♖e5 22 ♖h4+ ♘h7 23 ♕h3 ♕xh4 24 ♘xh4 is very good for White) 22 cxd3 ♖b8 23 ♖h4+ ♘h7 24 ♕h3 ♕xh4 25 ♘xh4 ♖xb2 26 ♖f1 and Black is worse but still alive.

18 ♕xd3

Now Black must lose a tempo moving his king, which allows White to bring his other rook into the attack with gain of tempo.

18...♔h8 19 ♖ae1 ♕b6

There is no defence: 19...♖e8 20 ♕h3+ ♘h7 21 ♘h6 wins at once, while 19...♘xd5 20 ♕h3+ ♔g8 (20...♗h4 loses to 21 ♖e4) 21 ♕h6 ♗f6 22 ♖e4 mates quickly.

20 ♕h3+ ♘h7 21 ♖xe7

Regaining one piece while retaining a tremendous attack.

21...c4+

21...♕b4 22 c3 is decisive.

22 ♔h1 ♕xb2 23 ♖e4 ♖g8

Allowing an attractive conclusion, but even 23...♕f6 24 ♖h4 ♕g6 25 ♖g4 ♕f6 26 ♖g7 ♕xg7 27 ♘xg7 ♔xg7 28 ♕c3+ is hopeless.

24 ♕xh7+! (D)

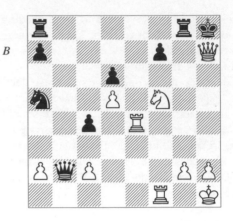

B

1-0

Mate is forced after 24...♔xh7 25 ♖h4+ ♔g6 26 ♖h6+ ♔g5 27 h4+ ♔g4 28 ♘e3+ ♔g3 29 ♖f3#.

Game 114

Judit Polgar – Ferenc Berkes
Budapest 2003
French Defence, 4...dxe4

1 e4 e6 2 d4 d5 3 ♘c3 ♘f6 4 ♗g5 dxe4 5 ♘xe4 ♗e7 6 ♗xf6 ♗xf6 7 ♘f3

In this system White gives up the two bishops in order to gain a lead in development and attacking chances on the kingside.

7...0-0 8 ♕d2 ♘d7 9 0-0-0 ♗e7

The most popular line has been 9...b6 10 ♗d3 ♗b7, in which Black continues his development without delay. The text-move is more ambitious; at the cost of a tempo, Black retains the bishop-pair.

10 ♗d3 b6 (D)

Black has to tread carefully in this variation, since even a slight misstep can result in disaster. One example is Topalov-Bareev, Monaco (Amber blindfold) 2003, which continued 10...c5 11 ♘xc5 ♘xc5 12 dxc5 ♕d5 13 ♔b1 ♕xc5 14 h4 b6? 15 ♘g5 h6 16 ♗h7+ ♔h8 17 ♗e4 ♖b8 18 ♕f4 ♗b7 19 ♗xb7 ♖xb7 20 ♕e4 and Black lost material.

11 ♘eg5!?

White has tried various ways to break through on the kingside, but most of them have started

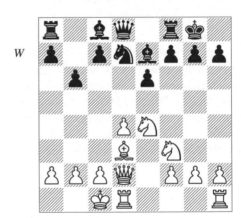

W

with 11 h4. This game was one of the first in which 11 ♘eg5 was played, and with new problems to solve it wasn't long before Black went wrong.

11...h6?!

Black's safest line is 11...♗xg5 12 ♘xg5 ♘f6, reaching a position which can also arise via other move-orders. It may appear illogical to play ...♗e7 and then ...♗xg5, but exchanges generally benefit the defender and in this particular position the reduction in White's attacking force is worth the apparent loss of time. After 13 h4 ♗b7 14 ♖h3 ♕e7 the position is roughly level.

12 ♗h7+!

This check was played for the first time in the current game (12 h4 had been preferred in earlier encounters). It forces the black king onto the dangerous h-file and leaves the f7-pawn with but a single defender.

12...♔h8 13 ♗e4 *(D)*

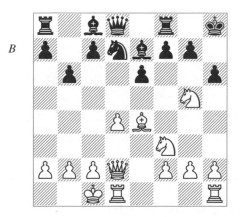

13...hxg5?

This turns out to be a fatal error, thanks to White's brilliant reply. Alternatives:

1) 13...♖b8 14 h4 ♘f6 (14...♗a6 15 c3 gives White a dangerous initiative) 15 ♘e5 ♘xe4 16 ♘gxf7+ ♔h7 17 ♘xd8 ♘xd2 18 ♘dc6 ♘e4 19 f3 ♘f2 20 ♘xb8 ♘xd1 21 ♔xd1 leaves White a pawn up for insufficient compensation.

2) 13...♗xg5! is still the best defence, when 14 ♘xg5 ♖b8 15 h4 ♘f6 gives Black good equalizing chances.

After the text-move, it is hard to see what White can play, since 14 ♗xa8? g4 leads to the loss of the f3-knight (moving it would allow ...♗g5).

14 g4!! *(D)*

This is Polgar's brilliant idea. By preventing ...g4, White prepares to play h4 to blast the h-file open. Moreover, since White is now genuinely threatening to take on a8, Black must waste a tempo saving the rook.

14...♖b8

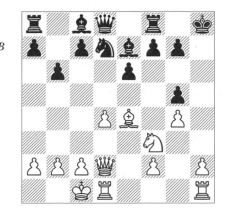

Black can also rescue the rook with other moves, but it doesn't make much difference; for example, 14...♗a6 15 h4 gxh4 16 g5 ♔g8 17 ♕f4 f5 18 ♕xh4 fxe4 19 ♕h7+ ♔f7 20 ♕h5+ g6 21 ♕h7+ ♔e8 22 ♕xg6+ ♖f7 23 ♖h7 or 14...c6 15 h4 gxh4 16 g5 f6 17 ♖xh4+ ♔g8 18 g6 f5 19 ♖h3 and White wins in both cases.

15 h4 *(D)*

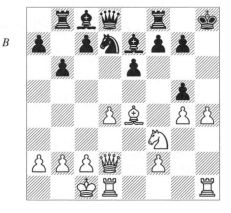

15...g6

There is no real defence:

1) 15...gxh4 16 g5 f5 (16...♔g8 17 ♗h7+ ♔xh7 18 ♕f4 f5 19 ♕xh4+ ♔g8 20 ♕h7+ ♔f7 21 ♕h5+ g6 22 ♕h7+ ♔e8 23 ♕xg6+ ♖f7 24 ♖h7 wins for White) and now White can win by 17 ♕f4 fxe4 18 ♕xh4+ ♔g8 19 ♕h7+ ♔f7 20 ♕h5+ g6 21 ♕h7+ ♔e8 22 ♕xg6+ ♖f7 23 ♖h7 ♗xg5+ 24 ♘xg5 ♕xg5+ 25 ♕xg5 ♖xh7 26 ♕g6+ ♖f7 27 ♕xe6+ ♔f8 28 ♖h1 or simply 17 ♗c6, when Black has no helpful moves.

2) 15...f5 16 hxg5+ ♔g8 17 gxf5 transposes to line '3'.

3) 15...♔g8 16 hxg5 f5 17 gxf5 ♖xf5 18 ♗xf5 exf5 19 g6 with an enormous attack for no material sacrifice.

16 hxg5+ ♔g7 17 ♕f4

The threat is 18 ♖h7+! ♔xh7 19 ♕h2+ ♔g8 20 ♖h1.

17...♗b7 (D)

Black misses the threat, but the game could not be saved in any case:

1) 17...♖h8 18 ♖xh8 ♕xh8 19 ♘e5 ♗xg5 (19...♕e8 20 ♖h1) 20 ♕xg5 ♕h6 21 ♕xh6+ ♔xh6 22 ♘xf7+ ♔g7 23 ♘e5 with an easily winning ending.

2) 17...♗d6 18 ♘e5 ♗e7 19 ♕e3 ♗xg5 (19...♘xe5 20 dxe5 ♕e8 21 ♖h7+ should be a familiar idea by now) 20 f4 ♘xe5 21 dxe5 ♕e7 22 fxg5 ♖h8 23 ♖xh8 ♔xh8 24 ♖h1+ ♔g8 25 ♕f4, followed by ♕h2, and White wins.

18 ♖h7+! ♔xh7

18...♔g8 19 ♖dh1 mates quickly.

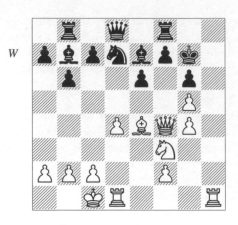

19 ♕h2+ ♔g8 20 ♖h1 ♗xg5+

The only way to avoid mate, but Black must surrender his queen.

21 ♘xg5 ♕xg5+ 22 f4 ♕xf4+ 23 ♕xf4 ♗xe4 24 ♕xe4 1-0

White retains the h-file attack, so at the very least the loss of some further pawns is inevitable.

Game 115

Boris Gelfand – Alexander Shabalov

Bermuda 2004

Queen's Gambit, Semi-Slav Defence

1 d4 d5 2 c4 c6 3 ♘c3 ♘f6 4 ♘f3 e6 5 e3 ♘bd7 6 ♕c2 ♗d6 7 g4

This move provoked a few smiles when it was first played, but it has now become one of the main lines of the Semi-Slav and has been used by Kasparov and Topalov, amongst others.

7...dxc4

The most common reply.

8 ♗xc4 b6

Black aims to develop his bishop at b7 and prepare counterplay on the long diagonal. But why not then play 8...b5? That is in fact the more common move, but although ...b5 gains a tempo, it can make it awkward to play ...c5 later because the b5-pawn is hanging. By playing ...b6, Black gives up a tempo but makes it easier to push the c-pawn. Although there is some logic behind the text-move, giving up a tempo in such a sharp position involves a risk.

9 e4 (D)

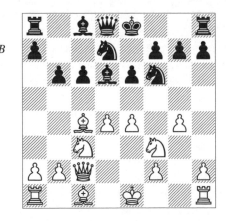

9...♗b7

Aiming to exploit White's weakness on the long diagonal. 9...e5 10 g5 ♘h5 11 ♗e3 and

9...♘xg4 10 e5 ♗b4 11 ♖g1 are inferior and give White a clear advantage.

10 e5

The critical move. 10 g5 is less effective because 10...♘h5 11 ♗e3 b5!? gives Black sufficient counterplay.

10...c5

The point of Black's play, but although he doesn't lose a piece, he has not solved all his problems.

11 exf6 ♗xf3

Not 11...♕xf6? 12 ♗e2 ♗xf3 13 g5 and the f3-bishop falls. The next few moves are more or less forced for both sides.

12 fxg7 ♖g8 13 ♕xh7 ♘f6 14 ♗b5+ ♔e7 15 ♗g5 (D)

The best move, since 15 ♕h6 ♘xg4 16 ♕h3 ♗xh1 17 ♕xg4 cxd4 18 ♕xd4 f6 leaves White struggling for compensation.

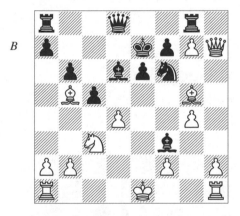

B

15...♗f4!

This surprising shot is the only move, since 15...cxd4? fails to 16 ♕h6 ♗e5 17 ♘e4! ♗xe4 18 f4 and Black's position collapses. Not, of course, 15...♗xh1? 16 ♕h6 and White wins at once.

16 ♕h3!

Gelfand's innovation, which is much stronger than 16 ♗xf6+?! ♔xf6 17 ♘e4+ ♗xe4 18 ♕xc4 ♕xd4, as played previously.

16...♗xh1

Black is obliged to accept the sacrifice, since 16...♗xg5 17 ♕xf3 cxd4 18 ♖d1 gives White a dangerous initiative for no sacrifice.

17 ♗xf4 ♕xd4

After 17...♖xg7 18 dxc5 bxc5 19 ♖d1 ♘d5 20 f3 the h1-bishop is shut out of play and White has a decisive attack.

18 ♕g3

Threatening both 19 ♖d1 and 19 ♗e5, so Black must react vigorously.

18...♘e4

18...♖xg7 19 ♖d1 ♖xg4 20 ♖xd4 ♖xg3 21 ♗d6+ ♔d8 22 ♗xc5+ ♔d5 23 ♗xb6+ axb6 24 fxg3 leaves White with a clear extra pawn in the ending.

19 ♕h4+

White even had a second promising line in 19 ♘xe4!? ♕xe4+ 20 ♗e2; for example, 20...♖ad8 21 f3 ♗xf3 22 ♕xf3 ♕b4+ 23 ♔f2 ♕xb2 24 ♗g5+ f6 25 ♖b1 and White will retain the g7-pawn.

19...♕f6

Forced, as 19...♘f6? 20 ♖d1 ♕xf4 21 ♖d7+ and 19...f6? 20 ♖d1 win for White.

20 g5 (D)

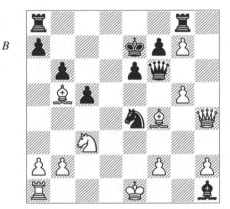

B

20...♕f5?

After this mistake Black loses quickly. The priority was to remove the dangerous g7-pawn so Black should have played 20...♕xg7. Then White can try:

1) 21 0-0-0 ♖ad8! (21...♖h8? loses to 22 ♘xe4!! ♖xh4 23 ♗d6+ ♔d8 24 ♗e5+ ♔e7 25 ♗xg7 ♗xc4 26 ♖d7↑ ♔c8 27 g6! fxg6 28 ♖xa7+ ♔d8 29 ♗f6+) 22 ♖xh1 ♖h8 23 ♗e5! ♕xe5 24 ♕xe4 ♕xg5+ 25 f4 with just a slight advantage for White.

2) 21 ♘xe4! ♗xe4 22 ♗c7 ♗d5 23 g6+ f6 24 ♕f4 e5 25 ♕d2 ♖gd8 26 0-0-0 ♕g8 (or

26...♛xg6 27 ♗xd8+ ♖xd8 28 ♗c6 and White wins) 27 a3 and White has a clear advantage thanks to his two connected passed pawns on the kingside.

Thus even with the best defence Black's position remains unpleasant.

21 0-0-0

Now White has a decisive attack.

21...♖ad8

21...♘xc3 22 g6+ f6 23 ♖d7+ ♔e8 24 bxc3 is winning for White.

22 ♖xd8

Or 22 ♖xh1 ♘xc3 23 bxc3 ♛d5 24 ♛h6! ♛xh1+ 25 ♔b2 and White wins.

22...♔xd8

22...♖xd8 23 ♘xe4 ♛xe4 24 g6+ f6 25 g8♘+! ♖xg8 26 ♛h7+ mates.

23 ♗d3! *(D)*

This simple move leaves Black helpless as he cannot unpin his knight.

23...♖xg7

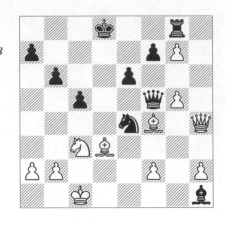

Desperation.

24 ♘xe4 ♖h7

Or 24...♗xe4 25 ♗xe4 ♛xe4 26 ♗c7+.

25 ♗c7+! 1-0

Since 25...♔xc7 26 ♛g3+ e5 (26...♔c6 27 ♛d6+ ♔b7 28 ♛d7+ leads to mate) 27 ♘f6 will leave White a piece up.

Game 116

Boris Gelfand – Kiril Georgiev
Calvia Olympiad 2004
Catalan Opening

1 d4 ♘f6 2 c4 e6 3 g3 ♗b4+ 4 ♗d2 ♗e7 5 ♗g2 d5 6 ♘f3 0-0 7 0-0 c6 8 ♗f4

The most popular moves have traditionally been 8 ♛c2 and 8 ♛b3, but in recent years this bishop move has gained many followers. In several lines White is prepared to sacrifice the c4-pawn for the sake of rapid development.

8...♘bd7 9 ♘c3 *(D)*

White can still back out with 9 ♛c2, but this is the consistent continuation.

9...dxc4

Accepting the challenge. This is a typical modern gambit in that White's compensation does not consist of a direct attack on the king or a massive lead in development. Instead, White hopes that his central control and chances to break through with d5 will provide at least enough for the pawn. More cautious players might prefer 9...♘h5 10 ♗d2 ♘hf6, although White can avoid the repetition by 11 ♛c2.

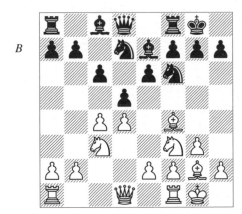

10 e4 a5

A rather odd move. Although White has no immediate threats, in such a position it is risky to spend time on moves which are of marginal usefulness. Although this move does not by itself offer White a definite advantage, it flirts with danger and means that any further slip by Black is likely to be severely punished. This is a typical example of a pattern we have seen several times in this book. One side makes a risky move which is not bad if followed up very precisely. When this precise play is not forthcoming, the result is disaster. The lesson here is that it is often better to leave a safety margin and not put yourself under pressure, since no one can guarantee absolute accuracy. The most promising defences are 10...b5 11 d5 ♕b6 and the solid 10...♖e8.

11 ♖e1

The immediate 11 d5 can be met by 11...exd5 12 exd5 cxd5 13 ♘xd5 ♘xd5 14 ♕xd5 ♘c5 and Black escapes, so White first builds up his position.

11...♖e8

11...b5 is too weakening and can be strongly met by 12 d5.

12 d5!? (D)

Gelfand criticizes this move in *Informator*. It is true that it allows Black to equalize with accurate play, but it certainly puts pressure on him to find the right defence. The alternative was 12 a4, followed by ♕c2 and ♖ad1, quietly building up before trying to punch through in the centre.

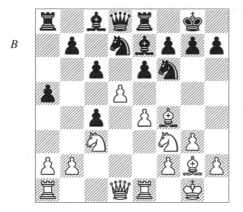

12...cxd5 13 exd5 ♘c5

Further exchanges are not helpful; for example, 13...exd5 14 ♘xd5 ♘xd5 15 ♕xd5 h6 (15...♕b6? 16 ♘g5 is very strong) 16 ♕xc4 and White's lead in development gives him unpleasant pressure.

14 ♘e5

14 d6 is tempting, but after 14...♗f8 15 ♗f1 (15 ♘b5 ♘d3 16 ♘c7 ♘xe1 17 ♕xe1 ♗d7 is also about equal) 15...♘h5 16 ♗g5 ♕xd6 17 ♘d2 ♘f6 18 ♘xc4 ♕xd1 19 ♖axd1 White has adequate play for the pawn, but not more.

14...exd5

14...♖a6 is also sufficient for equality; for example, 15 ♘xc4 exd5 16 ♘xd5 ♘xd5 17 ♗xd5 ♗e6 and the exchanges relieve the pressure. At least in this line Black would have made use of ...a5.

15 ♘xd5 ♘xd5?! (D)

Overlooking Gelfand's spectacular reply. The correct line was 15...♗e6! 16 ♘xe7+ ♖xe7 17 ♕c2 ♖c8 18 ♖ad1 ♕e8 with an unclear position.

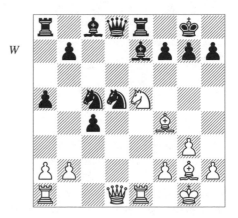

16 ♘xf7!!

Not 16 ♗xd5 ♗e6 and Black's problems are over.

16...♔xf7?

Taken aback by White's sacrifice, Black immediately blunders into a forced loss. However, White is better in any case:

1) 16...♘xf4 17 ♘xd8 ♖xd8 18 ♕c2 ♘fe6 19 ♕xc4 ♖d4 20 ♕c2 gives White some advantage; for example, 20...♗d7 21 ♖ad1 ♖d8 22 ♖xd4 ♘xd4 23 ♗d5+ ♗e6 24 ♗xe6+ ♘cxe6 25 ♕e4 and Black will have trouble defending all his pawns.

2) 16...♘e3 17 ♕xd8 ♗xd8 18 ♘d6 ♗c7 19 ♗d5+ ♗e6 20 ♘xe8 ♗xf4 21 ♗xe6+ ♘xe6 22 gxf4 ♘c2 23 ♖xe6 ♘xa1 24 ♘d6 and White has the better ending.

17 ♗xd5+

The correct choice; 17 ♕h5+ ♔g8 18 ♗xd5+ ♔h8 19 ♗f7 ♗e6 20 ♗xe6 ♘xe6 21 ♖xe6 ♗f6 offers White little.

17...♔g6

The king must come out, because 17...♗e6 loses to 18 ♕h5+ ♔g8 19 ♖xe6! ♘xe6 20 ♗xe6+ ♔h8 21 ♗f5, while 17...♔f8 18 ♕h5 is an immediate disaster.

18 ♖e5! *(D)*

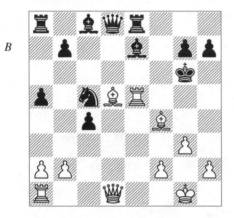

18...♗f5

18...h6 19 ♗xh6! gxh6 20 ♕h5+ ♔g7 21 ♖ae1 gives White a winning attack.

19 ♖xf5!

It is unusual to see a 19th-century-style king-hunt in a game between two contemporary grandmasters.

19...♔xf5 20 ♕h5+ ♗g5

Other moves allow a quick mate.

21 ♕xh7+ ♔f6

Or 21...g6 22 ♕h3+ ♔f6 23 ♗xg5+ ♔xg5 24 ♕h4+ ♔f5 25 ♕f4#.

22 ♗xg5+ ♔xg5 23 ♗f7

White could have forced mate by 23 f4+ ♔f6 24 ♕h4+ ♔f5 (or 24...♔g6 25 f5+ ♔xf5 26 ♕f4+ ♔g6 27 ♗f7+ ♔h7 28 ♕f5+ mating) 25 ♕h5+ g5 26 ♕h7+ ♔g4 27 h3+ ♔xg3 28 ♕f5, but the move played is also adequate.

23...♕d6 *(D)*

23...♔f6 24 ♕g6+ ♔e7 25 ♖e1+ ♔d7 26 ♖xe8 wins too much material.

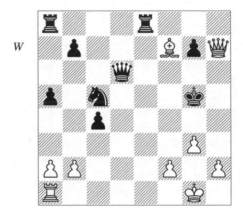

24 ♕xg7+ ♔f5 25 ♗xe8 1-0

25...♖xe8 26 ♕f7+ leaves White with a massive material advantage.

Game 117
Peter Svidler – Loek van Wely
Wijk aan Zee 2005
Sicilian Defence, ♘c3

1 e4 c5 2 ♘f3 ♘c6 3 ♘c3

This move-order is primarily directed against the Sveshnikov, since after 3...e6 4 d4 cxd4 5 ♘xd4 ♘f6 White can play 6 ♘xc6, a line which is held in considerable respect. If, on the other hand, 3...♘f6 then White will continue 4 ♗b5 (see Game 111, in which Van Wely suffered in this line).

3...e5

In a way, the most thematic response; Black takes advantage of White's omission of d4. In the resulting semi-blocked position, White intends to exploit the weakness of d5 and possibly to develop kingside play by a later f4 (after ♘d2, for example). Black aims to complete his development and to exchange off any pieces which arrive on d5.

4 ♗c4

Taking aim at d5 and (after a possible later f4) at f7.

4...♗e7 5 d3 d6 6 ♘d2 *(D)*

In recent years this has been the most common move, clearing the way for the f-pawn while at the same time intending ♘f1-e3 to increase White's control of d5. However, the older line 6 0-0 ♘f6 7 ♘g5 0-0 8 f4 remains popular – see Game 113.

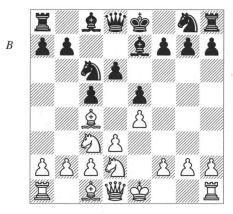

6...♗g5

Black aims to exchange his dark-squared bishop. While this is positionally desirable, it often happens that a 'bad' bishop provides essential defensive cement, so swapping it off entails some risk. The manoeuvre also costs some time hence 6...♘f6 is a more solid alternative.

7 h4

The critical reply, which forces Black to make an awkward decision.

7...♗xd2+

Black really wanted to exchange his bishop for White's c1-bishop and not the d2-knight, so this is something of a concession. However, the alternative 7...♗h6 8 ♕h5 g6 9 ♕d1 ♘f6 10 ♘f1 also has defects, not the least of which is that the move ...g6 has weakened Black's kingside and gives White the chance of a later h5.

8 ♗xd2 ♘f6 9 0-0 *(D)*

9...♗g4?!

A critical moment. 9...♗e6 10 f4 ♗xc4 11 dxc4 h5 looks like the best line, as played in Kasparov-Leko, Linares 2005, a game which Black drew without too much trouble. Playing

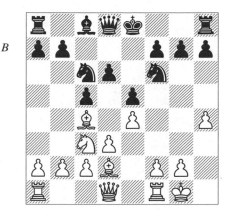

for exchanges is a logical way to reduce White's pressure.

9...0-0 is another possibility, but looks risky after 10 f4. For the moment Black has control of g4, but this doesn't compensate for White's kingside attacking chances. Part of Black's strategy in this line is to keep his king in the centre for the time being, because he does not want to give White a target by castling kingside and he wants to retain the option of castling queenside. However, care is always necessary when leaving your king in the centre and in this game Black pays a heavy price for a couple of faulty moves which result in his king being marooned far from safety.

10 ♕e1

A novelty at the time. Svidler had previously played 10 f3 ♗e6 11 f4, transposing to the 9...♗e6 line. The queen move poses new problems for Black, which Van Wely failed to solve over the board.

10...♗e6?

This acquiescent move is definitely wrong. Black after all puts his bishop on e6, but it turns out that White's queen is much better placed on e1 than on d1. The critical line is the odd-looking 10...♘d4 11 ♖c1 ♗f3!?, which prevents White's f-pawn from advancing by the most direct means possible. Then the position is totally unclear; one line is 12 ♕e3 ♕d7 13 ♗b5 ♘xb5 14 ♕xf3 ♘d4 15 ♕g3 0-0 with a murky position. However, at any rate the exchange of light-squared bishops has reduced White's attacking chances.

11 f4 ♗xc4 12 dxc4 *(D)*

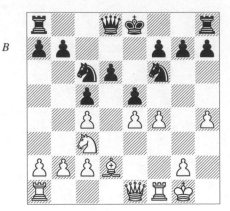

12...h5?!

Securing the g4-square for the knight is a logical idea, but here it is too slow. However, White retains at least a slight advantage after the alternatives:

1) 12...0-0 13 ♖d1 ♘d4 14 fxe5 ♘g4 15 ♕g3 ♘xe5 16 ♗h6 ♘g6 17 ♗e3 gives White good attacking chances.

2) 12...h6 13 ♘d5 0-0 14 ♖d1 with continuing pressure for White.

3) 12...♕d7, aiming for queenside castling, may be Black's best option.

13 fxe5 dxe5 14 ♗g5

Now the difference in the position of White's queen becomes important. If White had adopted the same line in Kasparov-Leko (with the white queen on d1) then Black would have been able to exchange queens here. As it is, Black faces a White's rapidly growing initiative.

14...♘e7

This move leads to an immediate loss, but even after 14...♕d4+ 15 ♔h1 0-0-0 (15...♕xc4 16 ♗xf6 gxf6 17 ♖d1 ♘d4 18 ♖xf6 0-0-0 19 b3 ♕b4 20 ♘d5 ♕xe1+ 21 ♖xe1 gives Black a

poor ending in which he will inevitably lose a pawn within a few moves) 16 b3 ♕d7 17 ♘d5 White wins a pawn on f6.

15 ♖d1

White's development is completed with gain of tempo and Black faces disaster.

15...♕b6

15...♕a5 loses after 16 ♕f2 or the more direct 16 ♖xf6 gxf6 17 ♗xf6 ♖g8 18 ♗xe7 ♔xe7 19 ♘d5+.

16 ♕g3 *(D)*

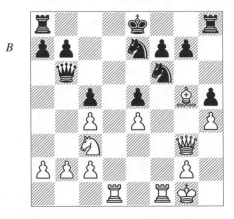

Black's king is trapped in the centre and the e5-pawn is hanging – all without any material sacrifice by White.

16...♘g6 17 ♗xf6 gxf6 18 ♘d5

Here *Fritz* gives White more than ten pawns' advantage, which is not a good sign.

18...♕xb2 19 ♘xf6+ ♔f8 20 ♘xh5 1-0

The end might be 20...♔g8 (20...♖xh5 loses to 21 ♕xg6) 21 ♖xf7 ♔xf7 22 ♖d7+ ♔e8 23 ♘f6+ ♔f8 24 ♕xg6. A crushing game, but one which well illustrates the dangers of leaving your king in the centre.

Game 118
Peter Leko – Lazaro Bruzon
Wijk aan Zee 2005
Ruy Lopez, Chigorin Defence

1 e4 e5 2 ♘f3 ♘c6 3 ♗b5 a6 4 ♗a4 ♘f6 5 0-0 ♗e7 6 ♖e1 b5 7 ♗b3 d6 8 c3 0-0 9 h3 ♘a5 10 ♗c2 c5 11 d4 ♕c7

The Chigorin Defence in the Ruy Lopez, which aims to support the e5-pawn, has been played for more than a century. It is one of

Black's most solid continuations in the Closed Ruy Lopez and hardly seems likely to lead to a miniature, but just watch what happens.

12 ♘bd2

White starts his standard knight tour to g3.

12...cxd4 13 cxd4 ♗d7 14 ♘f1 ♖ac8 *(D)*

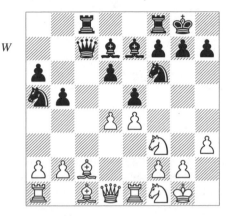

W

Black's attack on c2 forces White to take a critical decision.

15 ♖e2

One of three main options for White. The most popular line is 15 ♘e3, whereby White abandons his ambition to play ♘g3 but does not lose time. This move takes away the most natural square from the c1-bishop but it does mean that the knight can sometimes move to d5. The third possibility, 15 ♗d3, is currently out of favour due to 15...♘c6 16 ♗e3 exd4 17 ♘xd4 ♘e5 and Black's active piece-play compensates for the isolated d-pawn. The text-move looks rather artificial, but it allows the knight to move to g3 and keeps the c1-h6 diagonal open for the bishop. The basic rule for the Closed Ruy Lopez is that if White can complete his development while maintaining his central pawn duo on d4 and e4, then he will have the advantage.

15...♘c6

It is hard to say which move-order is most accurate for Black. The most popular line has been 15...♖fe8 16 ♘g3 ♘c6 when both 17 a3 ♘xd4 18 ♘xd4 exd4 19 ♕xd4 ♗e6 and 17 ♗e3 exd4 18 ♘xd4 d5 leave White with at most a minimal advantage.

16 a3 exd4?!

I don't like this move. Exchanging on d4 is a positional concession, since it leaves Black with an isolated d-pawn, but it can be justified if it gives Black compensating piece-play or if Black can quickly force through the liberating ...d5. Generally speaking, playing ...exd4 is more of a concession when White's bishop is on c2 than when it is on d3, because on c2 the bishop can easily move to the active square b3, while on d3 it has fewer dynamic prospects. In the current position Black has no particular piece-play, so his hopes are based on playing ...d5; however, as we shall see, it is not easy to achieve this in a favourable way. The flexible 16...♖fe8 looks best to me. In that case, play similar to the note to Black's 15th move might arise, although here White does have the additional possibility of 17 d5.

17 ♘xd4 ♖fe8

Black cannot play 17...d5 at once due to 18 exd5 ♘xd5 19 ♘xb5 axb5 20 ♕xd5, when Black has little to show for the pawn.

18 ♘g3 *(D)*

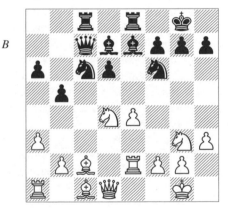

B

18...d5?!

The thematic move, but thanks to Leko's novelty at move 21 it doesn't have the desired effect of freeing Black's position. He should have contented himself with 18...♘xd4 19 ♕xd4 ♗e6, preventing ♗b3, although White has an edge after 20 ♗e3.

19 ♘xc6 ♗xc6 20 e5 ♘e4 21 ♗f4! *(D)*

This important innovation casts doubt on Black's strategy of playing for ...d5. Hitherto White had accepted Black's pawn sacrifice by

21 ♘xe4 dxe4 22 ♗xe4, but after 22...♖ed8 23 ♕b3 ♗xe4 24 ♖xe4 ♕c2 Black's active pieces and better development gave him excellent play for the pawn. Instead of grabbing material, Leko plays to complete his development.

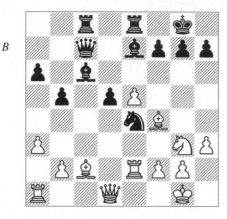

B

21...g5?

Many players, when faced by a positionally unattractive situation, seek to solve their problems tactically. If it works, fine, but it quite often happens that initiating tactics from a weaker position only leads to catastrophe. If this move won the e5-pawn then it would be justified, but it does not and the weakening of Black's kingside proves fatal. The alternatives were unfavourable for Black but at least not disastrous:

1) 21...♘xg3 22 ♗xg3 gives White an automatic attack based on f4-f5.

2) 21...g6 22 ♘xe4 dxe4 23 ♗b3 (23 ♗xe4 ♗xe4 24 ♖xe4 ♕c2 25 ♖e2 ♕f5 26 ♗d2 leaves Black with some play for the pawn, but objectively not enough) 23...♖ed8 24 ♖d2 ♖xd2 25 ♕xd2 ♖d8 26 ♕c2 with a clear positional advantage for White.

22 ♘f5! (D)

The refutation.

22...gxf4

There is no satisfactory move:

1) 22...♗c5 23 ♗xe4 dxe4 24 ♖c2 ♗f8 25 ♕g4 h6 26 ♖d1 gives White a crushing attack; the immediate threats are 27 ♗xg5 and 27 ♖d6.

2) 22...♕d7 23 ♖xe4! dxe4 24 ♕g4 h5 25 ♘h6+ ♔f8 26 ♕xh5 ♕e6 27 ♘f5 ♔g8 28 ♕g4 ♗d5 29 ♘xe7+ ♕xe7 30 ♗xg5 ♕e6 31 ♕h4 ♕g6 32 ♗f6 ♕h7 33 ♕g4+ ♕g6 34 ♕e2 and

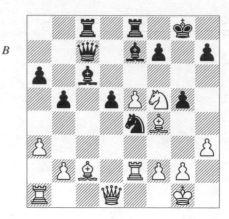

B

White has two pawns and a strong attack for the exchange.

3) 22...♗f8 is relatively best, but after 23 ♗h2 Black has no compensation for the serious weakening of his kingside.

23 ♖xe4! (D)

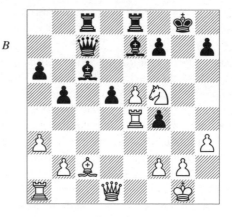

B

23...♔h8

Or 23...♗f8 24 ♖xf4 ♕xe5 25 ♖g4+ ♔h8 26 ♕d3 with a knight move such as ♘d6 or ♘e7 to come.

24 ♖e1

This simple move threatens the crushing 25 ♕h5.

24...♗d7

24...f6 25 ♕d4 ♖f8 26 e6 leaves Black's position a total wreck, while 24...♗b7 25 ♗d3 also doesn't help.

25 e6! 1-0

Winning a piece since either capture on e6 loses to 26 ♕d4+.

Game 119

Konstantin Landa – Evgeny Shaposhnikov

Russian Team Ch, Sochi 2005

Caro-Kann Defence, 4...♗f5

1 e4 c6 2 d4 d5 3 ♘c3 dxe4 4 ♘xe4 ♗f5 5 ♘g3 ♗g6 6 h4 h6 7 ♘f3 ♘d7 8 h5 ♗h7 9 ♗d3 ♗xd3 10 ♕xd3 e6

One of three main moves for Black here, the other two being 10...♘gf6 and 10...♕c7. At the moment 10...e6 is very much the most popular choice.

11 ♗f4

11 ♗d2 is also frequently played and after 11...♘gf6 12 0-0-0 ♕c7 (12...♗e7 is another important line) we reach a key position of the 4...♗f5 Caro-Kann, on which no verdict has yet been passed.

11...♕a5+

Black plays to pull White's bishop back from the active square f4. It is also possible to continue more quietly by 11...♘gf6 12 0-0-0 ♗e7 (see Game 25).

12 ♗d2 ♗b4 *(D)*

A relatively recent idea which has become quite popular. Previously Black had preferred 12...♕c7 13 0-0-0 ♘gf6, when we reach the same position as mentioned in the note to White's 11th move. The point of the text-move is to induce White to push his c-pawn, which gains space but also weakens White.

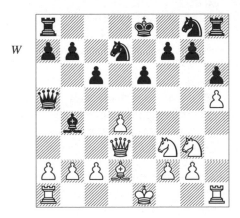

13 c3 ♗e7 14 c4 ♕a6

With this move the game follows a distinctive course, but it looks a little doubtful to me, since it is far from clear that the queen is better on a6 than on the conventional square c7. 14...♗b4?! also looks artificial and after 15 ♘e4 ♘gf6 16 ♘d6+ ♔e7 17 c5 White's powerful knight gives him the advantage.

14...♕c7! is best. The queen returns to its natural square and after 15 0-0-0 ♘gf6 we reach a position which can also arise via other move-orders. However, the modern way to play this whole line for White involves postponing the weakening move c4, so Black's cunning 12...♗b4 has induced White to go in for a line which is no longer considered critical for Black, all without losing any time (both sides have lost the same number of tempi). Black's practical results after 14...♕c7 have been satisfactory, and the burden is currently on White to come up with a new idea.

15 0-0 *(D)*

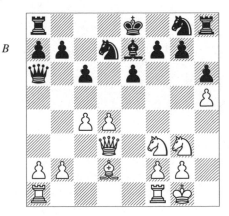

15...♖d8

The combination which White plays in this game is worth knowing because it can arise in a variety of situations. For example, let's follow the game Leko-Bareev, Dortmund 2002: 15...♘gf6 16 ♖fe1 0-0 17 ♘f5! ♖fe8 (17...♗d8?

fails to 18 ♘xh6+! gxh6 19 ♗xh6 ♖e8 20 ♘e5 ♘xe5 21 dxe5 ♘g4 22 ♕g3 ♔h7 23 ♕xg4 ♔xh6 24 ♕f4+ ♗g5 25 ♕xf7 ♖g8 26 ♕xe6+ with four pawns and an attack for the piece) and now Leko played 18 ♘xe7+ ♖xe7 19 ♗b4 with an edge. However, he could have continued 18 ♖xe6!! fxe6 19 ♘xg7 ♗f8 (19...♔xg7 20 ♗xh6+ ♔h8 21 ♘g5 leads to mate in a few moves) 20 ♘xe8 ♖xe8 21 ♕g6+ ♗g7 22 ♗xh6 ♖e7 23 ♗f4 (23 ♘e5 is also good since White has three pawns plus a dangerous attack for the piece) 23...♘f8 24 ♕g5 ♘8h7 and at this point 25 ♕g6 led to an immediate draw in Van Beek-Speelman, Gibraltar 2007. However, 25 ♕h4! would have been very good for White; for example, 25...♕xc4 26 h6 ♗f8 (26...♔h8 loses to 27 ♗d6) 27 ♗e5 and White regains the piece while keeping a couple of extra pawns.

16 b4

White's queenside pawn advance exposes the dark side of the black queen's position.

16...♘gf6 17 a4 *(D)*

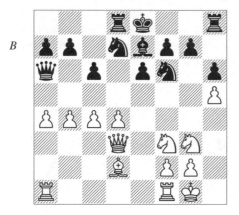

17...b6?

This is simply too slow and Black should have chosen one of the alternatives:

1) 17...0-0 18 b5 ♕b6 19 ♗f4 and White has pressure on the queenside but Black's position remains solid.

2) 17...♕b6 18 ♖fe1 0-0 and now 19 ♘f5 ♖fe8 is an interesting line because White can again play the ♖xe6 sacrifice, with or without c5. After 20 ♖xe6 (20 c5 ♕c7 21 ♖xe6 fxe6 22 ♘xg7 ♗f8 23 ♘xe8 ♖xe8 24 ♕g6+ ♗g7 25 ♗xh6 ♘f8 is also unconvincing because on c7

the queen is well placed to defend along the second rank) 20...fxe6 21 ♘xg7 ♘e5! (thanks to the attack on d4 Black has this defensive resource) 22 ♘xe5 ♕xd4 23 ♕xd4 ♖xd4 24 ♘xe8 ♖xd2 25 ♘xf6+ ♗xf6 26 ♖e1 White is a pawn up, but Black's active pieces give him good drawing chances. Since the sacrifice appears doubtful in this position, White would probably do better to play more modestly by 19 b5, with an edge. This analysis bears out the point that each position must be treated on its own merits; something that works in one position may not work in an apparently similar one.

18 ♖fe1

With Black's queen out of play on a6 and the c6-pawn weak, the omens for the coming sacrifice on e6 are promising.

18...0-0 19 ♘f5 *(D)*

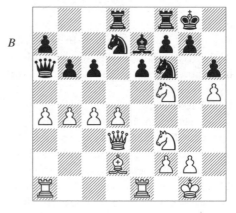

19...♖fe8

19...exf5 20 ♖xe7 ♘e4 is met by 21 ♗xh6 gxh6 22 ♘h4 ♘df6 23 ♘xf5 ♕c8 24 ♘xh6+ ♔g7 25 ♕e3 with a large advantage for White.

20 ♘xg7!!? *(D)*

I'm not quite sure how to annotate this move. We should be familiar with the ♖xe6 and ♘xg7 idea by now (although it was unfamiliar at the time this game was played), but generally speaking it is better to sacrifice on e6 first because Black is less likely to be able to decline the second sacrifice. In this particular position, the favourable circumstances mean that even played 'the wrong way round' it gives White the advantage. However, in my view 20 ♖xe6!! fxe6 21 ♘xg7 was the clearer move-order since if

Black declines the sacrifice by 21...♗f8 22 ♘xe8 ♖xe8 23 ♕g6+ ♗g7 24 ♗xh6 ♖e7 25 ♗d2 (threatening h6), then White has a large advantage, while 21...♔h8 22 ♘xe6 ♗f8 23 ♘xd8 ♖xd8 24 ♕g6 ♘g8 25 ♕xc6 gives White four pawns for the piece and a clear advantage.

3) 21...c5 22 ♖ae1 ♗f8 23 ♗xh6+ ♔g8 (23...♔xh6 24 ♕f5 ♖xe6 25 ♖xe6 is more unpleasant for Black) 24 ♖xe8 ♖xe8 25 ♖xe8 ♘xe8 26 ♕e3 and White has a clear advantage, but the game is not yet over.

22 ♗xh6+!

The third sacrifice proves to be Black's downfall.

22...♔h8 (D)

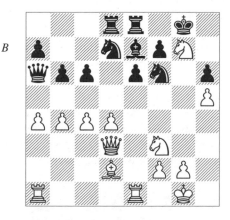

20...♔xg7 21 ♖xe6! fxe6?

Black stumbles into a forced mate. He should have declined the second sacrifice, although White retains some advantage in any case:

1) 21...♖c8?! 22 ♖ae1! ♗f8 (22...fxe6 23 ♗xh6+! is decisive) 23 ♖xe8 ♖xe8 (23...♘xe8 loses to 24 ♕f5) 24 ♖xe8 ♘xe8 25 ♗xh6+! ♔xh6 26 ♕e3+ ♔g7 27 ♕xe8 should win for White.

2) 21...♗f8 22 ♖xc6 ♕b7 23 b5 ♔g8 is a reasonable defence; White has three good pawns in return for the piece but at least Black will not be mated.

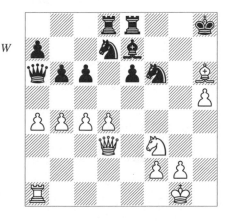

23 ♗g7+!

Perhaps Black missed this move, without which the whole combination would have failed.

23...♔xg7

23...♔g8 24 ♕g6 also leads to mate.

24 ♕g6+ 1-0

After 24...♔h8 (24...♔f8 25 ♘g5 mates next move) 25 ♘g5 ♖f8 26 h6, White mates by ♕g7# or ♘f7#.

This spectacular attacking game has considerable significance for opening theory.

Game 120

Alexander Motylev – Mircea Parligras

European Ch, Warsaw 2005

Sicilian Defence, ♘c3

1 e4 c5 2 ♘f3 ♘c6 3 ♘c3 ♘f6 4 ♗b5 ♕c7 5 0-0

We have already met this opening line in Shirov-Van Wely (Game 111). Van Wely played 5...e6, but this time Black goes in for what has become established as the main continuation.

5...♘d4 6 ♘xd4

White has tried quite a few moves here, but the most popular continuation has been the modest 6 ♖e1 a6 7 ♗f1. Exchanging on d4 gives White a temporary lead in development, but if he cannot make something out of it quickly then Black will almost certainly equalize. White should also be aware that Black can win a pawn by force in this line, so if he is not prepared to play a gambit then he should avoid 6 ♘xd4.

6...cxd4 7 ♘d5 ♘xd5 8 exd5 ♕c5 *(D)*

Attacking the bishop and pawn is the most forcing continuation, but Black doesn't have to adopt such a blunt approach. The more modest 8...g6 9 ♖e1 ♗g7, with the idea of ...♗f6 followed by ...0-0, is also playable.

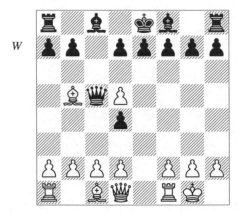

9 c4

The best way to give up the pawn.

9...a6

These days this is the preferred way to take the pawn. In Anand-Leko, Linares 2003, Black chose 9...dxc3, but after 10 ♕b3 a6 11 ♗e2 White developed a dangerous initiative and eventually won.

10 b4!?

This is not the only possibility although it is the most dynamic and popular. After 10 ♗a4 b5 (10...♕xc4 11 ♗b3 ♕c5 12 d3 gives White fair play for the pawn) 11 cxb5 axb5 12 ♗b3 White has avoided giving up a pawn, but Black has fewer problems with his development.

10...♕xb4 11 ♗a4

In return for the pawn White has opened lines for his queenside pieces.

11...b5!?

A double-edged move which attempts to disrupt White's plan, but which opens lines which may be useful for the attacker. The alternative is 11...g6 12 ♗b3 (12 d3 is also possible) 12...♗g7

13 a4 d6 14 ♗a3 ♕a5 15 ♖e1 ♕d8 with an unclear position.

12 ♗c2!?

The most aggressive move. After 12 cxb5 g6 13 ♗b3 (13 d6 axb5 14 dxe7 ♗xe7 looks safe for Black) 13...axb5 14 d3 ♗g7 15 ♗d2 ♕d6 16 ♕e1 ♕f6 White may have enough for the pawn, but I doubt if he has the advantage.

12...bxc4 *(D)*

Although this move may not be objectively bad, it is certainly risky to allow White's a1-rook to enter the game with tempo. As we have noted before, putting yourself under the burden of finding 'only moves' is often unwise. 12...♕xc4! 13 ♗b3 ♕d3 is more modest but quite effective. White can of course force a draw by 14 ♗c2, but it is not easy to see how he can realistically hope for an advantage.

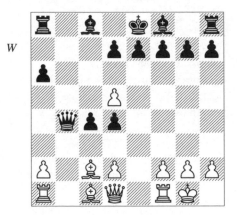

13 ♖b1 ♕d6

Black temporarily blocks White's d-pawn, although he may be forced to lose a tempo later if White plays d3, ♕f3 and ♗f4. Two other queen moves were also playable; after 13...♕a5 14 d6 (14 d3 c3 15 d6 ♕c5 16 ♗f4 e6 17 ♕f3 ♕c6 18 ♕g3 f6 19 ♗d1 ♕c5! looks fine for Black) 14...♕d5 15 dxe7 ♗xe7 16 ♕g4 or 13...♕c5 14 ♕f3 (14 d3 c3) 14...d3 15 ♗a4 f6 16 d6 ♖a7 17 ♖b8 ♔f7 the position is very unclear.

14 d3 *(D)*

14...cxd3?

A serious misjudgement; now Black wins a third pawn but he opens too many lines and White's attack suddenly gathers pace. 14...c3!

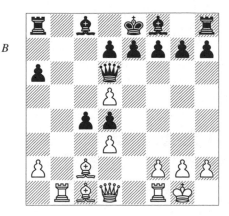

B

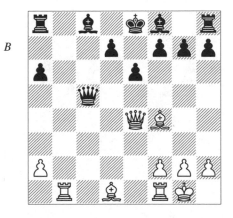

B

was the only move, keeping some lines closed. After 15 ♕f3 ♖a7 16 ♗f4 (16 ♕e4 e5 17 f4 f6 18 fxe5 ♕xe5 19 ♕g4 ♔d8 is also unclear) 16...♕c5 17 ♖b8 ♖b7 18 ♖xb7 (18 ♖a8 f6) 18...♗xb7 19 ♖b1 ♗c8 Black is under pressure but he can take consolation in his two extra pawns and the fact that there is nothing clear-cut for White.

15 ♕xd3 ♕xd5

Forced, as otherwise White plays ♕xd4 followed by ♗f4 with a crushing initiative.

16 ♗d1!

This was probably what Black had over-looked. Now he must deal with the threat of ♗f3 and so has no time to tackle the problem of his non-existent development.

16...♕c6?!

Black collapses, but even the best line 16...♕c5 17 ♕e4 d5 (17...♕a7 18 ♗f3 ♖b8 19 ♗f4 d6 20 ♖xb8 ♕xb8 21 ♖b1 ♕a7 22 ♕c6+ ♗d7 23 ♖b7 wins for White) 18 ♗a4+ ♗d7 19 ♗xd7+ ♔xd7 20 ♕f3 ♔e8 21 ♗f4 ♕c6 22

♖bc1 ♕a4 23 ♕xd5 ♖d8 24 ♕e4 f6 (24...e6 25 ♗c7 d5 26 ♗b6 ♕d7 27 ♖c7 f5 28 ♕e2 d3 29 ♕h5+ g6 30 ♕g5 and White wins) 25 ♗c7 ♖c8 26 ♖c6 ♕xa2 27 ♕xd4 ♔f7 28 ♕d7 ♖a8 29 ♖e1 leaves White with tremendous pressure in return for the pawns.

17 ♕xd4

Now all the lines are open and Black is de-fenceless.

17...e6 18 ♗f4 ♕c5

Or 18...f6 19 ♗h5+! g6 20 ♗f3 d5 21 ♖fc1 and White wins.

19 ♕e4 (D)

19...♕a7

There is no defence; e.g., 19...♕c6 20 ♕xc6 dxc6 21 ♗f3 ♗d7 22 ♖fd1 ♗e7 23 ♖b7 ♖d8 24 ♖dxd7 ♖xd7 25 ♗xc6 or 19...d5 20 ♗a4+ ♗d7 21 ♗xd7+ ♔xd7 22 ♕a4+ ♔e7 23 ♗g5+ ♔d6 24 ♖b7 and White wins in both cases.

20 ♗e3 d5 21 ♗a4+ ♗d7 22 ♕f4! 1-0

Black's queen is trapped.

Game 121
Alexei Dreev – Artashes Minasian
European Ch, Warsaw 2005
Pirc Defence, 4 ♗g5

1 d4 d6 2 e4 ♘f6 3 ♘c3 g6 4 ♗g5 ♗g7 5 f4

This is one of White's most direct and aggres-sive lines against the Pirc. Given that it demands accurate play by Black right from the beginning, it is surprising that it is not more popular.

5...c6

A perfectly respectable move, preparing to play ...b5. The other main lines are 5...0-0 and 5...h6.

6 ♘f3

At one time 6 ♕d2 was more popular, but now the knight move is regarded as more flexible, since in many lines White will castle kingside.

6...♕b6?! *(D)*

Not a good idea. This move only makes sense if Black is prepared to take the b2-pawn, but even a glance reveals how risky this is likely to be. White already has a dynamic pawn-centre and if this is combined with a substantial lead in development then Black is likely to run into trouble. The main lines are 6...b5 7 ♗d3 b4 8 ♘e2 and 6...0-0 7 ♗d3 ♗g4 8 ♕d2, with a modest advantage for White in both cases.

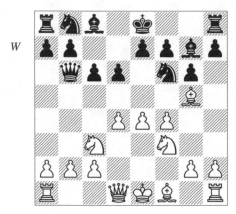

W

7 ♕d2

Dreev makes no effort to save his b-pawn since he is assured of good compensation.

7...♕xb2

Black is committed to this because after any other move ...♕b6 serves no purpose – indeed, it is even harmful since it blocks Black's b-pawn.

8 ♖b1 ♕a3 9 ♗d3

White need not rush; he calmly completes his development and only then looks for a way to launch a direct assault.

9...♕a5

9...0-0 is strongly met by 10 e5 dxe5 (after 10...♖e8 11 0-0 ♘d5 12 ♘xd5 cxd5 13 ♖b3 ♕xa2 14 ♕c3 Black loses his queen) 11 fxe5 ♘d5 12 ♖b3 ♕a5 13 ♘xd5 ♕xd2+ (13...♕xd5 14 ♗xe7 ♖e8 15 ♗h4 f6 16 0-0 gives White a dangerous initiative for no sacrifice) 14 ♔xd2 cxd5 15 ♗xe7 ♖e8 16 ♗d6 with a clear advantage for White in view of his more active pieces

and better development. The fact that castling is awkward due to the undefended e7-pawn impels Black to retreat his queen to c7 to cover e7, but this costs further time and in fact Black never does manage to castle.

10 0-0 *(D)*

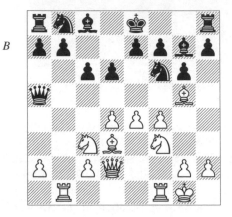

B

10...♕c7

10...0-0 is even worse now due to 11 e5 dxe5 12 fxe5 ♘d5 13 ♘xd5 ♕xd5 14 ♗xe7 ♖e8 15 c4 ♕e6 16 ♗d6 with a crushing initiative for White.

11 e5

Black is finally ready to castle, so it is time for White to take direct action in the centre.

11...♘d5 12 ♘e4 f5?!

This move has unpleasant consequences, but there was nothing totally satisfactory:

1) 12...f6 13 ♗xf6! exf6 14 ♘xd6+ ♔f8 15 c4 ♘e7 16 ♘g5! fxg5 17 fxg5+ ♔g8 18 ♕f2 ♘f5 19 ♘xc8 ♕xc8 20 g4 and White regains one piece with tremendous compensation for the other; e.g., 20...h6 21 gxf5 hxg5 22 f6 and wins.

2) 12...0-0 13 c4 f6 (13...♘b6 14 exd6 exd6 15 ♘f6+ ♗xf6 16 ♗xf6 ♘8d7 17 ♗e7 ♖e8 18 ♖be1 gives White a total stranglehold) 14 cxd5 fxg5 15 dxc6 bxc6 16 ♘fxg5 and White has regained his pawn while retaining a dangerous attack.

3) 12...dxe5 13 fxe5 0-0 (13...f5 14 exf6 exf6 15 ♘xf6+! ♘xf6 16 ♖be1+ ♔d8 17 ♗f4 ♕d7 18 ♗c4 with overwhelming threats) 14 c4 ♘b6 15 ♗f4 ♕d8 16 ♗h6 ♘a6 17 ♕f4 gives White a strong attack, but nevertheless this line was probably Black's best chance.

13 ♗xe7! *(D)*

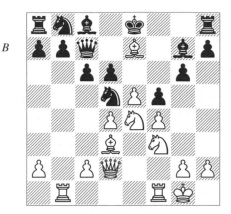

This move refutes Black's play. For the sacrificed piece, White obtains two pawns, traps Black's king in the centre and obtains a mobile central pawn-mass.

13...♘xe7

13...fxe4 14 ♗xd6 ♕d8 (14...e3 15 ♕e1 ♕d7 16 ♘g5!, with c4 to come, is also horrible for Black) 15 ♗xe4 ♗f8 (15...♘e7 16 ♘g5 0-0 17 ♕b4 and White wins) 16 ♗xb8 ♖xb8 17 c4 ♘e7 18 d5 speaks for itself.

14 ♘xd6+ ♔f8 15 ♘g5

Preventing ...♗e6 and threatening 16 ♖xb7 ♗xb7 17 ♘e6+.

15...b6 16 ♕b4

Now the threats are 17 ♘xc8 ♕xc8 18 ♗c4, followed by ♘e6+, and simply 17 ♕b3.

16...h6

Or 16...♘d5 17 ♕b3 ♕d7 (17...h6 18 ♘gf7 transposes to the game) 18 c4 ♘e7 19 ♘gf7 ♖g8 20 d5 and White wins.

17 ♕b3 ♘d5 18 ♘gf7 ♗e6

Black decides to give up the exchange, but this does not solve his problems. However, by now there was no defence; e.g., 18...♖h7 19 ♘xc8 ♕xc8 (19...♕xf7 20 ♘d6 ♕d7 transposes) 20 ♘d6 ♕d7 (20...♕e6 21 g4 breaks through) 21 c4 ♘c7 22 g4 ♘e6 23 gxf5 ♘xd4 24 ♕a3 and White wins.

19 ♘xh8 ♗xh8 20 c4 ♘e7 21 g4! *(D)*

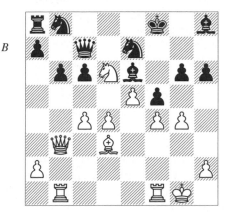

The same type of breakthrough also works here.

21...♘d7

After 21...fxg4 22 ♕c2 Black cannot defend against the threats of 23 ♗xg6 and 23 f5.

22 ♕a3!

The simplest. The line-up along the a3-f8 diagonal makes gxf5 into a genuine threat.

22...c5

22...fxg4 23 ♗xg6! wins, as does 22...♔g8 23 ♘xf5! ♘xf5 24 gxf5 ♗xf5 25 ♗xf5 gxf5 26 ♔h1 ♘f8 27 ♕h3, etc.

23 d5

The final triumph of White's massive pawn-centre.

23...♘xd5 24 cxd5 ♗xd5 25 ♖bd1 1-0

Black is the exchange down with a terrible position and decided to throw in the towel.

Game 122

Boris Gelfand – Bartlomiej Macieja

Spanish Team Ch, Merida 2005

Queen's Indian Defence, 4 g3 ♗a6

1 d4 ♘f6 2 c4 e6 3 ♘f3 b6 4 g3 ♗a6 5 b3 ♗b4+ 6 ♗d2 ♗e7 7 ♘c3

Originally this was one of White's main lines, before 7 ♗g2 c6 8 ♗c3 became by far the most popular continuation. Now that the 7 ♗g2 lines have been analysed almost to death, it may be that 7 ♘c3 is due for a revival.

7...0-0 8 ♖c1

The main line used to be 8 e4 d5, but recently White has been trying other possibilities, amongst them the semi-waiting moves 8 ♖c1 and 8 ♕c2, which anticipate the opening of the c-file after a later ...d5.

8...d5

This direct reply has been the most popular move for Black. After 8...c6 9 e4 d5 White's extra tempo ♖c1 is of more than value than Black's ...c6, so White gets a favourable version of the 8 e4 d5 line.

9 cxd5 ♘xd5

9...exd5 10 ♗g2 ♗b7 11 0-0 is similar to some other lines of the Queen's Indian and should give White an edge.

10 ♗g2 *(D)*

More critical than 10 ♘xd5 exd5 11 ♗g2 ♖e8, which gives Black a relatively comfortable game.

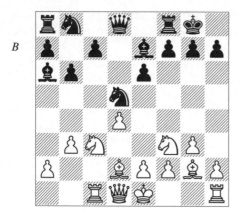

10...♗b7

Experience with this position is limited, and Black's best continuation is not clear. The other moves which have been tried are 10...♘xc3, 10...♗a3 and 10...♘d7.

11 0-0

11 ♘xd5 ♗xd5 12 ♕c2 is the alternative, but then Black can continue 12...c5 13 dxc5 ♘a6!? with a comfortable position, since 14 cxb6 ♘b4 15 ♕b2 axb6 16 a4 b5 gives White no advantage.

11...♘d7

The position appears rather harmless for Black and it is amazing that he gets into serious difficulties so quickly. Playing for ...c5 is the obvious plan, but Black implements it poorly. Here two reasonable ideas are 11...c5 straight away, with just a faint edge for White after 12 dxc5 ♗xc5 13 ♕c2, and 11...♘xc3 12 ♗xc3 ♘d7, preparing a later ...c5.

The text-move delays the exchange on c3, but this gives White the chance to play ♕c2 and then the idea of ♘xd5 (meeting ...♗xd5 by e4) starts to become a worry for Black.

12 ♕c2 c5

12...♖c8?! is inferior because 13 ♘xd5 ♗xd5 14 e4 ♗b7 15 ♖fd1 gives White significant pressure; e.g., 15...♘f6 (15...c5 transposes to the game) 16 ♘g5, threatening 17 e5. However, 12...♘xc3 13 ♕xc3 ♖c8 is still satisfactory for Black since after 14 ♖fd1 c5 15 ♕b2 ♗f6 White's pressure is evaporating.

13 ♖fd1 *(D)*

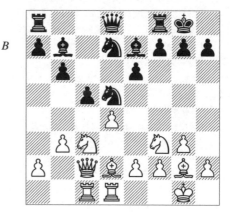

13...♖c8?!

Now Black really starts to goes wrong, allowing White to play ♘xd5 followed by e4 under favourable circumstances. He could still have equalized by 13...cxd4! 14 ♘xd5 ♗xd5 15 ♘xd4 ♗xg2 (15...♖c8? 16 ♕xc8 ♕xc8 17 ♖xc8 ♖xc8 18 ♗xd5 exd5 19 ♘f5 gives White strong pressure; e.g., 19...♔f8 20 ♗f4 ♘f6 21 ♘e3) 16 ♔xg2 ♗a3! 17 ♗b4 (17 ♘c6 ♕e8 18 ♗b4 ♗xc1 19 ♗xf8 ♗g5! 20 ♗d6 ♘c5 is fine for Black) 17...♗xb4 18 ♘c6 ♕e8 19 ♘xb4 ♘c5 and Black's problems are solved.

14 ♘xd5 ♗xd5?

14...exd5 would have been the lesser evil. After 15 ♕f5 or 15 ♗h3 White would have some pressure, but nothing too serious.

15 e4 *(D)*

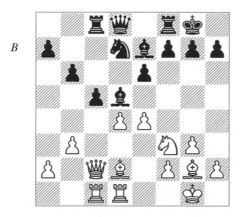

Now White pushes forward in the centre and creates a passed d-pawn.

15...♗b7 16 d5! exd5

16...♘f6 is no better due to 17 ♗c3! exd5 18 exd5 ♘xd5 19 ♘e5 and White has tremendous pressure for the pawn.

17 exd5 *(D)*

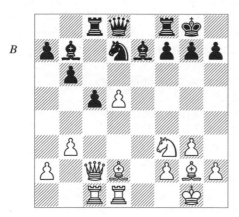

It is clear that Black is in trouble; White is ahead in development, has a dangerous central passed pawn and can look forward to attacking chances on the kingside.

17...♕c7?!

Other moves also fail to solve Black's problems:

1) 17...♗xd5 18 ♗f4 ♗e6 (18...♗xf3 19 ♗xf3 ♕e8 20 ♕e2 completely ties Black up) 19 ♘e5 ♕e8 20 ♘c6 will cost Black the exchange after ♘xe7+ followed by ♗d6.

2) 17...♘f6 18 ♗c3 transposes to the note to Black's 16th move.

3) 17...♖e8 18 d6 ♗f6 19 ♘g5 ♗xg5 20 ♗xb7 and the d-pawn gives White a large advantage.

4) 17...c4 18 ♘d4 cxb3 19 ♕xb3 and the weakness of c6 causes serious problems for Black.

5) 17...♗d6 18 ♘g5 g6 19 ♘e4 is very good for White.

6) 17...♗f6 is relatively best, but after 18 ♗f4 Black's position remains unpleasant.

18 ♘d4!

From here the knight can reach a whole range of tempting squares: b5, c6 or f5.

18...♗d6

The text-move blocks the dangerous d-pawn but leaves the kingside undefended. However, there was nothing better:

1) 18...g6? loses to 19 d6 ♗xd6 20 ♘b5.

2) 18...♗f6 19 ♘f5 ♖fe8 20 b4 and Black's position is creaking.

3) 18...a6 19 ♗f4 ♗d6 20 ♘e6! fxe6 21 ♗xd6 ♕xd6 22 dxe6 ♕xe6 23 ♗xb7 and White wins the exchange.

19 ♘b5 ♕b8 20 ♕f5 *(D)*

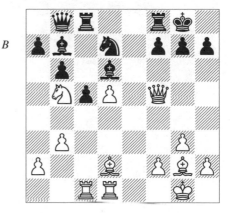

20...♘e5?

This loses at once, but even after 20...♘f6 21 ♗g5 ♘e8 22 ♖e1 a6 23 ♘xd6 ♘xd6 24 ♕d7 White has crushing pressure.

21 ♗f4 ♖ce8

21...♖fe8 22 ♖e1 f6 23 ♗e4 h6 24 ♕h7+ ♔f8 25 ♖ed1, with ♗g6 to come, wins for White.

22 ♗e4 g6 23 ♕f6 1-0

The threat of 24 ♗h6 and mate on g7 costs Black a piece.

Game 123
Magnus Carlsen – Alexander Beliavsky
Wijk aan Zee 2006
Ruy Lopez, Arkhangelsk

1 e4 e5 2 ♘f3 ♘c6 3 ♗b5 a6 4 ♗a4 ♘f6 5 0-0 b5 6 ♗b3 ♗b7

This line of the Ruy Lopez has been a favourite with Beliavsky for almost 30 years, but rarely can it have been so harshly treated as in the current game.

7 d3 ♗c5?!

The text-move leads to a position which can also arise via the move-order 6...♗c5 7 d3 ♗b7, but this move-order hardly ever occurs. The reason is that after 6...♗c5 7 d3 Black almost invariably prefers 7...d6, so as to leave open the option of playing either ...♗b7 or ...♗g4. This point is an indication that the current position offers Black less flexibility than he could obtain by other routes, and therefore with this move-order it is preferable to play 7...♗e7.

8 ♘c3 d6 9 a4 (D)

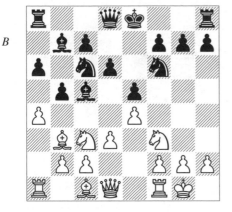

B

9...♘a5

An unusual continuation. Black normally prefers 9...b4, which may be met by 10 ♘e2 or 10 ♘d5. The latter is more popular, but the former is probably more dangerous.

10 ♗a2 b4

In one of the early games with this line, Savon-Bronstein, Odessa 1974, Black played the curious move 10...c6? defending the b5-pawn, but blocking in his b7-bishop and taking a square away from the a5-knight. After 11 ♗d2 0-0 12 ♘e2 bxa4? 13 ♕e1! ♗b6 14 b4! axb3 15 ♗b1! Black's misplaced forces had cost him a piece.

11 ♘e2 ♗c8

Relatively few games have reached this position, but that hasn't stopped Black trying six different moves here. 11...b3?! looks bad after 12 ♕e1!. 11...♖b8 has been played most often (although that is only three times); after 12 ♘g3 0-0 13 ♗g5 h6 14 ♗h4!? a very sharp position arises which should offer White some advantage. The text-move, returning the bishop to c8 in order to move to e6, bears out the point made in the note to Black's 7th move that ...♗b7 and ...♗c5 don't really fit together in this line, at least not at such an early stage.

12 c3

White starts to push forward in the centre.

12...bxc3 13 bxc3 (D)

13...♗b6

Anticipating White's d4, but Black's offside knight and loss of time with his bishops mean that he has no chance of equalizing. However, the alternative 13...♗e6 14 ♗xe6 fxe6 15 d4 ♗b6 16 ♕c2 exd4 17 cxd4 0-0 18 ♘f4 ♕e7 19 ♗d2 is also miserable for Black.

14 ♘g3 ♗e6

Beliavsky criticized this move in his *Informator* notes, but in my view White has a clear advantage whatever Black plays. Beliavsky gave the line 14...0-0 15 ♗g5 h6 16 ♗h4 ♗g4 17 h3 ♗xf3 18 ♕xf3 g5 19 ♘h5 (stronger than

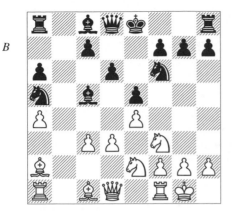

19 ♘f5, as played in de Firmian-Lugo, USA Ch, San Diego 2004) 19...♘xh5 20 ♕xh5 ♕f6 (20...gxh4 21 ♕g6+ ♔h8 22 ♕xh6+ ♔g8 23 ♔h1 followed by f4 gives White a winning attack) 21 ♗g3 ♔g7 as leading to equality, but I don't believe this. The two bishops, out-of-play knight on a5 and chances to break through with d4 and e5 combine to give White a significant advantage; one possible line runs 22 ♕e2 ♖ab8 23 ♗d5 (to force the knight to retreat to the inferior square b7) 23...♘b7 24 ♖fd1 a5 25 d4! exd4 26 e5 and Black is in trouble.

15 d4 ♗xa2?!

This mistake plunges Black into a critical situation. He should have maintained the bishop on e6 in order to cover f5; after 15...0-0 16 ♕d3 White is better, but Black can still hope to defend.

16 ♖xa2 (D)

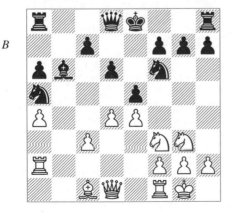

16...0-0

Black cannot even bring his knight back into play since 16...♘c6 17 a5! ♘xa5 18 dxe5 dxe5 19 ♖d2 ♕b8 20 ♗a3 traps Black's king in the centre and gives White a crushing attack.

17 ♗g5! exd4?

Now Black's position collapses. 17...h6 was essential, but 18 ♗h4! makes it hard to find a decent continuation; for example, after 18...exd4 (18...♘c6 19 ♘f5 and 18...g5 19 ♘xg5 are terrible for Black, while 18...♖e8 19 ♘h5 g5 20 ♘xg5 ♘xh5 21 ♕xh5 hxg5 22 ♗xg5 gives White a decisive attack) 19 cxd4 ♖e8 (19...g5 still loses to 20 ♘xg5) 20 ♖e1 Black still can't play ...g5, so there is no real answer to the threat of 21 ♘h5.

18 ♘h5

Black's problem is not so much the impending disintegration of his kingside, but the fact that White can bring up his reserves before taking on f6. Black's other minor pieces, stuck far away on the queenside, can do nothing to help.

18...dxc3 (D)

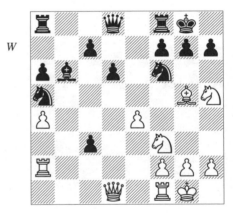

Black may as well indulge himself – by this stage it can't make any difference.

19 ♘h4!

The 15-year-old Magnus Carlsen finds a finesse which makes the win much easier. Now White threatens not only 20 ♗xf6 gxf6 21 ♕g4+, but also simply 20 ♘f5 followed by ♘fxg7.

19...♔h8 20 ♘f5 1-0

After 20...♘c4 21 ♘fxg7 ♘xh5 22 ♗xd8 ♘xg7 23 ♗f6 the win is easy.

Game 124
Vasily Ivanchuk – Peter Svidler
Morelia/Linares 2006
Grünfeld Defence, 4 ♗g5

1 d4 ♘f6 2 c4 g6 3 ♘c3 d5 4 ♗g5

This line against the Grünfeld has been played occasionally for many decades, without ever becoming really popular. Nevertheless, as we shall see, it can still pose Black some problems.

4...♘e4

The almost universal reply, since few players like to give up a pawn by 4...♗g7 5 ♗xf6 ♗xf6 6 ♘xd5 ♗g7.

5 ♗h4 ♘xc3

The most popular move, although 5...c5 is also playable.

6 bxc3 dxc4

This is considered best, since 6...♗g7 7 cxd5 ♕xd5 8 e3 gives White fair chances for an advantage.

7 e3 *(D)*

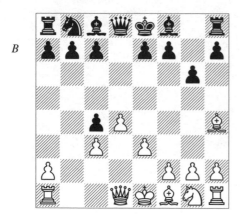

B

7...♗e6

Black makes White fight to regain the pawn, since if he simply allows ♗xc4 then White's better central control and actively posted bishop on h4 should give him an advantage.

8 ♕b1

This has been the favoured continuation in recent years, superseding the older moves 8 ♖b1 and 8 ♘f3.

8...c5

A novelty which turns out badly for Black, although the current game is probably not a fair indication of the assessment of the move. 8...b6 and 8...♕d5 are the most common continuations and in two later games played in 2006 Svidler turned to 8...♕d5, winning both games.

9 ♕xb7 ♗d5 10 ♕b5+ ♘d7?!

A later game Sargissian-Naiditsch, Bundesliga 2006/7 continued 10...♕d7 11 ♖b1 ♕xb5 12 ♖xb5 ♘d7 13 ♘f3 e6 14 ♗e2 ♗e7 15 ♔d2 and now 15...f6 16 e4 ♗xe4 17 ♗xc4 cxd4 would have given Black a very comfortable position. White could certainly have played better in this line, for example by 14 ♘d2, but perhaps this indicates that 8...c5 might reappear one day.

The move played allows White to continue his development while maintaining the pin along the a4-e8 diagonal.

11 ♘f3 ♖b8 12 ♕a4 *(D)*

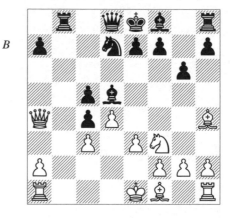

B

12...cxd4

Ivanchuk gives some lengthy analysis suggesting that 12...♕c8 13 ♘e5 cxd4 14 cxd4 ♗g7 15 ♗xc4 0-0 is only slightly better for White. However, I am rather doubtful about this since 16 ♘xd7 ♗c6 17 ♕d1! ♗xg2 (17...♕xd7 18 0-0 favours White since 18...e5 may be met by 19 d5) 18 ♖g1 ♕xc4 19 ♖xg2 ♕b4+ 20 ♕d2 ♕b7 21 ♘xb8 ♕xg2 22 ♕b2! clearly favours White. For example, after 22...e5 23 dxe5 ♕g1+ 24 ♔d2 ♖d8+ 25 ♔c2 ♕xh2 26 ♗xd8 ♕xf2+ 27 ♔b3 ♕xe3+ 28 ♕c3 ♕xc3+ 29 ♔xc3 ♗xe5+ 30 ♔d3 ♗xa1 31 a4 White will win Black's a-pawn, after which his own a-pawn will be a tremendous force.

13 cxd4 ♕c8

Both kings are in the centre but White's development is better. Another Ivanchuk suggestion, 13...c3 14 ♗b5 a6 15 ♗d3 ♗g7, looks very dubious after 16 ♕a3 hitting both c3 and a7.

14 ♖c1! (D)

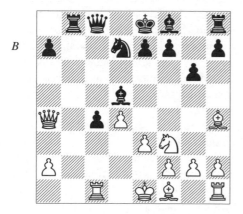

14...e6?!

Here Ivanchuk proposes 14...♗g7 and this time I agree with him. After 15 ♗e2 0-0 16 ♗xe7 ♖e8 17 ♗b4 ♘b6 Black has some play for the pawn and can at least considerably confuse the issue.

15 ♗xc4!

Ivanchuk correctly grabs the pawn, triggering great complications which end up favouring White.

15...♖b4 16 ♕a6 ♗b7

A second key line runs 16...♕c7 17 ♘e5! ♖b6 18 0-0! ♖xa6 19 ♗xa6 ♕b8 20 ♖c8+ ♕xc8 21 ♗xc8 ♘xe5 22 ♗f6 ♖g8 23 ♗xe5 with a healthy extra pawn for White.

17 ♕a5! (D)

The only square for the queen, but it proves sufficient.

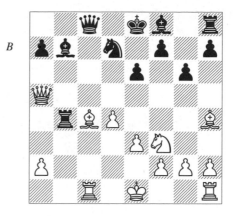

17...f6

17...♗d5 18 ♘e5! ♗xg2 is spectacularly refuted by 19 ♔d1! ♕b8 20 ♗b5! ♖xb5 21 ♕xb5 with mate on c8 and 17...♖xc4 18 ♖xc4 ♕xc4 loses at once to 19 ♕d8#, so Svidler blocks the h4-d8 line so that he is genuinely threatening the bishop.

18 ♘d2 (D)

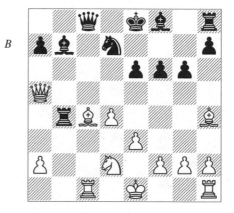

Threatening both 19 0-0, unpinning the bishop, and simply 19 ♗xf6.

18...♗xg2?!

Perhaps the best chance was 18...♖b6, but even then 19 0-0 ♗b4 20 ♕xa7 ♗xd2 (20...♕c6 is met simply by 21 ♘f3) 21 ♗b5 ♗xc1 22 ♕xb6 ♗e7 23 ♗xd7 ♔xd7 24 ♗xf6 ♖f8 25 ♗g5 gives White three pawns and a strong initiative for the piece.

19 ♖g1 ♕c6

There is no escape for Black; e.g., 19...♗d5 20 ♗xf6! ♖g8 (20...♖xc4 21 ♘xc4 ♕b8 22 ♕a4

♕b4+ 23 ♕xb4+ ♗xb4+ 24 ♘d2 leaves White well ahead on material) 21 ♗xd5! ♕xc1+ 22 ♔e2 ♕c8 (22...♕xg1 23 ♕d8+ mates) 23 ♖c1! ♕b8 24 ♗xe6 and wins.

20 ♖xg2! ♕xg2 21 ♗xe6
White has a decisive attack.
21...♗d6 22 ♖c8+ ♔e7 23 ♖xh8 ♔xe6 24 ♕d8 ♕g1+ 25 ♔e2 1-0

Game 125
Vasily Ivanchuk – Francisco Vallejo Pons
Morelia/Linares 2006
Queen's Gambit, Vienna Variation

1 d4 ♘f6 2 ♘f3 d5 3 c4 e6 4 ♘c3 ♗b4

This is often called the Ragozin Variation and can lead to a variety of Queen's Gambit systems.

5 ♗g5 dxc4

Transposing into the Vienna Variation is a slightly unusual choice here, with 5...h6 and 5...♘bd7 being played more frequently.

6 e4 b5

The main line of the Vienna Variation runs 6...c5 7 ♗xc4 cxd4 8 ♘xd4 ♗xc3+ 9 bxc3 ♕a5 and is believed to give White a slight advantage.

7 a4 c6 *(D)*

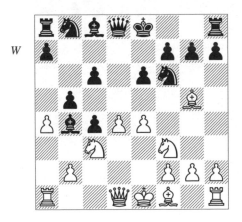

W

Now we have transposed to a position which more often arises via other move-orders, such as 1 d4 d5 2 c4 c6 3 ♘f3 ♘f6 4 ♘c3 e6 5 ♗g5 dxc4 6 e4 b5 7 a4 ♗b4, and which is considered to be part of the Semi-Slav. In this Semi-Slav move-order, White's 7 a4 is an attempt to avoid the complexities of the main line of the Botvinnik System (which arises after 7 e5), while Black

has various alternatives to 7...♗b4, such as 7...b4, 7...♕b6 and 7...♗b7. Although 7...♗b4 has been the most popular move, it has scored rather poorly for Black and if this reflects the true evaluation of the position, one should criticize not only 7...♗b4 in the Semi-Slav move-order, but also 6...b5 in the current game, since Black cannot then avoid arriving at the diagram position. However, as evaluations in opening theory tend to be mutable, I shall refrain from any such criticisms.

8 e5 h6 9 exf6

The only real test of Black's set-up.

9...hxg5 10 fxg7 ♖g8 11 g3

This move has recently been increasing in popularity, but the older preference 11 h4 is also critical.

11...♗b7 12 ♗g2 *(D)*

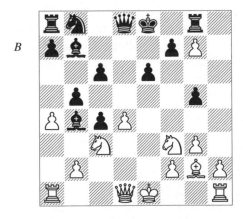

B

12...c5?!

Black takes the chance to eliminate White's d-pawn, but this ambitious move opens the position while Black's king is still firmly stuck in the centre. This clearly involves a risk which White could have exploited at move 14. I prefer the quieter and more pragmatic 12...♘d7 13 0-0 ♗xc3 14 bxc3 ♖xg7, which eliminates the g-pawn, while for the moment keeping the position more closed.

13 0-0

13 dxc5 has been played a couple of times, but after 13...♕xd1+ 14 ♔xd1 g4 15 ♘h4 ♗xg2 16 ♘xg2 the simplification of the position allows Black to equalize.

13...g4

Now, however, 13...♖xg7 14 dxc5 ♕xd1 15 ♖fxd1 is very good for White, since both white rooks occupy active positions and 15...g4 can be met by 16 ♘d2, because now White can recapture on g2 with his king.

14 ♘h4?!

In Kramnik-M.Carlsen, Monaco (Amber rapid) 2007, White unveiled the stunning novelty 14 axb5!, which gave rise to another miniature game: 14...gxf3? (accepting the piece is very risky; 14...♖xg7 must be critical, but even then 15 ♘e5 ♗xg2 16 ♔xg2 cxd4 17 ♕a4 looks at least slightly better for White) 15 ♗xf3 ♗xf3 (15...♕c7 16 d5! ♖xg7 17 dxe6 fxe6 18 ♖e1 is another unpleasant line for Black) 16 ♕xf3 ♘d7 17 dxc5 ♗xc3 (17...♖xg7 18 ♖fd1 ♗xc5 19 ♖xd7! wins for White) 18 bxc3 ♘xc5 19 ♖fd1 ♕c8 20 ♖d6 ♕b7 21 ♕h5 (the threats to c5 and e6 prove too much) 21...♖c8 22 ♖c6 ♘d3 23 ♖xc8+ ♕xc8 24 ♖xa7 1-0.

14...♗xg2 15 ♘xg2 *(D)*

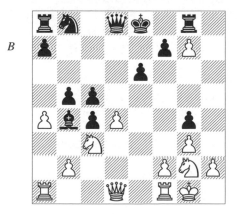

15...♖xg7

This innovation is an attempt to improve on the previously played 15...cxd4, after which 16 ♘xb5 ♘c6 (16...a6 17 ♘xd4 ♗c5 is strongly met by 18 ♘f5!) 17 ♕xg4 gives White a dangerous initiative; for example, 17...a6 18 ♕e4 ♖c8 19 ♖fd1 ♗c5 (19...axb5 20 axb5 ♘e7 21 ♖xd4 ♕b6 22 ♘e3! ♗c5 23 ♘xc4 ♕b8 24 ♖d2 is also very unpleasant for Black) 20 ♕h7 ♔d7 21 ♘a3 ♗xa3 22 ♖xa3 left Black's king seriously exposed in Yusupov-Van Wely, Groningen 1994.

16 axb5!?

The later game Vallejo Pons-Perez Candelario, Spanish Ch, Leon 2006 continued 16 dxc5?! ♗xc5 17 axb5 ♘d7 18 ♖e1 ♕c7 19 ♕d5 ♘b6 20 ♕e5 ♕xe5 21 ♖xe5 ♘d7 with equality. It is a mystery why Vallejo Pons deviated from Ivanchuk's play in the current game, although the note to Black's 17th move below may offer a clue.

16...cxd4

16...♘d7 17 ♘e4 ♕c7 18 d5 is unpleasant for Black; his bishop is shut out of play and there is no really safe spot for his king.

17 ♘e4 f5? *(D)*

In this double-edged position, Vallejo Pons makes an aggressive stab which allows White to sacrifice a piece to launch a vicious attack. Ivanchuk suggested two better alternatives for Black: 17...♗e7 18 ♖e1 ♕b6 19 ♖c1 ♘d7 20 ♘d2 c3 21 bxc3 dxc3 22 ♖xc3 ♕xb5 23 ♕c2 and White has enough for the pawn but not more, and 17...♕b6 18 ♖c1 (18 ♕a4 a5 defends) 18...♗e7 19 ♖xc4 ♘d7 20 f4 with an unclear position.

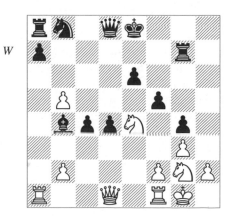

18 ♘f4!

The refutation. Ignoring the attacked knight, White plays against the weak e6-square.

18...♔f7

There is nothing better:

1) 18...♕b6 19 ♕c2! ♘d7 20 ♕xc4 ♘e5 21 ♕xb4 fxe4 22 ♖a6 ♘f3+ 23 ♔g2 ♖h7 24 ♖h1 and Black's position collapses.

2) 18...♗e7 19 ♘g5 e5 20 ♕c2 exf4 21 ♕xc4 ♘d7 22 ♕xd4 with a clear advantage for White.

3) 18...fxe4 19 ♘xe6 ♕f6 20 ♘xg7+ ♕xg7 21 ♕a4 ♕e7 22 b6+ ♔f7 23 ♕xa7 and White will end up two exchanges ahead.

19 ♖c1! *(D)*

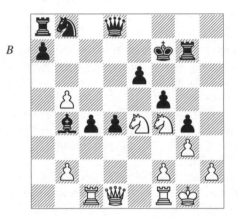

An astonishingly calm move which renews the piece sacrifice.

19...fxe4

Black may as well accept since 19...a5 20 ♖xc4 fxe4 21 ♖xd4 ♕c8 22 ♖xe4 ♘d7 23 ♖xe6 gives White three pawns and a tremendous attack for the piece.

20 ♖xc4

This piece sacrifice is remarkable in that White's attacking force looks far from decisive, and Black still has a barrier of pawns in the centre of the board. However, White's rook can munch through the c-, d- and e-pawns with gain of tempo, not only regaining much of the sacrificed material but also opening lines against the enemy king.

20...♗c5

Black returns the piece straight away in the hope of keeping his pawn-mass intact. 20...♗e7 21 ♖xd4 ♕b6 22 ♖xe4 ♕xb5 23 ♖fe1 is hopeless because all White's pieces can now join the attack.

21 ♖xc5 ♘d7 *(D)*

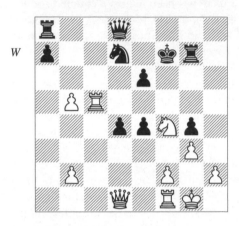

22 ♖h5?!

This finesse is actually less clear-cut than the direct 22 ♖c6! ♘e5 23 ♕b3 ♘xc6 24 ♕xe6+ ♔f8 25 bxc6 ♕e8 26 ♖e1, when Black's position is a total wreck.

22...♘f6?!

Now White can take aim at the e6-pawn. 22...d3?! 23 ♕b3 ♕e7 24 ♖a1, threatening both 25 ♖f5+ ♘f6 26 ♖a6 and the immediate 25 ♖a6, is decisive, but 22...♕b6 would have made White work harder. However, even in this case 23 ♕b3 ♖c8 24 ♖e1 ♖c5 25 ♖xc5 ♘xc5 26 ♕c4 ♕d6 27 b4 ♘d7 28 ♖xe4 ♘e5 29 ♕c5 ♘f3+ 30 ♔g2 ♕xc5 31 bxc5 e5 32 b6 axb6 33 cxb6 ♖h7 34 h3 is enough for White to win.

23 ♖e5

The fall of the e6-pawn, coupled with ♕b3, means the end of Black's resistance.

23...♕d6

23...♔g8 24 ♕b3 ♕e8 25 ♘xe6 ♔h8 26 ♕b4 is also winning for White.

24 ♖xe6 1-0

Index of Players

Numbers refer to pages. When a player's name appears in **bold**, that player had White. Otherwise the FIRST-NAMED PLAYER had White.

Index of Openings

Numbers refer to pages.

Other Books from Gambit Publications

Perfect Your Chess
Andrei Volokitin & Vladimir Grabinsky
"I am determined to solve this excellent training book from cover to cover..." – GM Jonathan Rowson, NEW IN CHESS
160 pages, 248 x 172 mm; $28.95 / £15.99

How to Defend in Chess
Colin Crouch
"...get to see a glimpse of the minds of two of the greatest defenders of all time, and how they still managed to cause problems for their opponents. I whole-heartedly recommend it – for not buying this book there is no defence!" – John Lee Shaw, CHESSGATEWAY.COM
224 pages, 210 x 145 mm; $24.95 / £13.99

Modern Chess Planning
Efstratios Grivas
"Some books just work; they do exactly what they set out to do. Efstratios Grivas's *Modern Chess Planning* is one of them" – David Kaufman, CHESSCAFE.COM
144 pages, 248 x 172 mm; $24.95 / £14.99

Winning Chess Explained
Zenon Franco
"Made unique by the exceptional quality Franco has put in to explain the ideas and characteristics of the positions ... altogether a **very** instructive book" – Andy May, NSGCHESS.COM
192 pages, 248 x 172 mm; $26.95 / £15.99

50 Essential Chess Lessons
Steve Giddins
"One of those books I wish I had 30-40 years ago. I would've become a master (if I had taken the time to study it)." – Bob Long, ChessCo
160 pages, 248 x 172 mm; $24.95 / £14.99

How to Calculate Chess Tactics
Valeri Beim
"Combines well-selected games and fragments with instructive problems and studies – a trademark of Beim's previous excellent books. It also includes 100 positions for the reader to solve." – GM Lubomir Kavalek, WASHINGTON POST
176 pages, 248 x 172 mm; $26.95 / £15.99

Secrets of Positional Chess
Dražen Marović
"A feast of instructive examples, including demonstrations of power and coordination among pieces and pawns" – GM Paul Motwani, THE SCOTSMAN
224 pages, 248 x 172 mm; $23.95 / £16.99

Decision-Making at the Chessboard
Viacheslav Eingorn
"Eingorn deals with a completely neglected subject in chess literature ... The reader gains an insight into the thinking process of a grandmaster" – Thomas Schian, ROCHADE
208 pages, 210 x 145 mm; $24.95 / £15.99

Understanding Chess Move by Move
John Nunn
"Beautifully put together. Anyone who plays over the games in it slowly and carefully is bound to improve his understanding of chess" – Peter Connor, CHESSVILLE
240 pages, 248 x 172 mm; $19.95 / £14.99

Secrets of Modern Chess Strategy
John Watson
"Marvellously written, scholarly and persuasive ... the best available discursive history of strategic developments in modern chess" – John Hurley, SUNDAY TRIBUNE
272 pages, 248 x 172 mm; $29.95 / £19.99

About the Publisher: Gambit Publications is passionate about creating innovative and instructive chess books, including a unique selection of middlegame titles to assist intermediate-level players. Gambit specializes in chess, and the company is owned and run exclusively by masters and grandmasters.

www.gambitbooks.com